Coningham

CONINGHAM

A BIOGRAPHY OF
Air Marshal Sir Arthur Coningham
KCB, KBE, DSO, MC, DFC, AFC

Vincent Orange

METHUEN

First published in Great Britain 1990
by Methuen London
Michelin House, 81 Fulham Road, London SW3 6RB

Copyright © 1990 by Vincent Orange

A CIP catalogue record for this book
is available from the British Library

ISBN 0–413–14580–8

Printed in Great Britain
by Mackays of Chatham plc, Chatham, Kent

Contents

For
Jane-Mari and Sal
'Let the end try the man'

Illustrations

Illustrations

Acknowledgements and thanks are due to Eileen MacAndrew for plate 2b; to Barry J. Gray for plate 3a; to the Central Flying School, Wittering, Lincolnshire, for plate 4a; to 55 Squadron, RAF Marham, Norfolk for plate 4b; to Lady Frank for plate 5a; to Sarah Brinton-Whittaker (via Denis C. Bateman) for plates 5b, 7a, 7b and 15b; to the Controller of Her Majesty's Stationery Office for plates 6a, 6b, 9a, 9b, 10a, 10b, 12b, 13a, 13b and 14a (Crown Copyright); to the *Daily Express* for plate 8a; to Air Chief Marshal Sir Kenneth Cross for plates 8b and 11a; to Roger Elmhirst for plates 11b and 14b; to The Imperial War Museum for plate 12a; to Air Marshal Sir Victor Groom for plate 15a; to the Hulton-Deutsch Collection for plate 16a; and to Sir Nigel Tapp (via Denis C. Bateman) for plate 16b. Plates 1a and 1b are from *The Secret History of the Coningham Case* by 'Zero' (Daniel Green); plate 2a is from *Wellingtonian*, 1910 (via Ray Michael, College Archivist); and plate 3b is from *British Fighter Units, Western Front, 1917–18* by Alex Revell.

The maps were redrawn from the author's roughs by Neil Hyslop. Map 1 is adapted from C. G. Jefford and W. E. Morgan, 'British Airfields on the Continent', *Cross and Cockade*, Vol. 10. Map 8 is adapted from Air Historical Branch Map No. 424.

Acknowledgements

It is always a pleasure to reach this stage in writing a book, when everyone who helped to make it possible can receive grateful, public thanks. Above all must come my friend Denis C. Bateman, who provided some of my best material and pursued numerous ends, living and dead, with great determination. Air Chief Marshal Sir Kenneth Cross revealed to me the existence of Sir Thomas Elmhirst's papers and put me in touch with Sir Thomas's son, Roger: without their help, this would be a much poorer book. My wife, Ann Margaret Orange, has again done more than the best of friends to help me in every way and her brother, David Jeffery, must once more be thanked for his prolonged hospitality in London, without which I could not even contemplate biographies of RAF officers. Mrs Jane-Mari Shearing (Coningham's daughter) and Sarah Brinton-Whittaker (his grand-daughter) gave me vital information and to them jointly I dedicate this book. Neither lady has attempted to restrict or influence in any way the use I have made of the material they provided.

Air Commodore Henry Probert (head of Air Historical Branch, Ministry of Defence, London), Fred Lake, Alan Vine and Duncan Webster (Ministry of Defence Library (Air) London), Andrew Cormack, Matthew George and Peter Murton (RAF Museum, Hendon), Patricia J. Methven (Liddell Hart Centre for Military Archives, King's College, London), John Wing (Christ Church Library, Oxford), Jean Buckberry (Cranwell College Library), Christopher Dowling (Imperial War Museum, London) and Ken Scadden (National Archives, Wellington) were all more helpful than I had any right to expect. I gladly record my gratitude to the ever-obliging staff of the University of Canterbury Library and Photographic Department, and to the University Council for research grants and study leave.

Among the many New Zealanders who helped me, I must single out (in alphabetical order) John Blechynden, Carolyn Carr, Peter and Nancy Coote, John Crawford, David Gunby, Errol Martyn, Ray Michael, Gerald Orchard, Trevor Richards, Arnold Wall and Lorraine Wilson. My British friends include Brian Bond, Chaz Bowyer, Ivor Calverley, Frank Cheesman, Sir John Colville, Bob Coles, Lord Deramore, Larry Donnelly, Andrew Geddes, Mike Goodall, Barry Gray, D. J. Harrison, Ray Honeybone, Francis Howitt, Kevin Kelly, Stuart Leslie, Peter H. Liddle, Lord Loch, 'Laddie' Lucas, G. C. McCarthy, J. M. McNeill, Mervyn Mills, Lady Belinda Montagu, Frank Sayer, Sir Nigel Tapp, Lord Tedder, Mrs H. M. Waterhouse, George

Acknowledgements

Westlake, Sir Frank Whittle, Donald J. Wiseman, Humphrey Wynn and an anonymous member of Coningham's staff, July 1941–June 1942. Terry Copp (Canada), Dudley Dove (South Africa), Joan Mulholland (Australia) and Mme Lucienne Rolando (France) were also very helpful.

From the United States, I received nothing but the most wholehearted cooperation (a fact which would have delighted Coningham). In particular, I thank Lynn O. Gama and Warren A. Trest of the USAF Historical Research Center, Maxwell AFB, Alabama, and Duane J. Reed of the USAF Academy Library, Colorado. Grateful thanks are in addition due to Richard G. Davis, Carlo D'Este, Robin Higham, I. B. Holley Jr., Will Jacobs, Mrs Laurence S. Kuter, David R. Mets, Daniel R. Mortensen, Mrs Mary Lee Strickland O'Neal, James Parton and Richard J. Sommers.

Last, but not least, come the Air Marshals who have given so generously of their time and hospitality: Sir Harry Broadhurst, Sir Gerald Gibbs, Sir Victor Groom, Sir Edmund Hudleston, Sir Wallace Kyle, Sir Theodore McEvoy, Sir Kenneth Porter, Sir Ranald Reid, Sir Frederick Rosier and Sir Laurence Sinclair.

Sarah Hannigan and Ann Mansbridge of Methuen have helped me cut the text to a manageable length, suggesting many improvements.

All the men and women mentioned above are collectively responsible for whatever merit this book has; I made all the mistakes and misjudgements myself.

VINCENT ORANGE
July 1989

Flight of the *Star Tiger* I

London to Lisbon, 27–28 January 1948

To ease the pain of numerous separations during the twenty years that they had known each other, the Air Marshal and his Lady gradually perfected a routine. By January 1948, it had long been agreed that departure plans should be completed the night before; so, too, should discussions about the prospects and hazards of whatever journey lay ahead; tender farewells should be expressed privately and the next day should at least begin normally.

On the morning of 27 January, therefore, Sir Arthur Coningham (known to everyone as 'Mary', for reasons which will be explained later) rose early, made himself a large pot of 'desert tea' (poisonously strong and nauseatingly sweet), leafed quickly through *The Times*, pausing only on the sports, society and business pages, before turning briefly to his correspondence and for much longer to the telephone. Lady Coningham (whose name was Nan) emerged shortly before a taxi arrived to carry him from their Mayfair home to London's recently-opened airport at Heathrow. They parted quickly and calmly, though well aware that this parting marked the start of a new life for both of them. Coningham, recently retired from the Royal Air Force, was off to Bermuda for a fortnight 'on private business'.

Not since he was a lad of nineteen – back home in New Zealand, before the outbreak of the Great War – had he been a civilian; except, that is, for some anxious weeks, never to be forgotten, in the middle of that war. Now, for the first time in more than thirty years, he could come and go and dress as he pleased every day; but he had no job and fifty-three was not an ideal age at which to start again. However, Coningham was famous (in some quarters, notorious) for living in style and began his second career with all the panache that marked his first. He had booked a passage aboard a new airliner (an Avro Tudor IV, named *Star Tiger*), operated by a new company (British South American Airways), pioneering a new passenger route across the Atlantic under the direction of another brilliant airman, Air Vice-Marshal Don Bennett.

Among the passengers was Tony Mulligan, formerly a Squadron Leader Navigator in Bomber Command, who telephoned a friend just before takeoff. 'We're in luck,' he said, 'Mary Coningham is on board. That means we'll get plenty of VIP treatment. It's going to be a terrific trip.' *Star Tiger* was bound for Lisbon on the first stage of a flight to Havana via Santa Maria in the Azores and Bermuda, that proved anything but 'terrific'. Everyone on board (a crew of six and twenty-three passengers) suffered acute discomfort throughout the journey to Lisbon because the cabin became so cold that icicles formed from condensation on the ceiling. 'I am trying to write this letter', wrote one passenger, 'at 21,000 feet over the Bay of Biscay. We cannot see anything because we are in thick cloud and the windows are frosted over inside. The heating has broken down and the thermometer is reading 34 degrees.' The crew was also having trouble with one of the compasses. A scheduled overnight stop in Lisbon was therefore doubly welcome, both as a chance to thaw out and to tackle these problems.

During that night, Coningham wrote to Nan. He kept quiet about the miserable flight – it was, in fact, nothing like so cold or noisy as many he had endured in the past – for he knew that Nan's anxiety about the dangers of flying did not diminish with the years, and set himself instead to amuse her, as usual, with scandalous sketches of his fellow passengers. He then told her that the pilot, Brian McMillan, was very much a man after his own heart: a skier of international standard in the Thirties, who had ended the war with a most distinguished record as a Wing Commander Pathfinder in Bomber Command, and was, moreover, a New Zealander.

The Coninghams were devoted sailors and often talked, not altogether idly, of sailing their own yacht to New Zealand. Chatting with McMillan put this idea back in Coningham's mind. It would be wonderful to return there, now that he was famous. In September 1945, he had made a triumphant tour of North America, as guest of the US Army Air Force, for three exhilarating weeks. Wherever he went, he had been a centre of attention – interviewed by press and radio reporters, invited to make speeches, shown the sights – and yet his name meant little to most Americans. How different it would be in Wellington! The transformation from farmhand to Air Marshal would in itself make the visit worthwhile. Better still would be the knowledge that he had overcome not only poverty but mockery. To be received with honour in Wellington by the masters and boys of his old school, by the senior officers of all three services and by the country's leading politicians would be experiences to savour, especially with Nan at his side. He wanted to see the faces of men and women who remembered his parents and had seen his name in headlines that shamed him as well as headlines that praised him.

During his tour of the United States, Coningham had been urged to read some Damon Runyon stories and did so, finding to his surprise that he enjoyed them. One sentence in particular stuck in his mind. 'Many citizens

2

of this town', he read, 'are compelled to do the best they can.' It certainly summed up the lives of his own parents very neatly. Coningham was not normally given to reflecting on the past, but at this pause in his career, marooned in a hotel bedroom, his thoughts may have turned to Arthur and Alice, doing the best they can.[1]

CHAPTER ONE

'Doing the Best they Can'

Arthur and Alice, 1863–1912

The Air Marshal's father, also named Arthur, was born on 14 July 1863 at Emerald Hill, South Melbourne, and Bede Nairn, an Australian historian, would later describe him as a 'cricketer and notoriety'. A fast-medium left-arm bowler and left-hand batsman, Arthur migrated to Queensland in December 1884 and was selected to represent Australia in 1893 as a member of the eighth team to tour England. The tour lasted for eighteen weeks and was a hard one, with two three-day matches arranged for every week. There were only fourteen players and Arthur was one of three poorly regarded by the team's managers. He upset them while fielding on a cold day early in the tour by gathering papers that had blown on to the ground and burning these to warm his hands. The incident happened at Lord's of all places, the London headquarters of the game, and was long remembered. It is typical of Arthur's unlucky life, on and off the cricket field, that a feat far more deserving of memory – when he dived into the Thames to save a boy from drowning – was soon forgotten.

At the end of the following year, however, Arthur at last received the call that still delights every Australian cricketer: he was selected to play in a Test Match against England. The second of a series of five fought out during that summer, it proved to be one of the most exciting in the long history of a famous sporting contest. In Melbourne, between 29 December 1894 and 3 January 1895, England, scoring 75 and 475, beat Australia (123 and 333) by 94 runs to take a 2–0 lead in the series. Arthur's performance was nothing exceptional. He was one of four players dropped for the third Test and would never be chosen again. Even so, he set three records in that single appearance which can never be taken from him. He was the first Queensland player to represent Australia and he took a wicket with his first ball, which was also the first ball of the match. Neither feat had hitherto been performed in Tests.[1]

So much for Arthur the 'cricketer'; his subsequent 'notoriety' was shared with his wife. Alice Stanford Dowling, born in Devonshire, England on 29 September 1869, was the daughter of a Warrant Officer in the British Army. She went to Australia at the age of sixteen to live with her married sister, Mary Bostock, in Brisbane. Arthur Coningham met Alice there and on 3 March 1893 a Catholic priest agreed to marry them in the parlour of his presbytery in Paddington, Sydney. They could not be married in the church, for this was to be a 'mixed' marriage: Alice having obtained a dispensation to marry a Protestant and Arthur having agreed that their children would be brought up as Catholics. At the last moment, Arthur refused to go through with the ceremony, despite repeated urgings from Alice. He was shortly to leave for England with the Australian cricket team and offered to give her money while he was away and marry her on his return. Eventually, the priest told them to get out and they went off to a 'Coffee Palace', still wrangling.

They were actually married a week later, on 11 March 1893 in St Matthew's Anglican Church at Bondi, Sydney. Arthur left for England the same day and Alice went to live with her mother in Brisbane. He returned seven months later and their married life began in that city. Their first child – named Arthur – was born in Brisbane on 19 January 1895, the proud father arriving from the Test Match in Melbourne just in time to meet the future Air Marshal. The family moved to Bondi in September and a second child – Mabel – was born there on 9 May 1896. On 10 November 1899, the Coninghams' third child – Vincent Francis – was born. With three children under five and no steady income, they faced a bleak future. In order to improve it, Arthur and Alice concocted a plan that would cost Alice her reputation, brand Arthur a cuckold, their son Vincent a bastard, ruin the career of a priest (if successful) and generate sectarian strife throughout Australia even if it failed. It would reveal much that was best hidden about their private lives (more, perhaps, than they bargained for), but it would also, they hoped, release them from poverty. They agreed that Arthur would allege and Alice admit that she had committed adultery on various dates in 1898 and 1899 with Father Denis Francis O'Haran, secretary to Cardinal Moran, Archbishop of Sydney.

The Coninghams had chosen their target shrewdly, for O'Haran was notoriously vain: 'more often photographed than a fashionable actor', it was said, and much too eager to hand round copies of these photographs to a wide circle of admiring ladies. Arthur sought damages from O'Haran of £5,000, custody of the two children whom he acknowledged as his (Arthur and Mabel) and a dissolution of his marriage; Vincent, he said, was O'Haran's son. The trial began in Sydney on 3 December 1900 before Mr Justice Simpson and a jury of twelve men – ten Anglicans and two Presbyterians.

According to the Coninghams, Alice met O'Haran at a St Patrick's Day concert in the Sydney Town Hall in March 1897 and as their friendship warmed during the next two years, Arthur began to feel unwanted. One day in May 1900, while Alice was out, Arthur searched her possessions, finding a signed photograph of O'Haran and two tiny green harps. Confronted with this evidence, Alice broke down and confessed all – confirming her infidelity in letters which Arthur (who conducted his case in person) produced in court. On leaving the witness-box, Arthur took his seat at the barristers' table and called his wife.

O'Haran first kissed her, she said, on 22 June 1898, but actual adultery – graphically described in court – began on 3 July. Alice next visited him in September. 'Now you are here,' he said, 'we may as well indulge.' Thereafter, they indulged regularly, usually on Fridays because O'Haran went to confession on Saturdays. By May 1899, she was pregnant and told O'Haran that he was the father. Though pleased, he refused to baptise the child when it was born. Gilbert Probyn Smith, a Sydney journalist, thought Alice quite nerveless. 'The strain on her must be very great,' he wrote, 'for the first day after her evidence, when she went out to her cab, a mob of howling men and women hooted and used all sorts of vile epithets to her.'

Father O'Haran denied all charges and his alibis were well supported by witnesses who freely admitted, however, to discussing their evidence with him before giving it. Arthur's cross-examination of O'Haran was thought by one observer 'a wonderfully able effort on the part of a man unversed in law'; he was 'as unfair as a big QC and as resourceful as a cat'. Arthur even summoned Cardinal Moran himself as a witness, but the Cardinal stoutly supported his secretary. Arthur raised one issue which took up hours of court time and provoked sharp criticism of the judge for indulging him. Was it possible, asked Arthur, for a Catholic to commit a sin, go to confession, receive absolution and then afterwards swear – without fault – that he had never committed the sin?

According to O'Haran's counsel, Jack Want, QC, the Coninghams were blackmailers and it was his duty to expose their sordid lives, which he did with great gusto. They branded, he concluded, 'to all time and eternity these two children [Arthur and Mabel] who at all events they claim to be respectable and legitimate, for the sake of screwing out this wretched sum of money from Dr O'Haran, with which I suppose they will regale themselves to the end of their lives.' Arthur answered boldly, praising Alice for her resolution in the face of a savage attack and defending her character. His strongest card he played last: no woman, he declared, could stand so undaunted by such a disgraceful story unless it were true.

The judge, in a summing up lasting five hours, made much of this point, though observing that 'women did cool things sometimes'. Shortly after 11 am on 14 December 1900, the tenth day of the trial, the jury retired. A large crowd gathered outside the court to await the verdict and as the day wore on, there were angry exchanges between Catholic and Protestant partisans. At 10.42 pm the jury returned and the foreman announced that there was no possibility of a 9–3 majority (the minimum allowed) no matter how long they deliberated. The jury was therefore discharged and the crowd, of some five to six thousand, reluctantly dispersed. For days afterwards in trains, trams, buses and ferry-boats the case was vigorously discussed. 'To a positively indecent extent,' complained the Melbourne *Argus*. 'Protestants and Roman Catholics ranged themselves on either side simply because of the doctrines they professed.'[2]

The second trial began on 11 March 1901, the Coningham's eighth wedding anniversary, with Arthur again representing himself. Two Catholics, two Jews and eight Protestants made up the jury. The first trial lasted ten days, the second fifteen, even though a different judge – Mr Justice Owen – forbade the theological debates which greatly extended the first trial. It soon became clear that a changed issue would go before the jury, for Mr Want had obtained documents from the enemy camp and was able to make the trial pivot not on the conduct of Alice and O'Haran *before* the first trial, but rather on the conduct of the Coninghams *between* the trials. O'Haran's supporters, assuming that he was the victim of a conspiracy, organised a formidable counter-conspiracy. Its organiser was Paddy Crick, a lawyer and politician with wide experience as a jury-rigger and evidence-faker who occupied a vital position as Postmaster-General of New South Wales. He stayed in the background, deputing active command to Daniel Green, a Sydney-born 'commission agent and promoter', who sought out witnesses and paid them to appear or disappear as required.

Green learned that Arthur was receiving letters of advice from one 'Zero', who had a deep knowledge of the Catholic Church and an even deeper hatred of O'Haran. Zero's letters were shown to Green, who had them photographed before passing them on to Arthur through an informer whom he had bought in the Coningham camp. Arthur's replies, signed 'Delta', were addressed care of a suburban post office and Green, following the collector home, was astounded to learn that Zero was a well-known priest. Green hastened to inform Cardinal Moran, who exacted a confession and had the unfortunate priest taken away in a state of mental collapse to the care of 'the good brothers of Hunter's Hill'.

The unmasking of Zero proved a turning point in the campaign. Arthur was robbed of a valuable ally and a secret weapon was put into his enemies' hands because Green took the place of Zero and continued the correspondence, sending misinformation and false advice to Arthur. For example, two of the men on the jury panel were, in Green's opinion, 'bitter black Orangemen and would have sat till they were blue mouldy before they found O'Haran innocent'. The new Zero therefore advised Arthur to have them struck off. Green actually met Arthur one night in a secluded part of Macquarie Street. He wore dark glasses and gave himself a clerical appearance; Arthur had a revolver on his hip; passwords were exchanged and Green then gave Arthur two dates when he was certain that O'Haran was in his presbytery and might well have received Alice. They were, of course, dates when the priest had cast-iron alibis.

Green's next attack was on Alice. Having been cooped up for weeks with her children and a woman friend in a tiny cottage in Paddington, Alice needed a change of scene. She fled to the country, to visit an old friend of both Coninghams – a Mr Miller – who lived at 'Burrilda', a boarding house in Fairfield, some fifteen miles out of Sydney. Miller was about to lose Burrilda until Green kindly found him the money to pay off his mortgage. Green also found him a boarder: a private detective who played the part of Captain Smith, retired sea-dog, and organised a party to celebrate 'the Relief of Burrilda'. Alice had several glasses of wine, porters and brandies, then collapsed, perhaps drugged as well as drunk. While she slept, her letters were stolen. In court, Alice said of the Burrilda Incident that she knew only 'what was told me the next day by my little boy'. The judge at first rejected Arthur's suggestion that 'little Artie' (then aged six) be called as a witness. Next day, however, he ruled that the boy *could* be called and that he would then decide if Artie was 'fit to be examined'. In the event, Artie was spared this ordeal.

For his address to the jury, Want now had a great deal more evidence on which to found his charges of blackmail and conspiracy, though he was apologetic about his 'informers'. Arthur's address (which lasted five hours) dwelt long upon this point: he could not, he said, employ an army of thieves, as did his opponents, to manufacture evidence. The judge, in his summing up, focused on the major question: had the adultery alleged taken place? The onus of proof lay on Arthur. His case depended upon the story told by his wife. Had the defence destroyed that case? The jury retired at 3.05 pm on 2 April 1901 and returned at 5.20 pm with a unaminous verdict for O'Haran. There were loud cheers in court. The judge thanked the jury, adding that he agreed with their verdict. Arthur sobbed briefly and then tried to grapple with the priest, but was overpowered and carried out of court.

Although the jury found for O'Haran, the foreman had added that it also thought there was insufficient evidence to prove conspiracy. On the face of it, a perverse finding, it indicated the jury's distaste – shared by the judge – for the means employed by the defence to achieve a victory it deserved. Later in 1901, Green published his account of the case under the name 'Zero', which he had so cleverly appropriated. Many copies were ordered by Cardinal Moran and other eminent churchmen, even though reviewers drew attention to numerous instances of theft, impersonation, subornation and perjury, all related with evident exultation.[3]

The Coninghams fled to New Zealand, starting a new life in Westport, on the west coast of the South Island, but in November 1903 Arthur was sent to prison in Hokitika for six months. He had been employed to sell copies of a medical guide. For each order, he got nine shillings (plus a further nine when the customer actually paid for the guide), but many of his orders were found to come from non-existent people and the assistant whom he blamed for these false claims could not be traced. Arthur, who conducted his own defence, appealed in vain for leniency 'on account of his wife and three little ones'. The Sydney *Bulletin*, picking up this story, sneered 'it wasn't any fault of Coningham's that he has a wife to base an appeal on'.[4]

By 1906, the family was living in rooms in a block of apartments rather grandly called the 'Mansions' in Ghuznee Street, Wellington, and 'little Artie', now 'young Arthur', obtained a Junior Free Place at Wellington College in February 1909, when he was just fourteen. These places had recently been instituted to oblige schools to accept 'a wider range' of pupils; that is, pupils whose parents could not afford fees. Young Arthur's record shows many absences in his first year and for 'conduct and diligence' he received a very poor grade. In 1910, he held a Senior Free Place and was again frequently absent, especially during the winter term, but his conduct and diligence improved to an average level. Although making no mark academically, he proved himself an excellent shot, winning the senior grade championship in October 1910, while still a fourth former. The College shooting team were the New Zealand secondary schools champions that year and he appears in a photograph marking the triumph: at fifteen, he is still slightly-built and has a serious, reserved look. He was often absent in 1911, his assessment declined again and he had left the College by 10 November, missing the end-of-year exams.[5]

Alice, meanwhile, was struggling to keep open a small hairdressing business in Cuba Street with little help from her husband. Their relations worsened during that year and on 11 October 1911, 'Con' wrote to Alice from Hastings, reminding her of his recent apology and his ready forgiveness of her misdeeds, but all he had received in return, apart from anonymous letters, was 'an abusive letter from Arthur, with your work behind it'. They patched up their differences sufficiently well to spend Christmas of 1911 together, but early in the new year Alice suspected her husband of carrying on an affair with Mrs Mary Ryman, who also had rooms at the Mansions. Alice consulted a solicitor, who recommended to her an agent, one Samuel Free. Samuel followed Arthur and Mary to a bathing-shed on the beach at Lyall Bay on 19 January – young Arthur's 17th birthday – and next evening, arranged for Alice to confront her husband and Mrs Ryman while they were cuddling on a bench at another beach; after Alice had had her say, Samuel presented Arthur with a divorce petition. Alice would later admit to pointing a revolver at Arthur, but denied breaking a water-bottle over his head.

The case, heard in Wellington on 13–14 May 1912, was widely reported and attracted full-scale attention from a popular weekly, *New Zealand Truth*, under banner headlines. All accounts recalled the sensational trials in Sydney in 1900 and 1901, though *New Zealand Truth* admitted that the present case attracted no comparable public interest. The judge rejected Alice's appeal for a hearing *in camera*. 'As far as the children are concerned,' he said, 'they are at school, and there is no reason why any scandalous news should reach them if there is proper discipline.' A letter from young Arthur was produced in court which began: 'Look here, Coningham, although you are my father, I am ashamed of you.' As in Sydney and Westport, Arthur conducted his own defence. Nervous and garrulous, he tried the judge's considerable patience while making the best of a thin defence. The jury took forty-five minutes to find him guilty of adultery and Alice was granted a decree *nisi*. Speaking to reporters after the verdict, Arthur claimed that divorce laws were too much for him: 'In Sydney,' he said, 'my wife said she did and a jury said she didn't. In Wellington, I said I didn't and a jury said I did.'

Little is known about the rest of their lives. Arthur spent at least some part of the Great War as a Corporal in the Salvation Army, working in the soldiers' institute, Rotorua. After that war, he returned to Australia and was admitted to Gladesville Mental Hospital in Sydney in November 1937, dying there on 13 June 1939: in another month, he would have been 76. The *Sydney Morning Herald* printed a kind obituary, recording only his career as a 'cricketer'; the 'notoriety' had been allowed to die. Alice kept in regular touch with her children for the rest of her life, though she saw young Arthur only rarely after 1916. She spent her last years in Bicknoller, Somerset, dying there in July 1959, her 90th year.[6]

CHAPTER TWO

'A Wonderful Life'

From Lake Rotoiti to Castle Bromwich, 1912–18

Young Arthur Coningham, having left Wellington College late in 1911 with no academic or technical qualifications, was obliged 'to do the best he could', like his parents before him. From his father, he inherited exceptional ability in all sports; his mother gave him her equally exceptional public presence; from both of them he took quick wits, plenty of bounce in hard times and cool courage; adding his own well-concealed determination to get on. Unlike his parents, he had the good luck – or perhaps merely the opportunity – to make the best use of his gifts. He landed a job as a general farmhand at the Roundell, a large sheep station lying around the northern shores of Lake Rotoiti, about fifty miles south of Nelson in the South Island. Coningham would spend eighteen months there and the hard, open-air life transformed a pale, slight lad into the big, confident man who so impressed – not always favourably – everyone who met him. For the rest of his life, he would often be described as *handsome:* a description that must owe more to force of personality than regularity of feature, but he certainly had a most brilliant smile and eyes that many found compelling.

Coningham quickly became good friends with Jack Coote (who managed the station), Jack Tomlinson (whose mother owned Top House hotel, near the station) and John Blechynden (son of the station's owner) who was a boy of eight when the new hand arrived from Wellington. All three had vivid memories of young Coningham and took great delight in following his rise to international fame. It was a rise that also astonished them because in the days when they knew him he seemed no more than a bright, rough lad: a typical hill-country sheepman in the making, with a boisterous sense of humour that would gradually be deadened by work and worry. Meanwhile, he was always looking for excitement and tried many stupid experiments, such as finding out how large a piece of gelignite could be hit with a hammer before the explosion became dangerous. Only a little less stupid was his device linking a clock to a pair of shotguns that fired them at exactly midnight to celebrate the new year of 1913. A wholly physical man, he loved wrestling, boxing, swimming, sailing, working with dogs and horses – the wilder the better – and was a superb shot. At party time, after shearing or mustering, he played the accordion with great vigour and joined readily in all singing; unusually for such a young, high-spirited man who loved company, he was never seen the worse for liquor. In the middle of 1913, Coningham left the Roundell to try his luck on North Island farms, but kept in touch for years with Tomlinson and Coote, whom he next met in France during the Great War.[1]

On the outbreak of that war, Coningham was working on a farm near Dannevirke, but hurried home to enlist in the 5th Wellington Regiment on 10 August 1914, naming his mother as next-of-kin, making no mention of his father. At that time, when the authorities could pick and choose their men, Coningham's selection owed much to his years at Wellington College, where he had been a champion shot; his subsequent experience of compulsory part-time military training would also have helped.

He sailed aboard HM Transport *Monowai* for an unknown destination on 15 August. Another transport and two escort vessels made up the expedition. Excitement at being so promptly – and mysteriously – involved in the war soon gave way to misery, for it was midwinter, the sea rough and many of the 800 men crammed aboard were helplessly seasick, and when they found their sealegs, they realised that the food on offer was dreadful. A week out from New Zealand, they learned to their surprise that they were to visit a French colony – Noumea, in New Caledonia – and only on arrival there did they hear that their purpose was to seize the German colony in Samoa, at the request of the British government, and so prevent a squadron of German warships known to be loose in the Pacific using either its harbour or its wireless station. Coningham spent much of his time on the voyage in hard drilling and shooting practice, in renewing old school friendships and making new ones.

The fleet arrived off Apia, Samoa, on 29 August and Coningham saw two naval officers go ashore, carrying as a flag of truce (according to one observer) 'a scrap of table linen annexed to a broomstick'. The German Governor refused either to surrender or to offer resistance and at length the troops were loaded into boats and towed into shallow water under the interested gaze of Germans and Samoans alike. Scrambling ashore, they were drawn up on a road near the beach by their commander, Lieutenant Colonel Robert Logan, who distrusted German assurances that there would be no shooting and conducted a properly military advance on and occupation of the enemy capital: the first to fall to British arms in the Great War. 'The Pearl of the Pacific,' lamented someone in the Reichstag, was now 'in the hands of the vile invader'. Once the British flag had formally replaced the German flag, Logan informed an assembly of Samoans that government would continue along lines established by the Germans.

The Wellington regiment occupied one end of Apia, including the cinema and Vailima House (built by Robert Louis Stevenson), while the Auckland troops occupied the other end, including the wireless station. After a week, the Wellingtons moved to a racecourse and set up tents there. On 14 September, Coningham had his first and nearly his last sight of an active enemy when the German cruisers *Scharnhorst* and *Gneisenau* arrived off Apia. Cleared for action, they covered the town and beaches with their guns for about an hour before departing, having decided that the recovery of Samoa was worth neither the time nor the ammunition. The decision left the conquerors deflated, their prisoners wryly amused and both sides aware that the war had passed them by. No further warlike incidents took place and Coningham was soon anxious to get away from Samoa. A routine of parades, physical training, route marches and rifle practice was introduced to fill up as much time as possible and a wide variety of tropical diseases quickly appeared to take up the rest. Thick clothing and heavy food further demoralised men obliged to occupy quarters in humid, low-lying areas near the beach amid swarms of flies and mosquitoes. After seven wearisome months in Samoa, Coningham gratefully went aboard HM Transport *Talune* on 3 April 1915 to return to Wellington, arriving early on the 14th.

The men paraded on the wharf and were warmly congratulated by several politicians for their splendid services, but Coningham – like many of his comrades – was acutely conscious of a need to take a positive part in the war and spurned the chance to relax in Wellington, the centre of loving attention from his family. Having already volunteered for further active service, these men were immediately marched off to barracks at Trentham. Coningham there made a fresh start to his military career, enlisting in the New Zealand Expeditionary Force (4th Reinforcements) with effect from 15 April. He was a trooper in C Squadron with the Canterbury Mounted Rifles from the 17th and sailed that day for Suez. They arrived at the end of May and went on to Anzac Cove early in June.

As a fine horseman, an excellent shot and a man of great courage, Coningham might well have made his mark in major campaigns, but in fact his second venture as a soldier ended even more lamely than the first. His health, undermined in Samoa, collapsed entirely in the Middle East: sunstroke, dysentery and typhoid put him in one hospital after another until September, when the authorities decided to send him home. He arrived in New Zealand on 26 October and spent his last months in that country deeply depressed as successive medical boards considered his condition. Finally, on 10 March, he was recommended for discharge with effect from 1 April 1916. From that date, he was once more a civilian: after twenty months of undistinguished service, hardly any of it in contact with the enemy, Arthur Coningham, now twenty-one and supposedly in the prime of life, was officially considered indefinitely unfit even for *home*, let alone *active* service.[2]

During April, however, Coningham sailed for England at his own expense and was admitted to a School of Instruction at Reading in Berkshire for prospective officer pilots in the Royal Flying Corps (RFC). Nothing is now known about the making of this decision, the most crucial in Coningham's life, except that he must have had a strong recommendation from an influential patron, either at Wellington College or in the army units with which he served, for he had had no flying experience in New Zealand.

From Reading, having been granted a commission as a Second Lieutenant on probation on 8 August, he moved to Salisbury Plain in Wiltshire, to Upavon and Netheravon, where he learned to fly. There was not then a standard method of instruction and few instructors were both keen and competent. As for the skills of methodical reconnaissance, formation flying and aerial combat, Coningham graduated from the Central Flying School at Upavon on 25 November without the slightest notion of such matters. In theory, he would have spent at least fifteen hours solo in the air; completed a cross-country flight of sixty miles, making two supervised landings en route; climbed to 6,000 feet, remained at that altitude for fifteen minutes and landing in a designated area; and made two night landings with the aid of flares. He had sent to Wellington College in September 'a very fine account', according to the school magazine, 'of his life in barracks and his experience as an air pilot'. Sadly, that account is now lost.[3]

Coningham must have done well in Wiltshire, for he was sent to a squadron of single-seat fighter aircraft, held to be much more prestigious – if not more useful to the war effort – than the squadrons of two-seaters which worked in close cooperation with the artillery. No. 32 Squadron was one of the first to be equipped with an aircraft specifically designed (by Geoffrey de Havilland) for air fighting: the DH 2, a 'pusher' biplane, with the engine mounted *behind* the pilot to give him a wide forward field of fire for his Lewis machine-gun. During 1916, this machine had proved itself superior to the Fokker monoplane, the first fighter armed with a machine-gun synchronised to fire through the propeller arc. Consequently, the DH 2 squadrons were hard worked and it was not until December, after six months in the line, that 32 Squadron (commanded by Major Tom Cairnes) was withdrawn to rest.

During this quiet time, on 19 December 1916, Coningham and four other new pilots arrived at 32 Squadron's airfield: Lealvillers, north-west of Albert. William Falconer, an air mechanic in C Flight, had been distinctly unimpressed by his first sight of Lealvillers, some two months previously: 'What a mud flat!' he wrote. 'Nothing here but four aero sheds and old beetroots and mud.' Gwilym Lewis, one of the squadron's original pilots, agreed: it was ideal, he thought, for anyone who wanted to become thoroughly miserable. 'The whole countryside is a mere bog; for real genuine high-class mud I doubt if our variety can be beaten.' However, a nearby prison camp provided ample German labour and by the time Coningham arrived many wooden huts had been built. Although sparsely furnished and unheated, they were at least clean and dry (in comparison to the trenches) if not quiet, for a battery of heavy guns made a shattering noise at irregular intervals throughout the day and night.[4]

15

Corporal Charles Dalton wrote to Lewis (then in England) from Lealvillers on Christmas Eve. The squadron, in his opinion, was now 'a wash-out': three aircraft had been wrecked *in practice* during the last week alone. Few of the original pilots were left and Dalton, like other members of the ground staff, felt at a low ebb and had little time for the new men. Gales and heavy snowfalls did nothing to cheer up anyone and it was not until the morning of 5 January 1917 that Coningham, with two other pilots, took part in his first offensive patrol.[5]

Thereafter, his personal 'firsts' came thick and fast. That afternoon, he saw his first enemy aircraft; on the 7th, he reported his first train movements; on the 10th, he got lost for the first time and had to land at another airfield; and on the 23rd (four days after his twenty-second birthday), came the first aerial victory in which he took part. He was one of a formation of seven DH 2s which dived on an unlucky Halberstadt two-seater, causing it to crash between Courcelles and Ervillers. By the 25th, Coningham was already making the first of many lifelong service friendships: he and Captain James Robb carried out an escort patrol that morning and would often serve together during the next thirty years as they made their way up to the highest ranks in the Royal Air Force. A week later, on 2 February, he lost his first squadron friend: Harold Blythe. Captain William Curphey, leading Coningham, Blythe and Charles Eccles, spotted two German aircraft at about 10,000 feet over the British lines, heading north-east. The DH 2s climbed towards them until they were themselves intercepted by several enemy fighters and a brief, desperate dogfight followed. Blythe was seen going down east of Puiseux, apparently under control, but close to the ground and with an enemy following him. Although Coningham tried to drive this machine away, he was obliged to turn and defend himself. He and Curphey got home safely, Eccles made a forced landing, returning to Lealvillers next day; but Blythe was wounded, shot down and captured, dying in hospital on the 10th.

During twenty bitterly cold days, up to and including 11 February, 32 Squadron's total flying time was 440 hours and eleven enemy aircraft were 'crashed or driven down' in that time in exchange for as many losses. Given the fact that the latest German fighters outclassed the DH 2, it was a creditable achievement. Although a wonderfully agile machine, the DH 2 was under-powered and unable to reach a high altitude; which meant that it usually fought at a disadvantage. Moreover, the pilot's position was so exposed that flying – let alone fighting – in winter was a severe physical trial. Coningham, who had flown on twenty-eight patrols in six weeks, was granted a fortnight's leave from 16 February and Robb, writing to his father on the 18th, admitted that everyone in the squadron, pilots and ground crews alike, needed a rest and welcomed a couple of days of steady rain. While on leave, Coningham sent another 'very interesting account of the work of the Flying Corps' to Wellington College. Before leaving for France, the school magazine recorded, he had seized the chance of a sightseeing flight over England in a

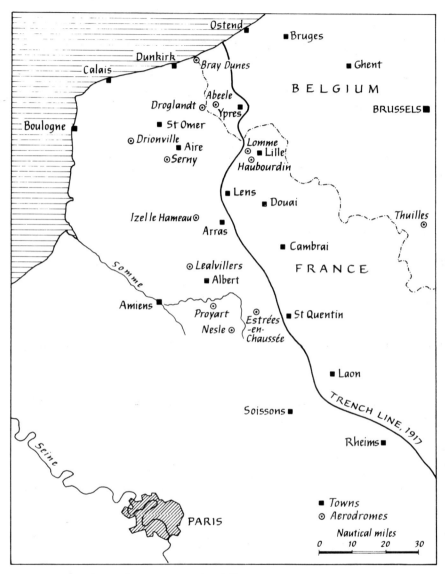

1. Aerodromes on the Western Front, 1917–18

monoplane and while in France had been doing patrol work, 'of which he gives a vivid account'; it was not, unfortunately, vivid enough to merit preservation. As the German withdrawal to the newly-completed Hindenburg Line got under way at the end of February, 32 Squadron was kept busy by urgent demands for the escort of reconnaissance machines, reports on the movement of trains, troop columns and the construction of new trench lines, all in the face of intense opposition from a German Air Service that had been greatly strengthened by reorganisation and re-equipment in recent months. In these days, the squadron certainly lived up to its motto, *Venite Pueri Ardua Ferre Possumus*, which might be rendered as: 'Come on, boys, we can handle this.'[6]

Nevertheless, the squadron suffered heavy blows in March, the worst on the 11th when Robb, leading a patrol of six machines, encountered nine enemy aircraft flying in formation east of Bapaume. Coningham and another pilot reinforced the patrol before a brisk battle began that cost the squadron dear: four DH 2s shot down and a fifth lost as a result of engine failure. Robb was among the casualties, making a forced landing at La Boiselle and being admitted to an Australian hospital. He wrote to his father on the 13th, telling him not to worry: 'just a small hole in the left leg,' he said, 'and am very doubtful if it is bad enough to get me back to England,' but it was. Robb already had a high opinion of Coningham, recalling later that year an occasion when Coningham led a flight of five machines that was attacked by fifteen, far over enemy lines. Everyone obeyed his orders (given before takeoff) to circle and climb in tight formation if outnumbered, firing only when directly threatened, and everyone got home safely.

It was during his service with 32 Squadron that Coningham found himself a new name. Leonard Rochford (a famous pilot in No. 3 (Naval) Squadron) recalled that Coningham was always known as 'Mary', a nickname worn down from the original 'Maori', given him because he was from New Zealand, but Rochford once heard Coningham tell someone that he was called Mary because his mother had wanted a girl. However, Christopher Musgrave, a New Zealand friend, later claimed that the name was given while Coningham was convalescing in a Cairo hospital in 1915. He was discovered by a fellow-patient sharing cocoa and kisses with a nurse, Mary Steele of Auckland, in an office at the end of the ward. On returning to his bed, he was met with a chorus of 'Connie loves Mary' and somehow *he* became 'Mary'. Whatever the truth may be, the fact remains that for reasons best known to himself he *wanted* to be called Mary and made sure that his friends knew this; except for official purposes, he never again answered to 'Arthur'. Already one of the squadron's leading personalities, Coningham helped to teach Rochford and his naval colleagues the rules of 'Cardinal Puff' during a party at Bertangles. Each player had to toast the Cardinal thrice, carrying out a complicated sequence of hand movements accurately between each toast on pain of draining his glass and starting again. Needless to say, wrote Rochford, 'few people got through the ordeal successfully and the game usually broke up and turned into a rough-house after only a few had had a turn'. Although a willing starter whenever the furniture began to fly, Coningham remained as abstemious as ever.[7]

By the end of March 1917, recorded 32 Squadron's history, 'work which normally would have been regarded as outstandingly severe was undertaken as a matter of routine' in preparation for the Battle of Arras, which began in a snowstorm on Easter Monday, 9 April, and lasted for five weeks. Despite dreadful weather, many 'special reconnaissances', to gather information about traffic movements and gun positions, were flown and with them began the newer duty of 'ground strafing' by pilots diving to below 1,000 feet to attack infantry and horse transport with machine-gun fire. Coningham himself carried out this dangerous but important duty many times in this war; in the next, he would see that it was carried out with far greater impact by numerous brave pilots trained under his command. More important in both wars than the direct casualties were the delays caused to the movement of men and supplies by overturned vehicles blocking roads; local panics compounded the disorder. At 1 pm on 14 April came orders for the squadron to pack up, ready to move at 4 pm, but it was only a trial, wrote Falconer, 'in case we need to make a hurried move, as we are now rather far back with the advancing'. As with ground strafing, so with the mobility of squadrons, Coningham would learn the art in this war and teach it in the next.

Second Lieutenant Coningham received the first of many promotions in the British air forces when he was appointed a Flight Commander and Temporary Captain with effect from 10 May. Two weeks later, the new Captain was granted his second leave. Since returning from the first on 2 March, Coningham had flown a further fifty-seven patrols, making a grand total of eighty-five in five months. On forty-six successive days in April and May, he flew forty-four patrols, sometimes two a day. He also carried out several air tests and flights to collect replacement aircraft as well as flights in the late afternoon with friends to visit other squadrons, usually staying about three hours. Despite this intense activity, actual combats in the air were uncommon. Many enemy aircraft were seen, most were chased, few were caught. According to a 'Summary of Work' for the year ending 7 June 1917, the squadron claimed thirty enemy aircraft crashed and forty-nine driven down out of control in more than 6,500 hours of flying time. It is not likely that all these claims were valid, but even if they were, each victim was taking the squadron nearly eighty-three hours in the air to achieve. Many observation balloons were also seen, though these were rapidly lowered as the British fighters approached and just as rapidly raised after they departed. Although visibility was often bad, determined efforts were made to report whatever could be seen in the air or on the ground.

While Coningham was on leave, 32 Squadron received the first of a new type of aeroplane which would replace the obsolete DH 2 by the end of June. This was the DH 5, a small single-seat 'tractor' biplane (with its engine mounted in front of the pilot), equipped with a single Vickers

19

machine-gun synchronised to fire through the propeller arc. The new type's most distinctive feature, intended to combine the excellent forward view of the 'pusher' design with the superior performance of the 'tractor', was a pronounced backward stagger of the upper wing. The feature was successful, but at the cost of the pilot's view of danger threatening from above and behind. Although the DH 5 was faster than the DH 2 and much more comfortable, its ability to dive steeply and recover quickly meant that 32 Squadron's pilots found themselves concentrating more than ever on ground strafing. The DH 2 and DH 5 were such markedly different designs that several accidents occurred while pilots were learning to handle the new machine.

The first two DH 5s arrived in mid-May and both, wrote Falconer, were 'smashed on the 'drome, pilots not used to them', on the 25th; five days later, four more had been 'smashed', though no pilot had yet been seriously hurt. Coningham had his first flight in nearly three weeks on 9 June in the DH 2 (No. 7926) which he had flown regularly for five months. That evening, he had his first flight in a DH 5 (No. A9179). The new type was still being used for practice and on 26 June Coningham carried out his ninetieth and last patrol in his faithful old bus. Next day, Falconer noted, six of the 'new buses' carried out an offensive patrol twenty miles over the German lines. Coningham led the patrol, which was joined for part of the time by Major Cairnes, the Squadron Commander, who rarely flew because he had only one eye – the result of a polo accident before the war. Gwilym Lewis met Cairnes in London a few weeks later and was invited to return to 32 Squadron: 'I told him I would be only too pleased to join him if he would get a decent aircraft, but not those things!'[8]

After the Battle of Arras, the main fighting on the British front moved north, to the Ypres Salient, where the Third Battle of Ypres would begin on 31 July in an attempt to clear the Germans from the Belgian coast. Early in that month, 32 Squadron was one of many moved to assist the armies and settled in a new home on 8 July at Droglandt Farm, about fifty miles north of Lealvillers and ten miles west of Poperinghe. The new home, wrote Falconer, was 'a nice farm house where we get milk, coffee, eggs, beer, etc.,' and although there is no village nearby, only scattered farms, 'we are in decent huts and the aero sheds are good'. When 32 Squadron arrived in the north, German aircraft were patrolling the area between their own balloon line and forward trenches in considerable strength. A system of 'Inner Offensive Patrols' by four aircraft working continuously throughout daylight hours at heights between 6,000 and 10,000 feet was therefore devised to drive away enemy artillery observation and photo-reconnaissance machines and protect British machines carrying out the same duties. Four fighters were to stand by daily to intercept intruders reported by wireless intelligence. The remaining fighters were employed on 'Outer Offensive Patrols' (up to 15,000 feet), sent out as the situation required with the sole duty of finding and engaging enemy aircraft.

At about 5.30 pm on 11 July, the squadron achieved its first success with the DH 5. Captain Coningham, leading an Outer Offensive Patrol of eight machines, sat patiently over an enemy aerodrome between Becelaere and Courtrai to wait for fifteen Albatros fighters (which had been observed leaving the ground) to get their height. The British fighters were at 13,000 feet when the Germans reached 12,000 feet and Coningham then led his men to the attack. He fired at three aircraft in succession, driving one down 'completely out of control'. Although not seen to crash, this Albatros was reckoned to be Coningham's first confirmed personal victory, achieved on his ninety-sixth patrol. Surviving records do not reveal an exceptional performance by Coningham thus far on the Western Front and yet General Sir Hubert Gough (commander of the 5th Army) sent for him that evening, as was officially recorded, to congratulate him 'on his gallant work, but did not realise how much he had done – he did splendidly all day (not once)'. Records for the rest of July certainly justify Gough's praise, especially in view of the fact that Coningham was flying a machine ill-suited for aerial combat.[9]

No fewer than twelve patrols, of two or three aircraft in each, were carried out on 20 July; about fifty enemy aircraft were seen and most were attacked. Coningham enjoyed a spectacular triumph during the morning, claiming three opponents destroyed. First, he and Lieutenant Wells dived on a two-seater, firing hard; they last saw it falling through cloud over Zandvoorde. Then, at 10.15 am, Coningham came upon four Albatros fighters attacking an RE 8 reconnaissance machine. He fired a long burst into one, 'which had a red tail and coloured fuselage,' he wrote later. 'It half looped, then spun down, completely out of control . . . When making back to the lines, patrol noticed three enemy machines circling low over the place where the coloured machine had gone down,' north of Comines. Finally, while on the way home, Coningham spotted a yellow Albatros far below. Getting the sun behind him, he dived on it, opened fire at close range and saw the left top wing fold back. The machine hurtled straight down from 2,500 feet, crashing near Wervicq.

'A very successful day's air fighting,' commented General Gough. 'Collishaw and Coningham did splendidly – as usual.' On 22 July, Brigadier General Charles Longcroft (commander, V Brigade) recommended Coningham for the immediate award of a Military Cross in recognition of his splendid efforts on the 20th. On four occasions besides these, added Longcroft, he had sent down aircraft that probably crashed and forced numerous others to flee. The award was confirmed a week later (and announced in the *London Gazette* on 17 September) for 'conspicuous gallantry and devotion to duty in attacking enemy aircraft. On numerous occasions he has displayed great dash and a fine offensive spirit in engaging the enemy at close range and driving them down completely out of control.'[10]

Coningham's career with 32 Squadron had meanwhile ended in a blaze of glory and a hail of bullets. Early on 27 July, while leading a patrol of two

21

'fighting pairs', he spotted a German two-seater protected by several scouts north of Polygon Wood. Instructing one pair to hold off the escort, he and his partner attacked the two-seater. Coningham hit the observer with his first burst and together they drove it down, 'in a succession of dives, smoking badly, evidently being hit in his engine', until it crashed near Zonnebeke. That evening, he destroyed another aircraft east of Houthulst Wood and Gough again commended him 'for his good and gallant leading, as well as his success'. On Monday, 30 July, the weather was very bad and only one patrol of four machines went out, at 5.50 pm. One of the four returned early, but the other three, Coningham, Wells and Albert Gordon of Auckland, engaged five Albatros fighters near Langemarck about 7 pm. Coningham got very close to one and saw his shots strike home. The Albatros went down, but he did not see it crash because he was himself attacked and suffered two head wounds. He lost consciousness, began to go down, and only came to on being attacked again by another Albatros. It overshot and Coningham got on its tail, hitting the pilot and sending it spinning down. Gordon, meanwhile, was wounded and crashed, while Wells was forced to hide in cloud. Although 'rapidly losing blood', as Longcroft later recorded, Coningham joined Wells and continued the patrol for another half hour until he was sure the enemy had been driven off.

Longcroft recommended Coningham for the Distinguished Service Order on 2 August, an award confirmed on the 10th and announced in the *London Gazette* on 26 September. Since 22 July, wrote Longcroft, Coningham had had numerous engagements with enemy aircraft, three of which were shot down. 'His bravery has at all times been of the highest order,' he concluded, 'and his splendid example of the greatest value to the squadron.' On 3 August came a message from Gough, congratulating all squadrons on their excellent work and ending: 'I hope Captain Coningham is getting on? His action showed the same great spirit, in spite of wounds.'

By then, Coningham had been invalided home to England, but was well enough at the end of August to visit Buckingham Palace, where the King invested him with both the DSO and the MC. These were awarded, according to contemporary report, for bringing down ten enemy aircraft in the course of sixty engagements in fifteen flying days between 11 and 30 July. He had also been mentioned in French Army Orders four times in a fortnight. However, a more critical scrutiny of the records suggests that Coningham was personally responsible for the destruction of no more than seven enemy aircraft during his seven months with 32 Squadron; he shared in the destruction of three others and damaged or drove away an unknown number. Whatever the actual figures might be, 'Mary' Coningham had undoubtedly emerged from anonymity in little more than a year since his first arrival in England. He would make it his business to see that that emergence was not temporary.

Coningham was admitted to Chalfont Park hospital in Buckinghamshire in August, suffering from 'Stress of Service', in the words of his Record of

Service, and unfit for any duties. A colourful interview with him was widely reported in the New Zealand and Australian press in November. News of his awards, he said, reached him while he was in the New Hospital at Hazebruck, recovering from wounds suffered in desperate combats on 30 July. His leave had been due to begin on the 31st, but on the previous evening he is said to have decided on a 'joy ride' as a suitable preliminary. The aircraft he encountered were commanded, according to the press, by 'Wolf, one of the "crack" enemy airmen'. 'Nerves,' said Captain Coningham, 'there wouldn't be any if the flying men would only try to see the funny side. For even the most exciting fight possesses amusing incidents. I was laughing nearly all the time I had the four Germans tackling me and popping at me from all directions.'

More seriously, he wrote to Wellington College from London in that same November. 'I am prouder of being spared to keep up the reputation of the College and of New Zealand than of anything else,' he wrote. 'It is a treat to have one's efforts recognised, but at the same time very saddening to think of all the other real top-notchers not so fortunate.' He looked forward eagerly to each issue of the *Wellingtonian* to catch up with school news and the fortunes of his contemporaries. 'I am due for a medical board again in about a week,' he ended, and 'am counting the days and living in hopes of being overseas again before the New Year. It is a wonderful life, with equally wonderful lads of our glorious country to share it with you.'

By the end of November, he was out of hospital and permitted to resume 'limited flying', but it was not until January 1918 that he was declared 'fit for general service after one month of high flying at home'. By then, he had been told that command of a newly-formed squadron in France would be his if he could show that his health and nerve were sufficiently restored to permit him to handle fighters again. For three months, therefore, he commanded a Fighter School at Castle Bromwich in Warwickshire, flying practically every day and proving – not least to himself – that he was once more ready for the Western Front.[11]

CHAPTER THREE

'A Very, Very Happy Lot'

Coningham and 92 Squadron, March 1918 to January 1919

'Mary' Coningham, a newly-promoted major, took command of a newly-formed squadron on 26 March 1918 at Tangmere in Sussex. Within a week, they were all members of the newly-created Royal Air Force, replacing – in name, if not in spirit – the old RFC and RNAS. No. 92 Squadron had slowly been taking shape for six months and was now to be equipped with a fighter far superior to either of the de Havilland types in which Coningham had made his mark in 1917. This was the SE 5a, which had a much more powerful engine (a Wolseley Viper of 200 hp) and *two* machine-guns: a Lewis mounted to fire over the centre section of the top wing and a Vickers mounted on the left side of the engine cowling to fire through the propeller arc. It could also carry four 25-pound bombs.

Sholto Douglas (an outstanding fighter pilot of the Great War) thought the SE 5a 'superior in performance to any enemy fighting machine on the front . . . the most successful of any of the single-seat fighters that we employed during the war'. It was also 'a singularly comfortable machine. The pilot sat in a roomy, well-padded seat, well protected from the wind. The engine was exceptionally silent and there was little of that nauseating smell of castor oil that is so apt to affect a pilot endowed with a weak stomach.'

Coningham's friend 'Robbo' – Captain James Robb – with whom he had served in 32 Squadron, joined him as his senior Flight Commander on 6 May. During their time in Sussex, Coningham and Robb led their pilots on numerous training flights to practise formation flying, controlled diving, aerial combat and cross-country navigation at ground level; essential preparation for battle and also a great deal of fun for men still young in years, if not experience: Coningham, 'the old man', was all of twenty-three and Robb was a week younger.[1]

The squadron's ground personnel embarked at Southampton (under Robb's supervision) on 29 June, landing at Le Havre next day and travelling

24

on by rail to the aerodrome at Bray Dunes, near Dunkirk, to join 65 Wing in X Brigade. That brigade was commanded by Edgar Ludlow-Hewitt, a man of forbidding personality who became one of the RAF's most influential officers. Never an easy man to satisfy, much less impress, he kept a close eye on his squadron commanders and by the end of the year had decided that Coningham was the pick of them. Ludlow-Hewitt did not make his decisions lightly, nor did he forget them, as Coningham would learn – to his advantage – some twenty years later.

The pilots flew their aircraft from Tangmere to Marquise and thence to Bray Dunes on 1 July. Practice patrols began on the 6th and at 6.15 am on 12 July Coningham led the squadron's first line patrol. The young major made his first solo patrol on the 17th and during the rest of the war would frequently fly on his own. He was responsible for many men and machines: 25 officers, 154 men, 46 machine-guns, 6 motor-cars, 9 lorries, 8 trailers (for carrying aircraft and other heavy equipment), 8 motor-cycles, 4 sidecars and – not least – 19 aeroplanes. For the first, but not the last, time in his career, Coningham commanded American airmen. Six of 92 Squadron's pilots were American and he kept in touch with some of them for the rest of his life: in February 1941, Robb would write to tell him of the arrival of the annual card from 'Rusty' Rogers, who was trying to get back into the RAF.[2]

On 19 July, 92 Squadron moved to Drionville in 80 Wing, commanded by Louis Strange, a famous airman who taught Coningham lessons which he would apply with excellent effect in the Western Desert during the next war. Strange had taken command of 80 Wing on its formation in June and 'although the squadrons were a more or less fortuitous collection', in the words of a subsequent commendation, 'his high influence and unexampled leadership' soon made of them an efficient weapon in aerial combat, attacks on airfields and the disruption of supply columns far behind enemy lines. Offensive patrols began on 22 July and the squadron's first victory came that evening, when Robb shot down a Fokker D.VII fighter south of Bailleul railway station. The Combat Report, signed by Robb, Coningham and Strange, has 'First Blood' scrawled across it in blue pencil. Coningham had followed Robb's victim down almost to ground level, getting in several bursts from both guns before his boiling engine forced him to turn away.[3]

A celebration that night was followed by a wake only four days later, on 26 July, when Major Mick Mannock, Commanding Officer of 85 Squadron, was killed. One of the war's great fighter pilots, Mannock's loss was felt throughout the RAF and that night, wrote Ira Jones, 'lots of fellows turned up at No. 85 to cheer up the lads. Among the star fighters were Mary Coningham and Collishaw, both of whom assisted considerably in making the evening cheerful.' Although Raymond Collishaw was an undoubted star in aerial combat, Coningham was not: out of the front line for nearly a year, his record was unexceptional, but it may be that a commanding personality already distinguished him and certainly his effervescence would have been welcome on such a grim evening.

Neither celebrations nor wakes, however, could be permitted to interfere with daily flying or fighting and Coningham led a 'Voluntary Offensive Patrol' (that is, one not ordered by higher authority) over the lines on 29 July. He spotted an enemy two-seater below the British fighters and dived, firing hard, until turning aside at 2,000 feet. Evander Shapard (one of the American pilots) had followed him and was hit in the wings by fire from the two-seater's brave observer, but moments later it crashed into a shell-hole north of Estaires. This was the eleventh victory, conservatively estimated, in which Coningham had had at least a share. Next evening, 30 July, exactly one year since the combat which so nearly cost him his life, he was in action again: seven Fokker D.VIIs were seen over Estaires and he immediately led his patrol of five fighters to the attack; one was driven down, apparently out of control, and the rest fled eastwards.[4]

On 2 August, 92 Squadron moved to Serny, six miles south-west of Aire. There a plan was made to improve cooperation between the SE 5as (which performed well at high altitude) and the Camels, at their best against low-flying or ground targets. It was arranged that Coningham's SEs would work with 46 Squadron's Camels whenever possible, as would the SEs and Camels of two Australian squadrons, Nos. 2 and 4: in theory, the Camels would destroy enemy aircraft driven down by the SEs, while at the same time the presence above of these formidable machines would make it easier for the Camel pilots to concentrate on two-seaters, observation balloons and ground targets.

On an evening early in August, Coningham drove to St Omer, about twelve miles north of Serny, to collect two replacement pilots, one of whom – James Gascoyne – later recalled life at the new airfield. Physically, he said, Serny was a wholly typical airfield, with the usual portable hangars and a litter of wooden huts for sleeping, eating, stores and repairs, but the atmosphere was something special. The squadron, he wrote, 'included Americans, Canadians, New Zealanders, South Africans, one or two common English and an Irishman or two; so we were a very mixed crowd indeed and a very, very happy lot'. Coningham, said Gascoyne,

> was a very liked man. He talked to everyone and did everything he could to help you. The fact that he came to pick us up shows the kind of man he was. Every pilot in the squadron was right on his toes and morale was very high indeed. You felt you had joined something worth joining . . . they were a wonderful crowd. You had every confidence in practically every man you flew with.[5]

On the evening following his arrival at Serny, Coningham took Gascoyne up to show him round. During that flight, Gascoyne got into difficulties: the machine was as unfamiliar as the landscape, he became too nervous to do himself justice and quite failed to realise that his compass was faulty. Coningham shepherded him to a landing in near-darkness at the airfield of a

Bristol Fighter squadron, calmly arranged for him to spend the night there, without revealing to these strangers the greenness of his new pilot, and then flew home, landing by the light of flares. Gascoyne came to regard Coningham as 'one of the greatest men I have ever met,' a man who 'instilled confidence in everybody'. Coningham 'advised me on everything that was likely to happen in the war in the air and the whole squadron just loved him. He was a really wonderful man.' Gascoyne was no starry-eyed boy, fresh out from Blighty and overwhelmed by his first sight of a bemedalled fighter ace who treated him as a human being. He was, in fact, three years older than Coningham and one of the RFC's earliest recruits, having joined in 1913; he first saw services in France in August 1914 as a ground crew member of 3 Squadron and learned to fly in 1917.

The squadron's main duty during the summer was two-hour patrols, usually in flights of five aircraft. 'We flew in the usual V-formation,' recalled Gascoyne, 'and, of course, had no direct form of verbal communication with each other; but there were recognised signals which made it necessary to keep a continuous watch on the leader.' While watching him,' Gascoyne added in the pilot's characteristic deadpan, 'one sometimes missed seeing things it would have been better for one to have seen.' In Gascoyne's opinion, 92 Squadron had six effective pilots, of whom Coningham and Robb – in that order – were the best.

> Your purpose was to attack any German aircraft doing observation over your own troops, directing artillery fire and that kind of thing and then, if you came across a fighter squadron over the line – we always flew on their side of the line, I don't ever remember meeting a German over our side – you would engage these people and fight it out. When the fighting had finished, you would each go home . . . If anyone was shot down, there was nothing you could do about it.

Coningham led twelve aircraft to the German airfield at Nesle on 11 August, arriving over it at about 11.30 am, just as fourteen Fokkers, warned of their approach, were taking off. Our method, wrote Coningham later,

> was to attack the top enemy aircraft all the while and not to keep following down on the tails of any who were diving under the majority. At the critical moment, when five SEs were fighting twelve Fokkers (the other SEs were circling above to keep off another party of enemy aircraft higher up), Lieutenant Rogers, after looping, got one Fokker in flames. Everyone saw this as the enemy, a mass of flames, looped and then half-rolled before the pilot fell out.

The episode, Coningham concluded, demoralised his comrades and they fled. Coningham, having already attacked three Fokkers (two of his pilots

27

thought he destroyed one and he himself saw another crash near the airfield), now attacked 'what appeared to be the stoutest of the three,' but 'owing to misjudgment my machine got shot about badly and I had to return'. Robb confirmed that Coningham 'got one crashed and one out of control'. All told, the squadron certainly accounted for three Fokkers, damaged others and strafed the airfield vigorously, but several of its own machines suffered and one pilot was shot down and captured.

Fifteen years later, Louis Strange vividly recalled the appearance of both Coningham and his machine after that raid:

He was covered with blood all over, although his only wounds were a grazed forehead and a damaged finger; but this was something in the nature of a miracle, because his machine had been shot about in the most amazing manner. In fact, I simply cannot imagine how it held together; bullets had ripped it in scores and clusters until there was hardly an untouched portion anywhere. He had accounted for two Huns, but from his own appearance and that of his machine, one might have imagined him fighting the whole German Air Force single-handed. At any rate, the state in which this skilled, daring and experienced fighter returned indicated the hottest and most desperate fighting.[6]

On 16 and 17 August, Coningham (now flying D/6993, his personal aircraft for the rest of the war) took part in two major air raids planned and led by Strange, though the original idea was Ludlow-Hewitt's. Their targets were airfields at Haubourdin and Lomme, both west of Lille and about two miles apart. No fewer than sixty-five aircraft from four squadrons assembled over Reclinghem on the 16th before flying to Haubourdin. The Bristol Fighters of 88 Squadron, flying at 13,000 feet, provided high cover and at intervals of 2,000 feet below and some distance ahead were Coningham's SE 5as, those of the Australian 2nd Squadron and the Camels of the 4th. The Camels arrived over the target at 12.50 pm and as soon as Coningham and the leader of the Bristols realised that no aerial opposition was forthcoming, they added their weight to the Australian attack.

The raid on Haubourdin lasted thirty minutes, all four squadrons attacking in turn. Only a few enemy aircraft were seen, including one which dived into trees near the airfield without being attacked, and ground defences were silenced as soon as they revealed their positions by opening fire. Six phosphorus bombs (40 pounds each) and 136 explosive bombs (25 pounds each) were dropped from various heights between 50 and 400 feet and over 12,000 rounds of machine-gun fire kept most Germans in their trenches. Three large iron hangars were completely burnt out and two aircraft standing outside were set on fire. All told, thirty-seven aircraft were thought to have been destroyed. A big building, taken to be the Officers' Mess, was blown up. Best of all, an irreplaceable petrol dump was left blazing. Many soldiers and mechanics were hit by machine-gun bullets as they ran from all directions towards the hospital. A train heading for Haubourdin was shot up and stopped; the railway station itself was strafed and troops waiting on the platform scattered. Nearby, further strafing caused one staff car to drive into a ditch and another to run off the road and up a bank; in neither case were the occupants seen to get out. Horses were killed and roads blocked by overturned transports.

The same four squadrons attacked Lomme next morning. This was a lighter raid (sixty aircraft dropping two phosphorus bombs, 104 explosive bombs and firing about 9,000 rounds), but once again some pilots bravely bombed from as low as fifty feet and this time a strong wind enhanced their efforts. Three canvas hangars and several wooden sheds containing aircraft were set on fire; direct hits were also scored on workshops and living quarters. 'Casualties were caused amongst a party of about fifty mounted troops,' reported Ludlow-Hewitt, 'who disappeared into Lille at full gallop.' Two enemy aircraft, attempting to land during the raid, 'crashed hopelessly'. Several photographs were taken, despite dense clouds of smoke and a much more intensive barrage than Haubourdin's defences could manage. Guns of all kinds opened up in Lille and shrapnel from this fire, thought Ludlow-Hewitt, must have caused casualties among German troops billetted in the neighbourhood. Even so, only one of the attackers was shot down.

Major Carl Degelow (Commanding Officer of *Jasta* 40, based at Lomme) remembered Belgian civilian workers diving into flooded trenches and cursing 'the Tommies' as they swept across the airfield. Belgians and Germans were at last united, but Degelow was unable to do anything to cheer them or even to save his precious aircraft or the burning buildings because, he wrote, 'as soon as one of us dared to come out of the covered trenches, a Tommy would come down and "spray" us'. German prisoners later said that seventeen Fokkers had been destroyed and many casualties caused. Both Haubourdin and Lomme were abandoned, 'the first of several steps of gradual withdrawal in a north-easterly direction,' wrote F. M. Cutlack, historian of the Australian Flying Corps, 'that, at war's end, put us not far from Aachen in Germany itself'.[7]

Until late in August, 92 Squadron's patrol area had lain in a rough triangle between Lille, Lens and Douai, but heavy fighting farther south, around Cambrai, then required the squadron to move twenty miles south to Le Hameau to patrol an area from the Scarpe river to the Arras-Cambrai road. On 5 September, while patrolling north of Cambrai, Coningham observed a Fokker D.VII that was leading an enemy patrol come up behind a formation of eighteen Camels and fire at the rearmost, sending it into a spin. Unwisely, the German pilot followed his victim down. Ordering his men to engage the rest of the patrol, Coningham singled out the unwary victor, whose machine was distinctively marked with a yellow stripe along the fuselage. By firing as soon as he could, he caused the Fokker to leave the spinning Camel and head for Cambrai, 'wriggling' desperately until Coningham got in a close burst. The Fokker, he wrote later, at once 'did a vertical zoom, hung upside down and the pilot half fell out, hung by his arm and then dropped clear of the machine. He hit the ground about one mile west of Cambrai.' Coningham was then forced to fly very low all the way back to the British lines, wriggling desperately himself to avoid the bullets of several enemy aircraft.

Three weeks later, on 27 September, Coningham's squadron moved again, to Proyart South. There it joined 22 Wing, now commanded by Tom Cairnes (formerly Commanding Officer of 32 Squadron) in V Brigade, commanded by Lionel Charlton. From a British viewpoint, the most important battles were those aimed at the Hindenburg Line. Charlton had issued orders on 26 September that were read to all pilots on the evening of the 28th. The attack due to begin next day, he wrote, was expected to have 'wide and far-reaching results'. Accurate, detailed reports from the battle area and the country immediately behind it would be urgently needed. Cairnes added that aircraft reserved for low-level work – among them Coningham's – would only be sent when and where good targets were *known* to exist and escort patrols to protect them would be arranged. The battle area was carefully defined – between Honnecourt and St Quentin – and patrols were not to be drawn away from it under any pretext, nor were they to drift so far east that enemy aircraft might slip unobserved into the battle area.

Such restrictions had rarely applied before 1918. Until then, patrols were simply ordered to seek out opponents as far over the lines as possible. Throughout the battle, mist and drizzle hampered all aircraft, but the British enjoyed a local superiority that greatly aided the Allied advance and impeded the German retreat. Aircraft were already cooperating with tanks as in the Second World War and field armies could no longer operate successfully until air superiority had been achieved over the battlefield. 'While large-scale strategic bombing operations and the widespread employment of aircraft in naval warfare remained in the future,' wrote Peter Simkins, a British historian, 'the tactical use of air power in land warfare was already coming of age.' And 'Mary' Coningham, who would become an outstanding advocate of tactical air power in the next war, was among its brave executants in this one.[8]

As the advance continued, so 92 Squadron moved again – to Estrées-en-Chaussée – on 7 October. Greater emphasis than ever was now being placed on ground attack and Coningham's fighters regularly carried four 25-pound bombs. 'If you could shoot up transport and block the road,' recalled Gascoyne in words echoed a thousand times by pilots under Coningham's command in the next war, 'that was a fine thing; you stopped the whole lot. So personally I used to try and attack them from the front.' As for the bombs, 'You just pulled a plug and away they went,' but 'they were really only a great success when you had a line of transport . . . If you tried to bomb a motor-cyclist, for example, you wouldn't stand a chance in hell of getting him.' The morale of Coningham's men was evidently high, for they pressed home numerous attacks and as many as seven of them were decorated for outstanding skill and bravery during the last weeks of the war. Coningham himself attacked two trains between Bazeul and Le Cateau on 9 October, reported the location of a hostile battery and silenced a rocket battery. Troops and horse-drawn transports were bombed and machine-gunned every day from as low as twenty feet; roads were blocked and occupied trenches and strong points identified for artillery bombardment.

Coningham wrote to Cairnes on the 15th, commending Robb's 'great skill and determination' in attacks that day. 'With one other pilot,' Coningham said, 'he silenced an enemy three-gun Howitzer Battery. He then carried out a valuable reconnaissance from 600 feet under very heavy machine-gun fire. Though his machine was badly hit, he successfully attacked infantry and transport waggons before returning.' As for air fighting, Coningham added, Robb had seven victories to his personal credit and his 'magnificent leading' was largely responsible for the destruction of at least a further twenty-five; his had been 'the main contribution towards the Squadron's success'. Despite this generous praise, Robb ended the war with only the newly-instituted Distinguished Flying Cross to show for services that, as Coningham well knew, were neither less gallant nor versatile than his own. This disparity in official recognition weighed on Coningham and throughout the next war he made it his personal business to watch for similar instances and also to see that prolonged service of a high order as well as acts of great courage were properly rewarded.

In common with many other fighting men, Gascoyne had no idea that the war was about to end and two days before the Armistice was on patrol as usual, attacking enemy troops, guns and transport from below 500 feet. As with Robb, his 'splendid daring and accurate shooting' (in Coningham's words) might well have earned him more than the DFC awarded on 17 November. Even so, the award took him completely by surprise: 'I walked into the Mess one day for lunch,' he recalled, 'and found a note on my plate which read as follows: "Lt Gascoyne, DFC. Congratulations. A. Coningham."' Having been rather pointedly ignored all morning, Gascoyne now found his Commanding Officer bearing down on him, hand outstretched, beaming broadly. It was a typical example of the care Coningham always loved to devote to the 'special occasions' – birthdays, marriages or awards – in the lives of his friends.[9]

At 2.30 pm on 10 November, Coningham took off on his last patrol of the war and, as was often the case during his time with 92 Squadron, he flew alone. He dropped four bombs, fired a hundred rounds into transport moving along a road at Rance, saw no enemy aircraft and landed safely at 4.30 pm. It was his 176th patrol in eleven months at the front – an average of four per week, allowing for leaves – quite apart from countless test and practice flights. He personally destroyed nine enemy aircraft, shared in the destruction of four, damaged at least four and drove away scores of others. That night, just after midnight, he and Robb burst into the pilots' billet (both, for once, somewhat the worse for wear) and woke everyone up, demanding loudly: 'Have you got a job to go to?' Although 92 Squadron spent only four months on active service, it was very hard worked throughout that time from six different airfields. Its pilots fired 12,400 rounds in aerial combat, 22,400 at ground targets and dropped 340 bombs during a total war-flying time of 2,650 hours. Three of its thirty-five pilots were killed; eleven others wounded or captured and seven decorated. Between them, they claimed thirty-seven enemy aircraft destroyed and sixteen driven down out of control.

Coningham enjoyed a few days' local leave and Ranald Reid recalled a prolonged celebration in Paris that ended with himself and an Australian trying to keep up with Coningham in a race round the Champs Elysées in three hired cars: 'He was the wildest of us three,' wrote Reid, 'and on *water* alone.' Coningham then took his squadron to Thuilles (between Beaumont and Charleroi) in Belgium on 2 December, where it was closely inspected by Sir John Salmond, head of the RAF in France, on the 19th. All must have been well, including the 'recreational arrangements' upon which Salmond placed great emphasis, for Coningham was permitted to go to England next day, leaving Robb in temporary command. While in England, the Air Ministry extended his leave to 13 January 1919 and he resumed command of his squadron two days later. Coningham and Robb, having decided that they wanted to remain in the peacetime air force, returned to England together on the 30th for a two-month 'Course of Instruction in Administration and Organisation' at Halton House, near Aylesbury, Buckinghamshire. The course, attended by squadron and flight commanders, was designed (as Robb recalled) 'to instill into them some discipline' as well as practical knowledge. As for 92 Squadron, it was disbanded in August. Twenty years later, in October 1939, it would be re-formed, again as a fighter squadron, and in North Africa would again be under Coningham's command.[10]

In February 1946, when Air Marshal Sir Arthur Coningham addressed the Royal United Services Institution in London on the development of tactical air forces, a subject in which he was by then an acknowledged master, he recalled his early experience. By the end of 1918, he said, fighter squadrons in close cooperation with tanks were leading the advance and fighter-bombers were making the German retreat 'expensive and chaotic'. Coningham stressed this period 'because the principles there thrashed out have remained constant, only their degree and their application changing in accordance with the technical advance of aircraft, weapons, modern aids and the method of control'. The command of air forces during that war, in Coningham's opinion, and the concentration of effort in support of land forces compared more than favourably with modern practice. Contact between soldiers and the airmen was very close and mutual appreciation cemented both forces into a team. Much of Coningham's best effort in the next war had been devoted to restoring that 'mutual appreciation'.[11]

CHAPTER FOUR

'The Qualities of a Senior Officer'

Coningham in England, Iraq and Egypt, February 1919 to May 1926

The nine months between the signing of the Armistice on 11 November 1918 and the publication of the RAF's first list of permanent commissions on 1 August 1919 were critical in 'Mary' Coningham's life. A man without qualifications (academic or professional), without property or income, he could see no future for himself in New Zealand, now that the war was over, except as a worker on someone else's farm. Since his arrival in England in the middle of 1916, however, he had found – perhaps to his surprise – that he remained cool and brave in a crisis and was able to command both aircraft and men with a skill widely praised. He loved flying as well as plenty of company, cheerful gossip, dancing and parties that went on till morning, even though he never smoked and drank little. Although not in the least effeminate, he rejoiced in his odd nickname and made sure that it carried over into peacetime. He had already made many good friends in London and enjoyed the bustle and glitter of life in a great city. Coningham therefore applied for a permanent commission, but months passed while the Cabinet considered whether or not to retain an independent air force.

As late as July 1919, there were *no* permanent officers: those *forming* the RAF were either seconded from the Army or the Navy or held *temporary* commissions in the new service. Eventually, the Cabinet decided to sanction a maximum of 1,500 permanent commissions and the Air Ministry offered these to 1,065 of the 6,500 officers who had applied. To his great relief, Coningham was among the chosen few. And few they were: on Armistice Day, he had been one of a force of 290,000 officers and men in the RAF; a year later, its total strength had fallen to 35,500 and three-quarters of its officers held only short-term (two-to five-year) commissions.[1]

Despite his enthusiasm for a career in the RAF, Major Coningham made a very poor impression on his first peacetime superior. He had arrived at the Officers' School of Instruction at Halton House on 17 February 1919 and two months later the Commandant noted that

> his work and general behaviour were most unsatisfactory. He returned
> late from weekend leave on more than one occasion and just before his

33

final examination absented himself without leave, returning too late to sit for the first paper. Displayed an entire lack of discipline and from this point of view appears to be unfit for any senior rank.

Coningham was only twenty-four and, no doubt, still enjoying the relief from being regularly shot at as well as the end of his responsibility for the lives of so many other men. These criticisms from Halton evidently cut no ice in the Air Ministry because although he reverted to the rank of Captain on 1 May, he was awarded the Distinguished Flying Cross on 3 June as a further tribute to his courage and leadership under fire and in July was offered and accepted a permanent commission in the newly-created rank, equivalent to Captain, of Flight Lieutenant.[2]

Coningham was among the first generation of permanent air force officers: an important point, helping to shape his character and attitudes in three ways. Firstly, these officers shared a fear throughout their *lives* – let alone their active *careers* – of the Army and/or the Navy ending the cherished independence of their beloved service. Portal, Tedder, Dowding, Douglas, Harris, Slessor, Leigh-Mallory, Park, Coningham and the rest quarrelled vigorously among themselves, but stood shoulder-to-shoulder against all outsiders. Secondly, these early RAF officers were well versed in Army–Air cooperation: either in clearing the battlefield sky of hostile aircraft or in the even more dangerous skills of low-level attack on ground targets chosen by the Army in the front, rear or lines of communication of enemy forces. It had been their main task during the Great War and remained so (made far easier by complete air superiority) throughout the Twenties and Thirties in many parts of the British Empire. And thirdly, many of the first generation of RAF officers were anxious to find a new role for their service after 1918, especially as an independent peace-keeping or war-winning force.

Theories about strategic bombing were devised in the Air Ministry or imbibed in staff college courses at Andover and devotion to these theories is said either to have won or nearly lost Britain the next war. The arguments are endless, but Coningham had no part in them. Of all the RAF's senior commanders in the Second World War, he was unique in that he received no formal, theoretical service education. By the end of that war, he was inordinately proud of the fact that he had neither served in the Air Ministry nor studied at Andover. His entire career was practical. He was a marvellous pilot and navigator, a gifted teacher (even though he had never been taught how to teach) and, rarest of all, a natural leader. His practical gifts helped to make him an exceptional athlete and sportsman – at polo, shooting, sailing, swimming and golf in particular – as well as an exceptional airman.

By February 1920, Coningham was an instructor at Manston in Kent, where a school for the technical training of mechanics had been established under the command of Keith Park, a fellow New Zealander who would also make his mark. Sholto Douglas was then serving at Manston and remembered them well: 'tall, handsome men,' he wrote, 'with fine records as

34

fighting pilots during the war . . . curiously alike in their temperaments'; a surprising opinion, but only at first sight, for though they moved in quite different social circles, both were ambitious men with forceful personalities and, thought Douglas, the fact that Park and Coningham were 'colonials' released them from 'the inhibitions which put so much restraint on the style of our own people'.

Both took prominent parts in the first RAF Aerial Pageant at Hendon on 3 July 1920, a spectacular display attended by at least 40,000 paying spectators and watched also by 'thousands who thronged the neighbouring hills and country – as far as Hampstead'. Coningham and Flying Officer Gerald Gibbs, in Sopwith Snipes, 'fought' two other officers in a Bristol Fighter. 'This display was very exciting to watch', reported *Flight*, 'making one realise what skill and daring our pilots must have possessed to have achieved what they did during the War'. Spectators thought it a dangerous display, recalled Gibbs, 'but in fact it was not, because as we didn't fire guns so we turned away a little earlier than in a real combat'. Moreover, those taking part in the Pageant had spent the whole of the two previous days practising for their events.[3]

Coningham escaped from Manston and returned to the Central Flying School (CFS) at Upavon on Salisbury Plain, where he had learned to fly, in October 1920. The calm direction of ground training by Wing Commander Norman MacEwan combined well with the daring example of Squadron Leader Christopher Draper in the air to ensure that the CFS became an excellent school for flying instructors. The 'CFS patter' (standardised instruction) was based on a booklet compiled during the war by Major R. R. Smith-Barry, doyen of flying instructors, and emphasised that 'good and bad morale, confidence and the lack of it, are more easily caught than the most contagious of physical diseases'. Consequently, the words 'danger' and 'nerves' should be eliminated from an instructor's vocabulary because 'nothing that a pilot may do in the air is dangerous if he knows what he is doing and what the result will be'. Coningham endorsed these sentiments and drove them forcefully into the hearts and minds of countless pupil pilots during the next decade. Captain Norman Macmillan, who became a notable test-pilot and RAF historian, remembered Coningham in 1921 'as a brilliant fighter-instructor' at Upavon, handling the Snipe, which was then the world's finest single-seat fighter, superbly.[4]

Although a gifted and conscientious teacher, Coningham remained keen to develop his own flying skills and was rewarded by selection in a team of five exceptional pilots to demonstrate the Snipe at the Hendon Pageant in 1921. Coningham, Teddy Gerard, Roy Brading, 'Pedro' Mann and Draper himself practised intensively for a couple of weeks before the Pageant and on the day itself they took off in formation, looped, rolled, flew upside down and landed again, still in formation. The *Royal Air Force Record* was most impressed by 'the most wonderful formation flying that ever happened'. A few days later, the CFS team repeated their performance at Andover, earning praise from the *Aeroplane* for 'a splendid display' in which 'the Performing Snipes' from Upavon did all that they did at Hendon and did it rather better, considering that a strong gusty wind was blowing'. After their 'circus performance', the magazine continued, the Snipes attacked 'three perfectly innocent Avros in a most cowardly manner and shot them down (theoretically) in flames'.[5]

Coningham enjoyed himself immensely at Upavon, but on the eve of his departure in February 1922, a wholly unexpected rebuke from MacEwan, who was normally the most amiable of commanders, shook his self-esteem. At their final interview, instead of the usual exchange of pleasantries, MacEwan chose to wonder aloud whether Coningham had 'the qualities of a senior officer': no-one, he said, doubted his ability to handle aircraft, but at twenty-seven he was no longer in the first flush of youth and had exhausted the post-war indulgence allowed even to a decorated hero and was faced with four years' service abroad – in Iraq and Egypt – that would decide whether he was still fit to command others; since the war ended, his performance on the ground had in no way matched his performance in the air.

With MacEwan's cold words ringing in his ears, Coningham sailed for Iraq from Southampton on 24 February, arriving at Basrah, at the head of the Persian Gulf, on 10 April. The RAF headquarters were centrally placed in Baghdad and five squadrons were based nearby at Hinaidi, one in the south-east at Shaibah (near Basrah), one in the north-east at Kirkuk and one in the north-west at Mosul. This latter, 55 Squadron – which Coningham joined and would later command – became famous for its exploits in Iraq. Its motto, *Nil Nos Tremefacit* (Nothing Shakes Us), was more freely translated as 'You can't put the wind up 55'.[6]

Early in 1920, it had become clear that the military occupation of Iraq cost more than the British government wished to afford. It was therefore necessary either to find a cheaper method of control or leave. Winston Churchill, then Secretary of State for Air, directed that the possibility of making greater use of the RAF be examined. Opposition from the Army was overcome and in August 1921 the Cabinet sanctioned a scheme leading to air control: ground forces would be gradually reduced and the number of squadrons increased until October 1922 when an airman, Air Vice-Marshal Sir John Salmond, would assume command of all British forces in Iraq: eight squadrons of aircraft, four of armoured cars, a single brigade of British and Indian infantry and about 5,000 Iraqi levies. In that year, wrote Lieutenant General Sir John Glubb (who earned great fame in the Middle East as Glubb Pasha, commander of the Arab Legion from 1939 to 1956), Iraq became the scene of 'a new experiment, unprecedented in the world, the employment of air forces in place of ground troops for internal security duties'.[7]

In theory, airmen had an advantage over soldiers in a country with few roads and many armed tribes, but how were they to know which tribes or villages were friendly and which hostile? Officers were therefore based with

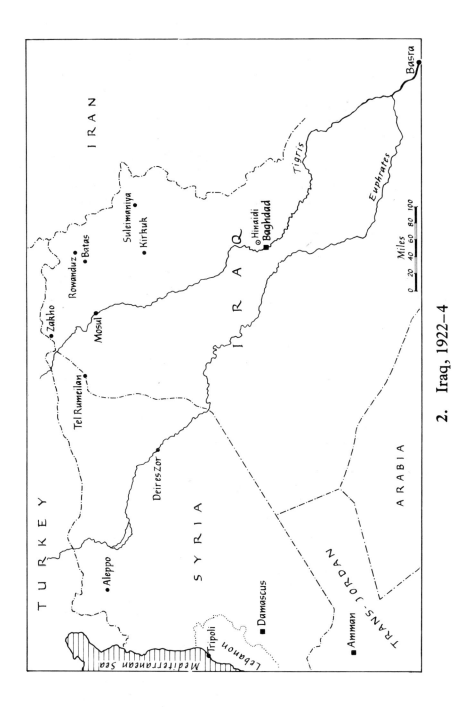

2. Iraq, 1922–4

37

government officials to collect information for passing on to their colleagues and to make arrangements for supplies of water, food, fuel, ammunition, etc. Without detailed, accurate information – obtainable only from the ground, by fixed observers or armoured car patrols – shepherds following winter rains with their animals to wherever grass had grown could not be protected from raiders well-mounted on camels or horses. But airfields were poorly-equipped, aircraft and men were few, maps and wirelesses virtually non-existent and forced landings in remote areas a common hazard made worse by the likelihood of death from thirst, hunger or Arab attack. Consequently, airmen who were slack or inept in the vital skills of navigation and engine care did not last long in Iraq and Coningham mastered four lessons there that were valuable to him twenty years later in more serious desert campaigns: without information, communications, supplies and close relations with ground forces, nothing could be done – and without continual attention from the officer in command, all four would fail when most needed.

When Coningham reached Mosul, 55 Squadron was flying DH 9a two-seater biplanes. The officers were accommodated in an old Turkish fort on the edge of the airfield, the airmen were in huts and tents nearby and their main task was dealing with unrest in the mountainous north of the country, where Kurdish tribes, encouraged by Turkey, sought their independence. Some British Army officers were murdered in June 1922 by Karim Fattah Beg, head of a tribe in southern Kurdistan, but 'the prompt appearance of aeroplanes,' in the opinion of the Iraq Record Book, 'undoubtedly subdued the waverers and hooligan element who might otherwise have thrown in their lot with Karim Fattah Beg and our machines continually bombed villages and localities where he was reported'. During July, 55 Squadron dropped five tons of 'instantaneous, delayed action and incendiary bombs as well as petrol' and fired 2,000 rounds of machine-gun bullets at ground targets. Much of this activity was directed at Rowanduz, about eighty miles east of Mosul, where the inhabitants 'have a good system of warning and get into surrounding caves, so delayed action bombs cause great nervousness among them'. The 'moral effect' of bombing, concluded the Record Book, has been 'excellent' throughout the region.

Nevertheless, unrest continued and on 5 September, Coningham helped to evacuate Britons from Suleimaniya, seventy miles south of Rowanduz, who had been threatened by 'rebels': his contribution was 'a Mr Turner and one machine-gun'. Altogether, sixty-seven persons, including non-Muslim government servants and a great deal of baggage, books and money, were taken to Kirkuk by a force of twenty-nine aircraft. The evacuation, completed without difficulty despite a strong gale, earned generous commendation from the Army and took place seven years before the much better-known evacuation of the British legation at Kabul in Afghanistan, often said to be the first air evacuation. Unfortunately, Coningham's pleasure in this feat was tempered by illness: he had spent twelve days in Mosul

38

hospital with sandfly fever in July–August and returned there for five more days in mid-September with a sharp recurrence.

There was, in fact, an undeclared war with Turkey in northern Iraq and all eight RAF squadrons were hard worked. They bombed and machine-gunned Turkish invaders, the villages and livestock of their local 'sympathisers' and cooperated closely with ground forces by dropping supplies and keeping them informed about enemy strength and movements. James Robb had now joined 6 Squadron (Bristol Fighters) at Kirkuk and enjoyed a boisterous reunion with Coningham at Christmas, 1922. Early in the new year, they took part in their first military operation together since the Armistice: a successful raid on Batas, a village south-west of Rowanduz. 'Hostile chiefs and Turks in village,' recorded Robb in his log book. 'Bombing good, then came down and shot up cattle and horses. Wood [Robb's rear-gunner] finished ammunition then used his revolver.' As a rule, however, their main opponent was a certain Sheik Mahmoud, a Kurd who had been governor of Suleimaniya under the Turks: 'We were always chasing him,' wrote Flying Officer Frank Long, a member of 55 Squadron, 'and trying to destroy him, but he always eluded us'; Mahmoud was therefore known throughout Iraq as 'the Director of Training' for the excellent practice he afforded the RAF in organising and carrying out raids on widely-scattered villages believed to be offering him support.[8]

Having recognised the merit in MacEwan's rebuke and with the distractions of London safely out of reach, Coningham had not found it difficult to revive the ambition which drove him out of New Zealand, and was promoted to the rank of Squadron Leader on 30 June 1923, taking command of 55 Squadron in July. On the 20th, he and Flight Lieutenant Sam Kinkead flew two DH 9as about 180 miles south-westwards from Mosul to Deir es Zor, a town on the Euphrates in Syria, taking with them a couple of officials who were to discuss frontier problems with the French authorities. As soon as the talks began, Coningham accepted an invitation to fly with a French officer a further 180 miles westward to Aleppo; Kinkead had to travel there by road, but both enjoyed themselves immensely, riding by day, partying by night and re-living old battles on the Western Front. Coningham was in his element, for he responded readily to the style and grace of French life, even in a remote colony, and returned reluctantly to the much drabber life of Mosul on the 26th. Kinkead, a highly-decorated fighter pilot and later a member of RAF teams competing for the Schneider Trophy, was killed nearly five years later, in March 1928, while attempting to break the world absolute air speed record in a Supermarine S.5 over the Solent off Calshot. His death shocked Coningham severely, for they had often served together and were the best of friends.[9]

On 22 August 1923, Coningham led a formation of six aircraft on a reconnaissance of Iraq's frontiers with Syria and Turkey. On reaching Tel Rumeilan, some seventy-five miles west of Mosul, on the 'provisional' frontier with Syria, he decided to land and instructed the other aircraft to fly on to Zakho, sixty miles north-east, near the Turkish frontier, and await him there. To his surprise, Coningham wrote later, he was confronted by 'a number of mounted tribesmen, who adopted a very threatening attitude'. They thought the machine a French one which had recently bombed them and though Coningham soon disabused them on that score, 'they made it obvious that they wished the machine to go away before the main body of the tribesmen, now approaching on foot, reached them'.

Coningham prudently departed, but returned next day with two other aircraft, 'in order to clear up the situation,' as he put it, 'and generally establish our prestige'. As they were about to land, heavy rifle fire opened up. Coningham refrained from returning the fire and ordered all three machines to carry on landing. The fire ceased, he climbed out of the cockpit and strolled calmly towards the tribesmen, enquiring politely what was amiss? The DH 9as having again been mistaken for French aircraft, some differences were pointed out; the tribesmen then apologised and produced coffee. Their leader was so impressed by Coningham's cool firmness that he wrote a message of goodwill in Arabic on the cowling of his aircraft. Coningham thanked him and later had the message copied, enlarged, reproduced in polished aluminium and riveted on to a conspicuous place. Throughout his career, men who served with Coningham often observed that he was never more cheerful and self-confident than when danger threatened.[10]

During September Sir John Salmond, Commander-in-Chief, visited Mosul to inspect units in that area and to observe a bombing demonstration by members of 55 Squadron. Coningham had been drilling them diligently since a fiasco in August when they came a distant last in a competition won by 45 Squadron, commanded by one Arthur Harris, later to make a name in Bomber Command. The demonstration pleased Salmond and a relieved Coningham flew south to take part in a display of formation and stunt flying, put on to impress a group of influential chiefs at Hinaidi on 12 September. All areas remained quiet in October and much time was devoted to training in bombing, machine-gunning, formation flying, cooperation with armoured cars, photography and setting up instructional classes for NCOs and airmen.

Victor Groom, then a Flying Officer in 55 Squadron (who served again with Coningham at the height of his career), liked the system whereby RAF officers could take over surplus horses from the Army and pay only for their upkeep. So did Coningham: a proficient horseman before he left New Zealand, he became a polo player of international standard in Iraq. Coningham also responded to what Squadron Leader A. T. Williams called 'the spirit of cheery enthusiasm' of all ranks in Iraq in the Twenties. It was, he thought, 'a revival of the war spirit of cooperation'. Squadron and Flight Commanders were encouraged to visit the air staff in Baghdad with a view to settling problems quickly, face-to-face, rather than allowing them to drag on while letters flowed back and forth. This system – or rather, attitude of mind – was very much to Coningham's taste and one he would follow, as far as he could, for the rest of his career.[11]

Off duty, he enjoyed river-bathing, weekend shooting expeditions in winter (sandgrouse and duck) and hunting pig. Social life, however, was limited: even in Baghdad there was only one jazz band and dances were rare, formal interludes in 'a somewhat monastic existence', as one officer recalled. Getting out of Iraq was a slow, expensive business. The Nairn Transport Company was organising a service using eight-cylinder Cadillacs from Baghdad to Haifa, a distance of nearly 600 miles, to connect with the Sunday train to Port Said and the P & O steamer to London. The journey took eleven days and cost £140 return: more than three months' pay, so Coningham stayed where he was. To a man who loved flying, it was no hardship, especially in the Mosul area in winter. Every minute in the air was then a treat, with miles of undulating green cultivation below and snow-capped hills in the distance. 'We lived for flying,' wrote one of Coningham's dearest friends, later Air Chief Marshal Sir Theodore McEvoy, 'and, taking no thought for the morrow, asked little more of life in our mid-twenties than to be spared for as long as possible from Marriage and Death.'[12]

Salmond reported to the Air Ministry in April 1924 on his eighteen-month stint as head of Iraq Command. The Army Commander, wrote Salmond in words which Coningham would make his own, 'should always work closely with an RAF officer, who will provide him with the information necessary to judge what services the air arm can give'. This officer would frame for the commander 'the requests to the RAF for conjoint and cooperative air action in accordance with the general plan'. Salmond emphasised the breadth of experience gained by airmen in Iraq, using aircraft of various types both independently and in conjunction with ground forces over every kind of country: open desert, deep valleys, rugged mountains, dense reed marshes and riverain areas closely intersected with irrigation channels. 'Aircraft prove of great value,' he wrote, 'in direct attack on ground targets by providing covering or supporting machine-gun fire; they disperse hostile forces and, when necessary, impede the escape of those forces by attacking bridges, fords or mountain defiles. Aircraft also perform such valuable services as transporting troops and stores, evacuating casualties, picking up and dropping messages and dropping supplies. Not least, they fly out the Army Commander at short notice to consult or instruct subordinates, assess the general situation and test the troops' morale, all without long absence from his headquarters.' Some soldiers, however, overrated air power. For example, George Pirie (another close ally of Coningham's in desperate days to come) was once instructed to kill a sheikh who had murdered a British officer: 'The pilot can't mistake him,' Pirie was told, 'for he is riding a dappled grey pony and his attendants are mounted on ordinary grey ones.'[13]

The Air Ministry emphasised that air action was 'a last resort', never to be initiated in any circumstances whatever except at the request of the local British civil adviser acting in concert with the local Iraqi administration –

and only when that request had been considered and approved in succession by the Minister of the Interior in the Iraqi government, his British Adviser and finally, the High Commissioner himself. Although the bombing of villages was strongly criticised in the British press and in Parliament, it was only resorted to when tribesmen deliberately disobeyed a Political Officer and even then only after they had been given ample warning (usually two or three days) to think about it. Then, when it was definitely decided to bomb, they were again warned, so that people could abandon the village if they wished or at least evacuate women and children. Sir John Glubb, who first learned to love the Arab people while serving in Iraq, emphasised the positive side of air action there. 'While everybody knows what we owed to the RAF in the Battle of Britain,' he wrote in 1960, 'its services in frontier wars in remote countries have not received adequate recognition.' British intervention in Iraq, he thought, was 'purely beneficial' in saving 'a poor, simple and hardy community from the terror of constant massacre' and establishing a peace that lasted for years. Unfortunately, the operations were not widely reported at the time because Iraq was difficult to reach and uncomfortable for press correspondents.[14]

In February 1924, Coningham, who had few happy memories of his earlier time in Egypt, now found himself sent there again. He arrived at Heliopolis, Cairo, on the 23rd, to undertake air staff duties at the headquarters of Egypt Group. When Coningham took command of what became the Desert Air Force in July 1941, he not only had years of practical experience behind him in Army–Air cooperation, he was also thoroughly schooled in handling air forces in the extremes typical of the desert: great heat, bitter cold, choking dust or mud like 'chocolate blancmange', as one former pilot described it. These severe climatic conditions generated extremes in personal performance and relations: men either did much better in their jobs than in Europe or much worse and their feelings about each other were also more intense. As no doubt MacEwan hoped, when rebuking him on the eve of his departure from England, Coningham's performance in Iraq and Egypt showed that he had in fact the qualities of a senior officer; in Egypt, however, Coningham carried out a pioneering flight that delighted MacEwan no less, for it confirmed his protégé's reputation as a great pilot and navigator.

By 1925, interest was growing in the problems and possibilities of opening up the African continent to civil aviation. The French and Belgians had plans for their own territories and Britain did not wish to be left behind. In September, the Air Ministry announced that three DH 9as of 47 Squadron (stationed at Helwan, near Cairo) would fly from there to Kano in Nigeria 'for the purpose of gaining experience in long distance flights over tropical countries, where few facilities in the way of the ground organisation required by aircraft exist, and with the object of allowing Nigeria to see the capabilities of British aircraft'. The venture would be led by Squadron Leader Coningham. His major problems would be navigation and engines. Although there were wireless telegraphy stations at some points along the route, the aircraft carried no transmitting or receiving equipment and had to rely on compasses and on maps which were nearly useless. The engines, reconditioned American 'Liberty' engines of 400 hp, had an unreliable record, so Coningham decided to run them gently, reducing the DH 9a's normal cruising speed from 90 to 80 mph.

The aircraft took off from Helwan at 7 am on 27 October, waved away by a large gathering of soldiers and airmen and landed at Wadi Halfa – 644 miles south of Helwan – after eight hours and twenty minutes in the air, all three pilots aching in arms and chest because, as Coningham frankly admitted, he had misjudged their weight distribution and they flew tail-heavy. Fortunately, this first day of their journey was both the longest and hardest of the sixteen they spent in the air. At Wadi Halfa, Coningham boldly reduced the load carried and, taking off at 4.50 am next morning, they reached Khartoum at noon. With a lighter, better distributed load, it proved a faster and more comfortable journey.

En route due west to El Fasher, a 'considerable range of hills' soon appeared and perturbed Coningham, for it was not marked on his map. Believing El Fasher lay east of such a range, he looked for it in vain and then decided to press on towards another range, some twenty-five miles farther west, which *was* marked. After fifteen anxious minutes, the town appeared and the flight landed safely (despite three punctures), everyone much relieved. Refuelling began at once, 'assisted by the officers, who had cancelled their polo, and the men of the garrison'. It was while in El Fasher that Coningham again contracted the malaria that would plague him at intervals during the rest of his life.

'The country from this point onwards,' he wrote, 'had never been traversed by aircraft.' Visibility as far as El Fasher had been 'phenomenal', but westward fires had been deliberately started to trap game 'and at times it was so smoky that at 4,000 feet one was now and then taken unawares and compelled to make sure that nothing in the machine was burning'. For some time after leaving El Fasher, they were able to follow a well-worn camel track, used by Muslim pilgrims making for Mecca, until it ran into mountainous country. After an overnight stop at Abecher, they flew over the landing strip at Fort Lamy, for Coningham had intended to press on to Maidugari, but noticing that more smoke than usual was coming from Herbert Rowley's exhaust, he decided to turn back. At Fort Lamy, he learned that Rowley had lost most of his fuel: had they kept going, 'he would have crashed in rather thick forest twenty miles beyond'. Not surprisingly, Rowley remembered the incident vividly, as we shall see.

It was not until 10.20 next morning that they were able to leave Fort Lamy and French territory for Maidugari in British Nigeria. 'Crowds had been out on the main road from Maidugari to Kano from dawn looking up into the sky,' he wrote, 'and people assembled in the towns on that road, coming in from considerable distances north and south.' Coningham landed

3. Coningham's flight across Africa, October–November 1925

to apologise for not having arrived the night before, but soon regretted his generous impulse because all three machines got stuck in soft yellow earth on the landing strip and it took forty-five minutes to free them, by a combination of engine and muscle power, and run them on to a harder polo ground. More harm was done to the engines during those minutes than would normally occur during at least twenty hours of flying time.

The flight had been expected to arrive at Kano about 10.00 that morning and would have done so but for Rowley's faulty carburettor. The Resident Representative in Kano of the Government in Lagos told the huge crowd which had assembled that the aircraft would now arrive about 5 pm. It was a rash promise, but Coningham redeemed it, landing on a polo ground outside Kano's ancient walls at 5.10 pm on 1 November 1925, the sixth day of the journey. The Resident, greatly relieved, afterwards told Coningham that 'we had saved their prestige'. The machines were carefully roped round to prevent damage and the whole airfield completely surrounded by troops holding back a crowd of at least 20,000 people. The airmen had flown the official distance from Helwan – 2,904 miles – in thirty-six hours and fifty minutes, but the actual distance covered, 'allowing for finding the way', was well over 3,000 miles at an average speed of about 83 mph.

Throughout the journey, Coningham closely observed the character of the country over which they flew and concluded that good landing grounds were few and far between. Distances and the time taken to cover them impressed him deeply. If a machine had come down near Lake Fittri, for example, the crew would have had to sit tight near the crash, living off what they could shoot or buy from the natives until rescued – and that would have taken at least forty-five days from Fort Lamy or Abecher: a distance the aircraft covered in two and a half hours. However, there was no possibility of a successful landing between Kaduna and El Obeid, except for a short stretch west of Abecher. 'The knowledge of this,' wrote Coningham, 'becomes a cumulative strain.' And yet, flying sometimes seemed to him the slowest means of transport. 'At 3,000 feet with visibility up to 150 miles, a hill comes into view quite two hours away. You know that your destination is some way beyond. There is no sense of speed and for hours the hill seems never to get any nearer.' The temptation to hurry, to risk damage to elderly engines, became difficult to resist towards the end of a long day, especially when an airstrip lay in view for up to an hour.

Flying from Kano 130 miles south-westward to Kaduna on 6 November, the airmen were met by 'everybody in full dress', taken to Government House and 'lived in the greatest comfort' until the 10th. 'A special grandstand had been erected and the preparations were such that the natives were convinced that the Prince of Wales liked Nigeria so much that he had come back . . . I was again given two days very good polo and well mounted.' Coningham took up the Emir of Zaria, Flight Lieutenant Humphrey Baggs took up the Sergeant Major of the Regiment and Rowley the Sergeant Major of the Police, a Hausa. 'He looked slightly thoughtful as he clambered into the machine,' wrote Rowley, 'but once in the air he broke into a great smile and then sang at the top of his deep voice until we landed.'

The three aircraft left Kano for Maidugari on the first leg of their journey home at 7 am on 12 November. They flew at 1,000 feet for much of the way 'to give the people a better view of the machines'. Having flown low over the native town, they landed or the same soft yellow sand as before, only this time making sure to run on to the polo field before stopping. The airmen were presented to the Emir of Bornu, who presented Coningham with two huge white rams, which he accepted with an enthusiasm made all the warmer by his knowledge that the Resident's staff would have to find some means of hiding them until long after he had gone.

They retraced their outward course without incident (except for strong head winds and punctures at every landing) until arriving safely at Helwan on 19 November 1925. Coningham and his men had flown on sixteen of the twenty-four days spent on the total journey, covering a distance that he estimated as about 6,500 miles. Exactly eighty hours were spent in the air (apart from a few courtesy flights) and all three of their much-maligned engines 'ran faultlessly' throughout, a fact that greatly pleased the crews for 'fifty-three successive hours were spent over country ordinarily called impossible'. The Air Ministry proudly announced two firsts: the first east-west crossing of Africa by air and the first appearance of aircraft in Nigeria. That same journey, 'by the normal methods of rail, steamer, camel and bullock transport', would take about six months.

Coningham got little immediate enjoyment out of his triumph, for he spent the last weeks of the year either in hospital or on sick leave, recovering from 'flying stress' as well a malaria. On New Year's Day, his restoration to full health was hastened by the award of the Air Force Cross 'for consistent and meritorious service and devotion to duty' in command of a flight 'mainly over dense bush country not previously traversed by aircraft'. Sergeant Henry Grant (who flew with Rowley) was awarded the Air Force Medal because 'it was largely due to his untiring zeal and ability that the whole journey was successfully completed'. So ended a flight described in the House of Commons by Sir Samuel Hoare (Secretary of State for Air) 'as a training exercise on an extended scale for a detachment of a squadron normally stationed at Cairo, using the ordinary service equipment of the squadron. The object would not have been met if a specially-equipped squadron had been sent out for the flight and greater expense would have been involved.' In a speech broadcast from London on 17 November, Hoare said that he had organised the flight and that next year there would be a flight by RAF machines to the Cape.[15]

'Considering that the DH 9as are of a design now some eight years old,' observed *Flight* on 26 November, 'and that the construction is mainly wood,' their performance was 'an eloquent testimony to British workmanship'. As for the flight's value, the magazine rated it much more highly than did the Air Ministry. 'It has linked up Nigeria with Egypt by air,' *Flight* emphasised, 'and must thus have done a great deal of good in causing the white population of that outpost of Empire to feel less isolated and much closer in touch with the rest of the world.' It had also

> welded another link in the chain which shall one day – of that we have not the slightest doubt – bind together the far-flung parts of the British Empire. Already one can foresee the time when British air lines will spread their net the length and breadth of Africa, linking up Egypt and Nigeria, with connections to the French air terminus at Dakar and the Belgian air lines in the Congo, not to mention the line from Cairo to the Cape.

Trenchard, addressing Dominion premiers a year later on 2 November 1926, took up this theme and Coningham's flight was among his examples of the new *reliability* as well as the proven *mobility* of air power. He therefore stressed the need to develop facilities throughout the Empire to exploit both advantages in the interests of civil communications and, above all, imperial defence.[16]

In fact, despite further RAF flights to Nigeria, the arrival of the first Imperial Airways aircraft in Kano was still ten years away. The full potential of the Takoradi-Khartoum-Cairo route would only be realised when the Second World War began. Once Italy had entered the conflict on Germany's side and British use of the Mediterranean had been severely curtailed, air access to the Middle East was possible only via Lisbon and Freetown to Takoradi and Kaduna and thence in Coningham's wake to Cairo where, from the middle of 1941 onwards, Coningham himself would give many thanks for the aircraft sent there.

In February 1948, shortly after Mary Coningham's death in a flying accident, Herbert Rowley (calling himself 'Polygon') recalled his flight across Africa in the *Aeroplane*. Not only an outstanding achievement in itself, he wrote, it showed clearly that Coningham 'had the essential qualities of a future great commander'. Consider the problems he faced: obsolete aircraft with engines needing constant attention; no radio aids on the ground or in the air; landing strips that were short and narrow even for the DH 9a; maps showing few landmarks accurately even where the country had been surveyed and slender chances of survival or rescue should a forced landing become necessary. Given a free hand to choose his crews, Coningham could have had specialists in navigation. Instead, he chose men who had served with him before: personal friends whom he could trust in emergency, a lesson he had learned in the Great War.

Coningham also had a rare courage, Rowley thought: 'the courage to delegate responsibility', handing over all the details of organisation, equipment, spares and stores to Rowley; having done so, he did not interfere. That courage would be characteristic of Coningham throughout his great commands in the Second World War. So, too, would be his confident good humour. On arrival at Abecher, for instance, he told his pilots that the maps were even worse than they thought: not only too small in scale, but wrong in such detail as they contained. Coningham laughed so heartily that everyone else joined in, but Rowley realised – later – that 'he must have been worried out of his life, for an error in navigation would probably mean the loss of the whole flight'. Finally, the ability to act quickly (which Coningham so often had to do under the stress of war) was seen after flying over Fort Lamy on the outward journey when he noticed the smoke coming from Rowley's aircraft 'and sensed immediately that the pilot was worried'; had he not turned back at once, 'one 9a would have crashed in thick jungle'. It was therefore 'right and fitting' concluded Rowley, that the young Squadron Leader who led this flight and pioneered the trans-African route should benefit from it when he commanded the Desert Air Force.[17]

CHAPTER FIVE

'An English Gentleman in Love'

Coningham and Nan, 1926–39

Coningham left Egypt in April 1926 and having accumulated twelve weeks' leave was able to enjoy his first English summer for five years untroubled by duty. His self-assurance was more soundly based than it had been in 1921, for he was now a senior officer, matured by strenuous and varied service abroad, while still – at thirty-one – enjoying a reputation, brilliantly enhanced by his flight across Africa, as an exceptional pilot. As well as professional ability and a commanding personality, Coningham was acquiring the social graces and interests helpful in achieving still higher rank. By nature a man well able to attune himself to any company, he was already an accomplished horseman and shot and now, during the summer of 1926, took up sailing, another pursuit that was immensely popular in circles within which he wished to move. Hitherto, in the ten years since leaving New Zealand, the need to fashion a career had left Coningham little time or opportunity for serious affairs with women, but his growing enthusiasm for sailing would soon lead him to the love of his life.

In December 1926, after three months at Sheerness in the Thames Estuary (where participation in a course on Army–Air problems was not allowed to interfere too seriously with sailing or socialising in London), Coningham took up a 'plum' posting at the RAF Cadet College at Cranwell in Lincolnshire. That college, opened in February 1920, was the main channel of entry to the Royal Air Force for regular officers. At the end of a two-year course, the graduate would officially have 'a general though somewhat elementary knowledge' of all three services, a solid grounding in squadron organisation and, above all, he would be a first-class pilot. The foundation stone of what would become a most imposing building was laid in April 1929, but cadets remained housed in wartime huts until September 1933, when the new building was ready for occupation. Cranwell offered few comforts in Coningham's time; cold and muddy even in summer and far

49

from either the bright lights of London or the sailing harbours of the south coast, it had nevertheless four supreme attractions as far as he was concerned: he could fly as often as he wanted, play as many games as he liked, ride horses till he dropped and cut a splendid dash between Lincolnshire and London in a spectacular sports car, more expensive than he could really afford.[1]

Coningham spent three and a half years as Commanding Officer of B Squadron at Cranwell and was warmly remembered by several officers who later served under him in North Africa and reached high rank: among them, Teddy Hudleston, Fred Rosier and Laurie Sinclair. Coningham, they agreed, had a pleasant manner, a splendid appearance and with his distinguished record in the Great War as well as his recent flight across Africa seemed to them an authentic hero. Sir Edmund Hudleston thought him a truly great pilot, for he had such good hands and often spoke of 'smoothing down' a cadet, showing him how to handle his aircraft more fluently. Sir Wallace Kyle remembered him as a centre of attention (not least from women, for he was a most eligible bachelor) and very interested in all games and social occasions. In addition to representing the RAF at polo in contests against the other services, Coningham regularly took part in Cranwell's sports tournaments, especially golf and squash, and usually won his matches.[2]

As a model for aspiring officers, the RAF could hardly have made a better choice, for Coningham's pride in the service's past and confidence in its future was total, nor did he hide the fact that he owed it everything: the revelation of unsuspected skills in flying and commanding that were deeply satisfying to exploit, and his transformation from a poor colonial farmhand into a convincing English gentleman, with accent and tastes to match. At that time, his most obvious affection was given to Bill, a shaggy black mongrel which accompanied him everywhere, even in the cockpit. Moreover, as Arnold Wall recalled, a Squadron Commander was rather like the housemaster of a public school: observing the overall conduct and performance of his charges and making final reports that would greatly influence their service careers. Although not required to give flying instruction, Coningham was 'a splendid exception'. By nature and experience a dedicated flying man, he made it his business to flight-test all cadets regularly, for he knew that young pilots were often in great danger *after* they became skilled and *before* they became experienced.[3]

From Cranwell, Coningham moved a few miles away to be second-in-command at the Central Flying School, then at Wittering, near Stamford, in July 1930: another plum posting. The CFS had 'a world-wide reputation,' wrote John Taylor, 'for all that was best in flying instruction' and attracted pupils from Commonwealth and foreign air forces. Once again, Coningham's exceptional merit as a pilot and teacher had been recognised and he was able to fly as often as he wanted in congenial company. This recognition meant far more to Coningham than, for example, a year at the Staff College in

Andover or a year at the Imperial Defence College in London. Very few officers of his generation who became senior commanders avoided either: indeed, many sought both assiduously, and Coningham was inordinately proud of the skill – or luck – which enabled him to avoid them without any adverse effect on his steady advancement. On 1 July 1931, after exactly eight years as a Squadron Leader, he became one of the RAF's ninety-four Wing Commanders and his pay rose from about £585 per annum to £760 (although it would be reduced by £40 in 1932 and was not significantly increased in the next three years). At that time, of the 2,145 officers in the service, only fifty-four were above his rank. According to *The Times*, Coningham was 'one of the most successful RFC pilots and squadron leaders in France during the War and it was there that three of his four decorations were won'.[4]

In July 1931, Coningham learned that in the following February he must leave England again, to go to Khartoum for three years. The new Wing Commander had already been in love for at least a year with Nan, wife of Sir Howard Frank, and she returned his love. Sir Howard, head of Knight, Frank and Rutley, one of the world's largest dealers in property, had married Nancy Muriel Brooks, formerly his secretary, in January 1922; he was then fifty, she nineteen. Sir Howard's only child by his first marriage, Mary, thus acquired a stepmother five years younger than herself. Nan's first son, Howard Frederick, was born on 5 April 1923; her second, Robert John, on 16 March 1925. Throughout the Twenties, the Franks owned several yachts and sailed or raced them regularly around the coasts of southern England. Coningham met them at Cowes and sometimes sailed with them, at first as a member of the crew. Throughout 1931, as their carefully-concealed love for each other increased, Coningham and Nan were tormented by their regard for Sir Howard, their fear of a scandal and by distress at their impending separation. At the height of their misery, Sir Howard died suddenly – on 10 January 1932 – at his home in Cheyne Walk, Chelsea.[5]

Among the terms of Sir Howard's will, which left Nan very well provided for, was one permitting her to sell that home and use the proceeds to buy another, if she wished. Nan did so wish and *The Times* announced on 2 February that 5 Cheyne Walk – a splendid Georgian mansion overlooking the Thames, thoughtfully and expensively modernised – was for sale. A few days later, Coningham bade her farewell at Croydon, where he flew to Paris on the first stage of a long journey by air and rail to Cairo – buoyed up at each stage by telegrams from Nan to which he replied with a flood of letters from 'Your loving and most completely Devoted Mary'. At 3 pm on the 20th, wrote Coningham, he 'again trod Egypt for the umpteenth time' – at Alexandria – and that evening attended a very smart reception in Cairo with Air Vice-Marshal Cyril Newall and his wife: wining, dining and dancing till 3 am. At lunch next day, a lady member of the Isle of Wight yachting set who was wintering in Cairo asked him, in perfect innocence, if he thought there was any chance of a mutual acquaintance marrying Lady Frank. 'My dear,' he wrote that evening, 'think of being asked that within twenty-four hours of arriving in Cairo! I said I thought not.'[6]

By 28 February, Coningham was writing to 'Nan, My Heart' from the Grand Hotel, Khartoum.

> Just nothing else approaches in importance the punctual arrival of the Air Mail tomorrow, bearing word from you. Your telegram made me the happiest person in the world – it greeted me on arrival, Beloved, and was the one great need and comfort in a quite surprisingly unfamiliar world. Precious, how wonderful life has been for the best part of two years. Since 16 July 1930. Being in love with you has meant so much.

Later that day, he wrote again, describing his journey to Wadi Halfa – 'flying in heat, sand and bumps for seven and a half hours' – where he dined with the Governor, the Countess of Warwick and Sir William Brass (a Conservative MP): 'a cheery feller, but lacking in "grey cells"' who was 'bucked at meeting me'.

Next day, Coningham reached Khartoum and met Sholto Douglas (newly-promoted to Group Captain, whom he was to replace as senior airman in the Sudan) and also Brigadier Stephen Butler, Kaid (Commandant) of the Sudan Defence Force. 'I have a lovely office,' wrote Coningham, 'best Wing Commander's office in the RAF. And a good staff.' Social life promised well, he thought: he had a speedboat for work with seaplanes which could be used as required for picnics, and a car which he had to be 'more conservative about as the auditors ask you nasty questions'. The arrival of 'the charming Mary Coningham' had long been expected and he was kept busy explaining to eager hostesses that he himself was the one and only 'Mary' Coningham. The dancing, he wrote, was better than the best in Cairo and more up-to-date in a delightful atmosphere. The Kaid took a personal interest in the band, fourteen strong and 'jet black in a gorgeous white kit with expressionless faces' under the direction of a white sergeant. 'My job is a terrific one,' he added, 'and much bigger than I thought', dealing directly with the Governor, the Kaid, his Chief Staff Officer and the Financial Secretary: 'I have my own budget.'

Coningham wrote again at 10 am on 2 March. 'Thank heavens I have arrived at the furthest distance from you,' he said, but every visit to Cairo would be a thrill 'as I'll be approaching you at 100 mph. Why must it stop at Cairo? Tomorrow is rather dreadful – with the exception of September – no, August and September – 1930, it is the longest time we have been apart.' He was still struggling to fix faces and names in Khartoum, aware that there were hundreds more for him to master out in the country, and had moved into Staff House, sharing it with three Army officers. 'It is gorgeous out here in our garden,' he wrote on the 4th, 'amidst lovely trees on the river front. An especial delight in this place are the birds – so many, varied in colour and for ever singing. The colours of the flowers and the blue sky and very green foliage – quite beautiful.' The country, he admitted, 'is really an unpleasant part of the earth, but the people running it make life most pleasant' and he looked forward to Nan joining him. 'Womenfolk,' he wrote, 'are smartly dressed' and then went on in a detail unusual for a man about the styles, quality and variety of the wardrobe she would need for riding, cocktails, garden parties, dances and formal balls. 'The main thing about clothes,' he concluded, 'is that all the womenfolk are here for a matter of five months or so and do think in terms of England.'

On 7 March, Coningham received a long letter from Nan, much delayed in transit, that was not only full of news but included the first of many 'marvellous little fairy stories' that so delighted him whenever they were apart; none, sadly, survive. During March, Nan sold the Cheyne Walk house and bought another in her beloved Chelsea, at 2 Wellington Square, about half a mile away. Between houses, she lived in Woodstock, a village near Petworth in Sussex. In a letter begun on the 12th, Coningham recalled their private engagement a year earlier, touched delicately on the shockingly sudden death of Sir Howard and turned quickly to explore their 'treasure box' of happy memories.

Sholto Douglas departed on the 16th and a week later, leading four aircraft of 47 Squadron (Fairey IIIF two-seater biplanes that could be flown either with wheels or floats), Coningham began an eight-day tour of the Sudan east and south of Khartoum. He wrote to Nan from Juba – 'just about plonk in the middle of Africa' – at 2.30 pm on Good Friday, 25 March 1932.

> Exactly six years ago to the day, Kink [Sam Kinkead] and I rode out five miles beyond here and hunted for four days, camped by the side of a Wady I can see from the hotel window. This place is only three years old and at that time there was not a human habitation nor any sign of anything other than wild life. Now it is the road terminus from Congo, Kenya and Uganda, the steamer terminus, the main airway stop, has an hotel, Governor, District Commissioner and is head of the province, etc. Mongalla, the previous capital, was too unhealthy.

Coningham, who often reflected on the vastness of the British Empire and the smallness of the community managing it, was invited to a small party in Malakal. 'As I walked in,' he told Nan, 'the only woman present, in the midst of eight men, said: "Hullo, Mary, I'm so glad to see you."' A daughter of the Chief Medical Officer in Cairo in 1926, she was now married to the District Commissioner of Malakal.

On returning to Khartoum, 'this old Maori' began another letter to Nan. His mother, like Nan's, had been glad to hear of his posting to Khartoum, hoping that it would end their affair, but he had just received a reply to his letter telling her of Sir Howard's death. She was, he said, 'quietly content to leave things in our hands and supposes we shall soon be married. She sees no reason why we should wait a year (as was the intention when I wrote) and was full of solicitude for you.' He was glad to learn that Nan had seen his dear friend 'Poley', Herbert Rowley, who flew across Africa with him in 1925: 'I hoped he would not mind my slipping quietly away from England,' wrote Coningham. 'As you know, nothing else but being with you counted during our last month together.' During April, however, Coningham was extremely annoyed to learn that their affair was being gossiped about by Poley at the Staff College, Andover, where he was a student that year. Although Nan was already willing to announce their engagement, Coningham was still anxious to keep it secret until November, when he next expected to see Nan. The opinions of Nan's boys, Howard and Robert (now aged nine and seven respectively), greatly concerned him. 'Have they no idea yet? They will like me, won't they? And, old Wollygobble, what are they to call me? Quite an effort, maintaining a degree of dignity while your wife's young sons call out "Mary" all about the place!! What fun. As I become their rather adoring father, they perhaps will count me as that.'

Coningham wrote to Nan from the Governor's House in Wau, Bahr-el-Ghazal province, on the evening of 17 May. It was, he thought, 'the English scene in perfection, the most beautiful and attractive place I have been in out here': they were on the edge of a lake 'with tropical foliage all around – trees, grass, flowers – all a glory and a mass of birds' while animals of all kinds abounded. 'I don't think I will ever shoot again,' he wrote. 'I hate the killing . . . The hunting and thrill and life generally are marvellous, but photography gives one all of that and avoids the killing of these lovely things. For they are beautiful and in many cases so tame and unused to danger from man that there is no difficulty or hunting required in bagging them. A poor sport.'

His brother Vincent (now known as 'Bill' and practising law in Sydney) had written to him and he enclosed a page from Bill's letter saying: 'A photo of your damsel has arrived. Looks very sweet and as I said before, intelligent.' Coningham added: 'Sorry, Honey, this is all the change you get from Brother Bill – but I can assure you it is *very* great praise!!!' Continuing the letter on the 22nd, he told Nan that someone had given him Huxley's *Brave New World* to read: 'Felt rather sick after a few pages and changed over to Churchill's *World Crisis*. That is nice meat to chew. Am giving Huxley's book to someone whose appetite it will suit better than mine.'

A week later, on 29 May, Coningham composed his most important letter to Nan: 'In deep solemnity, and with the biggest, most loving, and hopeful heart in all the world, I ask you, beg you: will you come and marry me at Alexandria in July?' She could return to England in August, to be with her sons for their school holidays, and news of the wedding could be delayed until November. July, he assured her, was the most perfect month of the year in Alexandria and 'I do want to be with you on 16 July. It is the 7th month and has always been best, by the powers-that-be, for me.' As for her late husband, Coningham thought he would have been the first to recognise that there was no need to wait longer.

He was so much older, you were such a good wife, you have done all that could be asked. And really, by planning marriage so soon after his death and telling friends and preparing for it – we have already defeated the customary reason for a wait – mourning; and reduced it to a conventional custom. Were we to have a London wedding with announcements, etc., in July – yes, that would raise objections. But this quietness is so much in keeping with the respect one feels for and wants to show him.

Aged thirty-seven and overwhelmed by love, Coningham was acutely conscious of precious time being wasted and feared to lose Nan, a most attractive – and wealthy – widow, still only twenty-nine and surrounded by potential suitors who had known her for years and were themselves attractive and wealthy. 'My only distraction is work,' he wrote, 'which I devour with a voracious appetite. But that is a makeshift and does not really ease what is a tortured existence.'

Coningham received her telegram, agreeing to do as he asked, on 9 June and spent the next month in a fever of concealed joy: 'I am so excited and thrilled,' he replied, 'but I'm dead calm and quiet and keeping to myself as if nothing out of the ordinary was ever going to happen. But the seething volcano underneath – I dare not let it one fraction of freedom.' Imagining the moment of her arrival, he intended to keep up his guard even then: 'You won't mind if I just quietly hold your hand only until we are alone, will you? No hurried little peck of a kiss in public.' His joy was tempered by continuing anxiety about ill-natured gossip at their haste to marry, about the absence of splendid ceremony and a full gathering of family and friends to make of their marriage a memorable occasion and, not least, about the difficulties of assembling the necessary banns and licences in time. In the event, the ceremony was less even than they expected, for the Anglican authorities in Cairo found themselves unable to take part and the happy couple were in fact married by an RAF chaplain in the station church at Aboukir, Alexandria, on 11 July 1932. Air Vice-Marshal Newall and his wife, both of whom liked Coningham very much, witnessed the marriage. The honeymoon was enjoyed in Alexandria, at the Hotel Casino San Stefano, with occasional visits to Cairo. Although Coningham gave up his hope of keeping the news secret until November, the announcement in *The Times* on 13 July – 'quietly, in Egypt' – was as brief as possible. The reaction of the Frank family, he learned from Nan, was 'kind and sensible'.

Nan returned to England on 4 August and no letters survive for the next fifteen months. By November 1933, she was living at Tutt Hill House, Hothfield, near Ashford in Kent and early in that month Coningham returned to Khartoum after leave in England. During the rest of his service there, his letters to her remained as tender as ever, especially when discussing the baby she was expecting: their daughter, Jane-Mari, was born on 5 May 1934, but Coningham had already made plans to provide both for her education 'should there be an accident to either of us' and 'to help her through the heavenly days of girl and young womanhood'. The gradual decline of his dearly-loved mongrel, Bill, also concerned him and he urged Nan not to keep him 'beyond the point where kindness says, "Go on, William, me lad, off to a long sleep and meet us later"'.

Now that he was no longer frantic about the danger of losing Nan, Coningham found more time to tell her about his work. He flew tremendous distances to every part of the Sudan in the most taxing conditions of heat and cold, dust and mud, often carrying doctors to deal with outbreaks of disease or other experts to tackle problems of irrigation or drought. Crises did not upset him – indeed, they inspired him – and he took the greatest delight in looking up old friends wherever he went. His relations with Newall (whom he now spoke of as 'Cyril') remained excellent and so, too, were his prospects of further promotion. Between them, Newall and Coningham exacted funds from the Sudan government to improve Khartoum's airfield. 'I am so glad,' he wrote, 'because it is something good to hand over when I leave. The airmen next year will be so much better off – two lots of talkie pictures, a swimming bath, good accommodation and the latest type of hangar in which to work.' At dinner recently, he told Nan on 10 February 1934, a lady had 'confessed to a complete change of opinion' about him: 'She thought I was just a "party" person – always in the swim, saying the right thing and always smartly dressed, etc.' He admitted the truth in what she said, but was glad to know that she now saw more in him than that. This year, he confided to Nan, 'I am not "no speaks" or out of sorts with one person in the country. In fact, it is very much the other way. And the great majority of them are grand people.'

Coningham took the keenest interest in gardens, especially flowers and bushes, discussing with Nan in loving detail the best position and likely performance of different varieties in the garden at Tutt Hill. At home in New Zealand, he recalled, Manuka bushes grew wild, flourishing on Wellington hillsides: 'We used to run and throw ourselves on them – like landing in a heap of hay! The smell is attractive and not unlike tea – in fact, it is called the Tea Tree as often as not.' He was also keen to have silk pyjamas and nightdresses made locally, at half English prices, and was seeking ways of getting them to Nan without paying duty: 'You are going to be surprised,' he told her, 'very pleasurably so, at yer old 'usband's skill at supplying such things as Nighties.' He chatted amiably, week after week, in numerous long letters about his love for her and their baby, the progress made by the boys at school, the challenges of his job, worries over money and his receding hairline; his prowess at tennis, golf, croquet and squash and the dinner parties he attended, especially those that proved so frigid they could be laughed about afterwards.

In return, he was always most anxious to hear news about their friends, among them three famous aircraft designers and manufacturers 'with large boats and yachts and huge incomes': Dick Fairey, Tommy Sopwith and Fred Handley Page (whom he invited to be Jane-Mari's godfather). Coningham shuddered whenever he thought about the expense of maintaining Nan's house in Wellington Square and was unimpressed by the sketchy, ill-written letters he received from Howard and Robert, but such criticisms were rare: by far the dominant theme of his letters is his great love for Nan and his interest in their home and children. 'Darling, darling, I am really looking forward tremendously to years ahead when we can make Tutt a real heavenly retreat.' As for the boys, 'I do want to shew them how to be good mixers and to do things – horses and cars and aeroplanes and simple things like walks and gardens and a general appreciation of all things combined with a love of games rather than sport. Shooting, hunting, fishing – no, I'm not so keen, but in games – yes.'

Nan told him in June that she had recently consulted a fortune-teller who declared that his fate would be decided in July. Coningham agreed: 'I was posted here in a July, you remember – it always (hooray, mail just passed over, so that means your letter by 8.30 – heaven) has been my fated month since I was a youngster.' Newall, he thought, would soon be promoted Air Marshal, a knighthood would follow and he was very much in the running for Chief of the Air Staff, a perfect position to 'help me on in my Group Captaincy towards Air Commodore. But all of that is lovely imaginings, though the cards are beginning to sort themselves out.' Meanwhile, Coningham proudly recounted to Nan 'an exciting journey south' in which he earned generous praise from influential civilians. He had taken a Fairey IIIF floatplane to Gambeila, to bring out Jack Maurice, the District Commissioner. This in itself was no light task, at a time of year when the river was so low that dangerous rocks were exposed, to say nothing of normal hazards such as floating logs and unpredictable crocodiles, but it was made far more difficult by news of fighting between Sudanese and Abyssinians in that region, fighting which also threatened the steamer carrying Auban, the relieving District Commissioner. Pawson, Governor of Malakal, was 'greatly agitated and really flapping', according to Coningham, both about the state of the river and the risk of attack from the east bank, but Coningham brought off two tricky landings and takeoffs – one to pick up Auban, the other to drop him and pick up Maurice – 'and there it is,' he concluded, 'another good job done for the RAF' and his own reputation.

That reputation was also high among soldiers in the Sudan. When the RAF authorities in Cairo criticised (wrongly, in Coningham's opinion) the conduct of Army–Air cooperation exercises in the Sudan, he was put to much trouble, though not as much as he would be in the next decade, to smooth ruffled feelings in both services. Nigel Tapp, a Major in the Sudan Defence Force, believed he did so successfully. 'We soldiers', he wrote, 'had a great admiration for Mary: he could not do enough for us.' Their exercises, though small in scale, covered huge distances and Coningham 'was constantly flying round to call on isolated soldiers or district commissioners. He never forgot to bring sausages and kippers – for we had no electricity and therefore no frigidaires, so these thoughtful presents were much appreciated!'[7]

At the end of June 1934, Newall told Coningham that a massive expansion of the RAF was likely during the next few years, news that delighted him. 'My hat,' he enthused, 'talk about going into the Navy! Were I a young man, I should go for the Royal Air Force every time. What a marvellous career because we are just at the start of the air age and it must go ahead quite rapidly.' It amused him to observe a change in attitude by the Army and the Navy: until recently, he said, 'they rather looked down on the RAF as nothing – now they are saying that they must expand to be able to help the RAF!' He also learned that he would be able to spend six weeks at home in August and September, but would not now leave Khartoum permanently until April; his next posting, however, would certainly be in England.

Coningham received his annual confidential report on 1 July and quoted to Nan the main points made by Air Commodore Geoffrey Bromet, Newall's Senior Air Staff Officer in Cairo. Bromet considered him 'exceptional' both in the performance of his duties and in flying skill, adding that he handled 'a very exacting and strenuous job with the HQ Sudan Defence Force with tact and marked ability'. In staff work, however, Bromet thought him merely 'above the average', and yet this assessment particularly pleased Coningham because, he wrote, 'I'm self taught and in a way it is better having it from Bromet, who is not so much of a personal friend as Cyril.'

No more of his letters to Nan survive and little more is known of his time in the Sudan. He suffered a severe attack of malaria in December and by 5 January 1935 was considered 'seriously' ill, but two weeks in hospital in Khartoum restored him and he was well enough to act as Air Liaison Officer at El Fasher during army cooperation exercises in February. At the end of March, he left Khartoum for the last time.

The tale of happy days is soon told. In England, Coningham was rewarded for his excellent service abroad with yet another plum posting: to the headquarters of Coastal Area at Lee-on-Solent, Hampshire, in May 1935. During the following year, the rapid expansion of the RAF led to the creation of functional 'Commands' (Bomber, Fighter, Coastal, Training), divided into 'Groups'; Coastal 'Area' therefore disappeared and was replaced by Coastal 'Command'. Coningham was promoted to Group Captain on 1 January 1937 and appointed Senior Air Staff Officer of 17 Group, newly formed at Lee with its headquarters in Wykeham Hall and responsibility for all on-shore training. Within six months, however, on 21 June, he left Wykeham Hall to take command of a flying-boat base at Calshot. Two squadrons were based there, but Calshot was also a centre for motorboat crew training, boat-building and marine engine fitting. Calshot Spit was purchased from its civilian owners and by Easter 1939 had been cleared of its many bathing huts.

For the Coninghams, the best of their few years together were those from the summer of 1935 to that of 1939. During that time, they enjoyed much of the happiness they had dreamt of before their marriage: they had a child of their own, sons who were thriving at Harrow and a home in a lovely part of Kent with a brilliant garden; they also had excellent health, plenty of money and numerous friends with whom they sailed on many summer days around the coasts of southern England and socialised on many winter evenings in London and in each other's homes. Coningham, however, worked as hard as he played, his ambition sharpened by happiness. During 1938, he was looking for a more demanding task than Coastal Command, so small and ill-equipped, could offer in the coming war. Two men whom he had impressed favourably were then in key positions: Edgar Ludlow-Hewitt, his patron at the end of the Great War, was head of Bomber Command: Cyril Newall, his patron while he served in the Sudan, was Chief of the Air Staff. Their patronage, together with his own merits, made it possible for Coningham to receive what seemed to be the ripest of his plum postings in July 1939 when he was sent to take command of 4 Group in Bomber Command.[8]

CHAPTER SIX

'An Endless Struggle to See in the Dark'

Coningham and the Early Trials of Bomber Command, July 1939 to July 1941

Coningham always regarded July as his lucky month and two events in that month of 1939 assured him that he was right to do so. He was promoted to the rank of Air Commodore (equivalent to Brigadier General) on the 1st and two days later took charge of 4 Group: 'the world's only specialised night-bomber force' (as an official historian claimed) in the RAF's élite arm, Bomber Command. His headquarters were at Linton-on-Ouse, five miles north-west of York, and at the outbreak of war on 3 September 1939 he commanded five 'mobilisable' squadrons (reduced to four by the end of that month) of twin-engined Whitleys at three bases around York. Each squadron had, in theory, twelve aircraft plus sixteen crews ready for operations. It may have been a uniquely specialised force, but it was certainly a small one and slow to grow: after seven months of war, Coningham had only five squadrons under command with no more than seventy operational crews between them. Sir Edgar Ludlow-Hewitt, his Commander-in-Chief, was stern and humourless and thus not, at first sight, a man with whom he would be at ease, yet in both world wars they got on famously. Coningham respected and admired 'Ludlow's' complete mastery of his profession, although an extreme sensitivity to casualties and accidents would handicap him as a wartime commander.[1]

In spite of its prestige within the RAF, Bomber Command was in fact totally unprepared for war against Germany in 1939. Its aircraft were inadequate in range, speed, defensive armament and bomb-load capacity; many of the few bombs it could drop (using inaccurate bomb-sights) would fail to explode; no plans had been made to use French airfields, without which raids over Germany would be a lottery, for most crews were untrained in navigation by day, let alone by night, and unlikely to find German targets from English bases except by chance; nor had they any flares with which to illuminate targets; their radio equipment, both on the ground and in the air, was poor; the problems of coping with enemy flak, searchlights or fighters had scarcely been considered; very little was known about either the

60

Luftwaffe's numbers or capability and the question of providing an effective escort fighter for vulnerable bombers was not even under discussion.[2]

Coningham's posting to that Command is surprising because, unlike many senior officers, he had never had anything to do with 'heavy' or 'strategic' bombers in practice or theory, neither commanding them on operations nor being indoctrinated in the True Faith about them as decreed in the Air Ministry and the Staff College. His disheartening experience during the next two years, as he gradually became aware of numerous hindrances to an effective strategic bombing offensive, did nothing to convert him and he left England before those hindrances were, in part, removed and before incontrovertible photographic evidence had confirmed that the standard of bombing accuracy was in fact much worse even than he had feared. Consequently, when Coningham returned to England after two and a half years away, years in which he had excelled in the management of other forms of air power, he was a confirmed heretic and would become involved in bitter disputation with the more manic devotees of the heavy bomber cult.

Meanwhile and mercifully, the Air Ministry had realised that it would be foolish to provoke the Germans into using their much superior air force against French or British cities. Fear of a knockout blow from the air had been a major worry among European politicians during the last years of peace, inhibiting them from standing up to Hitler. Now that they had at last done so, it made sense to accept the relative inactivity of the so-called 'phoney war' as a time for energetic construction at home, rather than attempted destruction abroad. There was also the moral question: bombing killed 'civilians' (non-combatants) as well as soldiers. Britain was reluctant to make the first move in a kind of warfare certain to arouse indignation, sincere as well as hypocritical, for she was anxious to retain the good opinion of neutral countries, the United States in particular, and make of them allies. All forms of warfare have, of course, always killed civilians and three in particular have long been aimed precisely at them – naval blockade, investment of a city, destruction of merchant shipping – but aerial bombing, being *new*, was then regarded with peculiar horror.

Two courses of action were open to Bomber Command in 1939. Firstly, attacks upon the German fleet, which no-one could deny was a legitimate military target; secondly, flights over Germany to drop not bombs but propaganda leaflets. Attacks on German warships required little penetration of enemy territory and a high degree of bombing accuracy. They were therefore carried out in daylight. Leaflet raids, on the other hand, called for long hours of flying over enemy territory and depended for their effect upon the widest possible scatter. They therefore took place at night. In the light of all that Bomber Command crews suffered during the war, these initial operations seem insignificant, but certain decisions were taken as a result of them which guided the subsequent offensive. For example, the Wellington (like the Whitley, a twin-engined bomber) failed to overcome German defences in daylight attacks in September and December 1939. The Air

Ministry naturally concluded that the bomber could not operate in daylight. At night, however, leaflet-bearing Whitleys ranged far and wide over Germany, encountering hardly any opposition either in the air or from the ground. The Air Ministry consequently concluded that the bomber could operate successfully at night.

The first leaflet operation, codenamed 'Nickel', actually took place on the first night of the war and most such 'raids' in the next eighteen months were undertaken by Coningham's Whitleys. Over a million copies of one leaflet were dropped over various towns on the night of 24–25 September 1939, inviting Germans to note that in spite of the blood already shed in the Polish war, 'Your Government's hope of successful Blitzkrieg has been destroyed by the British War Cabinet's decision to prepare for a three years' war'; British troops were already standing shoulder-to-shoulder with their French allies; British and French fleets had 'swept German merchant shipping from the oceans' and 'night after night, the British Air Force has demonstrated its power by flights far into German territory. Germans note.' Other leaflets quoted attacks on Nazi leaders in American newspapers or sought to separate German workers from their Nazi masters or to persuade Austrians to throw off 'the tyranny of the brown uniform . . . imported from Prussia' and all emphasised the unity of Britain and France. They harped on the heavy cost of war and on what had happened to Germany after 1918.[3]

Coningham thought widespread publication of such leaflets in the British press would have raised morale, but the government, so far from agreeing, did its best to keep their contents secret. As well as giving his crews essential training in night navigation, Nickel operations permitted them to report on the effectiveness of the German black-out, the degree of activity at various airfields and the trend of movements by road, rail and water. In fact, these tasks proved too much to ask of men tested severely by bitter weather in machines poorly equipped with internal heating or de-icing devices and it was during the first very cold winter of the war that Coningham began to realise that a precision bombing campaign on a destructive scale was, for the foreseeable future, no more than an ambition.

Early in the Nickel Campaign, on 9 October 1939, Coningham found an opportunity to raise 'personal matters' with Ludlow-Hewitt. Though holding an Air Vice-Marshal's appointment (equivalent to Major General), 'I am now,' he wrote, 'the only operational Group Commander in Bomber Command and Fighter Command not given that rank. Humility engendered by my recent promotion is tempered by the knowledge that my generation – Linnell, de Crespigny, etc. – have been moved up.' Two further consider-ations were local. Firstly, he had been trying to help the RAF socially in Yorkshire, by associating with civic authorities and the Army, but that was difficult because the Army, 'with its Command HQ in York, has sprouted an incredible number of Brigadiers and Major Generals. In the absence of an RAF makeweight, the Civic Authorities tend more than ever to confine their attention to the Army. Air Commodore means little, as they generally call me Commander.' Secondly, wrote Coningham, the expense of maintaining an official residence – Rufforth Hall, a house with sixteen bedrooms, two cottages and forty-two acres – was 'beyond an Air Commodore's capacity unless the standard is reduced to the discomfort-mark'. Ludlow-Hewitt's appeal to the Air Ministry and the ample furnishing resources of the Frank family jointly solved this problem, but nothing could be done for nearly a year about further promotion for Coningham.[4]

Throughout his time in Bomber Command, Coningham wrote many reports on night operations and training experience, reports from which both he and the Command gradually identified the numerous practical difficulties in strategic bombing that had been evaded in peacetime. He had to begin, on 11 October 1939, with basic principles. Experience gained during reconnaissance flights over Germany, he said, had 'clearly indicated the limitations of night bombing in relation to the specific order that the target must be seen'. These limitations were, obviously, light or its absence: 'moonlight or darkness, self-illuminated or blacked-out targets'. Bad weather and ground defences posed further problems. The period of 'useful moonlight' lasted for about fifteen days each month and during that period, the best time for operations over enemy territory varied from early evening to the last hours before dawn, the time advancing with the waxing and waning of the moon. He then went on to report what, if anything, could be seen in moonlight of rivers, canals, lakes, railway lines, trees, fields, bridges, small towns and villages at various heights. During the dark of the moon, only 'self-illuminated objects' such as blast furnaces, train engines and road traffic with lights could be seen. Weather was the 'controlling factor' in night operations and if unfavourable, he warned, 'our crews would be reduced to helplessness'.[5]

Coningham knew that 'at present' any suggestion that would 'lead us away from precision bombing of a visible target cannot be accepted'. With that restriction in mind, which had a far greater effect at night than by day, he thought the only suitable targets at any time of the month were coking plants, blast furnaces or illuminated industrial sites; targets on the coast or near big rivers or lakes were feasible in moonlight. Once the 'strictly visual limitation' was waived, however, and crews were better trained in astronomical navigation, the field of operations would broaden and targets could be bombed 'effectively and accurately by their known position in proximity to visible features'. He did not consider this method of bombing indiscriminate, drawing an analogy with the sniper who 'cannot see the man's head in the fork of a tree at 500 yards, but knowing it to be there he fires at the fork', hitting it as effectively as if he could see it.

On 9 December 1939, Coningham submitted a report to Command Headquarters on his Group's operations during the first three months of the war. Opposition from enemy fighters had been less than expected and both flak and searchlights were inaccurate. He had therefore adopted 'the gospel of operational opportunism' to take advantage of these weaknesses, but would not carry opportunism beyond the stage of reasonable trial and error because the defences would certainly improve. Nevertheless, at the moment, the 'real constant battle is with the weather and it would not be flattering to the Germans to know how much more we rate it as a protagonist than we do them'. Unfortunately, he lamented, there was never enough light on the target. 'Nothing artificial approaches good moonlight on a clear night, but the value even of perfect moonlight conditions must not be overrated. It is in fact only half way to dull daylight and the work possible should be judged in relation to that proportion. I foresee a never-ending struggle to circumvent the law that we cannot see in the dark.' His contribution to this struggle had to be abandoned in January 1940 because operational pressure became too intense and he lacked, in any case, staff with either the resources or qualifications to continue it.

Re-equipment with Merlin-engined Whitley Vs instead of Tiger-engined earlier models was coming along nicely, he reported, so that the old 'Tiger Complex' had given way to the 'Merlin Outlook'; a change from doubt to confidence. The performance and reliability of the aircraft heartened everyone, encouraging them to think of Nickel operations as far as Hamburg and the Baltic. Coningham's 'tale of progress', as he called it, in matters of oxygen supply, matt black painting, elimination of exhaust glow and improved interior heating, was 'tarnished somewhat' by difficulties in the supply of many items of equipment, details of which he forwarded separately. He discussed radio and armament problems and complained of the low standard of training in flying, navigation, wireless and air gunnery of too many men coming into his Group. Aerodromes were a major worry because wintry weather hampered work on runways and other essential facilities.

'As a Group,' he wrote, 'we have been fortunate in the volume of operational work we have had to do and this has countered any tendency to boredom. I think this is very important because the morale of a heavy bomber group has to be watched, particularly in a Yorkshire winter.' Medical officers at stations were 'a main link' in his contact with flying and ground crews. Adequate accommodation to meet the vast increase in numbers was gradually appearing and leave arrangements were working well. 'The stations have arranged their own concert parties and dances and in this sphere the presence of the WAAFs is a great asset. There was a tendency to segregate men and women, but I have changed this to the ordinary healthy association of airmen and WAAFS at cinemas, concerts, socials, etc.' Coningham then reflected upon the attitudes of the men under his command:

Our pilots are seldom worried by thoughts of engine trouble or a watery grave, their main concern being weather and landing conditions at their base. It means nothing to them that the journey of every two Whitleys to the Kiel Canal is the equivalent of an Atlantic crossing from Newfoundland with the addition of a certain amount of high explosive and a hostile reception.

This 'unworried outlook' troubled him deeply. 'One must never ease up,' he wrote, in the 'constant battle' against slackness because 'our young officers and airmen take too much for granted and they will quite casually hazard their lives and aircraft for want of a little care and preparation. We have to guide and supervise more and more and I am adopting the view that the crews' lives and aircraft are our active and direct concern at Group HQ and not their own.'

Six weeks later, on 19 January 1940 – his forty-fifth birthday – Coningham reported again on the general situation in his Group. The outstanding recent development, he thought, had been the introduction of 'security patrols' off the coasts to counter mine-laying by enemy aircraft. Despite bad weather, the patrols had provided good training and were carefully timed – in late afternoon hours – to ensure that German fighters could not attack and get back to their bases in daylight. 'Enemy defences at night continued to be comparatively ineffective' and the personnel position remained satisfactory, 'the principal reason being our lack of casualties'. In four months of war, he noted, 'our pilots have not had to fire a shot from their turrets'. During this period, attention had been focused on air gunnery and some squadrons had become so confident of their skill that they wanted to go into German waters in daylight to seek out enemy fighters. Coningham had rejected these suggestions 'with some firmness and reminded personnel of the experience of the day groups'. He had also stressed the fact that air gunnery was merely a means to an end, that end being to bomb, and had therefore made night bombing practice 'an urgent first priority task'. He was more than satisfied, he concluded, 'with morale and general keenness' and appreciated in particular the work of technical and maintenance personnel. 'My staff are excellent and very happy relations exist between them and the stations. There appears to be a feeling of mutual understanding and confidence which I value tremendously.'[6]

Two months later, on 16 March, he reported that January and February had been difficult from all points of view: 'operationally, physical and mental welfare and the general effects of boredom'. January in particular had been 'a dismal month', with airfields frozen solid under a blanket of snow and flying rarely possible. At least his crews were spared casualties and both they and their aircraft were gradually becoming better fitted for operations. 'Enemy defences at night remain ineffective, but aircraft are beginning to appear. No attack by fighters has yet been experienced, but I have warned our people to be ready, particularly during moonlight when hostile fighters would have a considerable advantage.' As nights shortened, distant targets would become impossible, given the Whitley's low speed. Although night bombing was now given priority in operational training, bad weather and a lack of both suitable equipment and practice ranges greatly handicapped his crews; training in air firing was similarly handicapped.

Bomber Command's first acid test at night came on 19 March 1940 and confirmed Coningham's fear that his crews, though brave and determined, still lacked the equipment and experience necessary to damage the enemy. On that night, a raid on a seaplane base at Hörnum (on Sylt Island, off the west coast of the Jutland Peninsula) was carried out in retaliation for the bombing of Scapa Flow by the Luftwaffe on the 17th. Hörnum was chosen as the most suitable *similar* target, in that it was remote from civilian centres. Thirty Whitleys and twenty twin-engined Hampdens took part in Bomber Command's first ever attack on a land target and the largest attack yet launched by either side. Forty of the fifty bombers employed claimed to have located and attacked aircraft hangars, braving heavy fire from the ground but none from the air. Many bombers reported hangars well ablaze, but photo-reconnaissance a week later revealed scarcely any damage.

The Air Ministry's Directorate of Plans had already pointed out on the day after the raid that as yet Bomber Command was incapable of causing substantial damage to German targets, whereas British shipbuilding yards and factories were extremely vulnerable to Luftwaffe attack. The bomber force should not be used 'as a mere political pawn', but conserved and expanded for use at the right time against *vital* targets. Ludlow-Hewitt, who had long been receiving the same message from Coningham, agreed and informed the Air Ministry on 30 March that the operation confirmed that 'the average crews of our heavy bombers' cannot identify targets at night, 'even under the best conditions'; it supported 'our previous experience that only those crews who have had long experience of operations at night over enemy territory can, under favourable conditions, find their way about by map-reading and identifying industrial or other targets.'[7]

Like Hugh Dowding, head of Fighter Command, Ludlow-Hewitt was too often too blunt about his Command's deficiencies in training and equipment for the taste of some senior Air Ministry and government officials; he was also right too often and too senior to be silenced. Unlike Dowding, however, who was suffered to remain at his post until the great crises of 1940 had eased, Ludlow-Hewitt was relieved on 4 April 1940, just before they began, by Air Marshal Peter Portal, a more optimistic proponent of strategic bombing. Ludlow's removal confirmed Coningham's belief (strengthened later in North Africa) that criticism, no matter how realistic, which reaches ruling circles must be well seasoned with a positive enthusiasm to succeed despite difficulties. Official historians of Bomber Command would draw attention to several conflicts between Coningham's detailed criticisms and his optimistic conclusions.[8]

Ludlow-Hewitt sent copies of confidential reports on some of his principal officers to Portal on 9 April. 'You may wish to glance through them,' he wrote. 'Please destroy them when you have done this.' Portal replied at once, thanking Ludlow-Hewitt and confirming that the copies had been destroyed.

Fortunately, Ludlow-Hewitt kept his own which survive. All his group commanders, he wrote, were able and experienced.

> I have no hesitation, however, in placing Air Commodore Coningham as first in order of priority of the five group commanders in my command, certainly as a war commander. I would not maintain that he would necessarily rank as the best of these group commanders in peacetime, but in war his rather exceptional qualities of leadership are conspicuous and are combined with a firm but sympathetic manner which exercises a strong influence on those under his command. His peculiarly personal qualities of leadership won the confidence of the operational crews of the group and he has therefore been able to maintain an extremely high state of morale while at the same time keeping everybody happy and contented. The work done by the group under his command is beyond praise and having had experience of the group under other commanders I feel sure that the success of the Whitleys is largely due to Air Commodore Coningham's personal influence.[9]

On that same day, 9 April, the German attack on the west had begun in Norway and Coningham's Whitleys could do nothing to repel it. During the six weeks of the campaign in France and the Low Countries which followed (from 10 May onwards) they could neither delay the rapid advance of German ground forces nor hit targets in the Ruhr, Germany's most vital region of war production, hard enough to draw fighters away from the front to protect it. On 11 June, thirty-six Whitleys flew via the Channel Islands over the Alps to attack the Fiat works in Turin, now that Italy had joined the war on the German side. Only eleven reached Italy and seven claimed hits on the works. Whenever possible, 4 Group made attacks on Milan, Turin and Genoa direct from England as well as on German cities. The weather was usually bad, anti-aircraft fire was vigorous, the bombers searched long and hard with the aid of flares for their designated targets and sometimes brought back their bombs if they failed to find them. Claims for success were frequent and crews undoubtedly believed that more serious injury was being done to oil production or lines of communication than was the case, but all operations, wherever directed, were small in scale and caused little damage, for at least half of the few bombs that were dropped fell in open country. The campaign was Coningham's first association with defeat. Two years later, he would experience – at closer range – a similar disaster.[10]

Political pressure, resisted by the Air Staff, grew during the summer of 1940 for indiscriminate bombing in retaliation for German raids on London and other towns. Up to 12 September, Germany had dropped 11,000 tons of bombs on Britain, but 'the injury to our war-making capacity', as Churchill informed the House of Commons on the 17th, was 'surprisingly small' because the Germans had not realised the importance of concentration on vital targets. The coming attacks on Berlin should therefore be aimed at such targets as power stations and gasworks – near misses would serve the purpose of killing and injuring civilians. This argument against indiscriminate retaliation was reinforced by self-interest: to reach Berlin, British bombers had five times as far to travel as German bombers to reach London from French bases. It made sense for Britain not to start something which would hurt her most, given that Germany had a striking force four times the size of Britain's.[11]

Coningham learned on 21 September that he had at last been promoted to the paid acting rank of Air Vice-Marshal with effect from the 12th. On 6 October, Air Marshal Richard Peirse became head of Bomber Command and Portal became Chief of the Air Staff at the end of October. Coningham wrote to Peirse on 12 November, in answer to his suggestion that aircrews be awarded operational chevrons. 'Now that our aerodromes are being bombed,' asked Coningham, 'is there any clear-cut hazard distinction between aircrews and maintenance crews?' The former had no 'monopoly of risk' and such an award would be 'an addition to the tendency to spoil aircrews', who already received too much preferential treatment: special living quarters off the airfield, extra leave, pay and rank, a monopoly of gallantry decorations and attention from journalists, photographers and broadcasters, 'in fact, a life of glamour compared to the maintenance personnel'. Most pilots, he added,

> want to be fighter pilots, most other aircrew want to be pilots, most other personnel want to be aircrew, particularly pilots. This pressure of ground personnel to go into the air, though perhaps not embarrassing to superior authority, tends to have an effect on their enthusiasm for their own job. This further distinction of air work would not help matters.

The contribution of *everyone* should be recognised, thought Coningham: chevrons on the left sleeve for aircrew, one for every 100 hours of operational flying: groundcrews, including women, to wear chevrons on their right sleeve, one for every year of service in the war area. In this way, he argued, the hazards of both air and ground personnel at war bases would be recognised and the distinction between the two, though evident, would not affect relations between them. Nothing, alas, came of this proposal, but it well illustrates Coningham's belief in equality of service, an attitude that helps to explain his outstanding success in North Africa.[12]

With the ending of the invasion 'season' in October, another attempt had begun to employ Bomber Command in its offensive role. By mid-November, Coningham commanded seven squadrons at four airfields north-west of York (Linton, Dishforth, Topcliffe and Leeming, Driffield having been relegated to a 'care and maintenance' basis) and claimed that the increased range of his Whitleys enabled him to penetrate far into Europe to attack such targets as Bratislava, an important oil refinery in Slovakia. If any target in southern Italy was thought particularly important, he could attack it and fly on to

Malta to refuel, returning home when opportunity offered. From 1 December, however, targets in Italy were allocated to 3 Group because of a shortage of Whitleys. Peirse assured Coningham on 30 November that there was no other reason for the change: 'I know that no opportunity has been lost of striking deeply into Germany and Italy and the results achieved are of the highest order.' Coningham replied on 2 December, agreeing that the change was advisable. He had sent to 3 Group details of his experience in such operations and hoped soon to have a squadron with the range necessary to reach Vienna and Breslau.

Oil targets had priority throughout the winter, but the continuing difficulty of 'precision' bombing at night, even in moonlight, led gradually to 'area' bombing – in the hope of hitting *something* important. Area attacks were carried out on a small scale in November, in retaliation for German attacks on English towns, but the first raid in which the intention was to cause maximum general destruction with no specific target designated was launched against Mannheim on the night of 16–17 December 1940, when 3 Group used eight Wellingtons, flown by the most experienced crews available, to 'fire raise' by dropping four-pound incendiaries: the first use of a pathfinder force. The raid began at 7.45 pm and went on for nearly eight hours. It was a clear, moonlit night and both Command Headquarters and the Air Ministry accepted optimistic – but inaccurate – crew reports at face value. So, too, did Coningham.[13]

On 7 April 1940, 4 Group Headquarters had moved from Linton to Heslington Hall in York, family home of Stephen de Yarburgh-Bateson, who managed to get himself posted there in August. Stephen, a London stockbroker in peacetime, was accustomed to dealing with high-powered city executives and by the end of 1940 had already been greatly impressed by Coningham: a 'perfectly charming' man, wrote Stephen, 'brilliant in all fields of RAF technique' he had one unnerving quality 'in that he never blinked his eyes'. Stephen was mastering a demanding job in the Operations Room, 'the "Holy of Holies" or nerve centre of the whole set-up', run by a team of Controllers under Coningham's direction. It was situated in the old drawing room at Heslington Hall, a room big enough to house all the telephones, maps and blackboards listing such information as the number and location of serviceable aircraft and crews and, most vitally, the supposed positions of aircraft out on operations. The most important piece of furniture was a complex switchboard, tended constantly by an officer assisted by three corporals who dealt with the endless stream of signals and also brewed continuous cups of tea, especially during the long night hours. 'The night duty was slow poison to some people,' recalled Stephen, 'they just couldn't stick it and the endless cups of tea with no food and far too much smoking played havoc with their insides.' It began at 5 pm and went on till 10 am next morning: 'It was really far too long, but continuity played a big part in an operation and you couldn't just hand over in the middle.' Only the Controllers had current flying knowledge and 'we stooges had to pick up what we could from them' – and did so quickly, for they were experienced, adaptable businessmen, used to working accurately under pressure.[14]

Peirse, writing on 3 January 1941, informed Coningham that an analysis by the Ministry of Economic Warfare, the Oil Board and the Air Staff had concluded that oil remained 'the most vulnerable target for an air offensive and that provided we are able to concentrate attacks on a selected number of synthetic plants, we may be able to bring about a critical shortage by the spring'. Peirse had therefore listed the major synthetic oil plants in order of priority and urged Coningham (and the other Group Commanders) to prepare attacks on them. Coningham replied on the 5th that he was already doing so and attended a conference in Peirse's office at 11 am on the 9th to discuss them further. Other matters discussed included the responsibility of Group and Station Commanders to discourage indiscriminate bombing and encourage a more determined search for primary targets. At 5 pm, they relaxed over a *March of Time* feature on the London blitz, followed by a Donald Duck cartoon.[15]

A month later, on 4 February, Peirse complained to Coningham about pilots who were reluctant to exchange 'the sniff of battle', as he called it, for what they considered the 'drudgery' of training. Coningham sympathised: when he first sent crews to Operational Training Units (OTUs) in May 1940, he had unwisely used the word 'rest', but within a month had corrected it to 'operational rest' and in interviews since had stressed the difference. Crews knew from their own experience as pupils that flying staff at schools had to work hard and all agreed – when it was put to them – that in wartime a spell out of the frontline *should* mean arduous work in compensation for comparative safety. Many pilots, he said, went gladly to OTUs once he told them that after six months he would be looking forward to their return. Let them keep their acting rank and give them a choice of postings, he advised, but make every pilot take his turn: 'It is the operational pot hunter, going from unit to unit on the plea of unsuitability for instructional duties, who upsets the rest.'

Heavy snowfalls during February left 4 Group's airfield situation 'unbelievably bad', as Coningham told Peirse on the 20th. Although reluctant to make a fuss, improvisation could only achieve so much: four airfields had to cater for seven squadrons, and of the four, only one – Linton – was partly runwayed and heavy snowfalls threatened to close the grass airfields at Dishforth, Topcliffe and Leeming. Coningham had personally visited, inspected and where necessary changed the runways and tracks of all aerodromes and satellites, built or building, and tested all defences: 'It was,' he added with feeling, 'a cold business.' The Germans had helped by making small daylight attacks, which kept everyone on their toes, and given fine weather, he added (remembering to temper complaint with cheerfulness), 'everything will leap ahead . . . there is an atmosphere of suppressed eagerness and expectancy which is healthy'.

In 1941, as Stephen de Yarburgh-Bateson emphasised, 'bombing was on a very small scale' and an attack by 4 Group consisting of twenty bombers was considered 'quite a big show'. Although wireless aids were undeveloped, airfields few and aircraft production still small in scale, 'the telephone lines were well and truly laid underground the length and breadth of England' and hostile action seldom interrupted communication with units, even though the switchboards themselves were antiquated. There were too few lines and they soon became overburdened with traffic and needed boosters on long distance and especially on broadcast talks. By 'broadcast' Stephen meant tying up all stations on one line to give the same message simultaneously to all. Sadly, said Stephen, some of the poorest broadcasters were to be found at Command Headquarters.

A conference took place at Heslington Hall at 9 am on the morning after each raid Stephen recalled:

> Every mortal detail was gone into by Mary Coningham, and each officer was questioned over the particular failure that concerned his department. Mary was unique in tha' he knew each subject far better than his subordinates and no slip-shod answer satisfied the great man. After he had assessed the value of the raid and duly given tribute where tribute was due, and admonitions where needed,

he rang Peirse to report. At about 10 am, Command Headquarters would broadcast information about the next raid: target, effort, bomb-load. Coningham was shown maps of the target and, knowing the effort required of his Group, decided which squadrons would be employed and which would stand down and continue training; all were informed by broadcast. Later came information about routes, timings and the effort proposed by other Groups. Coningham would consider this information with his senior officers, particularly his navigation, flak and weather experts, and seek any changes he thought fit, but the choice of primary target was always made by Command Headquarters. Once routes and timings were agreed, they were broadcast to stations which already knew the target and bomb-load required. About noon, the big weather conference would begin over the telephone, involving senior meteorological officers in all Groups and at the Air Ministry. Peirse would then decide whether the operation was on or off – or worse, whether a new target should be chosen. In Stephen's opinion, Coningham was the only RAF man of high rank who could read a weather chart as well as the experts. 'It may seem childish, but we loved to see a Met man cycling home in pouring rain without a mac.'

When Stephen visited a station,

> You would notice before an operation that many of the crews were busily engaged in the Mess writing letters, these were then left on the tables and just remained there till the morning, and were not touched. They almost seemed sacred to me, these epistles waiting for their owners to return;

some by the morning had become orphans and were duly posted by the Mess waiters, others were retrieved by their authors, the lucky ones.

As for interrogation on return, one picture always stays in my mind of a tired-out crew sitting smoking at their table and drinking their tea and in one chair sat a gollywog, their mascot. Someone happened to knock this chap off the chair and one of these tired men just picked him up, dusted him and sat this grotesque creature in his place. Golly had been on every trip and had never missed an interrogation, so I was told. This particular crew had an English Captain and all the rest were Colonials with an American rear gunner. I hope they all got through all right and when demobbed Golly got a new pair of trousers, he was in sore need.

During this second winter of the war, bitter experience of the effect of weather upon operations had been gained. Given the lack of accurate navigational aids, it was not easy for crews to find either their targets or their home bases. Increasing photographic evidence was beginning to shake opinions as to the destruction caused by bombing and led to demands for new aids to navigation and bomb-aiming, an increase in the size of bombs and in the size of aircraft. The command was also short of aircrews: for example, Coningham's group had 59 'operationally fit' crews (out of an establishment of 120) on 1 September 1940; on 1 December it had 60 and on 1 March 1941 would have only 82 out of an establishment increased to 140. In addition, the situation at sea was critical, Peirse told Coningham on 11 March. Churchill had issued a directive entitled 'The Battle of the Atlantic' in which he emphasised the need for Bomber Command to attack U-boats, Focke-Wulf aircraft, their bases and manufacturing plants wherever possible. Peirse had had a long talk the previous day with Portal and Churchill who made it clear to him that he must direct his principal attention to all targets threatening seaborne trade during the coming critical months. This new policy must be made known to stations, 'as otherwise they will be considerably mystified by the sudden change. At the same time, I would ask you not to give the reasons which have led to this change, which are for your information only and that of your immediate staff.'[16]

At this time, Coningham was proposing to increase the size of heavy bomber squadrons (to twenty-four aircraft with twenty-seven crews now and thirty later) for three reasons: to reduce overheads, make full use of airfields and bring on junior commanders. The average operational strength of a squadron, he said, was then ten to twelve aircraft; with twenty-four aircraft per squadron it would be sixteen to eighteen; also, casualties were more easily carried in a larger force. He had discussed the proposal with Ludlow-Hewitt (now Inspector-General of the RAF), and wished to pursue it with Peirse when next he came to Yorkshire. Overheads, wrote Coningham, had reached a 'fantastic stage and more than justify the PM's recent admonition to our Service'. Coningham had some 2,000 persons on each of his stations and out of this strength, he averaged no more than three sorties per station per night throughout the year; in other words, it was taking 700 men to send up one bomber. By increasing squadrons to twenty-four aircraft, one airfield would be saved for every two squadrons so enlarged and for every four squadrons a base station would be saved as well. Moreover, enlarged squadrons would give greater responsibility to junior commanders. The problem, he thought, was more serious than in Fighter Command: 'With heavy bombers, more organising ability, administrative knowledge and stability is required and the young flight commander who does superlatively well in the air often fails in this respect, generally through lack of training, for which he is blameless.' The Air Staff, however, chose to increase the number, rather than the size, of squadrons.[17]

Coningham wrote to Robert Saundby (Senior Air Staff Officer at Command Headquarters) on 12 April. He had, he said, been checking the routes into Germany used by his squadrons during the February moon and found that they were using well-known landfalls and paths across Holland. He named these 'rabbit runs' and forbade their use, not wishing his crews to behave predictably. For a recent attack on Düsseldorf, for example,

we fanned out all our aircraft over the French coast between Zeebrugge and Boulogne, with turning-points south of Lille and Liège. They would be expected to come back direct from Düsseldorf, so we brought them back the same way as they entered, fanning out on either side of Cap Gris Nez. Only one aircraft reported a fighter, though we had received prior warning that special patrols were out. With all of us dodging about, the German will doubtless lessen his concentration in Holland. We feel, therefore, that the governing principle must be to avoid doing the obvious.

But Coningham was concerned (as he told Saundby on the 17th) about a tendency for Groups to tackle problems without reference to each other. During the summer, increased opposition over targets could be expected and tactics would have to be changed quickly. Command Headquarters should therefore call for brief tactical reports from each Group, summarise and circulate the key findings. Unless this were done, Coningham argued, groups would cover the same ground independently.

As an instance of what I mean, 5 Group are experimenting with making passages at 16–18,000 feet. We were going to do the same thing with Halifaxes, but it may now be possible for 5 Group to have the data ready before we need to experiment. Then again, we are all tending to use the same strata of air – 9–12,000 feet – for attack and therefore the German concentrates in that layer. How are we countering him and with what success?

The contribution of 4 Group, Coningham warned Peirse next day, could not be great, for it is 'a rapidly wasting force'. Training had ceased at a time when demand was at its maximum: 'The good crews, on whom each squadron relies for results, are tiring and becoming jaded.' He quite realised the pressure on Peirse for constant effort, but 4 Group was down to only five and a half effective squadrons, all of them obsolescent Whitleys. By the end of May, however, his force was growing in size and quality. He then commanded 10 squadrons, of which 8 were operational: a nominal force of 160 aircraft, including 32 of the new four-engined Halifax bombers as well as 32 Wellingtons, which were more useful than the Whitleys.[18]

Coningham wrote to Command Headquarters on 3 May, proposing to make use of what he called 'the afterglow' in the northern sky in summer. He had taken special notice of it in 1940, 'for it limited the Norwegian operations and worried people during the Battle of France . . . the ground remains in pitch blackness, but the sky is full of light and to the north aircraft can be seen to a surprising distance. To the south there is normal darkness.' He therefore proposed to plan his approaches to the target area from the north and leave southward. For evasion, pilots must turn automatically to the south and darkness because a fighter that can intercept a northward-bound bomber will have it silhouetted against the light. The other Group Commanders, however, thought that such factors as the known location of ground and air defences, position of target and consequent length of route over enemy territory and weather conditions all weighed at least as much as 'afterglow'.[19]

Peirse wrote to Coningham on 28 May, telling him of cases of LMF (Lack of Moral Fibre) occurring on a *second* operational tour, where the men concerned had apparently unblemished first tours to their credit and even awards for gallantry. Had Coningham encountered such cases and if so, how should they be treated? It was, he replied on 1 June, a problem that he had carefully studied since the war began.

> Experience in the last war and in Iraq in the early Twenties convinced me that once a pilot or aircrew is allowed to crack he is permanently lost to air operations. No amount of rest, sanatoria, special treatment, etc., will effect a cure. I therefore watched closely and made arrangements to take people off operations when they were still fighting fit, with both they and their squadron commanders very angry at my action. We were the first operational group to do this and to send considerable numbers to the OTU.

His second object, Coningham continued, was to have a reserve of experienced personnel ready to return to operational units after their spell of training and operational rest. As the experienced captains of the 1939–40 winter were the majority of those sent away after that winter, Coningham expected to see many of them back again, six or nine months later, but this had proved not to be the case and he therefore concluded that it would be unwise to *require* a second tour of any aircrew. 'He should be sounded beforehand,' advised Coningham, 'preferably by a junior staff officer or operational friend. If I ask them, they feel they must say yes.' Most 'second timers,' he found, were 'the warrior type,' free of domestic ties and genuinely fond of operational life. The others, especially married men, settled readily into a safe training routine, particularly if they had a decoration, and were unwilling to move – unless on promotion and to a new type of aircraft.

In Coningham's view, the 'waverer' on his second tour should not be penalised. 'His frailty should be recognised by a notation that he is unfit for further operations, but his treatment should be governed by his first operational tour.' This was a matter for the Group Commander. Since the start of the war, Coningham had personally made all aircrew postings, 'the medium being a card index kept at this headquarters and consultation with unit commanders. The result, I think, is a happy group, an absolute minimum of waverers and a maximum of round pegs in round holes.'[20]

'Mary Coningham,' wrote Stephen de Yarburgh-Bateson, did not confine 'his great brain' merely to 4 Group problems. Stephen once saw him at lunch with his father 'draw the whole future strategy of the war on the tablecloth. It all came to pass and what man played a greater part than he in the Middle East?' He had a technique for dealing with 'naughty officers' that greatly impressed Stephen.

> First time, you were told how very silly you had been and surely you
> could see it, just a friendly chat. Second time, a good proper tick off,
> most unpleasant. Third time, there wasn't anything. You just went and
> what is more, what was no use to him was no use to anyone else, so you
> left the Service. He never handed on 'duds' to anybody. Pity others
> didn't adopt this plan instead of useless wasters always being kept in
> continuous circulation.

Coningham was the cleanest-minded man Stephen ever met, unable to abide anything dirty or sordid. When opportunity offered, Coningham and his wife were perfect hosts: 'She was a wonderful cook,' said Stephen, 'and insisted on always making all the little bits and pieces when they had a cocktail party.' Stephen once referred to Coningham as 'the Headmaster'; he overheard and threatened to buy a cane. He translated Bomber Command activities into Stock Exchange terms for Stephen's benefit and often discussed with him 'the State of the Market'. One thoughtful habit he had was to tootle his car horn on approaching Heslington Hall so that the staff was never taken unawares. Whole squadrons were invited to the hall and Coningham would show them round personally. 'He worshipped every stone in Heslington as his very own and woe betide anyone who abused the gardens,' nor did he ever forget to feed the ducks in the lake, no matter how cold or wet it was. 'We all loved him and it was a sorry day when he was suddenly whipped off to the desert to do greater things.'

Tragically, Coningham's last days in Yorkshire were spoiled by a disastrous raid planned and executed in his absence. On 24 July, fifteen Halifaxes carried out an unescorted daylight raid on the German battle-cruiser *Scharnhorst* which had just moved from Brest to the small port of La Pallice, over 200 miles farther south. It was thought necessary to attack her at once in case she was preparing for another Atlantic foray. The Halifaxes met fierce fighter opposition: five were destroyed, five badly damaged and the rest less seriously damaged. The fact that the *Scharnhorst* was obliged to return to Brest did not console Coningham. 'Mary came back,' wrote Stephen, 'to see the boards showing a shocking state of mutilation of all the best that he possessed and quietly said that if he had been present he would rather have sabotaged the aircraft than to allow such a monstrous idea ever to be perpetrated. This remark was said with tears in his eyes and not in anger.' He left that day for London, en route to Cairo, and was succeeded at 4 Group by another New Zealander, Roderick Carr.[21]

CHAPTER SEVEN

'Getting Together'

Coningham in the Western Desert, July 1941 to May 1942

Arthur Tedder, who would become one of the war's great commanders, arrived in Cairo on 10 December 1940 as Deputy to Sir Arthur Longmore, head of Middle East Air Command. He had flown from England to Takoradi on the Gold Coast (Ghana) in order to inspect and follow the route from there to Cairo which Coningham had pioneered fifteen years earlier. It was still, as Tedder found, a difficult journey: 'Nearly 700 miles of sheer nothingness' lay between Fort Lamy and El Fasher, he wrote, 'brown country, streaked with dry water-courses and dotted with bush; maps absolutely useless; nothing shown on them for the most part, for 200 miles at a stretch, and where something was shown, it was obviously incorrect. I must say I would have hated to have to do that trip without wireless', as Coningham and his companions had done. The experience greatly impressed Tedder and played its part in reminding him of Coningham's fitness for further service in Africa.[1]

Longmore was recalled to London in May 1941 and on 1 June Tedder's appointment as his successor was formally confirmed. 'Cooperation, sound administration and flexibility,' wrote Liddell Hart, 'were the keynotes of Tedder's air strategy and tactics' and he had the ear of the RAF's two most important officers, both of whom had earned Churchill's respect: Peter Portal (Chief of the Air Staff) and Wilfrid Freeman (Vice Chief, responsible for the day-to-day running of the RAF and Portal's closest service friend). Tedder compares well with Eisenhower as an *allied* commander, firmly resisting both national and service prejudices in seeking victory, but first he had to gather about him men who could 'cut the mustard' (as his American friends would say) during long, hard years when victory was a distant ambition. Having learned from Portal of Ludlow-Hewitt's glowing commendation, the first man he called for was Mary Coningham to replace Raymond Collishaw, a famous Canadian fighter pilot of the Great War, in command of 204 Group in the Western Desert. Although Collishaw had handled his tiny force with great enthusiasm and courage throughout a difficult year, he was, in Tedder's view, 'a bull in a china shop': too eager to attempt every task required in daily operations himself (a practice which left his staff officers 'frustrated and miserable') and too often foolishly optimistic about what could be done with the available resources in men and aircraft.[2]

In response to Tedder's summons, Coningham flew to Cairo at the end of July 1941. A great challenge – and opportunity – lay before him because Britain's position in the Middle East was then weak and likely to become weaker. The Germans had recently completed the conquest of Greece, Yugoslavia and Crete. Although threats to Egypt from Syria and Iraq had been rebuffed, they would certainly be renewed as soon as Germany completed her apparently imminent conquest of Russia. Rommel, who arrived in Tripoli in February, had already outwitted and outfought his opponents, advancing boldly to the Egyptian frontier, besieging Tobruk and skilfully repelling the first of many strong offensives laboriously mounted against him. All three British services were hard pressed, short of modern equipment and men experienced in combat. Wavell (Commander-in-Chief, Middle East) was replaced by Auchinleck on 1 July: his offence, like Longmore's, an inability to make bricks without straw, combined with over-readiness to tell this to Churchill; but the Army also suffered from the presence in vital positions of incompetent officers.

Peter Drummond, Tedder's Deputy, recorded in October 1943 that *all* operations in the Middle East during the past three years had been battles for airfields. 'Whoever held the airfields on the shores of the Mediterranean,' he wrote, 'could pass his own ships through that sea with reasonable safety and could forbid the route to the ships of the enemy.' At the end of March 1941, the Germans had taken Agheila and driven the British back to the Egyptian border, except for a garrison holding out in the fortress of Tobruk. The RAF had then a mere handful of squadrons in the Desert and was even weaker by mid-year, for airfields had been lost in Libya, Greece and Crete. The Axis Powers might well have conquered the Middle East by the end of 1941, closing the Suez Canal to Britain and her Allies and exposing to Axis exploitation the oil of Persia, the southern flank of Russia and the approaches to India – at that time under threat from Japan as well.[3]

Stanley Lee, a member of Drummond's staff, was impressed by Coningham: 'Big, masculine, confident . . . he had an easy, attractive personality, a ready and colourful flow of talk and a gift for decentralising the detail of his work and so leaving himself free to deal with broader issues.' Coningham was Tedder's 'most capable assistant' in North Africa, thought Sir Philip Joubert, under whom Coningham had served in Coastal Command. 'He was much given to sport and entertainment,' added Joubert, 'but his outstanding characteristic lay in his ability to keep his own counsel. I never felt I really knew what was going on behind his dark brown eyes, though we met daily at my headquarters and often at each other's houses.' Praise came also from Army circles. For example, Field Marshal Lord

Harding (Chief of Staff, Cyrenaica Command in 1941), surveying Britain's desperate position at that time, noted that 'two of our most able airmen,' Tedder and Coningham, 'had joined the British team – and none too soon at that.' And Liddell Hart, assessing Tedder's autobiography in 1966, wrote: 'The real hero of the desert war, in Tedder's view, is the New Zealander, Mary Coningham, and it is obvious that the trust and admiration was mutual.'[4]

After the war, in February 1946, Coningham recalled his arrival in the Western Desert. 'My headquarters,' he said, 'was a small hole in the ground five miles away from the Army Commander who had somewhat better quarters. There was no combined headquarters, but a good site had been half-prepared at a place called Maaten Bagush', 150 miles west of Alexandria. Tedder's last words to Coningham in Cairo had been 'get together'; the Army responded to his initiative and agreed to set up a joint Army-Air Headquarters when the 8th Army was formed in September 1941. This decision, wrote Coningham, 'was of fundamental importance and had a direct bearing on the combined fighting of the two Services until the end of the War'. Cooperation, however, as two recent historians have observed, 'whether between artillery and infantry, tanks and infantry or air forces and the army is a slow-growing and delicate plant, requiring time, much goodwill, regular human contact and careful training. It is a mood, not to be conjured into existence by decree or at a moment's notice.' Coningham, who fancied himself as a gardener, spent the rest of his career tending this plant with what he thought was loving care, though he had colleagues, notably in the Army, who were convinced that his pruning and weeding damaged it.[5]

Early in September 1941, Churchill ruled – in response to Tedder's arguments, relayed by Portal – that ground forces must not expect 'as a matter of course' to be protected against aerial attack. 'Above all, the idea of keeping standing patrols of aircraft over our moving columns should be abandoned. It is unsound to "distribute" aircraft in this way and no air superiority will stand any large application of such a mischievous practice.' Whenever a battle was in prospect, continued Churchill, the Army Commander was to 'specify' to the Air Commander the tasks he wanted performed both before and during the battle, but it was for the Air Commander to decide how best to carry them out. These rulings were to be widely publicised and vigorously enforced by Coningham with Tedder's wholehearted support, often in the face of angry or bewildered opposition from soldiers of all ranks, but they made his job no easier because, as Portal told Tedder on 2 September, the 'feeling persists here in the highest quarters that the Air Ministry are not sympathetic with the Army's requirements in air support' and criticism would redouble unless 'we put up a thoroughly good effort when the time comes'. Tedder assured Portal on the 5th that 'Mary Coningham is doing grand work in the Western Desert'. He had the soldiers 'eating out of his hand' and had already succeeded in getting fighter pilots and bomber crews to meet regularly and frame simple, clear plans.[6]

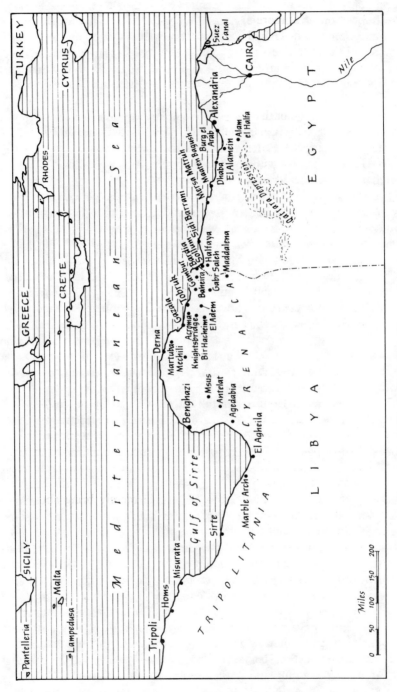

4. The Western Desert, 1941–2

At that time, Coningham was concerned about the weakness of his frontline force and still more about the methods of strengthening it. Middle East forces (Army and RAF alike) had to be supplied from Britain or – later – the United States. The shortest reinforcement route, followed by long-range aircraft via Gibraltar and Malta, was well over 2,000 miles. The main route lay around the Cape of Good Hope and through the Suez Canal; excluding detours caused by U-boat alarms, it exceeded 14,000 miles and generally took three months. A vital route, from Coningham's viewpoint, was the West African, opened late in 1940. His Hurricane and Blenheim aircraft arrived by sea at Takoradi where they were unloaded, erected, tested and flown across Africa via Khartoum – a place for him of bitter-sweet memories – to Egypt. His American aircraft were shipped to Port Sudan (on the Red Sea coast) for erection, testing and flight to Egypt. Having arrived safely in Egypt, these machines needed plenty of attention before Coningham's squadrons received them. A vast organisation, employing thousands of skilled men and mountains of spare parts was needed far from the fighting areas. Squadrons usually operated a long way from repair depots and therefore required more fitters and riggers with them than squadrons in Britain. Communication, being almost entirely by wireless, required a large number of operators. The observer and warning personnel to support the radar system was provided almost entirely by the RAF without civilian assistance. Finally, the incidence of sickness in the Middle East was higher than in Britain.[7]

Training units in the Middle East were too few, too small, too short of aircraft, instructors, pilots and ground crews. Moreover, graduates of these units, inexperienced in combat, could not be used freely in the frontline, least of all in machines outmatched in performance and armament by their opponents. The *need* for massive imports of modern fighters and battle-hardened pilots was as well understood in London as in Cairo and the Desert. Tedder and Coningham realised that the need simply could not be met in full; that they must nevertheless manage somehow with what was sent; and, not least, that undue moaning would merely bring about their own dismissal. The restraint they showed in these difficult times – quite apart from their outstanding skill in improvisation and in generating a determined optimism – would see them amply rewarded, in every sense of those words, when better times came. For Coningham, the rewards began on 24 September 1941 when the *London Gazette* announced that he had been made a Companion of the Order of the Bath (CB), an award made for precisely that combination of cheerful versatility with professional expertise while serving in Bomber Command that would carry him so far during the next four years. A fortnight later, on 9 October, his Group was transformed into a Command – as Air Headquarters Western Desert – both to recognise its growing size and range of responsibilities and to match its status with that of the newly-formed 8th Army.[8]

A joint Army-RAF directive on 'Direct Air Support' was issued on 30

September, following exercises in which Coningham took the keenest interest. There were two aspects of air support, the directive decided: defensive (to impede or halt the enemy's ground attack in general and dive-bombers in particular) and offensive (to destroy ground forces and so permit a counter-attack). For defensive support, the most suitable targets were often outside the range of ground observation and must therefore be selected by air reconnaissance. Air defence against dive-bombers could only be achieved by complete air superiority. There was no time for fighters to be summoned once an attack had begun; standing patrols were out of the question; fighter sweeps would be made at times when dive-bombing raids were thought most likely, but the only *constant* protection must be ground fire. For offensive support, light bombers would attack at various altitudes down to ground level, but the latter could only be attempted when the target was clear, surprise possible and expected resistance slight. Light bombers operating at low levels could assist formations which had outstripped their artillery, but were not to be called for when artillery or mortar fire was available. Their attacks could rarely be *sustained* and became less accurate the longer a raid lasted. Targets for them should never be chosen within 500 yards of friendly troops.[9]

The directive required an 'Air Support Control' (ASC) to be set up 'to meet, modify or reject' requests for support. Its Army component was to include a wireless organisation consisting of seven forward links known as 'tentacles' for communicating with the Control Headquarters where there were three wireless sets. Its RAF component included eight wireless sets known as 'Forward Air Support Links' (FASLs) for controlling air support aircraft in the air and for listening to reconnaissance aircraft; two sets ('Rear Air Support Links', RASLs) for communicating directly to airfields; and four for use at airfields. The headquarters of the ASC would be established as part of the headquarters of the formation fighting a battle and under Coningham's personal direction. Tentacles and FASLs would be allotted to brigades of infantry divisions to enable forward commanders to call for direct air support. ASC Headquarters would pass calls that were accepted via the RAF signal system to an appropriate airfield for action and inform the tentacle of the intended time and strength of the support on its way so that the forward commander could be ready to take advantage of it. Airfields were allowed one hour (for inspection, refuelling and rearming) after the return of a mission before reporting the availability state of their aircraft to ASC Headquarters. Sometimes support aircraft were given the exact location of targets before takeoff, sometimes a reconnaissance aircraft would lead them; most often, though, targets were indicated by R/T from a FASL. Clearly, an efficient recognition system, based on coloured lights and ground signs, between aircraft and ground troops was essential. Army officers, known as Air Liaison Officers (ALOs), began to arrive in the Desert in December 1941, specially-trained to explain air methods to soldiers, army methods to airmen and – as they became experienced and confident – to explain why things went wrong and how best they could be put right.[10]

Coningham and his men were still learning their jobs, as Tedder told Portal on 14 October 1941. He had sent 'young Cross' (later Air Chief Marshal Sir Kenneth, who had already made a name in Britain) to the Desert to take charge of fighter operations, but tactics evolved in Britain took too long to reach the Desert, where most pilots were still, as Tedder put it, at a 'village cricket' level of performance. In response to this plea, Basil Embry (a famous airman, well versed in recent tactics) arrived in the Desert a week later to be Coningham's Senior Air Staff Officer (SASO). As far as tactics and training were concerned, they agreed well enough and Embry later expressed 'the greatest admiration' for Coningham as an operational commander, but 'Basil was never cast as a second-in-command to anyone' in the opinion of a member of Coningham's staff and he returned to England in January 1942.[11]

Concern over Tedder's estimate of relative air strengths on the eve of Operation Crusader (a major battle planned to open in November) caused Portal, at Churchill's request, to send Freeman to Egypt in October. The New Zealand government, with memories of Greece and Crete still rankling, had asked for an assurance that the Army would have air superiority. Together, Freeman and Tedder agreed that probable serviceability on D-Day was 528 aircraft for the RAF, 385 for the Axis; all the enemy forces were said to be in the 'shop window' whereas the RAF, by stripping Iraq, Palestine, Cyprus, Aden and the Delta, expected to have about 50 per cent reserves 'behind the counter'. Churchill was thus able to offer New Zealand the assurance it sought. Coningham, like Tedder, found this 'numbers game' grimly amusing, for they knew that combat experience, quality of equipment, realistic training and determination to prevail (on the ground as well as in the air) mattered more in battle than arithmetic.[12]

Wing Commander Andrew Geddes (of Army Cooperation Command) had accompanied Freeman to Cairo and after two days there flew to Maaten Bagush, where the Army–Air headquarters 'were located in holes in the sand'. With only sixteen fighter and sixteen bomber squadrons available, Geddes agreed with Coningham that the task of maintaining local air superiority over the advance must not be jeopardised by trying to answer calls for direct air support. Air superiority would be difficult to achieve, given the fact that most pilots were short of flying and operational experience and ground crews, though willing, were inexpert. Other reasons for poor performance, Geddes reported, included the great distances between airfields and targets (up to 200 miles); the problems of navigation and target identification in a featureless terrain and the fact that targets often moved between first observation and actual attack or were obscured by a dusty haze. The need for close fighter escort for all bombing raids cost time in forming up and assembling over rendezvous points because it was rarely possible to base fighters and bombers on the same airfield. Clouds of dust made formation takeoffs uncommon: aircraft usually had to take off one by one, after the dust had settled, from widely-dispersed points.[13]

'In November 1941,' wrote Field Marshal Kesselring in May 1948, 'I was transferred together with *Luftflotte 2* to Italy as Commander-in-Chief South in order to support Rommel's army, but more particularly to reorganise the supply services which were in a bad state owing to British sea and air supremacy in the Mediterranean.' He also had the task of 'smoothing out differences between the Italian and German High Commands in Africa', where the Italians contributed little and consumed much. Another problem was 'the widespread and efficient enemy spy system', tipping off the British about most convoys. This, in fact, was Ultra information, derived from the interception and translation of German radio messages at Bletchley Park in Buckinghamshire. For the rest of the war, Coningham would be among those senior Allied commanders who benefited greatly from this reliable and detailed source of information about enemy strength, preparations and intentions. Whatever problems Tedder and Coningham had with their masters (service and civilian), with their colleagues in other services and later with their American allies proved neither as taxing nor as insoluble as those which the unfortunate Kesselring faced in dealing with Rommel, the Duce or Hitler. Worse still, in what Drummond rightly called a war for airfields, the Luftwaffe had no officer in Africa who enjoyed anything like Coningham's degree of independent authority.[14]

The chief aim of the Crusader offensive was to drive the enemy out of Cyrenaica. A successful offensive would reduce the danger from the west to Britain's base in Egypt; ease the passage of British shipping through the Mediterranean by capturing ports and airfields along the Libyan coast; relieve Tobruk, which hitherto had absorbed so much naval and air effort; and permit interference with Axis activities in Tunisia, Sicily, Italy, Greece and Crete. German armour, the backbone of Axis power, must be destroyed. To do this, a battle must be provoked at a time and place of British choosing. The obvious move was to send strong forces towards Tobruk to raise the siege – 30 Corps, with all the best tanks – aided by a well-timed sally from the Tobruk garrison. Meanwhile, the other main Army formation – 13 Corps – was to contain and cut off enemy forces holding the frontier defences and then advance to assist 30 Corps.[15]

For Coningham, Crusader began on 14 October with a campaign lasting thirty days, intended to win air superiority and impede the enemy build-up of weapons and supplies. It was also intended to locate enemy formations, particularly armoured divisions; to photograph airfields regularly; to identify defensive works, gunpits, petrol and ammunition dumps and minefields; to survey roads and tracks, keeping a check on the traffic using them; and to check as well the shipping passing through enemy ports. Then would come six days of intensive effort, up to and including D-Day (13–18 November), while the Army concentrated and moved forward. During these days, Coningham's squadrons proved remarkably successful in preventing the Axis

1a. Arthur Coningham (1863–1939): 'cricketer and notoriety'. He set three records in his only Test appearance for Australia and played a leading part in one of Australia's most famous court cases.

1b. Alice Coningham (1869–1959). Arthur's accomplice in that court case. She and Arthur were later divorced following another sensational case.

2a. Wellington College Shooting Team, New Zealand secondary schools' champion in 1910. Young Arthur Coningham, second from left in the back row, is still slightly built at fifteen and has a serious reserved look.

2b. Party time at Bognor Regis in June 1918, on the eve of 92 Squadron's departure for the Western Front under the command of Major Coningham, DSO, MC. Back row, left to right: Captain James Robb, Lieutenant Harveyson, Coningham and Lieutenant Flintoff. Front row, left to right: Lieutenants Good, MacAndrew, Randolph and Reed.

3a. Second Lieutenant 'Mary' Coningham of 32 Squadron in March 1917, standing in front of a captured Albatros D.1 fighter at Lealvillers, near Albert, on the Somme Front.

3b. During June 1917, 32 Squadron was re-equipped with the DH 5. A pronounced backward stagger of the upper wing gave the pilot an excellent forward view, but he was in serious trouble if attacked from above and behind.

4a. Flight Lieutenant Coningham (first left, front row) at the Central Flying School, Upavon, on Salisbury Plain. At their final interview in February 1922, the Commandant wondered whether Coningham had 'the qualities of a senior officer'.

4b. Squadron Leader Coningham, CO of 55 Squadron, flying his all-red DH 9A over Mosul aerodrome, Northern Iraq, in 1923. That squadron, famous for its exploits in Iraq, had as its motto *Nil Nos Tremefacit* ('Nothing Shakes Us' or, more freely, 'You can't put the wind up 55').

5a. Sir Howard and Lady Frank in 1931. Head of Knight, Frank & Rutley, the famous auctioneers and estate agents, Sir Howard was also Commodore of the Royal Thames Yacht Club. He died suddenly in January 1932 and six months later Coningham married his widow.

5b. Coningham and his new family outside Tutt Hill House, Kent, in August 1934. In front, his stepsons, Robert and Howard Frank; behind, his wife Nan smiles at their daughter, Jane-Mari, in the arms of Nan's mother. Nan's sister, Molly is on the right.

6a. Heslington Hall, York, Coningham's headquarters from April 1940 to July 1941, and now part of York University. 'He worshipped every stone in Heslington as his very own,' wrote one member of his staff, 'and woe betide anyone who abused the gardens.'

6b. An official photograph of 'RAF Staff Officers' planning a raid 'at a Whitley bomber station'; no date, no names. It actually shows a bespectacled Air Commodore Coningham, head of 4 Group, Bomber Command, with some of his senior assistants. The photograph may have been taken at Heslington Hall, in the summer of 1940.

7a. Nan Coningham. A photograph taken by Roger Forster in Paris in 1939. Her husband took it with him on all his travels during the Second World War.

7b. Air Vice Marshal Coningham in 1941, shortly before leaving England for the Western Desert. This photograph was specially taken for Nan, who kept it by her throughout their long separation.

8a. The British and American press hugely enjoyed the brief existence of this 'law firm' or 'contracting company'. Andrew Cunningham long remained head of the Mediterranean Fleet, but his brother Alan, commander of the 8th Army, was actually dismissed within a week of the appearance of Strubel's cartoon in the *Daily Express* on 21 November 1941.

8b. 'He doesn't like having his photo taken!' wrote 'Bing' Cross, one of the outstanding pilots and commanders of the North African Campaigns, seen here with Coningham, head of the Desert Air Force, at Landing Ground 110, sixty miles south of Sidi Barrani, in December 1941.

air forces from observing this concentration. Five days were allowed to cover the battle between the opposing armoured forces and the relief of Tobruk, followed by 'an indeterminate phase' covering, he hoped, the enemy retreat. But his squadrons had been employed for too long on purely defensive duties – covering shipping to Tobruk, patrols over troops in forward areas, escorting reconnaissance or bombing missions – and too many experienced pilots had been lost in Greece and Crete. They could not, in short, match the Germans in fighting or flying skill. Coningham was therefore obliged to withdraw squadrons in turn from operations for further training and to replace several commanders with men from England better versed in modern aerial combat. Lacking effective radar information, he had to operate sweeps by wings of two squadrons (twelve aircraft each) over areas considered vital by 8th Army headquarters. Greater numbers of Tomahawks and Hurricanes made up to some extent for their inferiority to the latest Messerschmitt Bf 109 fighters.[16]

On 17 November, the eve of the battle, the worst storm of the year broke out over the Desert and an ambitious bombing programme arranged for that night had to be abandoned. Torrential rain continued next day. Although bad weather hindered the air force, it helped the soldiers' initial advance and Coningham's sixteen fighter squadrons actually carried out 116 sorties despite rain and low cloud. Enemy air activity was nil, for the weather was even worse in the Axis area. A long and confused battle followed in which, after early successes, defeat threatened the British forces; but at last the enemy was compelled to retreat into Cyrenaica, leaving behind about 20,000 prisoners, a great many weapons and vehicles and ending the siege of Tobruk. It was a victory – and remained so, on balance, even after Rommel (having received reinforcements) pushed the 8th Army out of Benghazi and back to a position known as the Gazala Line, with its right flank on the sea some thirty-five miles west of Tobruk.[17]

'A New Name Appears', headlined the *Star* on 20 November over a brief note on Coningham's career and *Life*, *Time* and the *Daily Mail* all made play with the 'law firm' of Cunningham, Cunningham and Coningham: Alan, commander of the 8th Army (who would, in fact, be dismissed on the 26th), his brother Andrew, commander of the Mediterranean Fleet and Mary who, according to the *Daily Mail*, 'has a reputation in the RAF for dazzlingly brilliant flying. He knows enemy Europe well and can interview German and Italian pilots in their own languages', which was by no means true. When George Houghton interviewed Coningham, while gathering material for a book published in 1942, he spoke of him as 'scholarly'. Coningham smiled and replied: 'I'm an athlete, I'm no student. My friends will laugh when they see that.' Amid some equally laudatory and inaccurate comments, *Time* described Coningham as 'a dark, strong-faced, deep-voiced, wise-cracking, non-smoking, six-footer from New Zealand. He has a reputation for talent in cooperation – not a notable talent of previous RAF commanders in the Middle East.'[18]

On 23 November, Auchinleck (Commander-in-Chief, Middle East) received an urgent request from Alan Cunningham to visit 8th Army Battle headquarters, near Maddalena, about 100 miles south-east of Tobruk. Coningham had also asked Tedder to come up and he therefore accompanied Auchinleck. They found Cunningham distressed by the military situation and anxious to break off the offensive, but Auchinleck ordered him to get on with it. Rommel launched a surprise attack next day which broke through at once and Wing Commander Gordon Finlayson (Coningham's Senior Operations Officer) later wrote: '30 Corps lost control of the situation and there ensued a most interesting period which, as a study of panics, chaotics and gyrotics, is probably unsurpassed in military history.' During that day, Hurricanes and Tomahawks vigorously strafed enemy columns, but they also hit some British vehicles. Both sides used each other's vehicles and with everyone, friend and foe alike, charging along in an easterly direction, clouds of dust hung in the air and mistakes were inevitable. Cunningham himself was surprised and nearly killed when his aircraft took off from 30 Corps' Advanced Headquarters on the airfield at Gabr Saleh that day 'through a stampede of vehicles with tank shells bursting behind it'. No word of the German advance had reached Coningham and he was obliged to withdraw at a moment's notice to landing grounds farther east. 'I was loath to do any moves at all,' he told Tedder, 'but the force is so valuable that it could not be risked.' He had expressed himself forcefully to his Army colleagues, though recognising that 'in the prevailing confusion and lack of information' they could do little.[19]

For the next few days, aircraft of several squadrons were mixed up on various landing grounds, separated from their ground crews. Because it was feared that German parachute troops might attempt to seize landing grounds, pilots were ordered to sleep under the wings of their aircraft; guards were doubled and AA gunners prepared to use their guns against tanks. One Squadron Recorder reckoned that one night 'we had 175 aircraft on the 'drome and as the Hun column passed only ten miles north of us . . . they missed a glorious opportunity of wrecking most of our fighters'. The shambles was too much for Auchinleck, who replaced Cunningham with Neil Ritchie on 26 November. Cunningham was required to pretend to be sick, go into hospital for nine days incognito, move about Egypt in civilian clothes and travel back to England under an assumed name.[20]

Tedder wrote privately to Portal from Cairo on 4 December about Cunningham's dismissal. It came, he said, 'in the nick of time' for he was 'completely at sea as regards armoured warfare', constantly worrying about Rommel's plans and showing no confidence in his own. Before dismissing Cunningham, Auchinleck discussed the affair with Coningham, whom Tedder had told to speak frankly.

Mary's comment to me in a note the following day was, "the change in command has been made and the whole atmosphere has altered. The position was really becoming most serious and it was beginning to reach down to units" . . . Mary tells me that under the previous régime cooperation in the true sense was almost impossible since Cunningham would not discuss his plans or even disclose them except under extreme pressure. This has all altered and he and Ritchie are hand-in-glove.

When Tedder left the Desert, 'Mary and his fellows were in splendid form – as indeed they have been all the time.'[21]

Their form may have been splendid, but the enemy's westward movement made it increasingly difficult for Coningham to cover the British pursuit: either his fighters lacked the range to cover bombers assigned to direct support or information from advancing troops about possible targets took too long to reach him. 'The most intensive fighting on the front is here', he told Tedder on 10 December: 'my fighting for targets!!! Taken three and a half hours this morning.' He also reminded Tedder that 'we have practically no marksmen' among our fighter pilots 'because there is no practical air-to-air firing done until they are thrown into the battle when they are all worked up and do not know what they are doing. It is then too late, except for the lucky and perhaps more experienced ones who survive.' As a stopgap, he employed these pilots as a top cover for the novices below. They needed better aircraft, but Coningham did not receive his first Spitfires until May 1942.[22]

The pursuit was also hampered by the decision of 13 Corps headquarters, the formation responsible for forward operations, to fix bomblines as much as fifty miles ahead of the most advanced British troops and there were problems in supplying forward airfields, particularly with fuel, despite Coningham's use of RAF and captured vehicles to supplement supplies provided by the Army. Heavy rain delayed supply columns and made some landing grounds in the Derna-Benghazi area unusable; prolonged and intensive operations reduced aircraft strength and, not least, it remained very difficult for airmen to distinguish between friendly and enemy forces. Nevertheless, when Rommel retreated to Agedabia, Coningham urged an immediate advance, emphasising the moral advantage of the air superiority gained in Cyrenaica, the current disarray of the Axis air forces, the fact that they could receive no immediate reinforcement and the help Malta could give. 'This is the first occasion in the war,' wrote Coningham to Tedder on 2 January 1942, 'that we have overrun the German Air Force', but his own force was drastically weakened: by the 11th, he was down to twelve fighter and six bomber squadrons, able to muster between them no more than 107 fighters and twenty-six bombers. In the event, 13 Corps was held up at Agedabia until 6 January while Rommel prepared new positions seventy miles farther west in the marshes around El Agheila: according to Auchinleck, one of the easiest places to defend in Libya.[23]

Although British forces now held the whole of Cyrenaica for the second time, the need to send men and machines to counter disasters in the Far

East weakened the air force, while attacks on Malta meant that ships and aircraft based there were unable to prevent Rommel from receiving reinforcements through Tripoli. Worse still, he had what he called 'the good source', which began to flow to Rome and Berlin during the winter of 1941–2 from Colonel Bonner Frank Fellers, US Military Attaché in Cairo. The Italians had broken the code in which he reported to Washington and gave Rommel 'vital information on the Middle East battlefields', as Hans-Otto Behrendt, a member of his intelligence staff, recalled. 'In fact, it was stupefying in its openness' about British tank losses, the number of tanks operational and overall strength. For these reasons, Rommel launched a counter-offensive on 21 January 1942. This offensive, wrote Kesselring in May 1948, 'carried out by very weak forces with wonderful enthusiasm, supported in model fashion by the Luftwaffe in Africa', reached the Gazala Line on the 30th. 'All credit for this success must go to Rommel; he was unsurpassed in leading armoured formations and suchlike raids, provided his nerve did not desert him.'[24]

The enemy advance to Agedabia and Antelat, Coningham signalled Tedder on 23 January, was 'quite unopposed and due to serious blunder of Guards Brigade which opened road'. The first warning which 258 Wing at Antelat received came from Godwin–Austen's headquarters at 1 pm on the 22nd and simply said: 'Move back at once, enemy coming.' The place was being shelled as the last aircraft took off. Fortunately, Coningham had withdrawn most of his fighter force fifty miles north to Msus on the 21st, but if the attack had come on that day, the aircraft at Antelat would all have been lost, trapped on wet landing grounds. Even so, 'departure necessitated manhandling each aircraft by twelve men under wings to a strip 30 feet wide and 500 yards long'. During the 23rd, his fighters operating from Msus regained air superiority over the forward area, but Coningham no longer trusted the ground forces and decided to send all maintenance and heavy units back to the Egyptian side of the frontier. The Army, he told Tedder, intended to stand at Gazala and the fighter force was being kept wholly mobile to fight a rearguard action covering the withdrawal 'of the vast quantity of Mechanical Transport that abounds everywhere'. All this, he concluded, 'may sound very depressing, but it is the worst case and I can at any time about-turn any essential services that may be moving'. Tedder, reporting to Portal on the 26th, said 'Coningham's team working well, angry but keeping their heads.' The 'sole stabilising factors', he added three days later, were Auchinleck and Coningham: 'I have confidence in both, but wish the latter were stronger numerically.'[25]

Tedder wrote to Portal on 6 February, summarising the shambles of the past fortnight. Although Auchinleck's efforts to 'get at the truth' would probably be thwarted, nothing could hide the fact that Rommel's initial advance was 'literally unopposed', even though he could not move off the only road because of rough going and minefields at either side. 'From the time the enemy reached Antelat, our forces appear to have fallen into complete and utter chaos from which some of them are only now emerging.'

88

Perfectly sound British tanks were simply abandoned and port authorities in Benghazi panicked, destroying installations and supplies days before they were threatened. Army commanders also lost their heads, among them the Corps Commander at Antelat 'telling the RAF to cut and run', a Brigadier at Mechili 'telling Cross to move his squadrons back (about six days before it was necessary) and Cross having to tell him that even if we had no troops to cover our aerodromes he was quite satisfied to be protected by some 100 miles of empty desert'. The Army, concluded Tedder, had plenty of first-class men, 'but the old school tie and the bran-mash school and the Camberley drag have all got to *go*. Until they do, we shall have this sort of thing again and again.'[26]

Coningham informed Tedder on 8 February that he had been obliged to withdraw seven squadrons from the frontline either to re-equip or replace their aircraft. As his operations decreased, so those of the Axis air forces increased, directed mainly at forward landing grounds and the fortress of Tobruk. Anti-aircraft gunners there, sharing the general panic of the ground forces, shot down six of Coningham's scarce aircraft in two days (13 and 14 February), killing five pilots. Even though the Army's retreat had been checked at Gazala, by mid-February Coningham's landing grounds were being regularly strafed, day and night, by fighter-bombers. This weapon – 'a very difficult customer to overcome,' as he wrote on 18 February – would play a growing part in his thoughts and plans during the rest of the war. It forced him to construct new landing grounds farther east and to abandon several well-known, established airfields, though dummy aircraft were placed there to deceive the enemy and attract his attention. Hitherto, rapid movements forward and back in Operation Crusader had prevented Coningham from making continuous, effective use of radar, but now that the retreat had ended it could be used to detect enemy aircraft assembling over Martuba, thus enabling him to make economical use of his depleted force.[27]

By far the best news that came Coningham's way at this black time was the arrival on 14 February of Air Commodore Tommy Elmhirst to take charge of administration. Elmhirst, a most distinguished officer, began the war in 1939 under Coningham's command and would end it there in 1945, a record of which he was proud for the rest of his life. As a station commander in 4 Group, Elmhirst had despatched bombers to drop leaflets over Germany on the first night of the war; during the Battle of Britain he was a Controller in the Operations Room at Bentley Priory; and for the last ten months he had been responsible for the air defence of Egypt and the Suez Canal. 'On his arrival in the Desert,' wrote Sir Kenneth Cross (at that time Coningham's most outstanding fighter leader) 'he quickly created order where there had been disorder, supply where there had been shortage, confidence where there had been doubt and, above all, a belief amongst those doing the fighting that here was a man who understood what they needed.' Another contribution, less well known, was his influence over Coningham: a great commander, but somewhat haphazard in his methods. Elmhirst, wrote

Cross, would be seen 'making his way unbidden to the Commander's caravan to prevent or to remonstrate. It was seldom that the advice forthrightly given was ignored.'

In his own opinion, Elmhirst did 'probably his best job in the war' during 1942: 'reorganising the Desert Air Force into mobile fighter, bomber and reconnaissance wings, together with mobile supporting units'. He would set up similar organisations in Tunisia, Sicily and Normandy. 'Mary is a great leader,' Tedder had told him, 'and the pilots and aircrews under him are first class, but there is little organisation and not half the punch in the force that there should be, considering the number of men and machines we have sent them.' Elmhirst did much to solve that problem, with the help of Tedder's excellent staff in Cairo: Peter Drummond (his Deputy), Grahame Dawson and George Pirie, in charge of technical and administrative problems respectively.[28]

Elmhirst vividly recalled his arrival at Gambut, the joint Army–Air Advanced Headquarters some 40 miles east of Tobruk: 'From various corners of the large desert airfield,' he wrote, 'small columns of smoke were rising, smoke from burnt-out fighter aircraft of ours that had a couple of hours previously been subject to a low "shoot up" by German fighter aircraft.' Coningham, greeting him warmly, told him that he could either get himself a caravan for an office and work at Advanced Headquarters or, as his predecessor had done, work at the Rear Headquarters at Maaten Bagush, 200 miles farther east. Elmhirst wisely chose to stay forward. He then 'walked across the sand' to meet George Beamish, Coningham's personal choice as Senior Air Staff Officer to replace the unlamented Embry. Beamish, a man greatly admired by Coningham, was one of four brothers who were, recorded *The Times*, 'household names in every RAF mess and on every Rugby field between the wars'. He played twenty-six times for Ireland and on the first full-scale British Lions tour of New Zealand in 1930 had been the biggest and best of their forwards in all four Tests, one of which was won. An RAF champion at golf and boxing, Beamish had also received the Sword of Honour at Cranwell as the best all-round cadet of his year and in 1943 would become the first RAF-trained officer to reach the rank of Air Commodore. Not least, he was absolutely imperturbable: only shortages of tea or pipe tobacco upset him and he would gently chivy both Coningham and Elmhirst about the style and grammar of orders issued even at the height of panics. No-one, in his view, who had been in Crete in April 1941 should regard the odd setback in the Desert as a proper cause for alarm: as commander of RAF forces in Crete, he had escaped with Freyberg, the New Zealand Army Commander, at the last moment.[29]

Each evening, half an hour before supper in the Army Commander's mess tent, Beamish and Elmhirst would join Coningham in his caravan for a gin or whisky to discuss the day's events. These were improved by Nile water, which Coningham had flown up each week in a two-gallon tin. Elmhirst could remember only three occasions when Coningham said something 'really firm' to him. Firstly, he told Elmhirst to see that every officer and man was fully employed seven days a week. Out in the Desert, there were no distractions and work was the only alternative to boredom; those for whom there was no real work must be sent away, for food and water were too precious to waste on 'useless bodies'. Secondly, Coningham told him that he himself immediately sacked Squadron or Flight commanders whose mistakes cost lives: 'On your administrative side of the house, you can give an officer or man who fails you a second chance, but I wouldn't.' And thirdly, Coningham warned him that if he ever found on his visits to squadrons that they could not carry out orders because they were short of petrol, bombs or ammunition, 'then you, Tommy, are for the high jump'.[30]

Out on the main road, on his second day in the Desert, Elmhirst came across a Sergeant in charge of a Mobile Bath Unit, sent from Cairo 300 miles away to give airmen baths.

> A very good idea, but of course there was hardly sufficient water in wells to make cups of tea or fill radiators. I asked the Sergeant who he was under. He didn't know. Were his troops getting pay? No. Were they on anyone's strength so that they could draw rations or get their letters from home? No. It was an unhappy unit, with no chain of command to someone above who might help and direct it. It had no establishment, so no promotion or preferment for the men was possible.

Elmhirst learned that Coningham's Command had no written establishment, showing the purpose of all units, the number of aircraft, vehicles or weapons, officers and men needed in each unit to make the whole Command function. Within a week, Elmhirst had one compiled and approved by George Pirie in Cairo, 'an old friend of mine and my strong supporter'.

The establishment enabled Coningham to have Beamish promoted to Acting Air Commodore 'to give him that little bit of extra authority when dealing with our excellent but highly-strung commanders of wings and squadrons, let alone putting him on equal terms with his opposite number at Army HQ'. It allowed the posts of Coningham's driver, batman and clerk to be Corporals and his ADC and personal pilot to be a Flight Lieutenant. 'In fact,' recalled Elmhirst, 'there were celebrations in most quarters of the camp that day, with men in the correct rank for the job they were doing.' Better still, it was developed into a detailed Order of Battle in diagram form showing the chain of command and the location of every unit. 'No-one was left out or forgotten and consequently in retreats and advances, no-one failed to receive orders.' Constantly revised, it was the key to good control and administration: 'It seemed to bind the force together and I was never to be without one at my elbow in caravan or office for the next three years of war.'[31]

The reorganisation of the squadrons into wings with administrative staffs and supporting repair units was, in Elmhirst's opinion, 'without doubt the most important job I undertook in the Desert Campaign'. With Coningham's permission, he formed the fighter force into a Group (commanded by Cross) with two wings containing up to six squadrons of the same type of aircraft in each, all based if possible on the same airfield. This reorganisation had three purposes: to relieve wing and squadron commanders from office work and let them concentrate on leading their men in the air; to improve communications by reducing the number of units into which the Desert Air Force was divided; and to permit a stronger concentration of anti-aircraft defences around airfields. Coningham had himself served in wings during the Great War and saw the advantages in control of fewer and bigger formations, but Beamish, brought up between the wars to regard the squadron as the fighting unit, took a lot of persuading 'and Coningham would not agree until I had persuaded George'. The new wings then became the fighting units and Elmhirst's next task was to ensure that they were mobile: able to function, fight and move forward or back with sufficient petrol, ammunition, bombs, reserve aircraft and vehicles, stores and other equipment either on the airfields or within easy reach. Control of fighters in the air was exercised through a main operations room at El Adem and a forward one at Gazala, forty miles farther west. Both were identical in staff and equipment so that in advance – or retreat – one could leapfrog the other.[32]

'During the past five weeks,' reported Tedder to Portal on 11 March, 'Coningham has only had four fighter squadrons available for operations in the forward area, excluding one which is entirely occupied in covering Tobruk. Even in these the strength has been low owing to inevitable teething troubles with Kittyhawks.' He had that day discussed the general situation with Coningham and there could be no doubt that the enemy air force had rallied. The Army 'still seem incapable of providing ack-ack defence in any way comparable with that achieved by the enemy' and Coningham's fighters lacked the speed to intercept the Bf 109; Spitfires were badly needed. Nevertheless, he was returning to the offensive whenever he could, though targets were hard to find 'since we have certainly taught the enemy how to disperse and camouflage'. Coningham was looking for headquarters and similar vital spots and using Blenheims and Hurricanes as night intruders, but for strategic reconnaissance – a vital task from everyone's point of view – he needed aircraft with a range and performance superior to the obsolete Maryland. 'I gather from Coningham', he concluded, 'that there is rather a change of heart and recovery of fighting spirit in the Army, but I wish one could feel more confidence in them.' Apart from Gott, who had taken over 13 Corps, 'there is not much else besides Auchinleck himself. I don't know whether it is realised at home how much the Army really lost – quite apart from tanks and guns, they lost 1,600 MT. Recently-escaped officers report four out of five vehicles on the enemy L of C [Lines of Communication] as British.'[33]

No major battle was in prospect in April and Coningham was able to concentrate on essential training. Captured enemy pilots were impressed by his men's flying skill, but not their shooting. Coningham strongly advocated 'shadow firing' (at the aircraft's own shadow racing over the sand) as excellent practice, far more useful than firing at towed targets. An instructor could fly above his pupil to observe his approach, manoeuvre for position and bullet strikes. As well as firing practice, Coningham wanted pilots to receive intensive training in navigation, escort flying and ground attack. The bombers were based around Baheira, twelve miles east of Gambut: close enough for regular discussions between fighter pilots and bomber crews about aims and achievements. Particular attention was given to ground organisation during this quiet time and the force benefited greatly in later operations from hours of practice spent in rapid rearmament, refuelling and essential servicing. Coningham held weekly conferences with his Wing Commanders throughout the lull at which every aspect of operations, tactics, training and administration was discussed; not least, everyone was kept in touch with his thinking on these matters.[34]

Early in May, Group Captain R. H. Humphreys visited Coningham's headquarters at Gambut to study the use being made of Ultra. Coningham's Signals Intelligence Officer interpreted this information in the light of local intelligence, discussing his interpretation with Coningham and Beamish, who also read the original signals. As well as these, Bletchley Park periodically signalled summaries of recent intelligence derived from Ultra to remind recipients of the general picture because Coningham (like all other recipients) was required to burn signals as soon as they had been read. Humphreys told Coningham that the Luftwaffe might soon abandon the costly day bombing of Malta from Sicilian bases, concentrate on night bombing instead and thus release Bf 109F fighter escorts for use in the Western Desert. Coningham promptly asked Tedder to send him Spitfires from Malta to counter these excellent machines. Soon afterwards, just in time to face a new German offensive, Coningham received his first Spitfires.[35]

The main offensive against Malta, wrote Kesselring, had begun on 2 April and was 'completed' by 10 May: 'air and sea supremacy was assured on the supply routes from Italy to Africa' and it would then have been 'a simple task to capture the island'; without Malta, as he repeatedly told Rommel, operations in Africa could not prosper for long. Nevertheless, Kesselring 'gave way to a sudden proposal of Rommel's to launch an offensive in Africa before the attack on Malta'. This, he admitted, was a mistake. 'I ought to have known that a tactical success can only be exploited and sustained if the supply services are functioning faultlessly. I ought furthermore to have known that Rommel never stops when he has a success in his hands.' The situation, from Rommel's point of view, was certainly tempting and he received an accurate appraisal of Auchinleck's strength on 20 May, based on his 'Good Source', the signals sent by Colonel Fellers from Cairo to Washington. These signals were tapped until 29 June, when at last the source dried up. Rommel's armoured strength had vastly increased, owing to British inability to interfere seriously with his shipping, and he knew, as Auchinleck warned Churchill, that a British defeat in Cyrenaica would cause a retreat all the way to El Alamein because there was insufficient armour to hold positions prepared in the rear. The Battle of Gazala brought defeat for the British yet again, the shocking loss of the great fortress of Tobruk (with almost its entire garrison and an immense quantity of weapons, transport, food and clothing) and the retreat which Auchinleck had foretold.[36]

CHAPTER EIGHT

'Drastic and Immediate Changes'

Coningham in the Western Desert, May to September 1942

From 26 May, when the Battle of Gazala began, Elmhirst had 'forward' and 'retreat' plans on his desk on alternate days, for no-one could tell who was winning. By continual fighter sweeps over the battlefield, Coningham tried to prevent soldiers and tanks from being shot up and bombed; then, when enemy tanks appeared, he used bombers (escorted by fighters) against them; finally, whenever possible, he attacked airfields and intercepted air formations approaching the battlefield. 'The fighting spirit of our pilots and bomber crews at this time could not have been higher', thought Elmhirst, 'and they had complete confidence in Mary's handling of them. He had handpicked the leaders over the past ten months and all wing, squadron and flight commanders were his personal choices.' He visited them every day to invite their opinions on operations, but once decisions had been taken, he expected unquestioning obedience. The leadership of the 8th Army was not at that time in the same class: 'There was a lack of discipline', Elmhirst observed, 'not, as far as I knew, among the men, but among their leaders.' For example, he remembered Ritchie telling him one evening during this battle that he had sent out his orders for the next day, but 'my Corps Commanders will have a tea party on them and whether they comply with my exact intentions is questionable'. A tank battalion commander told Elmhirst that on one occasion when his Brigadier ordered him to withdraw he replied: 'Not a bit, George, I've got some good targets and I'm staying!' He lost his tanks and many of their crews were killed or captured.[1]

On 31 May, Coningham sent Peter Drummond in Cairo an account of the battle so far, beginning with his attacks on Rommel's airfields on the night of the 21st, five days before the offensive began, to which Rommel responded with heavy night attacks on Coningham's airfields. On the 27th, wrote Coningham, 'we had the first confirmation of the value of fighter-bombers when employed on fast-moving targets in the battle area. The Army were fighting very well and hard, overcoming the first shock of the attack', but many units were overrun. 'In the circumstances, which we fully appreciated, the Army could not ensure security for the Gambut landing grounds, so I played for safety and sent half the fighter force back to the base landing grounds for the night.' That night, the 27th, 'was fairly noisy with lots of low-flying Ju 88s bombing and shooting up the camps and roads', but little damage was suffered. Next morning, Coningham decided that enemy supply lines should be his main targets and soon his fighters and bombers were 'doing a shuttle service and thinking of nothing else but these ground attacks'. By the afternoon of the 30th, the enemy was trying to escape and bomber pilots reported 'a confusion of vehicles colliding, being shelled, bombed and running on to the mines, so it must have been quite a mess'.

Coningham had taken a considerable risk in ordering that enemy fighters were to be ignored and that no-one was to fly above 6,000 feet. It was, he added feelingly, as one former fighter pilot to another, 'a lot to ask a fighter force . . . to think only of the ground and to submit themselves to unmolested attack from above'. Further experience would teach him that the fighter-bomber, whose success had been 'phenomenal', according to Army reports, could only be used against targets that were badly dispersed or poorly defended. Large targets with well-organised flak were too danger-ous for attack by aircraft at low level with impaired manoeuvrability.[2]

'Mary must have all the credit', wrote Elmhirst on 31 May, for the 'fine Army–Air cooperation', which began when he asked Ritchie's predecessor if he could 'share the same wooden bench' in the mess tent. 'The fact that I now sit with them and the senior Army Staff is a normal follow on and so is the cooperation . . . Mary has stood the strain well, but I think his hair has gone a bit whiter.' Meanwhile, both soldiers and airmen in North Africa were once again receiving invaluable help from Malta. On the night of 30–31 May, a few hours before Coningham reported to Drummond, an Italian merchant ship had been sunk in the Gulf of Sirte by aircraft operating from Malta; four nights later, they sank a second ship north of Benghazi. These sinkings, the first since the end of February, marked the start of a new offensive against Rommel's sea supply lines that would never again be interrupted.[3]

On 1 June, Tedder congratulated Coningham 'most sincerely' on his recent handling of the Desert Air Force: 'Your decision to give close support to the Army at all costs was right and has been fully justified by results', but few replacement aircraft were available and Coningham would now have to return to 'normal' fighter operations. 'The most important lesson learned in the first round,' he told Drummond on 2 June, was 'the value of the fighter-bomber.' The Germans had realised this too and Coningham foresaw 'a race between us as to who can produce the greater numerical and tactical strength in fighter-bombers for the critical phases of future rounds'. He had no time for the twin-engined Boston as a daylight tactical weapon, except when air superiority was total, because it required a fighter escort to deliver a 1,500-pound bomb load whereas locally-modified 'Kittybombers' could carry two

250-pound bombs and take care of themselves. Coningham had three squadrons already equipped with bomb racks and wanted Grahame Dawson in Cairo to speed up the supply of American racks with which to equip every Kittyhawk squadron. 'I am sure everything is being done to send a few more Spitfires to us,' he added, most politely. 'One squadron would have made a great difference during the past week.'⁴

Rommel mounted a strong attack against Bir Hacheim, a fortified position held by Free French troops at the southern end of the Gazala Line, on 2 June. Coningham's fighters did their best to protect them and on the evening of 4 June, after a day of fierce fighting, General Koenig (the French Commander) signalled him: 'Bravo! Merci pour la RAF!' to which Coningham promptly replied: 'Bravo à vous. Merci pour le sport.' Even so, only six out of at least twenty-four Luftwaffe raids on Bir Hacheim were intercepted, although fighters were kept at readiness at Tobruk and frequent sweeps were flown over the French positions. Standing patrols were impossible because Coningham had too few fighters and the Germans too many. Moreover, he had to withdraw his forward radar unit from Gazala: this unit, with a range of sixty miles and low vision, was then the only one of its kind in the Desert and he could not afford to lose it. Another problem was the frequent breakdown of the telephone system between Coningham's headquarters at Gambut and his fighter wings caused both by enemy air attack cutting overhead wires and by British vehicles passing over ground cables.

However, Koenig's men were not driven out of Bir Hacheim until the night of 10–11 June. 'Those nine days,' wrote a German historian in March 1944, 'were irrecoverable.' Though 'stupidly insensitive' (in Roderic Owen's opinion) to the menace of Malta, Rommel determined at all costs to capture this far less important 'island' in the Desert. The victory so sapped the Luftwaffe's strength that it proved unable to exploit the British retreat from Gazala to Tobruk, thirty-five miles to the east. For two days and nights, wrote Owen, that road 'became one interminable slow-moving caterpillar of men and machines inviting air attack on a scale once so effective in France. Yet our retreating troops lost only six men through enemy air action. "Thank God you didn't let the Huns Stuka us", said General Freyberg to Tedder: "we were an appalling target."'⁵

Coningham had written to Tedder in Cairo at 10.30 am on 6 June about the worsening military situation. Neil Ritchie, he said,

> has mentioned possibility of a withdrawal to Tobruk line and he feels it
> will be necessary if Knightsbridge goes because his armoured forces are
> so reduced. Gott [13 Corps Commander] has been asking for Tobruk to
> be emptied and Norrie [30 Corps Commander] wanted Hacheim
> evacuated. Neil has had a very anxious night and looks worried. He says
> we are fully on the defensive.

All three, thought Coningham, were severely strained and a visit from Auchinleck would be psychologically opportune. Next morning, 7 June, he wrote again. Neil and his Corps Commanders were going without sleep, he said, working all day and up at every alarm most of the night. Coningham had therefore taken Neil 'for a stroll and suggested that these periodic offensives were as much a contest between the mental and physical welfare of the opposing commanders as between the fighting forces and then made him go to sleep. Much more of a grip of things was taken yesterday and I think prospects are much brighter.' That evening, Elmhirst wrote home from Gambut. 'Mary,' he said, 'is at his best on days of gloom': a recent lunch in the Army Commander's mess had started very silently, 'until Mary's cheerful voice was heard in the outside tent calling for a gin, followed by a loud laugh . . . What a gift, and no-one knew the situation better than he did.'[6]

The amount of intelligence available to Coningham from all sources – decoded signals, the tapping of wireless messages, prisoner interrogation and photo-reconnaissance – increased steadily and it was made available to him more swiftly, so that in planning operations he was well informed about the Luftwaffe's order of battle, airfield serviceability, fuel stocks, casualties and replacements. From June 1942 onwards, according to the official historians of British Intelligence, 'British forces in North Africa were supplied with more information about more aspects of the enemy's operations than any forces enjoyed during any important campaign of the Second World War'. Even so, Rommel could not be halted in June. On the evening of the 15th, strong enemy patrols came within twenty miles of Gambut, where there was no adequate ground force immediately available to resist an attack, but the El Adem area needed full air support and this could not be provided if the fighters withdrew from Gambut. Coningham therefore decided to stay as long as possible. 'We are all at one hour's notice to move,' he signalled Tedder next day, 'and owing to proved value of Force, Army has given one brigade for close defence, which helps my judgment of night security. I have prepared landing grounds all the way back to the frontier and plan is steady withdrawal of squadrons, keeping about twenty miles away from enemy.' That brigade, if provided, contributed little to Coningham's security and he made what use he could of his armoured cars, sending them out to form a protective and warning screen around forward airfields. When the fighters withdrew from Gambut on 17 June, they did so on information provided by an armoured car patrol.[7]

The days 15 to 17 June were the busiest yet experienced by the Desert Air Force. Hitherto, the nature of the land fighting had usually demanded a specific type of air support, as at Bir Hacheim, where targets were most suitable for low-flying fighters rather than light bombers. Along the Acroma-El Adem line, however, there were good bomber targets as well as scope for fighters armed with bombs and machine-guns. At the same time, defensive fighter patrols were in demand over Army units as they withdrew along the coast road. Liaison between Army units and Air Support Control was good, except with the garrison at El Adem. It was not until 3 pm on the 17th that

Coningham learned of the evacuation of El Adem, the last serious threat to Rommel's flank and rear: it had in fact been evacuated twelve hours earlier, making Gambut no longer tenable. Keeping his head, Coningham brought off 'a masterstroke', as Elmhirst described it. 'He spotted from reconnaissance that the enemy had moved up fighters to an advanced airfield before they had installed gun defence there. All our available fighters were sent in to attack and destroyed twenty of theirs on the ground. Accordingly, all our long lines of retreating columns have not been harassed at all by air attacks.' The Kittyhawks, recalled a South African airman, 'found the German fighters refuelling and rearming and virtually destroyed the entire force, with the result that our forces retreated nose-to-tail down Bardia Pass with not a sign of the GAF. I flew over the area. It was a bomber's dream.'[8]

Unfortunately, once Coningham had been obliged to withdraw to the Sidi Barrani group of landing grounds, Tobruk was outside normal fighter range. His light bombers had sufficient range, but unescorted daylight raids were out of the question with the enemy in possession of landing grounds from Gazala to Gambut. Tobruk, in consequence, was heavily pounded from the air and surrendered on 21 June, Auchinleck's fifty-eighth birthday. 'As far as I was concerned,' he said in 1974, 'it had no strategic value at all' and all the men captured there 'should have been taken out', but for Churchill it had emotional value. Worse still, he heard of its fall while a guest in the White House, from President Roosevelt himself. This was a humiliation which he found hard to forgive, even though he recognised that Auchinleck was right in regarding El Alamein 'as the only defensive position in which you could protect Egypt. Holding Tobruk didn't protect Egypt in the least'.[9]

Kesselring, however, considered Tobruk's capture 'among the most outstanding performances of the war'. Rommel was made a Field Marshal, General von Waldau (his principal airman) received the Ritterkreuz; Italian prestige was restored and massive stocks of supplies captured. 'This was a situation', wrote Kesselring, 'which would surely have induced any general, let alone Rommel so full of his triumph, to follow up his success.' A conference of Axis commanders was held at Gambut, where Rommel 'reported that there was practically no opposition of importance left and that he could promise that the Army would be in Cairo in ten days'. Kesselring disagreed. The Luftwaffe's men and machines, he said, were not ready for such a campaign. 'As an airman, I consider it madness to rush in against intact air bases. The cooperation of the air forces being of decisive importance in a battle, I must from this point of view decline to continue the offensive with Egypt as its goal.' His objections were overruled. Mussolini was coming to Africa to make a formal entrance into Cairo and Kesselring received 'a curt order from Hitler by wireless not to obstruct Rommel'. The Italian commanders, Bastico and Cavallero, 'were so enraptured with the certain "Cairo" success that they already considered it necessary to look up the best hotels in their guide books'.[10]

Tedder reported to Portal from Cairo on 23 June, writing the letter himself because he had things to say 'which one would not like to go through a typist'. The land battle, he wrote, had been

> a tragic series of lost opportunities and lack of inspired leadership. I did what I could to try and persuade the Auk to put the armour under Gott (who is far more of a leader than most of them) and not under Willoughby Norrie, who had been a complete and utter failure in the Crusader affair. The Auk hesitated a good deal over Ritchie, but I think finally left him in command for lack of a better. As I told him before and Coningham and I have told him since, Ritchie is a sound and solid staff officer; he is no commander to put up against a quick-witted and thrusting opponent. Willoughby Norrie and Messervy (who has now lost three armoured divisions) have gone, but the milk has been spilt once again . . . I have again and again, before, during and after this collapse, urged the Auk to go up and take command himself. I cannot get him to do more than go up for a day or so – which, of course, is no use. He feels himself tied here by all the other commitments, the signals for the PM, etc., etc.

Tedder feared a stalemate for months to come. 'On the other hand, if only our friend Rommel would run true to form and come bullocking on regardless, there might be a chance of knocking him right out,' but Tedder thought he would be leashed in while the Axis made a determined attempt to conquer Malta.[11]

'Coningham is doing very well,' Tedder told Portal on 25 June. 'I think his judgment has been excellent.' He and his men 'have been under intense pressure and though they feel right on top of the Hun, they may well get rather fed up with the Army – and that we must avoid.' 'Mary has been a tower of strength through the dark days,' wrote Elmhirst next day, 'and full of cheer and ability throughout. *A great leader* . . . he always stays forward until the last, ensuring that the fighters are put to the best use covering the retreat until the Hun is almost on their airfield and they have to move back.' From 23–26 June, contact between the British rearguard and the foremost enemy units was minor and did not call for air support, but the main Axis force – advancing in three columns across the Desert – presented an ideal bombing target. During these days, Coningham maintained a constant and increasing effort to impede the advance, despite the move eighty miles eastward of his fighters from Sidi Barrani to Mersa Matruh and his bombers from Mersa Matruh a further seventy miles to Dhaba. In contrast, the Luftwaffe proved slow to move forward to airfields within range of the fighting, either to protect Axis troops or to attack the British, retreating in a close-packed stream. Determined attacks might well have delayed them and given Rommel's land forces time to catch up.[12]

Tedder told Portal on 29 June that he and Coningham had met at Maaten Bagush on the 25th to review the situation with Neil Ritchie (not yet aware that Auchinleck would dismiss him and take personal command of the 8th Army that day). 'Poor Neil,' wrote Elmhirst, 'we saw him as usual in our mess tent one evening for supper at the end of the retreat and then he was spirited away, removed from his command.' The Australian historian, Chester Wilmot, had less sympathy for him. It was strange, he told Liddell Hart, how often in the British Army a man like Ritchie, who 'looks every inch a soldier' rose to the highest posts in spite of his stupidity. Ritchie, thought Tedder, was 'completely whacked' and after he went, 'passive bewilderment' was quickly replaced by 'active command'.[13]

About 7.30 pm on 26 June, wrote Tedder, we heard that 'large enemy columns had gone through the gap south of the main Matruh defences and that in consequence the enemy were within twenty miles of the aerodromes on which our whole fighter force was based'. As at Gambut, Coningham was ready for a sudden move, but with darkness coming on there was no time to get squadrons off and down again at their next landing grounds before dark. No soldiers were available to defend his aerodromes, so he could only send out a screen of armoured cars westward to warn him if the enemy pushed on through the night. If that happened, Coningham's pilots would have no choice but to take off and get down somewhere farther east as best they could; his motor transport drivers were likewise poised to carry away as many ground crews and operations personnel as possible; as for Tedder and Coningham, they proposed to take care of themselves, having no small opinion of their skills as drivers and navigators. Fortunately, Rommel did not for once press on and the fighters began to move back at dawn to landing grounds in the Dhaba area.[14]

Tedder and Coningham then learned that the Army had chosen a site for the combined Advanced Headquarters that was about half an hour's drive from the nearest airfield. 'This complete failure on the part of the Army even now to understand some of the most elementary principles of modern warfare frankly defeats me,' wrote Tedder, but Coningham's possession of a Fieseler Storch (a German aircraft able to take off and land in a very small space) enabled him 'not merely to be in touch with the General without losing touch with his squadrons, but also to visit isolated units and formations in two or three hours which could not by other means have been visited in under two days'. Auchinleck gave orders for the protection of landing grounds, but at 10 pm on 28 June Coningham rang Tedder to say: 'We've been had once again!' No British troops were in sight and his screen of armoured cars had just reported the approach of enemy tanks and infantry, obliging him to abandon his most westerly landing grounds.[15]

Next day, Tedder met Major General Lewis H. Brereton, USAAF, newly arrived in the Middle East with a few heavy bombers, who recorded Tedder's description of Coningham's 'brilliant withdrawal': a feat involving 'five separate displacements against the enemy's rapid advance, in the course of which only forty aircraft were lost – all out of commission on the ground. In a similar withdrawal of the Germans and Italians last year, over 450 aircraft were captured by the British.' This was the first Brereton had heard of Mary Coningham, an officer with whom he would work closely for the rest of the war. Tedder wrote once more to Portal on 30 June, expressing yet again his 'complete confidence in Coningham's handling of a very difficult situation. He is keeping his head extremely well and is adjusting his employment of his forces hour by hour as the ground/air situation changes.' Rommel had pushed forward remarkably quickly, helped by nearly 4,000 tons of fuel which the Tobruk garrison had failed to destroy. Army Headquarters, save for Auchinleck, gave Tedder 'a terrible feeling of apathy and ignorance. One hopes that, as seems possible, the Hun may bump into the New Zealanders at the outset. They at least will fight.'[16]

'We have very definitely suffered a severe defeat', wrote Elmhirst at this time. 'There is no argument about it, but a lot of argument about why.' At least the enemy would find nothing of use to him on airfields. 'None too easy to ensure, but my staff have worked magnificently on the job, though it almost brought tears to my eyes to give the order to put a pickaxe into the many fifty gallon drums we could not bring away.' Elmhirst shrewdly refused to *burn* anything: 'There is quite enough alarm and despondency,' he wrote, 'without adding columns of black smoke to it.' Nevertheless, if Mussolini and Kesselring had held firmly to their conviction that Malta must be subjugated before victory in the Desert could be achieved and if they had succeeded in carrying with them the German High Command, events in the Mediterranean would have run a course much more favourable for the Axis. Instead, the risk was taken of advancing into Egypt with Malta still able to interfere seriously with Rommel's supply lines. It might even be argued that the very extent of his success at Tobruk led to his eventual failure; that the supplies captured at Tobruk were a bait, unwittingly laid by the British, which led him to overreach. His tactical victory led to the cancellation of the one strategic project which could have guaranteed Axis command of the Mediterranean because Rommel failed to allow for the impact of Coningham's air force on both his advance and on his ever-extending lines of communication; he failed also to appreciate the strategic significance of Malta and, not least, the recuperative power of the 8th Army.[17]

Rommel reported to Berlin on 4 July that he must temporarily suspend further attacks and go over to the defensive for about two weeks in order to bring up men and supplies and regroup units. He then lay only sixty miles west of Alexandria and had advanced over 350 miles in six weeks to the last line of defence before the Nile valley. Both the 8th Army and the Desert Air Force had suffered heavily during that time: the force of 125,000 men confronting Rommel at Gazala on 26 May had been reduced by the end of June to 60,000 men and Coningham had lost about 600 fighters and 140 bombers. Early in July, the German radio announced that Rommel would be in Alexandria on the 6th and in Cairo on the 9th. Panic followed in certain circles, as Stanley Lee (a senior RAF staff officer in Cairo) recalled. 'There were long queues outside the banks, the luggage shops, the South African and other legations at which visas might be obtained. Car prices rose astronomically. Various officers' wives disappeared quietly in convenient aircraft.' Orders were given for secret documents to be burnt and Lee experienced 'a sense of improper satisfaction in seeing one's burdensome papers thrown cheerfully on the flames and their problems postponed indefinitely. All over that part of the Garden City where lay our headquarters and the Embassy, the air was full of tiny scraps of burnt paper.'[18]

The worst, in fact, was over, as Lewis Brereton recorded on 4 July after his first meeting with Coningham. 'No account of the British stand which stopped Rommel,' he wrote, 'can fail to record the fine part played by the RAF and the New Zealand Division under General Freyberg. These two undoubtedly saved the 8th Army from complete defeat.' It was on the evening of the 3rd that the enemy advance faltered as a result of persistent air attack and withdrawal began next day. The 'determining factors', thought Brereton, were the RAF's morale, shorter lines of communication and superior repair and salvage organisation.[19]

On a forty-mile front, from El Alamein on the coast road in the north, to the edge of the Qattara Depression in the south, Auchinleck turned his Army to stand and halt Rommel's advance. That the Army, tired and severely depleted in strength after its long retreat was able to do so, ranks as a major achievement. There can be no doubt, however, as Auchinleck readily admitted, that the RAF's role at this critical time was decisive in saving the Army from a disaster that would have vitally affected the whole course of the war. Our air forces, he wrote later, 'could not have done more than they did to help and sustain the 8th Army in its struggle. Their effort was continuous by day and night and the effect on the enemy was tremendous. I am certain that, had it not been for their devoted and exceptional efforts, we should not have been able to stop the enemy on the El Alamein position.' Sinclair (Secretary of State for Air) added his praise in a letter to Portal on 4 July. 'I am convinced,' he said, 'that no air force, even including Fighter Command in the Battle of Britain, has ever worked harder or fought harder than Coningham's men have during the retirement.' Numerous references were found in captured German diaries to the effect of round-the-clock bombing. 'The enemy air force is bothering us a lot,' recorded one diarist on 4 July. 'We are becoming like potatoes – always underground.'[20]

Tedder's personal contribution to this achievement was recognised by promotion to the rank of Air Chief Marshal on 3 July; nothing – except praise – came Coningham's way. Tedder, thought Stanley Lee,

could never have been as successful as Coningham as a field commander. He lacked Coningham's easy assurance and was too highly strung to be able to work continuously under the strenuous conditions in which Coningham flourished. But at Cairo, where he sat at the centre and held all the reins, he was able to fulfil his role of higher commander with the greatest skill, organising and disposing his forces, building for the future and devising machinery to work smoothly with the Navy and Army and help link the three Services together for a single purpose.[21]

On 4 July, after four days in the same place (a camp on the edge of the Delta) a more cheerful spirit was abroad and it was there that the build-up came 'for the battle which was to start the run to victory,' as Coningham wrote after the war. Mobile equipment was redesigned or rearranged on the basis of battle experience, radar was more extensively used and air support technique improved, but most important was the arrival of the first American fighter groups, 'bringing with them a promise of great strength to come and a fund of flying skill, keenness and good will. Their wish to use the same methods as the RAF enabled them to take their place quickly and naturally as a most valuable addition to the Force.' Week by week, to Elmhirst's delight, new aircraft arrived, including Spitfires. He was out every day, visiting units to find out where they needed help and to ensure that Coningham's instructions were being obeyed. At supper in the Army Commander's tent, he usually sat alongside his opposite number, the Quartermaster General (now Brian Robertson), to settle any problems about supplies of food, water, bombs or petrol. 'Everyone lower down on the "Q" side,' he wrote, 'both Army and Air, knows that their "tops" live and get on well together and that they will get no change from us if they don't get on well together all the way down the line!'[22]

Tedder reported to Portal on 12 July about his latest 'stimulating stay' with Coningham's force. Wings, he thought, had now developed a 'corporate identity' which in no way weakened squadron spirit but did permit the pooling of base maintenance parties. Squadrons had been divided into A and B parties: 'In the event of a move, the A party goes on by road, the squadron continuing to operate from its existing base with the B party, until the A party has reached the new landing ground and is ready to service the squadron.' This organisation, intended to make continuous effort possible, either in retreat or advance, depended upon the Army regarding the defence of landing grounds as a serious obligation. This had never been the case in the past and, as Tedder reminded Portal, 'on two occasions at least it was only our own armoured car screen that saved the fighter force from being wiped out on the ground by enemy land forces'. Coningham had to rely almost entirely on his own sources of information in order to give the Army the support it needed and found its 'complacent ignorance' about the positions and movements of forward troops infuriating. Though Auchinleck himself fully appreciated the position, Tedder feared that it would 'take some time to clean out the Army stable'.[23]

As for the Americans, Tedder thought Brereton was good: his experience in India had taught him 'how little he and his people know about real operations, both on the ground and in the air', but he was prepared to learn. With Tedder's approval, Brereton planned to employ his four-engined Liberator heavy bombers as a strategic strike force under his own command while his tactical strike force of Mitchell medium bombers and Kittyhawk fighters operated under Coningham's control. Brereton sent Colonel Auby C. Strickland to Coningham's headquarters, where he learned quickly and, better still, formed a friendship with Coningham that outlasted the war. Carefully primed by Coningham through Strickland, Brereton outlined the Desert Air Force's 'broad plan of employment': first, to defeat the enemy air forces and maintain air supremacy; next (though equally important), to assist ground operations by destroying enemy troops, artillery, transport and supply, thus permitting the Army freedom of action 'by nailing the enemy to the ground, immobilising him through loss of vehicles and supply'.[24]

'What you tell me', wrote Portal to Tedder on 21 July, 'about Army cooperation is of extraordinary interest and very helpful in our arguments here. So few people realise that cooperation must be mutual and that subordination is not what is required to achieve it.' Tedder agreed, sending Portal copies of an exchange between Auchinleck and Coningham which illustrated that essential mutual respect. 'Our pilots,' Coningham had signalled on the 18th, 'themselves intensely engaged over the front, refer continually to the gruelling trial of strength seen below and wish to do everything possible to help. We are proud of our land forces and have every confidence in the result of much hard battling that remains.' Auchinleck, replying at once, said: 'We are getting along slowly, but I hope surely, and we one and all know what we owe to you and your men. We shall not forget it and hope to prove we are worthy of such grand partners.'[25]

Nevertheless, as Elmhirst recalled, Auchinleck abandoned the joint Army–Air Headquarters and set up his own headquarters close behind the centre of the Army defence line.

> After a few days on our own, I don't think he was even asked to join up with the Auk, Mary decided that we were out on a limb: no close touch with the Army, no airstrip, poor communications with our own wings and squadrons and with AHQ in Cairo and, almost worst of all, an unpleasant camp site in the open flat desert with millions of flies around us. So, he and the Chief Signals Officer set off on a reconnaissance one morning and, back in the evening, told me that he had found a wonderful site for our HQ camp. In sand dunes on the sea coast (fifty yards to bathe in the Mediterranean) with an airstrip close by, close to the main desert road, water available and signals communications not difficult to connect to Cairo, Army HQ and to our wings and squadrons. Burg-el-Arab was the place: no habitations, but the odd palm tree – and no flies.

And, as Tedder told Portal on 26 July, the difference between Army meetings and Coningham's meetings was 'the difference between a funeral breakfast and a wedding breakfast. There's no life about them.' Tedder rightly suspected that 'people at home' were losing confidence in Auchinleck, even though he was 'honest, clear thinking and full of guts', but most of his senior staff and commanders were 'useless "good fellows"' and Churchill (taking with him Sir Alan Brooke, Chief of the General Staff) decided to visit the Middle East and judge for himself.[26]

The Prime Minister arrived in Cairo on 3 August. Accompanied by Tedder, Coningham and Brooke, he spent the morning of the 5th at Auchinleck's Forward Headquarters, wearing the uniform of an Air Commodore – a tribute noted by soldiers and airmen alike – and then lunched at a Fighter Control mess. Coningham was well aware that Churchill did not share Auchinleck's indifference to good food, personal comfort and pleasant surroundings. He had therefore instructed the officer in charge to have a double tent erected over a specially-laid concrete floor (to keep the temperature down) and produced a lunch sent out on ice from the best hotel in Alexandria. Next evening, having consulted Field Marshal Smuts (Prime Minister of South Africa) and a host of lesser lights in Cairo, Churchill decided that 'drastic and immediate' changes were needed. General Alexander became Commander-in-Chief of the Near East (a Command much smaller than Auchinleck's), General Montgomery became Commander of the 8th Army (after Gott, the first choice, was killed on 7 August) and three other generals were dismissed. Auchinleck learned of his fall on the 8th and a week later Alexander and Montgomery had taken over.

Both Churchill and Smuts had asked Tedder what should be done. 'Selection, promotion and removal of staffs and commanders', he replied, must be entirely based on results, not on seniority, personal friendships, old school ties, etc. Failures must be analysed and exposed – not, as invariably in the past, buried under many coats of whitewash.' 'Somehow and by someone,' he told Portal on 8 August, 'the whole attitude and atmosphere of the Army Staff needs changing.' He was 'very sorry indeed' for Auchinleck, but the decision to remove him was right. Churchill returned to England 'full of the exploits of your people' Portal wrote to Tedder on 26 August, 'and he cannot say enough for what you have done. He was also very pleased with Coningham and with what he saw of the squadrons.' Portal was convinced that the RAF 'saved Egypt'; everyone he met returning from the Middle East was 'loud in the praise of yourself and of your units. This universal praise is very comforting to all of us here and is doing the Air Force a great service at this time.'[27]

Coningham met Montgomery on 16 August, wrote Elmhirst, and was most impressed. 'Tommy,' he said, 'I have now been with the Army in this desert for over a year and have seen three Army Commanders and two Corps Commanders come and go, but we now have a man, a great soldier if I am any judge, and we will go all the way with him.' And they did, through four campaigns, ending in Germany in May 1945. Sadly, their relations with each other grew steadily worse as the triumphs in which they shared grew steadily greater. Elmhirst attended Montgomery's first conference with his Corps Commanders on 21 August.

At one side of a little table with a blackboard behind sat he and Mary and on benches opposite the rest of us, Freddie de Guingand (Chief of Staff), Brian Robertson (Quartermaster General), the two new Corps Commanders, Horrocks and Leese, and the only remainder of the old gang, Herbert Lumsden, together with George Beamish and me. George walked into the tent sucking his old pipe (long gone out) and was greeted with: 'I don't have smoking at my conferences.'

On first sight, Elmhirst had wondered if Montgomery could stand the racket, for he looked so pale and frail. By the end of that conference, he realised that the Army had 'a little tiger' for a commander. 'But I don't think he is the sort of leader that young lads will hero worship like Mary!'[28]

The keypoint of the Army's position was the ridge at Alam el Halfa. Rommel would be forced to fight on ground dominated by British artillery and aircraft. Coningham followed his now familiar tripartite plan of round-the-clock bombing to keep the enemy awake and dispersed; attacks on lines of communication and supply to isolate the battlefield; and a daily contest to win and keep air superiority by attacking airfields and threatening ground forces. Throughout August, Coningham noted Rommel's reluctance to employ his dive-bombers and a particular sensitivity to reconnaissance flights in the south, indicating a shift of armour southward in preparation for a right hook to the coast, behind British lines. The greater part of Coningham's force had been rested and time found for training, including familiarisation with the terrain. Maximum numbers had been concentrated on the airfields available and control was eased by excellent telephone links. Ample supplies had been established at all landing grounds and Air Support Control had a full disposition of tentacles to cover the battle area with rear links to all fighter and bomber wings. But the Kittyhawk squadrons remained under strength and prospects for replacement were poor. Coningham now had three squadrons of Spitfires, but they too were under strength. His Hurricane squadrons, though strong in numbers, were less valuable than either. There were plenty of Boston bombers, however, and both Baltimores and Mitchells were available as reinforcements. 'Morale was very high,' wrote Beamish: 'The battle could not open under better conditions.'[29]

'We sit awaiting a Hun attack,' wrote Elmhirst on 26 August. 'Last night in mess the betting was 6–4 on that it started that night. No attack came and Mary lost a bob. Tonight it was evens. Every day the Hun puts it off is better for us and there is a spirit of quiet confidence at HQ.' Nothing happened during the next two days and on the 28th, he wrote, Montgomery and Coningham were 'in good form in the mess at supper and we had a general discussion on the difficulty of bringing up the younger generation'. Two more days passed before Rommel ended their suspense. He began his attack during the night of 30–31 August, just as the worst dust storm for many weeks swept Coningham's airfields. Held up by unexpected minefields, Rommel did not advance as quickly as planned in the first few hours and, as

Kesselring pointed out, air raids on an unprecedented scale caused him very heavy casualties. Kesselring was therefore not surprised when the attack was called off on 3 September and Rommel, 'no longer the bold leader of old', went on leave after setting up a new defence line.

The Battle of Alam el Halfa – truly, the battle for control of the Middle East and the second largest oil-producing area in the world – had been lost. That battle, in Elmhirst's opinion, was Montgomery's greatest victory. Until then, the Army had not yet got over the long retreat after the defeat at Gazala and lacked confidence in itself, but Montgomery's careful location of armour, the well coordinated use of concentrated artillery fire with aerial bombing and, most important of all, his refusal to follow up Rommel's retreat, brought victory. 'All the old Desert hands,' recalled Ronald Lewin, 'the 7th Armoured Division for example, were screaming for us to rush after Rommel. If we had done so, it is as certain as anything that Rommel would have pulled back on to the fairly elaborate minefields in his rear, set up a quick but strong anti-tank defence as he had at Gazala and massacred our galloping armour.'[30]

Montgomery wrote to Coningham on 3 September, praising the RAF's skilful and determined efforts. 'It is clear to me,' he concluded, 'that such magnificent cooperation can produce only one result – a victorious end to the campaign in North Africa. Let our motto be: United we stand, divided we fall, and let nothing divide us.' Coningham replied on the 5th, congratulating him on winning the battle 'in such a flawless manner', and Montgomery responded at once, repeating his praise of Coningham's 'magnificent cooperation'. Brereton thought Coningham's handling of operations in this battle superb and Coningham, for his part, was quick to praise the bravery of his American allies. That night, Coningham brought out a bottle of champagne and he, Beamish, Dawson and Elmhirst drank to the Hun's 'further confusion'.

For the first time since he began his offensive at Gazala on 26 May, Rommel had lost the initiative. In that sense, the Battle of Alam el Halfa represented a critical turning-point in the Desert War. The decisive moment came on 21 June, when he chose to invade Egypt, even though his enemy enjoyed air superiority and was retreating to strongly-fortified positions supported by well-equipped bases. Once his attack had failed, Rommel should have withdrawn swiftly to shorten and strengthen his supply line. The Allied forces would not have pursued him with speed or conviction whereas a fixed battle, at a time of their own choosing, suited their deliberate methods of fighting admirably. Such a withdrawal would, of course, have been a severe blow to Axis prestige and, as Kesselring admitted, 'again and again one had to pay the penalty for allowing politics to influence strategy and operations'.[31]

Air Marshal Sir Arthur Barratt, head of Army Cooperation Command in England, was at the joint Army–Air Headquarters during this battle and able to watch the whole machine in action. Each evening, he later reported to the Air Ministry, Montgomery would give Coningham 'the clearest possible appreciation of the situation, the information as he knew it, what he intended to do himself and what he expected the enemy to do'. Coningham would then say what he could do himself and a general air plan was agreed upon. A further conversation took place next morning to consider events, ground and air, during the night. Coningham later told Barratt that he had never had 'such a clear and concise exposition of the military situation and needs during his experience in the Western Desert'.[32]

As for offensive tactics, Coningham told Barratt that day bombers now flew in formations of nine or eighteen aircraft with 'Kittybombers' as close escort on either side in line astern and 'bombless' Kittyhawks or Spitfires (if available) acting as high cover. Level bombing had been found superior to dive-bombing in that the target was not immediately obvious to the enemy; it was also less dangerous to air crews. If all went well, Barratt reported, the lorried infantry accompanying tanks would jump out of their vehicles and scatter, thus reducing the concentration of their light flak and so permitting the Kittybombers to attack at low level in fair safety. At night, excellent results had been obtained by using Albacore biplanes to find and illuminate targets with flares for the benefit of Wellingtons. Coningham liked the Albacore pilots to carry bombs as well, to give them 'a personal offensive interest'. In conclusion, Barratt expressed unbounded admiration for the organisation centred on Cairo and spread throughout the Middle East, which salvaged, repaired and serviced thousands of aircraft without which the Desert Air Force would collapse. Under the energetic direction of Grahame Dawson, it was run by junior officers and NCOs who were encouraged to show initiative and ingenuity. They had trained Egyptian labour 'and every difficulty and obstacle is only looked upon as something to be overcome'.[33]

Although the Axis air forces outnumbered Coningham's force and German fighters were superior in performance and armament, they failed to protect their own troops and convoys or to interfere seriously with the movement of Montgomery's troops. Hence, they were beaten in precisely the operations for which they had trained. The strategic force of Cretan-based long-range bombers, ideally placed for action against the 8th Army's rear, was misemployed on singularly ineffective convoy escort, on transport duties and even on dive-bombing. As for the Stukas, they enjoyed little success at heavy cost, frequently jettisoning bombs within their own lines or dropping them in level flight. The Luftwaffe fought hard, losing ten aircraft for every one lost by the Italians, but was frustrated by its own mistaken policies (especially the attempt at close support of ground troops without first winning air superiority) and its lack of an efficient maintenance organisation (the number of serviceable aircraft fell dramatically whenever operations began). Not least, in considering reasons for Rommel's defeat, there was a degree of mutual support between Montgomery, Coningham and their masters in Cairo and London quite unmatched on the Axis side. 'The tremendous power of the Air arm in close cooperation with the land battle was well demonstrated in the operation', wrote Montgomery. 'The Army and Air Force worked to a combined plan, made possible because the Army and Air Commander and their staffs were working together at one HQ.' It was, he thought, a vital action 'because had we lost it, we might well have lost Egypt. In winning it, we paved the way for success at El Alamein and the subsequent advance to Tunisia.'[34]

Coningham used the lull after 5 September to reorganise his force and absorb six American squadrons (three of Kittyhawk fighters, three of Mitchell bombers) into it. The Americans were thoroughly trained airmen, but lacked experience both in combat and in desert life. Coningham ensured that daily practice and nightly conversation soon made them a valuable reinforcement to his already well-mixed force of Britons, Canadians, South Africans, Australians and New Zealanders. Elmhirst wrote home on 19 September, reflecting – as he often did – on Coningham's personality.

> What a queer fellow he is! A brilliant leader and full of sound sense. But of the organisation, administration and supply of his force he knows nothing and never asks me or asks where or what I have been up to. But if anything went wrong and a squadron could not operate through failure or shortage of crews or supplies, he would know in a moment and be down on me like a ton of bricks. He is always on the go and spends his whole energy on the Army–Air operations aspect and the immediate object of defeating the enemy in the air by the personal control of the fighter and bomber boys, a great percentage of whom he knows personally.[35]

Coningham was also thinking ahead, about action following Rommel's forthcoming defeat 'in the El Alamein area' and circulated his plan, Operation Buster, on 26 September. He expected a great many Axis troops to avoid death or capture and flee westward. If North Africa were to be cleared 'without further deliberate operations,' he wrote, 'the speed of our advance must be very high'. It followed (for reasons of supply and organisation) that only a comparatively small force, composed exclusively of fighters and fighter-bombers, would be able to go forward immediately in direct support of the Army. But it also followed, in Coningham's opinion, that the Axis air forces would make a special effort to delay the Allied advance and so permit their land forces to retire in good order, receive reinforcements and supplies and establish themselves strongly in the vital Agheila positions. Nevertheless, as long as the Army kept the enemy on the run, Coningham thought the risk that weaker air forces might face stronger opponents was one well worth taking. By immediate and continual harassment in the critical initial stage of the enemy's retreat, Coningham hoped – wrongly, as it turned out – that his fighters and fighter-bombers would make up for the absence of light and medium bombers.[36]

CHAPTER NINE

'Close and Willing Cooperation; Exasperation and Complacency'

Coningham, the Battle of El Alamein and the Pursuit of Rommel, October 1942 to January 1943

'Mary turned on a blitz today,' wrote Elmhirst on 9 October. Learning on the 8th that enemy landing grounds at Dhaba and Fuka were under water, Coningham decided to interrupt training and mount a major raid next day. Unfortunately, the pools had evaporated by the time his raid began and the Luftwaffe, although surprised, reacted vigorously; so, too, did German ground defences. Coningham lost fourteen aircraft in exchange for ten enemy aircraft destroyed on the ground, four in the air and twenty damaged; but serious damage was done to supply dumps (ammunition, petrol and food), motor transport and gun batteries. Elmhirst thought the raid particularly useful in that 'our American friends' did well. Seven months later, Beamish reminded an American air general of this raid as an example of the value of an independent air force: had Coningham not been 'an independent commander,' he said, 'assessing the situation from day to day, he would have been influenced by the need for building up for the main Army offensive and would not have been in a position to order this attack at short notice.'[1]

The success pleased everyone and Elmhirst recorded 'another cheerful supper in our mess tent' on the 10th. 'Monty in good form and I managed to draw him out on the benefits or otherwise of a staff college education. He was a celebrated "directing staff" at Camberley while Mary rather prides himself on not being "staff" educated.' On another night, Elmhirst got a discussion going on the proper balance in life between work and play. 'I now try and open up on some topic every evening that will get everyone talking. It takes minds (including Monty and Mary) off the very serious business of the day.' Montgomery played along willingly, for at this time he approved of the RAF and its local management. Egypt, he wrote, is 'our only practical and active front . . . where intimate cooperation between Army and Air Forces in battle is actually practised; in England this subject is not on the map at all and the RAF cannot be got to play in the matter; in Egypt they play 100 per cent.' Jock McNeill, an Army officer who specialised in air

111

support systems, agreed. Coningham, he wrote, was 'always friendly and approachable' and so too were his staff officers. 'To all outward appearances at least, the two commanders worked well together and Monty was not an easy "comrade in arms"! I can confirm in Desert Air Force under Mary Coningham there was very close and willing cooperation with 8th Army, in marked contrast to that in higher places in UK at that time.'[2]

Nevertheless, there were still senior Army officers in key positions whose understanding of air support remained primitive. For example, at lunch on 18 October, a tank brigadier told Elmhirst: 'What a Corps Commander really wants is a squadron at his disposal to come up on his call and bomb something in front of him.' To which Coningham replied: 'Yes, and the whole lot would immediately be shot down by Me 109s because there would have been no one central authority to ensure a fighter escort for them.' Although Elmhirst agreed, he felt such ignorance was in part 'our fault' for not educating soldiers better. Freddie de Guingand, Montgomery's Chief of Staff, even claimed that the Air Force was no use in defence. Elmhirst roundly reminded him that he had not been with the Army during its retreat to El Alamein. De Guingand swiftly subsided, though whether he changed his mind, neither Coningham nor Elmhirst could say.[3]

Coningham held his monthly conference with his Wing Commanders at 9 am on 12 October. As usual, Elmhirst observed, 'allowing everyone else to have their say and, with his very human touch, more than once getting everyone laughing'. Coningham told them that the Army plan for the battle, codenamed 'Lightfoot', was complete and that from the 16th 'nothing remains to be done but the final concentration'. Although Rommel knew that an attack was coming, he did not know when and so tactical surprise could be achieved if secrecy was preserved. Army officers were being brought into the picture in stages and on 21 October all leave would be quietly stopped. The 21st and 22nd, he said, were being devoted to convincing the troops that this was 'probably the decisive battle of the war'; the Germans would be 'hit for six' right out of Egypt and Libya and we ourselves would drive on to Tripoli and Tunis.

> The Army have trained hard for this battle, they are on their toes and
> with their great preponderance of armoured strength, artillery and our air
> superiority, the result seems clear. But the enemy will not surrender and
> a killing match, lasting anything up to ten days, will probably result.
> Heavy casualties and hard fighting and then difficult exploitation.

Wing Commanders, said Coningham, were to inform Squadron Commanders of the coming battle on the 18th, emphasising that 'it is likely to be a hard, gruelling and extended fight and that the Army will require every possible help that maximum and continuous air operations can give.[4]

Kesselring, meanwhile, had begun a last attempt to neutralise Malta on 11 October, stung by the vigour and skill with which its air commander (Keith

Park) handled his small force of fighters and bombers. From an Axis viewpoint, Kesselring achieved the worst possible result: on the one hand, he was obliged to abandon his offensive on the 19th and Malta thereafter gave increasingly valuable support to operations in North Africa; on the other, the deployment in Sicily for that offensive of about half the Luftwaffe's first-line strength deprived Rommel of assistance badly needed in Egypt. Sadly, the Desert Air Force lacked the support of a strong force of night bombers. Despite the outstanding success of the Wellington-Albacore combination in helping the Army to stabilise at El Alamein and to win at Alam el Halfa, Tedder proved unable to maintain, let alone increase, that force: in July he had had 130 Wellingtons, but by the eve of El Alamein he had only seventy. At that time, Bomber Command in England had 600 bombers, medium and heavy. A strong night-bomber force, able to support Coningham's daytime efforts by attacking enemy ports, supply dumps, airfields and troop concentrations might have permitted the complete destruction of Rommel's army at El Alamein.[5]

On the eve of battle, Coningham had under his control some 420 single-engined fighters and 150 light bombers, including 37 fighters and 37 bombers of the USAAF, but half his fighter force was composed of obsolete Hurricanes and he had only about 50 of the much-superior Spitfires. Supper that night had again been a cheerful meal and Elmhirst got a conversation going on the young married officer as the curse of the services. 'It was the first time,' he wrote later, 'that any of us had seen the Army Commander really unbend and be very human.' Coningham had just returned from a four-day tour of all squadrons and Elmhirst had listened in to a couple of his talks. 'He is so sound, so cheerful and chatty that instead of being twice their age, one thinks he is of their age. He certainly has the gift of youth which is so necessary if he is to have these teed-up young lads behind him.'[6]

Coningham's airmen had achieved air superiority by October 1942 and Montgomery was therefore able to assemble and deploy infantry and armour as he thought fit, untroubled by worries over aerial attack or even reconnaissance. As numerous historians have observed, however, the land battle did not go according to plan and by insisting that it did, Montgomery founded a reputation for infallibility, but lost the credit he deserved for the skill, determination and rapidity of decision with which he reshaped it. His forces were vastly superior – at least in numbers – to those the Axis had available. Nevertheless, the initial assault (Operation Lightfoot, launched on 23 October) had failed by the 26th, obliging Montgomery to reshape battered forces and hastily devise a fresh assault (Operation Supercharge) for 1 November.[7]

While this extensive regrouping was taking place, the Army was vulnerable to counter-attacks and Rommel launched such attacks, but airmen disrupted them. Night bombing of enemy encampments and forward landing grounds by Wellingtons (assisted by flare-dropping Albacores) was supplemented by attacks from Malta and Egypt on supply ships making for North Africa.

Meanwhile, day bombing of enemy assembly areas and strafing of landing grounds, supply dumps and road convoys prevented Rommel from mounting a carefully-prepared, concentrated attack; at the same time, his aircraft were kept away from British troops, transports and tanks. Although the Luftwaffe's fighters and bombers were outnumbered and outfought, its fleet of Ju 52 transport aircraft enjoyed a major success. Throughout the twelve days of the battle, barely sufficient seaborne supplies of petrol and ammunition reached the Axis Army for a single day's fighting. On 23 October, however, the daily air lift from Greece and Crete began, supplemented by supplies carried aboard submarines and destroyers. Efforts to stop this air lift by night bombing raids on bases proved unsuccessful; so, too, did attempts at interception. The Ju 52s flew at night and El Adem (their principal destination twenty miles south of Tobruk) lay at extreme range for Coningham's handful of twin-engined Beaufighters which were, in any case, extremely busy on shipping strikes. The sinking of enemy shipping in the Mediterranean reduced the Axis Army to such a plight that it could not have sustained such a long battle without this air lift.[8]

On 11 October – twelve days before Montgomery began his offensive – Coningham's plan for an advance in support of a breakthrough had been circulated as Operation Buster. It provided for the split of the air forces employed into two main components, Force A and Force B: the former to operate in direct support of the Army, the latter to act as a reserve and protect lines of communication. Previous experience suggested that the Luftwaffe would be quickly reinforced to slow the British advance. Coningham therefore decided to leave his bombers behind and use all his fighters (to maintain air superiority and cover the advance) and rely upon fighter-bombers to disrupt the Axis retreat. Since bombers could not be moved forward as quickly as fighters or fighter-bombers, required more supplies and maintenance and could not operate unescorted, Coningham was obliged to accept the loss of their heavier punch. It would be essential to keep Montgomery moving because Malta's food and fuel reserves were dwindling rapidly. So many ships had been lost during the last relief of the island in August that another convoy from the west could not be attempted while the Axis controlled the Sicilian Narrows. A convoy from the east would only become practicable when airfields around Martuba (on the north-east coast of Cyrenaica) were captured, permitting fighters to cover the ships until they came within range of Malta's own fighters. Coningham knew that a convoy was planned to reach the island by 20 November. The Martuba airfields must therefore be occupied by the 18th at latest.[9]

Although the Army was responsible for carrying forward his main stocks of fuel and ammunition, Coningham had three supply and transport columns formed to accompany Force A and about sixty aircraft were held at Amiriya, thirty miles south of Alexandria, to ferry forward fuel, bombs, ammunition and other supplies needed by the Army to meet an emergency. Coningham was well aware that rapid movement would be difficult to make or sustain because the journeys in prospect were immense. It was 430 miles from Alexandria to Tobruk by road; 310 miles from there to Benghazi; a further 660 to Tripoli; Tunis, the ultimate goal, lay 600 miles beyond Tripoli and 2,000 miles from Alexandria. Almost the whole of this journey must be made along a single metalled road – a road inadequately maintained in peacetime and since then regularly mined, blown up, bombed and shelled by both sides. Movement off the road was at best hazardous and after heavy rain impossible. Neither the Army nor the Air Force had adequate transport. The Army had few trucks with four-wheel drive or the power, springing or gears needed for rough travelling; the RAF had no modern specially-designed transport aircraft and made do with converted bombers until American DC–3 Dakotas became available late in November. Port facilities and wells of drinkable water along the route westward were scarce and would certainly suffer from enemy demolition and booby traps. Not least, the precious petrol was transported in tins so flimsy that up to a third was lost.[10]

In the middle of the battle, on 26 October, Coningham made time to reply to a letter from Lord Trenchard, most famous of the RAF's founders and, as Chief of the Air Staff for more than a decade after the Great War, the man who made or marred the careers of Coningham and his contemporaries. Trenchard had been taken round several squadrons by Elmhirst on the 16th (a day of dreadful sandstorms, commemorated by a mock-heroic certificate which Coningham enclosed) and on the following evening Coningham arranged for him to be elected 'Lord Protector of the RAF' by acclamation. Coningham now sent him an account of the battle to date, emphasising points that he well knew would gladden the old air warrior's heart. The air forces, Coningham wrote, had been in action for weeks before the land battle began, impeding the enemy build-up, weakening the Axis air forces, ensuring that only one side benefited from regular aerial reconnaissance and covering the Army's advance. Nowadays, soldiers and airmen went into battle 'more as equal partners' and Coningham visualised future battles in which the Air would be the predominant partner with the Army or Navy in support. 'We shall have already reached that stage here,' he concluded, 'when the enemy breaks and tries to get away.'[11]

Brian Horrocks (Commander of 13 Corps) visited Montgomery's headquarters on 2 November, just as a squadron of medium bombers flew overhead. 'They are winning this battle for me,' said Montgomery. 'The RAF are doing a wonderful job.' By then, wrote Horrocks, 'Mary Coningham, that tough New Zealander,' had achieved air superiority and Horrocks recalled Axis prisoners complaining bitterly about the devastating effect of continuous air attack. Elmhirst had ordered his big supply column (200 lorries full of fuel and ammunition) to go forward on 1 November and tuck itself in, just behind the Army's leading patrols, ready for a dash to the Dhaba airfield to stock it for the first jump ahead. At about 10 am on 3 November, Rommel ordered a withdrawal.

But the British soon spotted our move and attacked the coast road with about 200 fighter-bombers. Their bomber squadrons were also extremely active that day. The Afrika Korps was attacked no less than eleven times during the morning by strong formations of bombers. At midday, I returned to my command post, only just escaping by some frantic driving a carpet of bombs laid by eighteen British aircraft.

This was the momentous day when enemy resistance was seen to crack and the retreat westward began. An astonishing effort had been mounted by airmen already exhausted by intensive operations beginning on 19 October: their losses (twenty-four aircraft destroyed and thirteen damaged) were by far the heaviest suffered since the early days of Rommel's Gazala offensive. 'Now we have to turn retreat into rout,' wrote Elmhirst on 3 November, 'and the Hun will not get back along the road to Tobruk scot-free as we got back here in June.' Although Coningham thought the tide had turned, he was not yet sure that victory had been achieved. Nevertheless, at 6.40 pm he warned his force that Operation Buster, the pursuit plan, was to be set in motion.[12]

On 4 November, however, Coningham refused to send the ground party of a fighter-bomber wing forward to Dhaba, which was expected to be captured next day. Elmhirst thought this a pity: all casualties suffered thus far had been replaced and he would have been prepared to risk further casualties to prevent the enemy having a day on the road out of reach of air attack. Coningham also refused permission for a Hurricane squadron armed with heavy cannons to join in the attacks on the coast road. It was trained and equipped for precisely this task, but such aircraft needed fighter escorts (which were not available) and were particularly vulnerable to ground fire. The coast road, as Coningham realised, 'was not merely an admirable target for attack, but also for defence'. Even so, his aircrews had not flinched. After his capture, General Ritter von Thoma said,

> never-ceasing bombing by day and by night had a terrible effect . . . Ground strafing was at times terrific. I do not know whether more damage was done by cannon or machine-gun. Personally, I should not think it matters much. It all happens so quickly – the planes come down near columns or concentrations and shoot at anything. They are sure to hit something, just by spraying their fire, and then you have the added damage caused by panic and confusion.[13]

Coningham ordered two wing ground parties to go forward on 5 November and Elmhirst had 400 tons of petrol, bombs and ammunition on the Dhaba airfields within six hours of the German departure: 'A good effort,' he thought, 'which means the fighters should be able to operate from there tomorrow, but it might have been today.' Tedder reported to Portal on the 5th that Coningham had resisted the temptation to accept successes against

116

the Luftwaffe in October as decisive and had therefore directed a proportion of his effort to keeping the enemy air down. 'The problem now,' thought Tedder, 'is to get the fighters right forward quickly in long bounds.' Coningham and he had repeatedly emphasised the importance of long swift moves to the Army and hoped the message had got across. Cooperation between fighters and bombers and between British and Americans was first class and so too was the operational organisation, but the Hurricane squadrons were 'completely outclassed', Tedder concluded, 'and it is hard to have to tell them they cannot have modern aircraft yet'. It was this fact, together with the heavy losses already suffered, that made Coningham reluctant to employ his light bombers. They needed fighter escorts; he was short of fighters and in any case preferred the fighter-bomber, a much more effective weapon.[14]

No-one foresaw the situation that arose directly after the battle. The Axis forces, in the first stages of disorderly flight, lay within easy range of bomber bases in Egypt and concentrated bombing might have immobilised them. Detailed Army and Air Force plans had been made for the battle and the pursuit, but not for a brief, though potentially vital, period of overlap. Had the Army and Air Commanders anticipated this overlap period, more use might have been made of escorted bombers, but Montgomery and Coningham planned to pursue, not annihilate, the enemy and therefore insured against aerial opposition which proved negligible. Consequently, the air force employed for day operations during the early days was too light to be effective in other than a protective or harassing role.[15]

On 8 November, four days after the battle of El Alamein ended, Operation Torch (the Anglo-American invasion of North-west Africa) began. That torch might well have been extinguished if a failure by Montgomery and Coningham had encouraged the French to offer determined resistance to the invaders and if Spain had swung round to full cooperation with the Axis. As it was, German land and air forces in Tunisia were massively reinforced, greatly prolonging the campaign and confirming Coningham's fears about the vulnerability of his obsolete Hurricanes and Kittyhawks to first-class fighters. One effect of the need to prepare for Torch had been a delay in the re-equipment of his force. He could have made particularly good use of long-range, heavily-armed Beaufighters to harass retreating columns effectively. Just as round-the-clock bombing proved to be one of the main reasons why Rommel did not reach the Delta in July or August, so – with the tables turned – similar attacks might have prevented his retreat. According to Montgomery, however, there were three principal tasks after the battle: to outflank Rommel's remaining forces, to establish the Air Force on forward landing grounds and to capture the port of Tobruk and thus ease supply problems. The role Montgomery assigned to the Air Force was subsidiary and protective: to act, 'in conjunction with the armoured cars, as the long-range hitting weapon and greatly increase the confusion of the enemy's withdrawal; at the same time, fighter cover could be given to the light forces operating in the van of the pursuit'.[16]

Although Coningham supported Tedder's desire to get the fighters 'right forward quickly in long bounds', bombers *were* used and the Germans themselves spoke of 'incessant raids, mainly on the coast road, causing delays and considerable damage among the retreating convoys', but most fighters were required to cover the pursuers, leaving few to escort bombers attacking the pursued. In the early stages of the enemy retreat, the difficulty of distinguishing between pursued and pursuers further inhibited bombing. The New Zealanders, for example, were reported active in an area of some seventy square miles around Fuka. No Air Commander could take responsibility for ordering concentrated bombing while Army Headquarters itself was doubtful about the position of its advanced units in the target area. On 5 November, however, the enemy might have been subjected to heavier bombing while negotiating a difficult escarpment at Fuka, some sixty miles west of El Alamein. Torrential rain next day changed sand into mud, halting armour and aircraft alike; the whole area from Fuka westward to Sidi Barrani, 120 miles of coast road containing what remained of the Panzer Army, was then closed to aircraft.[17]

The last opportunity for the day bombers to hit hard at the enemy came as he passed through the Halfaya and Sollum Passes on 10 November, but most activity that day remained defensive patrols to protect British troops from aerial attacks which never came. Throughout the first phase of the retreat (4–10 November), the Luftwaffe was so disorganised and short of fuel that it did little. Its lack of impact was in marked contrast to the orderly, fighting retreat of Coningham's force in June, which had fallen back stage by stage to landing grounds stocked in advance with fuel, bombs and ammunition. Between 2 November (when the Luftwaffe began to pull out of its Egyptian bases) and 12 November, it destroyed sixty-three of its own aircraft on the ground, several aircraft were abandoned intact and others left on trucks, still crated up at a time when the advancing 8th Army presented a magnificent target, with thousands of vehicles packing the main road for days on end. The Afrika Korps received little protection from the Axis air forces in daylight and none in darkness.[18]

A major problem at this time was lack of water. 'We have rationed down to half a gallon a day,' wrote Elmhirst on 8 November, 'but the units are saying they have to go fifty miles to the nearest well and always find the Army there first.' Elmhirst therefore signalled to Whitney Straight (head of a transport Group in Cairo), asking him to fly up enough Nile water for 2,000 men. By the 10th, the fighters were within striking distance of Tobruk, having covered 500 miles in five days, and on that day the Germans left Egypt for the last time and news was received of the Anglo-American landings in Morocco and Algeria. Montgomery, who had a bad cold ('at any rate a human failing,' Elmhirst noted), firmly told Tedder and Coningham over lunch that only the rain stopped him from catching the remnants of the

Panzers at Mersa Matruh. The 15th Panzer Division, however, thought the British Army had followed its 'accustomed misguided policy of extreme caution'. Although cooperation between artillery, infantry, armour and aircraft had been 'extremely good' (in German opinion), 'the effect of the air attacks was not exploited'.[19]

'Monty got his "K" [knighthood] yesterday,' wrote Elmhirst on 12 November, 'and a step up in rank. We in the air force are depressed that Mary did not get something for the sixteen months he has fought here so brilliantly', but Coningham hid his disappointment even from Elmhirst and Beamish, helped by the urgent need to keep both airmen and soldiers pressing hard on the enemy's heels. On the 15th, he sent a brief appreciation of the situation to Cairo. He was, he said, very short of water and rations. His MT fuel was seriously short and dependent on air supply; as for aviation fuel, he had just enough for limited fighter operations:

> Basic trouble with all supply is inability of Army to deliver. We are a long way ahead of Army supply base Matruh. Had it not been for air transport and our own MT columns, our forces would be using Bagush area and enemy would have been out of reach last four days. As it is, full punishment being inflicted with exceptionally small losses as far as Agheila and enemy air forces now being chased out of Cyrenaica.[20]

Tedder, with this appreciation to hand, reported to Portal the same day. He expressed his unease about the general situation, 'despite all the victory bells and headlines about our great generals'. The initial attack had achieved surprise, thanks to the efforts of airmen who prevented Axis aircraft from carrying out reconnaissance over the Army's assembly areas. By 4 November, unfortunately, the advance was bogged down, so Tedder had gone out to the Desert. He told Montgomery that the enemy's supply shortage might not last: he was making desperate attempts to remedy it and the RAF could not guarantee to sink every ship. Tedder also emphasised the importance of haste with regard to both the next Malta convoy and the success of the Allied landings in North-west Africa. It was no use. Montgomery saw: 'not the slightest likelihood of any big move for at least ten days.' Half an hour later, however, he said he had something important to explain to Coningham and would Tedder care to hear it? This proved to be allegedly 'new information' about enemy dispositions which would in fact permit him to resume the advance at once. Tedder wrote:

> Advice he will not take, even that from Coningham, who knows the Desert better than any of them, but fortunately he will quite often use the advice. That the great ideas should come from the great man himself matters little, provided they are acted on. Where we should be if it had not been for Coningham's continual, tactful but persistent, advice to the

soldiers I do not know, but I suspect that a 'slogging match' in the neighbourhood of Dhaba might still be going on.[21]

Even so, Tedder added, the enemy had got away time after time, as a result of Montgomery's slowness.

> For days now we have been trying to get across the importance of cutting off the enemy south of Benghazi. Coningham has put a couple of Hurricane squadrons out in the Desert north of Gialo to help cut this line, but so far Montgomery has failed to be 'inspired'. Now more than ever before, if that is possible, he knows all the answers and it is going to be more and more difficult to arouse the right inspiration in the great man's mind . . . Coningham is going on magnificently. The aura of greatness is not an easy one in which to live, but Coningham is coping with tact and at the same time with great firmness – not that Montgomery has ever been foolish enough to attempt to say what the air should or should not do.[22]

In the race for the Martuba airfields (needed to cover the convoy leaving Port Said for Malta on the 16th), Coningham's Force A reached Gazala, only fifty miles away, on 16 November. Although heavy rain that day flooded them, obliging him to operate from Gazala, the convoy got through safely and revealed how far Axis air and sea power in the Mediterranean had declined. Rommel, meanwhile, was heading anxiously for El Agheila, a place protected to the east by delaying-lines at Mersa Brega and Agedabia. Both sides having laboured to improve the natural defences of the whole area during earlier fighting in the Desert War, it offered Rommel his first opportunity to rest and regroup in relative security since the flight began. He therefore greatly feared that Montgomery might cut him off from that haven by striking across the Cyrenaican Hump to Agedabia via Mechili, Msus and Antelat. Had he done so, Rommel would have been caught and destroyed somewhere on the open road between Agedabia and Benghazi. To Coningham's bitter disappointment, Montgomery refused to risk a bold, outflanking movement in strength and Rommel gratefully occupied the El Agheila positions during the night of 23–24 November. No less gratefully did Montgomery settle down to prepare a massive frontal assault, the form of warfare in which he felt comfortable.[23]

As Coningham told the American historian, Forrest C. Pogue, in February 1947, Montgomery 'could have cut across in front of Rommel, but no: despite my advice to use his air, he pushed along, pushed along. My people would sometimes land fifteen miles ahead of him and come back and find his people still pacing along, looking for mines.' Montgomery, thought Coningham, was:

a competent general in positional warfare, but he never exploited his victories. Someday the truth will be written about him and the legend will be dispelled. It's a shame that he should be mentioned as important, when people like Ike and Alex worked so hard to do a good piece of work, worked modestly and without demands for credit and he goes along in his selfish way, building up these carefully-prepared legends.[24]

Robertson (Quartermaster-General) had told Elmhirst that if the Air Force moved out of Egypt it must look after itself and Coningham accepted the challenge: as Elmhirst wrote on 15 November, 'We are now the only force that can keep in touch with the retreating enemy and we cannot do that from airfields in Egypt.' Their Rear Headquarters, still in the Delta, together with Whitney Straight's transport aircraft, were functioning like clockwork and supplies were flown forward daily; from the 15th, they would be sent as far as Martuba to permit aircraft to attack Benghazi. Montgomery, however, refused to press on and most of Coningham's force stuck at Martuba for ten days. 'We are stretching ourselves to the uttermost,' Elmhirst wrote on the 18th, 'and making our lorries and their drivers do just double what they normally should do. Not so the Army, they are holding to the normal seven hours driving a day. I think they could stretch themselves more.' Looking through his letters years later, Elmhirst noted 'a continual fret' that the Air Force could not keep closer to the retreating enemy. The lorries did their best, but needed half their load forward to be petrol for the journey back. Coningham had aircraft in Benghazi, 170 miles beyond Martuba, but the enemy at El Agheila was almost out of their range and until Benghazi port was opened and supplies coming in, he could not supply even one wing further ahead.[25]

Coningham wrote by hand to Tedder from Martuba on 20 November, sending him a copy of an appreciation written by de Guingand, Montgomery's Chief of Staff. As 'a sample of defeatism', it would, he knew, shock Tedder: its message being, 'We have done our job, the rest can be done by the RAF or the Western Army'. The appreciation astounded Coningham (and Tedder, when he read it), for reliable intelligence sources made it clear that the Axis forces ahead of them were weak in everything except fighting spirit. 'As long as we hold Western Cyrenaica,' wrote de Guingand, 'the enemy requires the use of Tripoli in order to maintain a large army for use against Cyrenaica and Egypt . . . as long as the enemy have the use of Tripoli, the defeat of his forces at Agheila will not prevent him from building up other defensive positions between these and Tripoli.' Although the 8th Army should play a part in the *neutralisation* of Tripoli, its *capture* should be undertaken by the Western Army. The enemy, continued de Guingand, would probably hold Agheila, a very strong position. 'Given time to develop our maintenance and build up our reserves in Western Cyrenaica, we should, no doubt, be able to blast our way into the Agheila position,' but it would be better to 'await the time when he withdraws or capitulates from exhaustion or lack of supplies' as a result of air and sea attacks from the west. 'It is most important,' de Guingand emphasised, 'that those at home should be left in no doubt as to the problems facing 8th Army in an advance into Tripolitania'.[26]

This appreciation convinced Coningham, as he told Tedder,

> that Montgomery never wanted to go on beyond Agheila and that he still
> does not want to. Before the battle started on 23 October he was hedging
> and murmuring something about the 'Torch' operation doing Tripoli.
> The whole tone of past weeks has borne this out. Any competent general
> with overwhelming force can win a positional battle, but it requires the
> spark of greatness to do well in pursuit or in retirement.

Montgomery's suggested date for an attack on the Agheila position was more than a month away – 24–28 December – and although Coningham was disgusted he was also helpless. 'Both Montgomery and Freddie [de Guingand] are very sensitive and the latter is particularly scratchy at the evening staff meetings, where we have used the American Strickland to stir up the dust' by suggesting, for example, that if the Army's armoured cars 'weren't careful, they would be in time to see the last truck of Rommel's depleted force pass down the road into Agedabia'.[27]

De Guingand, added Coningham, 'has a guilty conscience and knows how much a failure they have been, but he is very loyal and the clash in his own mind causes extreme petulance. I suspect Monty is being prodded from high quarters and he is equally touchy, but the cloak of omnipotence protects him!!!' By delaying an offensive until at least 24 December, the hope was that the Western Army 'will have done the trick by then and that nothing will remain but a triumphal drive by Monty to Tripoli'. Coningham did not think this likely, but 'if it does happen, there will beforehand be a scramble by the enemy away from Agheila and we want to hit them. If it does not happen, there will be more intensive air fighting'. Meanwhile, despite heavy rain, he was driving on to Msus.[28]

Tedder wrote to Portal on 23 November, sending him Coningham's letter and a copy of de Guingand's appreciation. 'Coningham's remarks,' he said, 'are by no means an overstatement.' Montgomery's supreme self-confidence and personal drive had been invaluable when he arrived, the initial attack well-organised and led, but

> from that time on, there has been no spark of genius, no glimmer of an
> attempt to exploit the initial smash. The final breakthrough would never
> have taken place on the scale it did had Montgomery not, after much
> pressure, used the advice he ostensibly spurned and sent his mobile
> forces wide. After that one wide swing, the Army has settled down to a
> lumbering advance, trailing behind the enemy rearguards.

Coningham was unable to get his light or medium bombers forward because the supplies they needed had been diverted by Montgomery to his massive build-up around Tobruk. 'I have had another go at Alex on the subject,' Tedder continued, 'but I don't think he is capable of overriding Montgomery – so I have written him a 'posterity' letter pointing out the facts and sent a similar signal to Coningham, saying he 'may' show it to the Army Commander.'[29]

Given the Army's grudging support, Coningham had done splendidly to keep his fighters up with the forward troops. A week later, Tedder told Portal that Coningham had asked him for up to 3,000 tons of petrol to be flown forward to enable his fighters to operate in the event of an enemy retreat. Tedder had told Coningham that he must get Montgomery 'to give proper priority to the air or else say in black and white that he prefers to do without it'. With American help, Tedder would send as much petrol as he could, but he was 'determined to try and get Montgomery to face up to facts. It is no use bullying Alexander since he cannot say "boo" to Monty.' Portal sent these letters to the Army head, Sir Alan Brooke, on 13 December. 'The opinions expressed,' he wrote, 'may be attributable to the ignorance of airmen about a soldier's job, but I am sure they are not prompted by any but the worthiest motives'; they were borne out to a great extent by 'our best Intelligence reports' and though nothing could now be done, Portal thought Brooke should see them. Brooke, however, was unmoved by criticism from any source that 'Montgomery was too sticky in pursuit' and dismissed it, then and later, with airy generalities.[30]

As a preliminary to action at El Agheila, Montgomery asked Coningham for heavy bombing, but this could not be provided – as Coningham pointed out, with increasing asperity – without bombers and bombers could neither be brought forward nor employed unless Montgomery assigned to air supplies a far higher priority than hitherto. Totally exasperated, Coningham invited Tedder to send him a 'posterity' signal which he could show to the Army Commander. Tedder readily agreed, spelling out on 23 November, in the simplest words he could think of, the points Coningham had already made:

> You have, I know, been pressing for many days for arrangements to be made whereby our Wellingtons and light bombers can operate from Cyrenaica . . . I know Army Commander appreciates importance of securing forward landing grounds, but this is useless unless appropriate priority is given to the maintenance of squadrons which could use these landing grounds. A balance must be drawn between land forces and air forces. If your forces are to be properly employed and able to hit where it hurts, they must operate from and be maintained at forward landing grounds. Obviously, there is a price to be paid in terms of corresponding reduction of maintenance commitment of land forces . . . Surely the Air

has paid good enough dividends recently for Army Commander to realise necessity of paying the necessary price?

Next day, Tedder informed Portal that no bombers had yet been brought forward 'despite repeated requests on the part of Coningham for requisite priority of maintenance' because Montgomery preferred instead to build up an enormous force of 100,000 men in and around Tobruk.[31]

Coningham's 'main fear,' he told Tedder on 28 November, was that Rommel would leave El Agheila before Montgomery began his frontal assault and that the air forces would be unable either to pursue or cover the pursuers. 'The Army cannot advance without fighters,' he ended, 'and the fighters cannot move without petrol.' Tedder replied next day. It was, he said, 'entirely a matter of priorities': opportunities to weaken the enemy in Cyrenaica had already been lost because the air forces had been starved of supplies. He thought it 'incomprehensible' that the Army should be 'satisfied with a situation in which only a proportion of the available fighters and practically none of the available bombers can operate in the forward areas'. Tedder agreed with Coningham that unless 'drastic steps' were taken, the enemy would be able to withdraw unhindered and the Army pursuit would be unprotected. Should Montgomery choose not to take these steps, Tedder ordered Coningham 'to make the resulting situation unmistakably clear to him'.[32]

Meanwhile, on 23 November, Coningham received a telegram from Tedder telling him that he had been made a Knight Commander of the Order of the Bath (KCB). Quite apart from his personal delight, Coningham was profoundly gratified that his beloved Nan was onced more a 'Lady'. 'Mary very pleased,' wrote Elmhirst, 'no-one could have deserved it better, I think.' Trenchard wrote to Portal on the 25th, offering congratulations on honours 'at last' for the RAF in the Middle East: 'I am delighted that you have managed to get them through. I know how you must have felt at their omission when Alexander and Montgomery got their honours.' Churchill spoke of Coningham in the House of Commons as 'no mere technician, but a redoubtable warrior'; the *Daily Telegraph* printed a photograph of Sir William Rothenstein's drawing made at Heslington Hall, the *Daily Mail* published a long account of his views on air power at El Alamein and there was praise in other newspapers.[33]

On 12 December, after three weeks of careful preparation, the bombardment of Mersa Brega began, but the defenders slipped away unharmed. Next day, learning that Montgomery was attempting yet another outflanking movement, Rommel gave orders for El Agheila to be abandoned after sunset on the 14th. Montgomery and Coningham made a determined attempt to close the trap, but by 18 December it was clear that Rommel had again escaped and the pursuit resumed. It was slowed, as always, by thousands of cunningly-laid mines and booby traps; by the blowing of numerous craters in the road and the difficulty of moving heavy vehicles away from it; by

Montgomery's concern for his ever-lengthening supply lines and now by his awareness that he had no need of haste. Detailed, accurate intelligence information – from aerial reconnaissance as well as the interception of signals traffic – assured him that Rommel lacked the resources to mount a counter-attack and every mile he retreated westward took him closer to Anglo–American forces advancing eastward in Tunisia and spared the 8th Army a bloody encounter with a shrewd and savage enemy at bay.[34]

Consequently, four weeks passed before Montgomery was ready to mount another carefully-prepared frontal assault combined with an outflanking movement. This assault, on 15 January 1943, was aimed at Axis forces waiting for it behind a new defence line at Buerat, more than 200 miles west of El Agheila. They withdrew as adroitly as ever, though suffering some losses to both land and air attack. Rommel chose not to defend Tripoli, the capital of Libya, because by then practically every ship making for that port was being sunk. Extensive damage to the harbour area and regular air raids made successful unloading of any that did get through very difficult. He preferred instead to retreat into Tunisia, where he could at last receive supplies and reinforcements on a scale generous enough to permit the planning of serious counter-attacks.[35]

The British entered Tripoli unopposed early on 23 January to face days of hard work to clear the harbour and make the port usable again. 'BBC shouted all day about Monty and Tripoli,' noted Admiral Power in his diary, 'but of course the RAF did it all.' Bearing in mind the Allies' immensely superior strength, Kesselring thought they should have got there at least a month earlier. Montgomery, however, could move smartly enough when journalists and photographers were about and made sure that Coningham was nowhere to be seen while he personally accepted Tripoli's formal surrender and thereafter awarded himself a ceremonial tour, amid cheering troops. As usual, de Guingand was left to swallow his own embarrassment and explain away his master's latest discourtesy. In exactly three months since the offensive began at El Alamein, the 8th Army and the Desert Air Force had together advanced 1,400 miles and were at the Tunisian frontier by the end of January. 'For us in the Middle East,' wrote Peter Drummond in October 1943, 'Tripoli aerodromes represented the last long-coveted prize in the Battle for Airfields.'[36]

Thereafter, a new campaign began. As Coningham realised, that campaign and all those following would require the RAF to be on close terms not only with British soldiers but also with American airmen and soldiers. By December 1942, the 9th Air Force (formed under Brereton on 11 November to embrace all USAAF units in the Middle East) was already providing a vital transport service and on the 2nd Coningham arranged with Brereton something more: a 'flying pipeline' to the front. 'On one day,' noted Brereton, 'forty-nine C-47s carried 48,510 gallons of gas from El Adem to Agedabia, a distance of 425 miles by truck and 250 by aircraft. The flight was completed in an hour and fifty minutes. It would have been a three-day trip for fifty-nine trucks.' Coningham spoke enthusiastically to the British press about Anglo-American cooperation. 'We have a job to do,' he said, 'and we are doing it. We are a happy and I think competent family and the result is an efficient machine.' When Americans first arrived in the Desert, he had told them: 'I wish you to profit by the three years of experience that we have had. You profit by all our mistakes and by our successes.' He had already made friends with Brereton, Strickland and others and during December he greatly impressed Brigadier General Howard A. Craig, who became a distinguished staff officer in Mediterranean campaigns. Craig faithfully recorded, pondered and circulated Coningham's startling views on the equal status that should exist between Army and Air commanders, observing that direct support of ground forces had been only a small part of recent battles and that the Army had actually been in support of the Air most of the time 'in that it captures the essential landing grounds, prepares new ones, moves in and supplies and protects the airdromes'. These views would be much discussed in Tunisia.[37]

CHAPTER TEN

Anglo-American Muddles and Reforms; Coningham's 'Shield and Punch'

Torch and Tunisia, November 1942 to March 1943

Operation Torch began on 8 November 1942 with landings on the coasts of Morocco and Algeria. At that time, these territories – and Tunisia, farther east – were controlled by about 130,000 ill-equipped French troops with orders to defend them against any invaders, Allied or Axis. No attempt was made to land in Tunisia, to seize the key ports of Bizerta and Tunis, because these would be subject to heavy air raids from Sicily and Sardinia. Moreover, Anglo-American planners were uncertain about the response of either the French or the neutral (but pro-Axis) Spanish to their arrival in the Mediterranean and decided that a landing east of Algiers would be imprudent. Once established in Algeria, a subsequent advance into Tunisia could be covered from the air and supported by sea. Hopes were high that the French would welcome the Americans, if not the British, and that the Spanish would quietly applaud if the invasion prospered. In the event, some Frenchmen resisted it, the Spanish did nothing, but German and Italian troops prevented Anglo-American forces from seizing Bizerta or Tunis.[1]

By December, it had become clear that a long, hard campaign must be fought in Tunisia. A land only slightly smaller than England, Tunisia is dominated by two broken mountain ranges – the Western and Eastern Dorsale – running roughly north to south with a barren country between. Elsewhere, there is much hilly woodland and rolling pasture. Freezing cold in winter, with torrential rainstorms, it is a land easy to defend and demanded methods of warmaking quite different from those which had served both sides so well in the broad deserts stretching eastward to the Nile. In the Tunisian as in the Desert campaigns, the Allies enjoyed command of the sea, the air and an enormous advantage on land in numbers of troops, tanks, guns and supplies of all kinds (especially fuel). Not least, they continued to receive a steady stream of detailed, accurate information about enemy plans, strength and supply arrangements from codebreakers in

England who intercepted and deciphered the most secret German signals traffic.[2]

The Allied Commander-in-Chief was an American General, Dwight D. Eisenhower. A man of exceptional character and vision, Eisenhower would fight from then until the end of the European War not only against Germans and Italians but also against the xenophobia and self-regard common among his senior subordinates, American, British or French. At the same time, the political as well as military consequences of his every move would be minutely examined by his masters in Washington and London. Overall command of Allied troops in Algeria was given to a British General, Kenneth Anderson, head of the newly-created 1st Army. Anderson and his Chief of Staff (McNabb) were blunt Scotsmen, often rude when not silent and by nature gloomy; both were found wanting in the Tunisian Campaign. So, too, was Lloyd R. Fredendall, head of the American II Corps. Fredendall and his staff, wrote Omar N. Bradley (his next-but-one-successor) 'were rabidly, if not obscenely, anti-British and especially anti-Anderson'; Fredendall, moreover, was regarded by men well placed to judge as an incompetent coward. George S. Patton would replace Fredendall in March 1943. Patton, wrote Bradley, 'was in the best of times a bull in the china shop', but these had not been, for Patton, the best of times. Since Torch began, he had been stuck in Morocco, far from the action he craved. Eisenhower had already told him, forcibly, to think before speaking; he would go on telling him, with little effect, for the rest of the war. In Bradley's opinion, 'Patton was a notorious and outspoken Anglophobe, worse even than Fredendall, if that were possible'; immature and crude, 'excess was Patton's style'. The inadequacies or antics of these and many other officers in Tunisia would sorely perplex Eisenhower – and he had not yet met Montgomery.[3]

The men under command had little combat experience, but the Axis forces in Tunisia – well-trained and combat-hardened – proved stern teachers and the Allies learned quickly. Both British and American troops had to work out how best to use their own weapons as well as to combine effectively with each other and with other services, particularly airmen. Their French allies had few useful weapons and many were reluctant to cooperate either with Britons or Americans. The haste with which Torch had been planned and mounted meant that grievous errors of judgment were made in handling both military operations and the management of supply and communication lines; the command structure became a muddle and bitter recriminations followed. During December, realising that the race for Tunis and Bizerta had been lost, Eisenhower set up a headquarters in the St George Hotel in Algiers, manned by a huge staff of American, British and French officers, all charged to sort out the muddles before the campaign resumed. Luckily, rivalries between Germans and Italians in Tunisia, with their masters in Rome and at Hitler's court, were even sharper than those on the Allied side because they knew perfectly well that the campaign, however prolonged, could have only one result: an Axis defeat.[4]

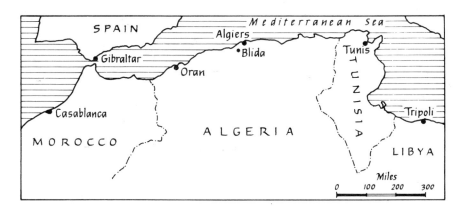

5. Operation Torch and the Tunisian Campaign, 1942–3

The original Torch plan had called for an overall Air Commander, but Eisenhower accepted the advice of his senior American airman, Carl A. Spaatz, that a unified command was impracticable. British and American airmen therefore fought separate wars, mainly at the behest of their respective Army Commanders, and signally failed to obtain air superiority. By the end of December, Eisenhower had become convinced that a single Air Commander was necessary to take charge of both the American 12th Air Force (James H. Doolittle) and the British Eastern Air Command (Sir William Welsh) and recommended Spaatz. Churchill and Portal were reluctant to accept Spaatz because of his inexperience in command or administration until 5 January 1943 when Eisenhower agreed to appoint James Robb, Mary Coningham's old friend, as Spaatz's British Chief of Staff.[5]

Air power was neither independent nor centralised because senior Army officers insisted upon control of their 'own' air power, to provide local protection and deal with local problems. No American ground units had air-ground training before leaving the United States and the plight of the British 1st Army was as bad, with less reason, for no notice had been taken of the combat-proven air support advances made in the Middle East. William Momyer, an American fighter pilot, recalled in May 1982 his early unhappiness in North Africa at the misuse of Allied air power. It seemed obvious to him, though not to the Army Commanders, that the winning of air superiority was an essential task. Instead, his fighter group was committed almost exclusively to flying 'umbrella patrols' over the frontline, leaving the Luftwaffe free to hammer Allied airfields undisturbed. Worse still, German airfields were left undisturbed while Allied bombers attacked ports and other targets as far away as Sicily and Italy. Mary Coningham, said Momyer, was the man who 'brought the thing together'; he was 'probably the most knowledgeable British officer on tactical air operations, as a result of his experience in the Western Desert'. Admiral Power, writing in his diary on 21 January 1943, opined that Torch is 'a really bad show . . . USA discipline is very bad, as is all their air administration. Anderson is not a good cooperator and Welsh (RAF) is a non-cooperator.' Power was impressed by the performance of the 8th Army and the Desert Air Force, which he thought far superior to that of the Anglo-American forces in Tunisia.[6]

Spaatz sent Tedder a message on 22 January in which he described the air support situation as critical. Until Coningham could arrive, Laurence S. Kuter was to be given command of an organisation known as the 'Allied Air Support Command', comprising 242 Group and the American 12th Air Support Command (ASC). Kuter, promoted Brigadier General in February 1942 at the age of thirty-six, was by four years the youngest general in the US Army and went on to enjoy a successful career. Arriving in Algiers on 14 January to serve as Spaatz's American Chief of Staff, he found in the St George Hotel an empty office: that, he knew, would be Spaatz's. No desk warrior, 'Tooey' Spaatz worked best at airfields, aboard aeroplanes or in his quarters, preferably late at night. 'Since all ground officers are expert Air Chief Marshals,' wrote Kuter on 26 January, 'my job is to keep ground forces from swallowing the air forces, to keep RAF from swallowing AAF, etc. Nice bunch of cannibals in Africa! And Casablanca. And London. And Washington.' Kuter met Coningham in Maison Blanche, near Algiers, at the end of January. They became good friends, but not at first sight: Kuter thought him 'a big, self-confident, forceful and clearly ambitious fellow. He made a long loud speech on the fact that he wouldn't be an 'Air Support' Commander and had changed the name to North African Air Force. He meant just that! Command of everything with wings.' Kuter replied that he was happy to fight both Anderson and the Germans, but not 'Tooey' Spaatz as well. 'Tooey,' thought Kuter, 'is going to have a tough time between the charming Tedder and the bellicose Coningham.'[7]

On 27 January, Portal formally proposed that Coningham take command of 'Air Support Tunisia' and Harry Broadhurst succeed him in command of the Desert Air Force. 'Pete' Quesada (an American fighter pilot, ultimately elevated to Lieutenant General Elwood R. Quesada) recalled that 'Mary Coningham was the logical person to head the tactical air command. There was just no doubt about it. We didn't have anybody that could even come close to him . . . his was the easiest of all the selections that had to be made.' Quesada made himself known to Coningham at a meeting with British Army officers where he responded tartly to their emphasis on the virtues of experience by drawing attention to their experience of numerous defeats. Coningham applauded warmly, and they became, in Quesada's words, 'everlasting friends'.[8]

Robb went to Maison Blanche on 31 January to meet Tedder and Coningham on their arrival in Tunisia. They had long discussions that night with Spaatz and on the following afternoon Tedder and Coningham left for England in a Boeing B–17 Flying Fortress, both taking ten days' leave; Coningham also took a letter to Robb's wife, as well as plenty of oranges, lemons and wine for their families. While in England, celebrating with family and friends his knighthood and, belatedly, his 48th birthday, Coningham was promoted – not before time – to the rank of Acting Air Marshal, equivalent to Lieutenant General. Nan and her children were then living with the Crossley family at 'Darkwater', Blackfield, about seventeen miles from Southampton. Whenever Coningham came home from the Mediterranean, recalled Belinda Crossley, he always brought plenty of supplies with him. Belinda's mother would meet him at the local airfield in her Morris 8 and a lorry-load of fruit, wine and cheeses would follow behind. Belinda well remembered Coningham's dynamic personality: he completely dominated everyone at 'Darkwater' and they had a hard time matching his energy or living up to his expectations of them.[9]

On 8 February 1943, Spaatz wrote to George E. Stratemeyer, US Chief of Air Staff. 'The new organisation here is about to go into effect,' he said, 'and there are many problems which can only be settled at very high levels', the most serious being the fact that it was difficult to treat aviation as 'co-equal with the Army and Navy in our set-up, whereas the RAF will not submit to being considered in any other way'; in particular, it will not accept that air support 'belongs' to an Army Commander or that he may dictate its employment. Coningham, 'a full-fledged veteran of the Battle of the Mediterranean', has plenty of prestige and 'it can readily be seen that something is bound to break out in a very short period'. Writing to his wife a month later, on 7 March, Spaatz described Coningham as 'somewhat like a combination of Bob Olds and Billy Mitchell, with possibly a bit of Mac-Arthur thrown in for good measure', naming the three most flamboyant officers he could think of. 'The problem of integrating these individuals,' he told her, 'with their ambitions, flair for the dramatic, etc., is, to say the least, not simple': bearing in mind, of course, the fact that Spaatz had ambitions and flair of his own.[10]

Changes in the North African High Command were announced by Churchill in the House of Commons on 10 February. When the 8th Army reached Tunisia, it would come under Eisenhower's orders and Alexander would move from Cairo to Algiers to become Deputy Commander-in-Chief of the Allied Force and head of 18 Army Group (including the British 1st and 8th Armies, the French XIX Corps and the American II Corps). A Mediterranean Air Command was to form under Tedder, represented west of Tripoli by North-west African Air Forces (NAAF) under Spaatz. NAAF comprised tactical, strategic, coastal, troop transport and training commands. Spaatz set up an operational headquarters in Constantine, 200 miles east of his administrative headquarters in Algiers, and throughout NAAF, down to squadron level, command and staff positions were alternated between British and American officers, setting a pattern for the rest of the war. Unfortunately, Churchill made a radio broadcast that night in which he spoke of the new tasks assigned to British officers and failed to mention even one American officer. At the end of the broadcast, there was dead silence in Spaatz's headquarters and Robb, who was present, realised that Churchill's blunder would not be forgotten.[11]

While Coningham was on leave, Kuter carried on as interim commander, though finding it impossible to apply Desert methods of Army–Air cooperation in Tunisia. 'Our tactical air units,' he wrote, 'would have been delighted to go after the Luftwaffe on its airdromes. However, their whole energies were required to keep enough airplanes in flying condition to maintain the umbrella that II Corps demanded,' nor did they have either the transport or organisation to move forward rapidly and efficiently. Patton was not interested in attempting to camouflage his command post and when it was located and strafed by a Luftwaffe patrol, he demanded that Paul Williams (12th ASC) extend the umbrella from dawn to dusk even if it meant an end to all offensive air missions. Ground forces, added Kuter, were even instructed to abandon their light anti-aircraft weapons and take cover if

Stukas appeared. These dive-bombers were regarded as invincible by men who had seen too many movie newsreels.[12]

Tedder and Coningham returned from London on 14 February, the day on which the command changes were announced, and Coningham flew next day from Algiers to Tripoli 'in an endeavour,' as Robb wrote, 'to put a little air sense into the mob of Generals there'. In a public lecture three years later, Coningham made the same point more politely. Montgomery, he said, 'had shown full understanding of air problems and the air work with his Army since the day of his arrival in the Western Desert. Before I left him in January 1943 to form an Air Force on Army Group level in Tunisia, we discussed some doctrine and checked up how far we had travelled along the road of Army–Air efficiency.' A pause in operations permitted them to arrange a conference at which this doctrine could be expounded.[13]

Judging by the great number of copies that survive, Coningham's address to senior American and British officers, both soldiers and airmen, in Tripoli on 16 February made a remarkable impact. 'The Soldier,' declared Coningham, 'commands the land forces, the Airman commands the air forces; both commanders work together and operate their respective forces in accordance with a combined Army–Air plan, the whole operation being directed by the Army Commander.' Certain 'fundamental differences' must, however, be recognised.

> The Army fights on a front that may be divided into sectors, such as Brigade, Division, Corps or an Army front. The Air front is indivisable. An Army has one battle to fight, the land battle. The Air has two. It has first of all to beat the enemy air, so that it may go into the land battle against the enemy land forces with the maximum possible hitting power.

The fighter, continued Coningham, governed the front and this fact required the centralisation of air control in the hands of a single air commander. He had no doubt

> that in this technical age it needs a life of study and specialisation for a sailor, a soldier or an airman to learn his profession. He is never free from the problems of development, particularly in war, and I therefore cannot accept the possibility that any man, however competent, can do the work of the other services without proportionately neglecting his own. In plain language, no soldier is competent to operate the Air, just as no airman is competent to operate the Army.

Coningham, however, was concerned to stress *mutual* support. The previous December, for example, a site for a landing ground was selected at Sedada, 120 miles east of Tripoli. Advanced forces of the 7th Armoured Division reached the area at dusk one day and by 9 am the next a landing ground was ready, provided with MT, an ambulance unit and anti-aircraft guns. A transport aircraft carrying RDF equipment was sent there, escorted by two squadrons flying on their auxiliary tanks. These were dropped and the squadrons were then at readiness. Two other squadrons flew on to bomb Tripoli, returning to land at Sedada. By this time, air transports were coming in with fuel, ammunition and personnel. The Ambulance Holding Unit had already received a number of the Army's casualties and as the transport aircraft unloaded, so the ambulance cases went on board and away without delay. During the three months between the battle of Egypt and the capture of Tripoli, he pointed out, 5,800 wounded soldiers had been evacuated by air. 'You can imagine the effect on the morale of the Army,' he added, 'when it is known that badly-wounded cases, if trundled over the desert, very often die.' By the following morning, work had begun on two more landing grounds, forty miles ahead of Sedada, and so the advance continued, airmen and soldiers working together.

During his recent visit to England, Coningham had been 'rather distressed to find that the home doctrine of Army–Air operations is confused and the subject of considerable feeling'. The main reason, he thought, was obvious: except for 'the cold shower of Dieppe' the Army at home was not fighting whereas the RAF was; the Army had time to spare and needed aircraft for training whereas the RAF felt itself fully occupied and needed aircraft for operations; the result, said Coningham, was 'mutual petulance'. Sadly, the views held in England had been transferred to Tunisia.

> The result you know. And now this Army, which has done so well and hoped more or less to catch the boat at Tripoli for a spot of leave at home, has the prospect in front of it of even heavier fighting than it has experienced in the past. The misuse of the Air in Tunisia has contributed to the present lack of success. Incidentally, we here still do not understand why some of the Army and Air officers concerned in the planning of Torch did not visit the Western Desert and learn at least some of the simple lessons which 8th Army mastered over twelve months ago.[14]

The views of Montgomery and Coningham were incorporated by Portal in a pamphlet, *Air Power in the Land Battle*, issued by the Air Ministry in May 1943 with a forword by General H. H. Arnold, head of the USAAF. 'Embodied in these pages,' wrote Arnold, 'are battle-tested fundamentals in the exercise of command and employment of Air Power, adherence to which has contributed to the success of two of this War's outstanding commanders. It is my express desire that these precepts be known to every officer in the Army Air Forces.' 'I was full of praise for Monty's pamphlet on air–ground cooperation, which he issued throughout the Army,' wrote Tedder to Liddell Hart. 'So I should have been, for Mary Coningham wrote it two months before.' Montgomery was much given to rejecting ideas and then promulgating them as his own.[15]

Although American airmen recognised that the British system of central-ising control of available air forces under an Air Commander equal in authority to the Army and Naval commanders had proved 'outstandingly successful' (in the words of an official history of the USAAF), they were unable prior to 1943 to get this system accepted by the US War Department, which regarded the air force as subordinate to the ground force. In the battle area, not only did the Air Commander come under the Army Commander, but air units might be *specifically allotted* to the support of subordinate ground units. Such principles fostered distribution (rather than concen-tration) of force; encouraged an 'umbrella' concept of defence which invited defeat in detail by opposing air forces; committed aircraft to missions ill-suited to their capacity and robbed the Air Commander of freedom to exploit the inherent *flexibility* of his weapon. This doctrine, which failed in the early months of the North African campaign, 'was rewritten with the advice of men trained in the school of the Western Desert' and became official US War Department policy on 21 July 1943: air and land power were recognised as 'co-equal and interdependent forces', neither of them 'an auxiliary of the other'. Those men who framed this doctrine tested it further in Sicily, Italy and North-western Europe 'in one of the most effective collaborations known to military history'.[16]

At the time of Coningham's address in Tripoli, the Allied land forces in Tunisia held a front of about 250 miles, extending from Cape Serrat (thirty-five miles west of Bizerta) on the north coast to Gafsa in the south. Under Anderson's 1st Army, 5 Corps held the northern sector; a mainly French force (also under 1st Army) occupied the centre; and II Corps held the southern sector. The RAF's 242 Group covered the 1st Army area, the American 12th ASC covered II Corps' area and the 8th Army (now moving towards the Mareth Line) was covered by the Desert Air Force. According to a history of the 12th Air Force, the enemy air forces were on top: 242 Group's airfields in the Medjerda valley were often closed by rain or low cloud, while the enemy operated continuously from all-weather airfields in the Bizerta, Tunis and Kairouan areas. Farther south, 12th ASC had been forced back by the enemy advance to Kasserine from the excellent Thelepte plain, where all-weather airfields were available, to a mountainous area around Tebessa 'where mud reigned supreme' and only one sealed runway, at Youks, was available. Not least, the American historian admitted, the units of 12th ASC 'were in a low state of efficiency and suffering from the cumulative effect of inexperience of mobile operations and the poor airfield situation'.[17]

About 9 am on 18 February, Larry Kuter learned that Coningham would arrive at the joint Army–Air Headquarters (about fifty miles south-east of Constantine, near Ain Beida) in fifteen minutes. 'He came in at full steam,' Kuter recalled. 'Coningham is all out for his unlimited authority as an *air force* commander. He said Spaatz agreed last night. Suits me, but I asked him to get our written charter revised.' Kuter then proposed to send an officer to 1st Army Headquarters to coordinate a programme of airfield construction with planned ground operations. 'To hell with that,' replied Coningham, 'we'll set up the airfields and 1st Army will conform to our plan.' Behind his self-assurance, force and ambition, wrote Kuter, 'there is remarkable blunt charm which enables him to refer to recent successful battle experience in a convincing manner which appears to be not at all grating or irritating to his ground-force listener.' He was 'a big, active, able, enthusiastic man for whom the nickname "Mary" was ludicrous'. Kuter forecast that Coningham's arrival, his close association with Alexander and the 12th ASC's recent successes might swing over some doubting soldiers. 'Even Anderson (who I believe will be afraid to tackle Coningham) and McNabb (who can recognise a winner) will be affected.'[18]

The headquarters of Alexander and Coningham lay among hills and scattered olive trees with a big pavilion tent in desert camouflage serving as a common plans and operations centre. It contained a large map which was, wrote Kuter, 'the heart of ground–air cooperation and collaboration'. Coningham had had his caravan transported by sea and land from Tripoli to Ain Beida (protected by threats of fierce reprisals against anyone who damaged it) and set up close to the pavilion tent; he had also arranged for Elmhirst and Beamish to join him again and so, when they arrived on 19 February, Coningham had his familiar home and staff once more about him. The initial atmosphere, however, as Elmhirst wrote a week later, 'was decidedly gloomy, other than the new Commander-in-Chief, General Alexander, and Mary, who were in no way dismayed'. Alexander observed that all his jobs began with disorder and retreat, 'but he had a cheerful smile on his face'. The food was better than in the Desert Campaign, for Coningham made sure that they drew both British and American rations and were never without good American coffee, sweetcorn and tinned fruit to supplement British tea and corned beef; his staff also included men skilled in procuring fresh eggs and vegetables.[19]

As NATAF consisted of British and American formations, the headquarters had a staff of British and American officers as well as an American Deputy Commander. Coningham's intentions were converted into action by three air force formations, each closely identified with an Army headquarters: 242 Group (Kenneth Cross) with 1st Army, the Desert Air Force (Harry Broadhurst) with 8th Army and 12th ASC (Paul L. Williams) with II Corps, US Army. Squadron Leader Donald Wiseman's role was to supply Coningham with air intelligence, including Ultra information. 'He handled this well,' Wiseman recalled, 'and never gave me concern by divulging sources.' Coningham, Kuter, Elmhirst and Beamish usually had a drink about 7 pm in Coningham's caravan to discuss the day's work. As in the Desert, supper was a time for relaxed conversation and Elmhirst would try to get a lively debate going. Neither Alexander nor Coningham had any liking for war talk on such occasions nor for blue jokes at any time. Kuter described Beamish as a big husky fellow who had once been the heavyweight boxing champion of the RAF and had acquired a badly broken nose on his way up. In sharp contrast with his appearance was his gentle, high-pitched and somewhat effeminate voice . . . George and an Army Brigadier had desks in Operational Control. They seemed never to sleep, but lived on huge pottery mugs of extremely strong tea.[20]

William Momyer, then with 12th ASC, remembered his first meeting with Coningham. 'Colonel,' he said, 'the first thing we are going to do is get out and destroy the German Air Force.' When that is done, 'we will do all the air support and anything else that the Army wants. But until we get those airfields and get those German airplanes off our back, we are not going to do anything else.' Until Coningham's arrival, 12th ASC had been for all practical purposes under II Corps control and, said Momyer, 'that accounts for the fact that we weren't going out hitting those airfields' because 'there was very little understanding of the importance of air superiority'. Quesada, Deputy Commander of the Coastal Air Force, agreed. Coningham, he said, 'was the first senior air force guy who established tactical air doctrine', he was 'the architect of it' and 'overcame the concept of using the air force as artillery and he established the doctrine that if an airman is left to use his own weapon and use his experience he would further the cause of the Army or the ground battle'.[21]

Rommel, meanwhile, had withdrawn into Tunisia and discovered that the Mareth Line (north of Medenine) was not as strong a position as he had supposed. Made up of decaying bunkers and pillboxes built by the French in the Thirties to keep out Italians, it was far too long to be held by his small forces: twenty-two miles from the sea to the Matmata Hills, with open desert beyond those hills. He wanted to base his defence of the southern approach to Tunis on a line at Wadi Akarit, forty miles farther north, but only fourteen miles wide: a position that could not easily be outflanked because its inland flank lay on the salt marsh of Chott el Jerid. Knowing that Montgomery would take plenty of time to clear the port of Tripoli, reorganise his forces and build up supplies, Rommel planned an attack on the Americans.[22]

So, too, did General Jurgen von Arnim, commander of the Axis forces in Tunisia. On 3 February, Arnim had seized Faid Pass in the Eastern Dorsale from its French garrison and struck westward on the 14th, routing large American forces. Rommel, having moved his army into the Mareth Line, sent a detachment to strike at Gafsa and caused another withdrawal. On the 17th, the Americans were driven out of Sbeitla and airfields at Feriana and Thelepte. Having fled in disorder about fifty miles across an arid plain from the Eastern to the Western Dorsale, the Americans (aided by British and French forces) made a stand at the Kasserine Pass. This pass gave access to supply and administration bases at Tebessa and Le Kef. If these were lost, the Allies might have to leave Tunisia, but Arnim failed to assist Rommel in exploiting an unexpected success with maximum force and speed.[23]

Alexander had flown from Cairo to Algiers on 15 February to take command of all ground forces in Tunisia. On the 19th, after a tour of the fighting fronts, he informed the War Office that the

> general situation is far from satisfactory. British, American and French units are mixed up on the front, especially in the south. Formations have been split up. There is no clear policy and no plan of campaign. The Air is much the same. This is the result of no firm direction or centralised control from above. British are in good heart and have fought well. Americans are ignorant, ill-trained and rather at a loss; consequently not too happy. French are badly equipped, but I believe have possibility to play a useful role if they can be armed. We have quite definitely lost the initiative.

Rommel's attempt to force the Kasserine Pass, rebuffed on 19 February, was resumed next day with staggering success. Arnim, however, had held aloof and by the morning of the 22nd the opportunity for a major Axis triumph had passed. Rommel, now anxious to return to the Mareth Line, withdrew.[24]

On 22 February, wrote Kuter, 'Ike came up to our HQ to discuss the situation in the Pass' with Alexander and Coningham. 'Alex, calm, quiet and thoughtful, did most of the talking.' The Panzers, he said, were moving in the Pass with apparent ease and there seemed to be no effort being made to stop or destroy them there.

> Alex extolled the American soldiers as big, strong, bright and very well-equipped. He then gently, but firmly, laid out his two points of worry. First, when in contact with the enemy, our troops were not fighting. Second, when not in contact, they were not training to fight. Ike said that he too was worried and didn't know what to do about it. [Alexander] did not suggest moving experienced commanders from Montgomery's successful 8th Army into our II Corps, but did offer some of the veteran non-coms and junior officers who had trained with those commanders and their troups. To this offer there was no spoken response. I believe that all concerned knew that it wouldn't work with George Patton's dash of anglophobia.[25]

The weather improved slightly during that day and Coningham's aircraft helped to stem the attack. That evening, the German retreat began, harassed with increasing effect from the air, as Allied ground commanders were quick to note. 'The Air Force is now better organised,' wrote Eisenhower on 25 February, 'is well sorted out and operating efficiently.' Nevertheless, his aide (Lieutenant Commander Harry C. Butcher) thought 'the proud and cocky Americans today stand humiliated by one of the greatest defeats in our history. This is particularly embarrassing to us with the British, who are courteous and understanding. But there is a definite hangheadedness.' Coningham, however, shared the opinion of experienced Desert hands that muddle and panic were only to be expected when untried troops – British as well as American – came up against a combat-hardened enemy. Formations that did poorly in Tunisia would prove themselves in subsequent campaigns. During this crisis, some B-17 Flying Fortresses accidentally bombed a 242 Group base at Souk-el-Arba, killing some British airmen, wounding many and destroying several aircraft. Kuter rushed to Spaatz's headquarters, but he was away. Joe Cannon, however, 'gallantly assumed responsibility', in Kuter's words, and went with him to express his very deep regrets to Alexander and Coningham, who were 'most gracious and told of RAF failures to identify targets and attacking friendly forces'. Later that year, Cannon became one of the closest of Coningham's many good friends among American officers.[26]

Despite heavy rain and bitter cold, wrote Elmhirst, Coningham was, 'as usual, in good form' and full of energy. He took Elmhirst with him on an inspection of the front late in February: 'He is a forceful driver and we often did thirty miles in thirty minutes, on slippery roads with convoys to pass.' The shortage of airfields concerned him. In the north, the only suitable area was a valley running east from Souk-el-Arba that was ideal in fine weather, with ample space for any number of landing grounds, but any rain quickly turned the heavy soil to mud and clouds hid nearby hills. Aircraft serviceability was low and greatly hindered a force operating against enemy aircraft located in open country with good all-weather airfields. In the centre, the country west of Kasserine was extremely bad for airfields. Good areas lay around Thelepte, Canrobert and Constantine, but these latter were out of fighter range of the frontline. It was therefore necessary to begin an ambitious airfield construction programme around the Axis bridgehead. Coningham was also concerned about the limited use being made of radar. No serious attempt, in his view, was being made to overcome problems caused by a mountainous terrain. He had the whole layout reorganised and augmented with gaps in the cover made good by extensive use of light mobile sets; telephone links between radar stations were also improved.[27]

'I saw Coningham's hand in recent operations,' wrote Churchill to Portal on 27 February. 'No doubt his control and Tedder's general organisation will bring about an improvement, but here is the place where we want to fight the Hun and where the Hun has to fight us *in the air* and every effort should be made by us, apart from the Americans, to bring the strongest forces constantly into action.' Hitherto, Churchill continued, Allied air operations in Tunisia had failed, but 'I am counting on you to retrieve it, now that you have the best men on the spot and in the right places.' Portal, replying next day, blamed 'the defensive "penny packets" policy imposed upon us by the inexperience of the 1st Army under air attack and by the ignorance of the High Command about the basic principles of Army and Air Force cooperation'. This misfortune, he thought, was attributable to the 'ideological' controversy which had been going on for so long in England, 'a controversy which I hope and believe has now been killed by Monty and Coningham'. On the same day, 28 February, Montgomery wrote to Brooke, inviting him to send out senior officers from England for instruction.

> They would see the teamwork at a HQ and how we tie up the staff work as between the Army and the RAF staffs; how we work the Army Air Support Control; how we fight for airfields; the whole technique of how we step up the RAF squadrons on to forward airfields, so as to give cover to the forward troops; the AA protection of forward airfields as you advance . . . In fact, the whole business. They will never learn these things in England; they would like to, but cannot as it is all theory; here it is all practical.[28]

'The only thing that was absolutely first class' in Tunisia in February 1943, thought Elmhirst, 'was the fighting efficiency and spirit of the air crews, American and British: all they required was to be organised and directed.' That was Coningham's task. On 2 March, as soon as he returned from an inspection of the front, he informed his subordinate commanders – Cross, Broadhurst and Williams – that his directive from Spaatz was 'to provide maximum air support for land operations', a task that could only be carried out when air superiority had been fought for and obtained. 'As a result of success in this air fighting, our land forces will be enabled to operate virtually unhindered by enemy air attack and our Air Forces be given increased freedom to assist in the actual battle area and in attacks against objectives in rear.'[29]

Coningham proposed to carry out a continual offensive against enemy aircraft and airfields. Escorted light and medium bombers would attack by day, interspersed with low-level sweeps by fighter-bombers; at night, light bombers would keep up the pressure: 'we will probably also be supported by the operations of the Strategic Air Forces operating independently but in conjunction with my plan.' Control, he said, could not be exercised without rapid and reliable communication between headquarters, commands and units.

> On a front of 250 miles, there will be a tendency for operations to be restricted to areas within ranges of aircraft from their home bases. It is necessary, however, that the main elements of the Force should be capable of providing mutual support and concentration as necessitated by operations. You are therefore to plan the movement or reception of units in detail from one sector to another and be prepared to implement your plan at short notice.

'I judge the efficiency of fighter squadrons solely on their abilities in air fighting,' Coningham emphasised.

Where fighter squadrons are employed mainly on escort tasks, bombing and ground strafing, they must first possess the basic qualifications in air fighting standard and their role must be changed frequently to afford opportunities for actual practice in air warfare. Efficiency in air fighting depends upon high morale, sound tactical unit and wing plans, good marksmanship and alertness in the air. High morale depends upon the three basic requirements of a fighting force: leadership, training and equipment.

He did not favour large patrols which merely chased enemy aircraft away, preferring a greater number of small – but well-drilled – patrols, giving more chance of actual combat and less chance for enemy pirate attacks. 'Fighters employed to escort bombers must never allow themselves to be lured away and must regard it as a point of honour that their charges are not attacked by enemy fighters.'

As for bombers, 'a very high standard of teamwork' was necessary, 'with emphasis throughout on navigation, formation flying, studied controlled bombing and defensive fire'. Fighter and bomber commanders must get together regularly with ground personnel both to decide the best methods of carrying out escorted raids and to ensure the most rapid refuelling and re-arming of aircraft. 'All light bombers should be capable of night operations. Much army movement, particularly supply, is covered by darkness. It is during this period that crippling blows may be struck. Moreover, night training permits the exploitation of dusk and dawn attacks – times when the enemy may well be found concentrated and off guard.'

The efficiency of 'the human machine', Coningham concluded, was essential for success in operations.

The appointment of commands and the allocation of honours and awards is therefore my personal task. Personnel matters come first in my thoughts . . . Spirit and confidence will spring from good leadership and training and can be safeguarded by consideration for the individual. The weak men of low morale are not to be tolerated in units as they taint the atmosphere. You are to remove such personnel immediately on discovery . . . I attach the very greatest importance to the dissemination of information and guidance to all personnel. You are my governing link with the units. I want you to explain my views to them and in this way inspire a cooperative spirit which will give us the strength of unified effort by the whole force.

Coningham summarised his aim and method for Lieutenant General Anderson on the same day, 2 March. My aim, he wrote, 'is to give maximum aid to our Armies; my method is to use air power correctly'. This could best be done through concentration of command and operation in the airman's hand. He was delighted at news of recent successes and hoped soon to be able to hit the enemy forces hard. 'We are not, however, a substitute for nor an appendage of land operations,' he warned, 'and, particularly with small formations, the laws of weather, darkness and topography make it necessary that the Army should rely on its own fighting qualities.' Coningham urged Anderson to see that such 'defensive slogans' as 'air cover' and 'umbrella' were dropped, because the air force was 'a combination of shield and punch' and could only really be efficient when acting offensively. The successful offensive, he believed, was inherently protective.[30]

General Arnim had begun his long-planned attempt to take Medjez el Bab, some thirty miles south-west of Tunis, on 26 February. It was repulsed with heavy losses. Worse, it caused delay in Rommel's attack on Montgomery at Medenine, south of the Mareth Line. Until the 26th, Montgomery had had few troops up forward, but by 6 March, when Rommel at last attacked, he had many forward, as well as ample air support and detailed information from Ultra intercepts about the attack plan, which was unusually inept. Montgomery was at his best when receiving an obvious blow about which he had been forewarned and for which he had time to prepare and plenty of men and materials assembled to meet it. At Medenine, wrote Kesselring in May 1948, the 'last trump' had been played and hopes of keeping the war away from Europe and especially from Germany for another year had been gambled away. Although a brilliant exponent of desert warfare and very brave, 'Rommel's nerves were very unstable' in Kesselring's opinion: 'The slightest reverse affected the whole frontline. The smallest success started him building castles in the air.' After El Alamein, sadly, he gradually lost both his belief in victory and his ability to *simulate* belief in victory, relapsing into 'the gloomiest forebodings, which in the long run became really hard to endure'. Tired and ill, Rommel left Africa for the last time on 9 March 1943. Like all his opponents, Coningham felt both relief and regret at the news of his departure. In theory, the end of German power in Africa had long been certain, but in practice few of the men whom he had so long harried or resisted were prepared to bet on it until they knew, for certain, that 'the Desert Fox' had gone.[31]

CHAPTER ELEVEN

'A Major Crisis in Anglo-American Relations'

The Last Weeks of the Tunisian Campaign, March to May 1943

The Allies were already assured of victory in Tunisia by early March. Air and sea power had virtually isolated the Axis forces, cutting them off from supplies of ammunition and fuel, whereas during the lull since the defeat at Kasserine, the Allies had assembled vast quantities of these supplies as well as greatly increasing their manpower. 'Our military problem,' wrote Bradley, 'was relatively simple: to defeat a hopelessly trapped Axis force with minimum Allied casualties in the fastest possible time, without allowing any of the enemy to slip out of Tunisia to fight again.' Alexander could either drive a wedge between Arnim in the north and the Afrika Korps in the south, encircling and destroying each separately, or he could squeeze them together into a smaller and smaller beachhead in the north, until they had no more usable airfields and no more room to manoeuvre. He chose the latter option because he lacked confidence in II Corps. Montgomery was to break through at Mareth and drive north; Anderson's 1st Army would advance in the north and centre; and II Corps would make noises and feints towards the east, drawing off troops in front of Montgomery by threatening their right flank. Alexander was right, thought Bradley, to assign the Americans a minor role; II Corps was not yet capable of anything better.[1]

Montgomery's attack began on the night of 20 March, when he outnumbered the enemy on his front by two to one in men and guns and four to one in tanks. Coningham had arranged for the air forces of Cross and Williams to distract the Luftwaffe's attention from the 8th Army front by attacking airfields day and night and so permit the Desert Air Force to devote its whole attention to direct support of that Army. Even so, Montgomery's usual frontal assault, as usual, failed. The New Zealanders, meanwhile, had once again been entrusted with an outflanking movement, this time making a very wide sweep from far behind their own lines. They reached the Tebaga Gap (about fifteen miles south-west of El Hamma) by nightfall on the 20th and were there checked. Early on the 23rd, Montgomery recast his plan (again, as usual) to concentrate on a flank attack. The Germans, realising that the frontal assault had failed and forewarned by the arrival of the New Zealanders at Tebaga, reinforced their defence there before the new attack was launched at 4 pm on the 26th. Arnim had withdrawn Messe's army from Mareth to Wadi Akarit on the 24th, so the defenders of Tebaga were only required to hang on until the non-mobile defenders of Mareth could withdraw. The path of the British advance on the 25th was swept by intensive low-level air attack by sixteen squadrons of Broadhurst's Desert Air Force. The British armour for once continued an attack in darkness, a sandstorm having covered their assembly and early advance. Even though the attack went well, most of the Axis forces reached Wadi Akarit safely, helped – as ever – by Montgomery's need to spend a week, from 29 March, reorganising and building-up.[2]

The attack on the 25th was Broadhurst's finest hour and he wrote immediately to Coningham to describe his men's splendid achievement. Their 'concentrated and continuous' attacks, he said, disorganised the enemy defences, permitting a breakthrough by Montgomery's armour. The number of prisoners taken and the amount of equipment left behind 'testified to the terrific moral and material effect caused by this air attack' which, as Broadhurst fairly pointed out, 'introduced no novel features, but merely used normal forms of attack closely linked to a normal army problem and which caught the enemy without well-prepared AA defences on an occasion when we enjoyed almost complete air supremacy'. Coningham described this action as 'an example of the proper use of air power in accordance with the principle of concentration'. Such results, he added, could only be achieved by hard training, long experience and first-class leadership – and when air force control was centralised in an Air Commander working closely with an Army Commander. Broadhurst, having got Montgomery out of a hole by risking his whole force, thereafter became his favourite airman, but in later years neither man allowed sufficient credit to Cross and Williams for occupying the Luftwaffe elsewhere.[3]

Kuter, meanwhile, was trying – with little success – to protect Williams from constant demands for defensive umbrellas over II Corps 'and to persuade Patton's staff and senior officers that NATAF's most effective support would be to destroy the Luftwaffe and gain control of the air'. Patton, however, had been brought up to believe in 'the sanctity of area command', as Kuter put it, and the idea that an airman working in the area of Patton's command should not be subject to Patton's orders was anathema to him; the fact that Montgomery accepted the idea merely stiffened his resistance. Though less abrasive than Patton, Bradley shared his views on air power. Coningham, he wrote, 'believed less in "close support" than in "strategic" air strikes deep at the enemy's rear bases and airfields and dogfights to achieve air superiority. Consequently, he was opposed to maintaining an air umbrella at all times over ground troops.' Worse still, Bradley alleged that Coningham juggled his resources 'disproportionately' in

144

Montgomery's favour. Like Patton and Bradley, Anderson (commander of the 1st Army) did what he could to control aircraft in his area, but Coningham had in Cross a 'bold and fiery' man to command 242 Group who was unimpressed, wrote Kuter, either by Army traditions or Anderson's three stars.[4]

Three USAAF officers were sent from England to North Africa by Major General Eaker (head of the 8th Air Force) to study operations there. Kuter told them, on 20 March, what he had learned from Coningham and from his own observations: that coordination between air and ground forces 'must be by liaison and not by command'. Army Commanders were unwilling to see the campaign as a whole and consequently wished to disperse the limited air power available on a variety of targets immediately in front of their troops, thus preventing the Air Commanders from striking an effective blow anywhere. American troops, said Kuter, 'demand and expect' fighter protection over the entire front from dive-bombers, but protection against Stukas was best provided 'by dispersion and light anti-aircraft fire from ground troops'. To date, he added, 'the Stukas have delivered but one effective attack on American troops'. Coningham told Eaker's officers that fighter pilots should have fighting experience before assignment as bomber escorts and must not devote their entire time to such work or their fighting efficiency would fall. Every fighter should be a *fighter-bomber*, with jettisonable tanks and bombs interchangeable; they should be based very far forward – not more than twenty miles from the front – and protected from air or ground attack by standing patrols, wide dispersion and frequent changes of airfield. Incidentally, said Coningham, too many US Army officers showed a casual attitude to field sanitation regulations and unless they smartened up, the coming of warm weather would have disastrous results.[5]

Coningham decided to place all his British and American bombers (except those allotted to the Desert Air Force) in a separate group under his immediate control to employ on whichever part of the front the situation demanded. Formed on 20 March under the command of Air Commodore Laurence Sinclair, it was named Tactical Bomber Force (TBF). Given the mixture of types – and the mixture of British and American personnel – as well as the shortage of equipment and spares, its achievements were a tribute to goodwill all round. Sinclair recalled that Coningham and Kuter told him they had decided to disband the Boston (A-20) Group and give the aircraft to his Bisley wing, provided he could train his crews to fly Bostons. 'This was a big feather in Mary's hat,' wrote Sinclair, 'and showed the confidence Kuter had in him as this was done with good grace.' When Sinclair offered to retrain the Americans himself 'in methods approved by Mary', Kuter agreed at once. Spaatz gave his full support to TBF and was a key background figure in its success in Sicily and Italy as well as Tunisia. Sinclair's relations with Americans, both staff officers and aircrew, in these operations were uniformly good and TBF gave excellent service. 'I think Mary should get much of the credit for setting this all up,' he wrote. 'As long as everything went OK, we were left to get on with it, but if things went wrong we were going to be the ones who carried the can – not Mary.'[6]

Although Elmhirst admired Alexander, finding him 'broad-minded, philosophic, cheery and most likeable', he doubted whether he had 'that vital leadership and the ability to "get it over" to the troops that Monty has, and I think Mary has too'. Even so, he wrote on 30 March, Alexander and Coningham made a first-class partnership, 'which should mean everything in the big battle-to-be when the units they control, the British 1st and 8th Armies, the American Army and the three Air Forces concerned, have to hit together'. By the end of March, said Coningham in February 1946, the days of mistakes in organisation and tactics were over: 'Everything was tidy and with the 1st Army and American forces pressing in from the west, the 8th Army coming up from the south and powerful air forces maintaining air mastery over Tunisia, the stage was set for a great victory.'[7]

Sadly, the stage was also set for what Tedder would call 'a major crisis in Anglo-American relations' when Patton and Coningham quarrelled publicly. Kuter remembered Patton telling him 'tearfully' that he had had to order Lieutenants to lead even the smallest units and still 'couldn't make the sons of bitches fight': 286 junior officers died doing work that Sergeants and Corporals should have been trained to do. These words, thought Kuter, spoke volumes for the state of the American Army early in 1943. Then, on 1 April, some German aircraft attacked one of Patton's observation posts, killing three men, among them his much-loved personal aide, Richard N. Jenson. They had three radios at the post and, as Patton later admitted, failed to move it regularly, so permitting the Germans to fix its position. Patton's command of II Corps was insecure: he had been 'pitchforked' into it, he complained, 'on one day's notice' and only commanded it for ten days before going into battle. This insecurity, together with the need to excuse yet another American failure to make progress, exasperation at the difficulty he was finding in winning fame and, perhaps most of all, grief at Jenson's death, provoked Patton to add an intemperate comment to a routine sitrep (situation report) signal and give it a wider distribution than normal. 'Forward troops have been continuously bombed all morning,' he claimed. 'Total lack of air cover for our Units has allowed German Air Forces to operate almost at will.'[8]

Kuter read the signal at Ain Beida that evening without too much concern: it seemed 'so obviously exaggerated and emotional' that he doubted if anyone would take it seriously. Nevertheless, he asked the operations staff to collect the facts and called Williams, arranging to meet him at Thelepte next morning. Together they would drive to Gafsa with the facts and urge Patton to back down. During the night, unfortunately, Coningham studied those facts and, wrote Kuter, became 'more and more inflamed'. He then wrote out his response and had it transmitted to every one of the sitrep addressees.

At 7.30 am on 1 April, wrote Coningham, 'an unspecified number of fighters' appeared over the II Corps front at El Guettar; at 9.50 am, a dozen

Ju 87s, followed a few minutes later by five Ju 88s and a dozen Me 109s, dropped a few bombs. 'Total casualties: four killed, very small number wounded.' In contrast, 362 Allied fighters operated that day, 260 of them over Patton's front. The sitrep, consequently, was at first regarded as an April Fool's Day joke. Coningham added:

> It is assumed that intention was not to stampede local American Air Command into purely defensive action. It is also assumed that there was no intention to adopt discredited practice of using Air Force as an alibi for lack of success on ground. If sitrep is in earnest and balanced against above facts, it can only be assumed that II Corps personnel concerned are not battleworthy in terms of present operations. In view of outstandingly efficient and successful work of American Air Command concerned, it is requested that such inaccurate and exaggerated reports should cease. 12th ASC have been instructed not to allow their brilliant and conscientious air support of II Corps to be affected by this false cry of 'wolf'.[9]

Spaatz and Tedder received copies of Patton's sitrep on 2 April. Its 'inaccuracy', 'unjustness' and wide distribution caused 'great concern', recorded Spaatz's Command Diary. Next morning, Spaatz and Tedder received Coningham's response. They flew to Thelepte, met Kuter and Williams and investigated Patton's claim, finding it quite unfounded. The four officers then drove to Patton's headquarters in Gafsa, where he dumbfounded them by remarking that he was satisfied with 'the good air support' Williams was giving him. An intruder bombed Gafsa while the conference was in progress; a raid which grew in telling to at least four enemy aircraft and delighted Patton: 'If I could find those sonsabitches,' he exulted, 'I'd mail them each a medal.' In Patton's version, they 'flew right down the street not fifty feet from the window, firing machine-guns and dropping small bombs'. And yet, no-one was hurt. A fleeting attack by *soldiers* on a target near the front would have been accepted as a normal hazard of war, but Patton believed that he was entitled to total immunity from *aerial* attack.

Kuter recalled this meeting vividly, with Patton 'wearing his fiercest scowl', throughout, even though both Tedder and Spaatz apologised and promised to make Coningham do likewise. 'Patton appeared to me to act like a small boy who had done wrong, but thought he would get away with it.' Alexander, however, was not deceived and telephoned Patton, telling him 'that he had read Coningham's message, that Patton had asked for it and got just what he had asked for.' But Tedder, thinking Coningham had provoked 'a major crisis' telephoned Eisenhower, assuring him that he had ordered Coningham to go at once to Gafsa and apologise. 'Ike apparently took the incident very, very hard,' wrote Bradley. 'Even though Patton had ignited the furor with the sitrep, Coningham's riposte stung him to the quick and for days he was in a towering rage.' This over-reaction astonished Kuter until he reflected that Tedder and Eisenhower 'hadn't seen as much of Patton as we had in the forward area'.[10]

Later that day, Coningham withdrew his signal and on 4 April visited Patton, who refused to accept an oral apology 'for your calling 60,000 American soldiers unbattleworthy and failing in their duty'; men who 'had been under barrage all day due to what I considered was his fault'. Patton demanded a specific retraction, sent to everyone who received the original signal, and Coningham – full of abject apologies – readily agreed. 'I can't thank you enough,' he said. 'You have been very generous.' 'It is always easy to be generous,' replied Patton, 'to a gentleman who admits his mistakes.' They parted friends and, thought Patton, 'we will now get better air support than ever before. I was rather proud of myself, as I was firm, but moderate.'

Not surprisingly, Coningham's account of the meeting, given later to Kuter, has a different tone. The Air Marshal countered the General's fierce scowl with his most brilliant smile, picked up the chair indicated for him and placed it directly opposite Patton, who had enthroned himself behind a huge oak desk, decorated at either end with II Corps's colours and standards. 'Mary said that they had shouted at each other for a while and each pounded his side of the desk. Finally, they concluded that each enjoyed a good fight, shook hands and had lunch together, all smiles.'[11]

Spaatz, who was well aware that Coningham's signal had been a defence of American airmen rather than attack on American soldiers, told Eisenhower on 5 April that 'Coningham's trouble was all caused by Patton's distribution of his sitrep of 1 April and that in view of its accusation notice had to be taken of it.' Eisenhower had already written to General Marshall in Washington about Coningham's 'very unwise and unjust criticism' of II Corps, but having listened to Spaatz, Eisenhower felt it necessary – not for the first or last time – to rebuke Patton.

> I realise how chagrined you were, and why you felt that some public retraction or apology was indicated. However, I realise also that the *great purpose of complete Allied teamwork must be achieved in this theater* and it is my conviction that this purpose will not be furthered by demanding the last pound of flesh for every error, when other measures should suffice . . . I am since informed that there was a certain amount of unwise distribution of your sitrep.

He advised Patton that if in future he felt critical of another service, it should be expressed in a 'confidential report to the next military superior *only*'. The rebuke angered Patton, who regarded Eisenhower as 'completely sold out to the British. I hope the Press at home gets on to it.' He also hoped 'the Boches beat the complete life out of the [British] 128th Brigade and 6th Armored Division. I am fed up with being treated like a moron by the British. There is no national honor nor prestige left to us. Ike must go.'[12]

Coningham, meanwhile, had addressed a long account of the whole affair to Philip Wigglesworth, Tedder's Chief of Staff in Algiers, on 5 April. The provocation, he wrote, was particularly intense: a solid forty-eight hours of sitreps, signals and telephone calls, not one addressed either to his own or Williams' headquarters and 'all based on false information because General Patton is living forty miles away from his airmen and does not know the air position'. By then, of course, Coningham realised the harm his outburst had done to Anglo-American relations, as well as his own reputation, and was anxious to repair his standing with Tedder, hitherto an influential patron.

> The Chief reproved me for my signal, and I think he was quite right because it does not help to throw grit in the works and no individual must be allowed to upset the machine. My main concern, however, is that I may have added to the load carried by our Chief or by the Commander-in-Chief. If you have the opportunity, would you kindly convey this aspect of the incident to General Eisenhower with my sincere regrets?[13]

Tedder would be slow to forgive Coningham. He sent a 'strictly private and personal' signal to Portal on 17 April 'about Coningham's ill-judged signal'. Eisenhower, he said, had taken the matter well, 'but it is clear that for some hours there was grave danger of very serious political and international repercussions', although the ultimate effect may be good. 'Patton is now certainly a friend of ours,' thought Tedder, 'and I think chance of belly-aching signals from Army greatly reduced. This, however, does not justify Coningham's original signal which must affect people's assessment of his judgment.' Tedder then came to the point that underlay his anger with Coningham. The 'repeated failure' of American troops to carry out offensives successfully was an 'unfortunate fact' and Eisenhower was 'very concerned that this situation may be distorted and developed by Hearst Press to support campaign for confining American military effort to Pacific theatre. We shall have to be careful to avoid over-stressing British contribution to present campaign.'[14]

Between 27 March and 4 April, a visit from Sir Trafford Leigh-Mallory (head of Fighter Command) had already strengthened Coningham's determination to show himself a good 'Anglo-American'. Leigh-Mallory had come to study the organisation of air forces in Tunisia with future operations across the Channel in mind; operations in which Coningham hoped to play a leading part. Leigh-Mallory's report to Portal, warmly commending Coningham's command as an excellent organisation in itself and one fostering good relations with other services, British and American, would have offset the damage done to his reputation by the squabble with Patton. The report was well received and on 14 June the Air Ministry announced that as a result of experience gained in North Africa, Army Cooperation Command (formed in December 1940) had been reorganised and would henceforth be known as the 2nd Tactical Air Force (Coningham's being the first). To take over that command, once a cross-Channel invasion became a realistic prospect, now became Coningham's prime ambition.

Leigh-Mallory had been favourably impressed by the direct contact in Tunisia between Army and Air Force commanders and their staffs, ensuring that 'both in strategy and tactics, land and air forces are directed and employed to the best advantage of a common plan'. He also liked the fusion of British and American staffs, although 'the importance of personalities and the selection of the right individuals for the key posts' was continually emphasised to him. Coningham, thought Leigh-Mallory, is 'fully in the mind' of Alexander and 'fits in the Air to meet the Army's main requirements'. By mutual consent, he noted, 'Army Cooperation' was taken for granted and the term suppressed in correspondence.

Although Alexander and Coningham shared the same mess, they did not find it necessary to be continuously in contact in an Operations Room. In general, they dealt with 'plans and main intentions', conferring as necessary, in addition to their daily meeting with Intelligence officers of both services. Coningham regarded his task 'primarily as one of coordination and supervision of operations', although he personally decided what effort each Group should employ and what reinforcement they should give to each other. He did not hesitate to intervene 'if a study of the day's operations convinces him that the forces are being wrongly employed'. His experience in the Desert and in Tunisia led him to place all his bombers, British and American (except those allotted to Broadhurst's Desert Air Force), in a separate Group under his own control to deploy on whichever part of the front seemed best to him. Coningham, observed Leigh-Mallory, dealt personally with such matters as the appointment of senior officers, authorisation of acting ranks, recommendations for honours and awards and the commissioning of air crews.

As for the conduct of operations, two key principles instilled by Coningham into his staff were 'simplicity' and 'avoidance of detailed control'. At each Army–Air headquarters were two trailers: one for Air Intelligence, the other for Operations (in which were maintained maps showing the *recent* positions – with bomblines – of Allied and Axis land forces and the location of their airfields). No attempt was made to plot the *current progress* of operations or the actual state of squadrons, but a telephone switchboard enabled the Group Commander to discuss these matters if necessary either with Coningham or Kuter or his own subordinates. Most operations, Leigh-Mallory noticed, were mounted as part of a pre-arranged plan, involving fighters, fighter-bombers, reconnaissance aircraft and bombers, light or medium, although there were always men and aircraft available to deal with unexpected opportunities or setbacks. Army Liaison Officers supplied – and transmitted – military information and submitted special requests which were accepted or rejected at the Army–Air headquarters level, never lower.

Actual operations, however, were handled at the Fighter Group level, where the emphasis was on the passing of information rather than control: a principle which Leigh-Mallory wanted to see adopted in England. The Fighter Group Control Centre was admirably designed to permit everyone concerned to do his job as easily as possible. The Centre, he wrote, 'is mobile and consists of four vehicles sited to form a square over which a canvas awning is placed and in which is located an operations table and triangulator table. In addition, one extra vehicle, sited adjacent to the others, houses the Intelligence staff.' The concentration of all fighter, bomber and reconnaissance operations in one Centre was excellent. At the same time, he added, 'the criterion is not the number of squadrons which can be controlled in the air, but rather the number of airfields with which the Control Centre has to communicate and the distance at which they are located. Both in Tunisia and in the Western Desert it has been possible to concentrate the airfields in a small area and to site the operations room adjacent to it.'[15]

Elmhirst was naturally delighted to hear Coningham tell Leigh-Mallory that 'The whole of our Western Desert show, and this one, revolves round three people – myself, George Beamish and Tommy Elmhirst.' Writing home on 5 April, however, he confided that his task in Tunisia was harder than it had been in the Desert, where 'a wonderful team' – Tedder, Drummond, Pirie and Dawson – supported Coningham's air force from Cairo. The support provided from Algiers in the supply of new equipment or the speedy repair of old was nothing like so efficient. A week later, Elmhirst wrote:

> The general handling of things here by Alex and Mary has been, I think, beyond praise. It has been the coordination of all air forces that has done the trick in the air. The Hun is nearly out of the sky and we have pushed our airfields forward so that we can pound the docks, dumps and airfields of Tunis and Bizerta in daylight with our light bombers escorted by fighters. Also we can cover ᵣrom the air his sea routes from Sicily.

Kesselring, writing after the war, confirmed that 'ever-increasing enemy air attacks' were making the Axis struggle more difficult. Coningham 'was finding conditions more and more favourable, allowing him to make concentrated attacks over very short distances'.[16]

The Wadi Akarit position, north of the Mareth Line, was potentially very strong, but insufficiently fortified. Also, the defenders were short of ammunition and other supplies as a result of the premature stand too far forward at Mareth. Montgomery, as ever, planned a frontal assault, but Francis Tuker (Commander, 4th Indian Division) urged a wider attack in darkness, intended to take high ground to the west. The attack began at nightfall on 5 April, but the enemy had not waited for it. Excellent initial penetration was therefore made and reconnaissance on the morning of the 7th showed the enemy in retreat northwards along the coast road and north-eastwards from El Guettar on II Corps's front. That afternoon, patrols from the western and eastern armies met for the first time. Coningham's aircraft were able to strike continuously along the whole flank of the Axis retreat for 150 miles to Enfidaville, where the coastal plain narrows between hills and the sea, but he could not prevent the enemy reaching that refuge on 11 April, two days ahead of the 8th Army's leading troops. Montgomery had striven ruthlessly, wrote Ronald Lewin, until restrained by Alexander, 'to steal a march to Tunis, and many New Zealanders, Indians and British troops died to no purpose' under Axis fire. The two Axis armies were now linked in defence of a 100-mile arc from Enfidaville to Cape Serrat on the north coast. Short of everything and vastly outnumbered, the area now controlled was too small for further manoeuvre and air cover was practically at an end.[17]

Where should the knock-out blow be delivered? Eisenhower, urged by Bradley, pressed Alexander on 23 March to make the main effort in the north, in 1st Army's sector, and transfer Patton's II Corps to take part in it for the sake of American morale (in the United States as well as in Tunisia) and in order to gain experience for future campaigns. Alexander agreed and on 10 April directed Anderson (1st Army Commander) to prepare an attack for the 22nd. He also agreed that Patton should continue to operate independently, subject only to Alexander's direction, and reduced Montgomery's forces, telling him that his role would be subordinate because there was more room to deploy and supply troops in the north than in front of Enfidaville. The whole of II Corps, covered all the way by Coningham's airmen, moved north under Bradley's command: bumper-to-bumper, in perfect weather, entirely uncamouflaged, entirely unscathed. Patton returned to Morocco on 16 April to resume planning for the invasion of Sicily and Bradley advised him 'to button his lip' in future, 'to stop criticising Ike and the British', but it was wasted breath. 'For all Patton's bravado,' said Bradley, 'the American GI had yet to prove himself in combat. There had been many isolated noteworthy achievements and acts of valor, but on the whole we had merely learned to walk.'[18]

Alexander's plan, issued on 16 April, was for a four-pronged offensive: Montgomery to strike north at Enfidaville on the night of the 19th; the British 9 Corps to attack on the morning of the 22nd; the British 5 Corps, on its left, to make the main effort at nightfall on that day near Medjez el Bab; and II Corps to attack next day, the 23rd. Coningham's air blitz was to begin on the 19th. 'As well as visiting our own air units,' recalled Kuter, 'Mary and I spent much of our time visiting Anderson and Bradley and their senior staffs. Ordinarily, we travelled separately. One of us remained in our operations control center while the other was on liaison.' Kuter made sure that Bradley was told about major bombing and strafing attacks 'in support of other troops as well as his own'. James Robb (Spaatz's British Deputy) also visited Bradley, finding him 'most unimpressive'. In spite of a 'continuous procession' of Allied aircraft overhead, wrote Robb, the American General looked up every time, 'expecting to see German markings'. One of

Bradley's divisional commanders asked if Hurricanes could drop their long-range fuel tanks full. Robb asked why. They could be shelled and set on fire, he was told, and the fire would destroy mines and booby traps. 'My God' was Robb's only comment.[19]

Throughout the Axis occupation of Tunisia, the Allies had interrupted – with increasing effect – attempts to supply troops there by air or sea. Airborne supplies came from Naples via Sicily to Tunis or Bizerta and Coningham helped to organise systematic attacks on these air convoys from 5 April. A week later, when the Axis armies were penned behind the Enfidaville-Cape Serrat line, a desperate attempt began to supply them, using Me 323s. These huge machines, though able to carry four times the load of Ju 52s, proved even easier targets, despite the efforts of their fighter escorts. Broadhurst's Desert Air Force, located on landing grounds north of Sousse by the 16th, could reach them in the Gulf of Tunis. The campaign against Axis shipping and air convoys was greatly aided by Ultra intercepts and the RAF's radio intelligence service in revealing times of departure, proposed routes, escort strength and cargo carried. 'Mary Coningham was very, very clever at this,' recalled Pete Quesada, Deputy Commander of Coastal Air Force, 'and this Ultra information was a great help to him and to us.' Losses in this campaign, together with those suffered during the same winter of 1942–3 in attempting to supply the Germans trapped in Stalingrad, crippled German air transport for the rest of the war.

Coningham congratulated Broadhurst on his 'exhilarating success' against air convoys on Palm Sunday, 18 April. 'The Ju 52s are somewhat coarse game,' he wrote, 'but very valuable at present. I presume that the premium on the air passage over the Sicilian Channel is rising astronomically.' These words were widely reported and provoked a tart signal to Tedder from Churchill on the 20th: 'Highly-coloured accounts of the air battle were issued by correspondents from Algiers and also from Cairo, setting forth in unusual terms AM Coningham's commendation of AVM Broadhurst's action. It is improper that HM's Government should be left to learn from the press and radio the result of important operations.' Portal also signalled Tedder that day. 'I do not get anything from Coningham,' he said, 'nor, of course, from Spaatz to tell me how things are going as a whole or what ideas are running in their minds.' He therefore wanted 'an occasional appreciation' from Coningham as well as copies of his reports to Spaatz. 'As much local colour and interesting detail as possible should be included, as raw material for PM's statement, but message need not be long or elaborate.'[20]

On the Allied side, when the last (scheduled) offensive began, was a combat strength of over 300,000 men and 1,400 tanks. Total German strength along the Enfidaville-Cape Serrat arc was about 60,000 men with fewer than a hundred tanks. Even so, the attack faltered. Montgomery's strike was repulsed with heavy losses and the three other thrusts had been checked by 25 April. Anderson demonstrated yet again how little he understood the use of air power. Coningham had placed his entire air force and all the medium bombers loaned to him by Spaatz under Cross's operational control, whose headquarters lay beside Anderson's, but Anderson did not even consult Cross in making his plans. Montgomery shared Coningham's exasperation. Anderson, he wrote on 24 April, 'is not fit to command an Army in the field; everyone knows it, including his own Army'. Tunis did not fall until 7 May and Axis resistance lasted until the 13th. About 150,000 Germans were captured, fewer than the first exuberant claims, but much of southern Europe was left bare of experienced troops, although the Allied leaders did not realise this at the time. Consequently, with Tunisia very much in mind, they expected a long, hard fight in their next major operation, the invasion of Sicily. This expectation sharpened their fears and quarrels, which left bitter memories even though they would achieve a surprisingly easy victory.[21]

Harold Balfour, Under-Secretary of State for Air, had climbed to the top of Grenadier Hill with Coningham early on 6 May to watch the start of the final drive on Tunis and described what he saw in London three days later. 'I never realised what complete air superiority meant,' he said, 'until I saw this example of military and air movements carried out without the slightest attempt by enemy aircraft at interference.' Above each group of ten to twenty bombers, flying in tight formation, were fighter escorts. The bombers flew beyond the Allied artillery barrage, swung round towards their targets in a shallow dive, dropped their bombs and turned away, still in formation. Balfour counted 500 sorties before he had to leave at 11 am. The Desert Air Force, meanwhile, was attacking enemy airfields around Bizerta, to ensure that the bombers remained undisturbed except by ground fire. The air weapon, Balfour enthused, was being used 'not in penny packets but in full force at the right time on the right objective agreed to by the military and air commanders in their predetermined plan. Our armoured forces carried out their work able to look straight ahead and not upwards to see if they were menaced from the air.' Under such pressure, wrote Coningham, the enemy front finally collapsed. On 7 May, he recalled, an American General on the northern front 'was fighting hard and calling for air support, which could not be spared from the main drive, and on the 9th he was wondering how to control and feed 40,000 prisoners'.[22]

'Prisoners by the thousand,' wrote Elmhirst, after a day touring Tunis. He felt guilty about spending so long out of the office until he saw Alexander and Coningham, at ease in the former's white Rolls-Royce coupé, also sightseeing: 'Neither had said a word about such a trip at breakfast!' Coningham, said Elmhirst, greatly appreciated the Army Commander's invitation to join him in a tour of the troops; it made up for a similar tour promised by Montgomery after the capture of Tripoli, 'but at the last moment Monty set off on his triumphal tour alone!'[23]

Alexander, Coningham and Kuter had flown to Tunis in a Boston on 11 May, landing at El Aouina airfield: 'our first captured airdrome,' wrote Kuter, 'and I enjoyed the sensation of landing thereon in the first combat

154

airplane', even though the hangars and buildings were 'a tangled shambles'. Driving through Tunis, Kuter was impressed by 'the intact modern beauty of the city in contrast with the smashed debris of the waterfront resulting from true precision bombing'. He was also impressed by the German prisoners he saw: marching smartly, singing lustily and staring boldly back at the Allied commanders as they drove past. 'Although they had been bombed, strafed, shelled and pressed since 22 March,' he wrote, 'their individual morale was good and they clearly had not been whipped.'

Reluctantly, Kuter left for Washington on 13 May. A year later, he flew over Tunisia once more. 'There are no caravans on the hills west of Le Kef,' he wrote nostalgicly to Coningham on 18 May 1944, 'but their tracks are clearly visible. Even from the window of a plush-and-chrome C-54 en route from and to the Pentagon, those hills were inviting. At Gafsa I could not swear that the great store of heavy AA ammunition has not been depleted. The desert from Benghazi to Cairo is still thoroughly scarred by tank tracks and the occasional outline of an Advanced Landing Ground is still visible.'[24]

Kuter took with him to Washington a report that was, in fact, an indictment of the handling of air power during the Tunisian campaign before the reorganisation in February 1943. On 18 February, wrote Kuter, when effective use of air power began, Rommel's armour was in the Kasserine valley; two months later, it was backed into the Tunis plain and on 19 April Coningham's air force 'initiated the air phase of the final battle to capture Tunis and Bizerta. More conclusive proof of military effectiveness could not be exemplified.' It is clear, Kuter concluded, echoing Coningham,

> that a modern battle is not fought or won by a ground force alone or by a naval force alone. Any modern successful battle consists of a battle in the air which must be won before the surface battle is begun. If the air battle has been won, the surface forces are freed from effective hostile air attack and the offensive power of the free air force can be applied directly in support of the surface forces.

Kuter reached Washington on 18 May. Hitherto, as Major General Barney M. Giles told Arnold (Chief of the USAAF), most accounts of the Tunisian campaign had come from the viewpoint of II Corps. 'Naturally,' said Giles, 'the views of ground troops who have never been the spearhead for the main effort on the ground are quite different from the views of either the main effort people or the top ground or air commanders.' Kuter had been eager to have Alexander and Coningham invited to Washington to speak for themselves, but he soon realised, as he wrote to Spaatz on 25 May, that there was no need: the dramatic improvement in the performance of Allied arms after 18 February had impressed the War Department more effectively than any argument.[25]

'The Allied success was absolute,' admitted Kesselring in May 1948, and resulted in giving the enemy an impression of superiority . . . a handicap for further operations in the Mediterranean zone which ought not to be under-estimated. The loss of Tunisia following that of Tripolitania hit the Italian High Command and the Italian people particularly hard. With the burial of their colonial aspirations the danger increased to their Motherland, which so far had hardly known there was a war on.

The successful assault upon Sicily, followed by the invasion of that 'Motherland', would shortly end that happy ignorance.[26]

CHAPTER TWELVE

'Getting into Europe is no Light Task'

The Sicilian Campaign, May to August 1943

Between the end of one campaign and the start of another, Coningham was determined to relax and enjoy some comfort. While freezing in Ain Beida in February, he had foreseen that at least part of the summer must be spent in Tunisia and decided to locate and seize the best residence on the coast. This, he learned, was the Sebastian Villa at Hammamet, about forty miles south-east of Tunis. 'Tommy,' he reminded Elmhirst, 'we've been living hard in the desert for two years and we'll be living hard again when we go into Europe, but we're likely to have a spell in Tunisia and I mean to have the best establishment close to the Tunisian beaches that can be found – and we won't live on rations, but on the best the country can provide.' Early in May, therefore,

> he bullied me to go to General Alexander and get him to sign a piece of paper saying that when Hammamet was captured, the Sebastian Villa was to be reserved for Commander-in-Chief, Tactical Air Force. Alex looked a little sideways at me and my request, but signed and the paper was handed to Mary's aide and pilot, John Lancaster, with orders to go to Hammamet and stake the claim as the Germans moved out.

Lancaster did so, greatly to the annoyance of the senior officer of the advancing British troops, who was all set to move in.

'The Villa,' wrote Elmhirst, 'was a delight': Moorish exterior, modern interior; freshwater swimming pool and fragrant gardens sloping down to a sandy beach. Built by a Rumanian, he was told, who had married *two* wealthy American ladies and was currently imprisoned in the United States – not for bigamy, but for pro-Axis sympathies. The lounge was decorated in black and white, with snow leopard skins on the floor. There was no dining room, but a large black marble slab served as a dining table under arches at the side of the swimming pool. Coningham, Elmhirst and Lancaster moved

157

into private suites, but Beamish spurned such luxury and had his camp bed set up in a beach hut. James Robb was a frequent visitor, splashing about in the pool, relaxing on the beach and relishing, as in pre-war days, Coningham's flair for making a special occasion of a break from work and worry: his food and wine were always the best available, served with style in beautiful surroundings and washed down with plenty of cheerful conversation.

A veteran of many top-level conferences, Robb had a stock of striking remarks to offer on such occasions. Admiral Cunningham, for example, had solemnly intoned at one recent conference: 'Everything at sea is pursuing its usual course,' to which Eisenhower replied: 'You mean you've had *another* ship torpedoed?' General Brooke, said Robb, had once asked: 'How do I know what I think until I've heard what I've got to say?' Doolittle described the morale of P-38 pilots as 'lower than a frog's posterior' and thought flying missions was 'the most fun I've ever had with my clothes on'. According to Robb's counting, Eisenhower's swearing record for a single conference was 32 'God dammits' and four 'Blast the bastards'. One day, an official artist turned up at the villa to draw Coningham, Elmhirst and Beamish, much to their amusement – and secret gratification. On 23 June, the *London Gazette* announced that Coningham had been made an Officer of the Legion of Honour with Croix de Guerre and a month later, on 27 July, he was made a Chief Commander in the Legion of Merit by President Roosevelt.

The villa attracted eminent guests during June, among them the King, the Prime Minister, the Foreign Secretary, a galaxy of Generals, Air Marshals 'and last but who shall say least,' wrote Elmhirst, 'Leslie Henson, Vivien Leigh, Dorothy Dickson and Beatrice Lillie'. Coningham, ever an imaginative host, set himself to produce for his guests the best meals and entertainment the area could provide. He encouraged the local mayor to go out fishing and to retrieve bottles of a special vintage buried for the duration of the German occupation. 'Our royal visit,' Elmhirst recalled,

> was a memorable one and I think we gave the King the relaxation he was in need of. He certainly enjoyed the bathing and the good food and the ENSA party we collected to entertain him after the evening meal. I remember being told by the equerries who were exhausted and going to bed early that I was to ensure that the monarch went to bed by 11 pm. The monarch had other ideas and at 1 am was still swapping stories with Leslie Henson while our young air force commanders were entirely happy with the company of the three ladies. Vivien Leigh's curtsy to HM on being presented that evening was unforgettable.

For all their comfortable quarters, they worked early and late, though Coningham was adamant that they should not work after noon on Sundays and sent Lancaster into Tunis to collect ENSA celebrities or French generals' daughters to be their guests. Mervyn Mills – then a Flight Lieutenant and Coningham's Camp Commandant at La Marsa (near Tunis), later an official historian of the Tunisian Campaign – thought very highly of Coningham, who had earned the respect of his men for his own achievements as a pilot during and after the First World War, for his shrewd tactics in the Second and most of all for never squandering airmen's lives. Any luxuriating at Hammamet – and such as there was grew greatly in the envious reports of men who were never there – was richly deserved after years of hard labour in the Desert and in Tunisia. Coningham, in Mills's opinion, 'had an endearing man-to-man approach and the sensitivity of the "artist in action" to the horrors of modern warfare' as he would shortly observe them in such beautiful, historic lands as Sicily and Italy.[1]

On 26 June, Larry Kuter – now Assistant Chief of Air Staff, Plans, at USAAF Headquarters in Washington – wrote to Coningham.

> You will be surprised and Tooey [Spaatz] will be amazed, at an official statement of War Department doctrine which is now being prepared for 'restricted' publication. It is based squarely on the statement, in capital letters, to the general effect that Air Forces and Ground Forces will work coordinately and coequally, neither subordinated to the other. More people were defeated in Tunisia than Germans and Italians.

Kuter sent copies of this 'extraordinary document' to Spaatz and Cannon on 2 July: 'Remember,' he said, 'that this is not an ordinary Field Manual designed for the general guidance, etc., but is a very special Field Service Regulation intended to be binding on American Forces.' That manual, said General William Momyer, 'was really the emancipation proclamation' of tactical air power, setting out in unequivocal terms the priority of missions: first, to gain and maintain air superiority; second, to isolate the battlefield; and third, to support the ground forces.[2]

Meanwhile, a meeting had been held in Algiers on 29 April to consider changes proposed by Montgomery to Operation Husky, the plan for invading Sicily. 'Essence of his objections,' recorded Harry Butcher (Eisenhower's naval aide), 'was that his part in Husky had to be so strong his risk of defeat would be nil.' Tedder and Admiral Cunningham, Commander-in-Chief Mediterranean, wanted priority given to the capture of airfields, but Montgomery disagreed. 'Ike sides with Air and Navy viewpoints,' wrote Butcher, but 'Monty is riding a wave of popular acclaim and seems to think he can't be wrong.' Oliver Leese (Commander, 30 Corps) appeared on behalf of Montgomery, who now began a practice that would become notorious by the war's end of ducking meetings with his fellow commanders. When the airfield question arose, Tedder interrupted Leese and said (according to Patton): 'Really, gentlemen, I don't want to be difficult, but I am profoundly moved. Without the capture of these airports, the operation is impossible.' Argument raged for nearly three hours. At last, it was suggested that Coningham visit Montgomery. 'Fine,' said Tedder, 'it will be good for Monty to hear his master's voice.' Clearly, the rift between Tedder and

Coningham had now healed. Over lunch, Tedder told Patton: 'It is bad form for officers to criticise each other, so I shall.' Montgomery, he said, 'is a little fellow of average ability who has had such a build-up that he thinks of himself as Napoleon – he is not.'[3]

That build-up owed much to a Captain Geoffrey Keating, met by Butcher when he tricked his way into Eisenhower's residence in Algiers on 3 June with a couple of photographers. Butcher wrote:

> Keating disclosed that he is the personal press agent of General Montgomery. Said he eats in the General's mess, knows all the plans and personally supervised the photographic units. He was responsible, he said, for *Desert Victory*, the film that has created such a popular impression of Montgomery in America. He said England had no hero, so he set out to make one and Montgomery was now 'it'.

Butcher was unimpressed. Men should not, he thought, be led to believe they were fighting merely to make a big shot of their General. Still, the highball given Keating was well invested because it led him to blab about the methods he used to impress the world with Montgomery's prowess and importance. 'These are typical of Hollywood, and to me stink,' Butcher concluded. Keating's boasts have been confirmed by Nigel Hamilton, Montgomery's authorised biographer.[4]

Tedder wrote to Portal on 5 May:

> The Husky/Monty affair has not been a very happy business and has, I'm afraid, rather debunked both Alex and Monty. In our first meeting to discuss Monty's proposal, Alex put up a show which was really pitiful. He seemed quite incapable of discussing the naval and air implications of Monty's 'plan' and had no word to explain his complete *volte face* regarding the original plan with which he had fully agreed . . . Monty's showing has been no better. Having put up his 'plan', which completely ignored the air aspect, and having been rather off-hand when Coningham put the air aspect to him, he came up here with the present plan and made great play with the air aspect and the need for immediate capture of the airfields.

Such 'gymnastics', added Tedder, have their humour, but do nothing for the reputation of British generals with the Americans.[5]

By contrast, Coningham was on excellent terms with most American Generals, Auby Strickland in particular. 'Whenever I am asked how the British and Americans get along,' wrote Lewis Brereton on 1 June, 'I recall the Strickland-Coningham answer. I don't know which one originated it. Their stories are the same, but sound differently according to which man is talking – Strickland in his Alabama drawl or Coningham in his combination British–New Zealand accent.' According to Coningham, Strickland 'toddles over to my tent in the desert and I inquire; "How are you this lovely morning, old boy?" He says: "Ripping, old chap." And I say: "What about a spot of gin?" Strickland answers: "Naturally, old topper." I produce a bottle of gin and he produces a can of grapefruit juice. That's how the British and the Americans get along.' Eisenhower himself thought highly of Coningham. 'He is impulsive, quick, earnest and sincere,' wrote Eisenhower on 11 June. 'He knows his job and, under the British system of cooperation, performs it well.'[6]

Tedder would control all air operations during Husky from a Command Post at La Marsa, on the coast north-east of Tunis. Spaatz and Coningham, together with the American commander of the heavy bombers (Doolittle) and the British commander of the coastal aircraft (Lloyd), therefore set up their headquarters nearby. Alexander's new headquarters, 15th Army Group, were also at La Marsa. Coningham's command (comprising Broadhurst's Desert Air Force, the 12th ASC under Major General Edwin House and Sinclair's Tactical Bomber Force) would be responsible for direct support to the Anglo-American assault troops. Alexander and Coningham would be in Malta at the time of the invasion. Keith Park (AOC Malta) would control operations from Malta, under Coningham's direction, until sufficient bases were seized in Sicily for Broadhurst and House to assume local control, the former concentrating on support for Montgomery's 8th Army, the latter on support for Patton's 7th Army. Sinclair would arrange escorted bombing raids by day and in moonlight from North African bases.[7]

During May, before Husky began, it was decided to capture the Italian-held islands of Pantelleria and Lampedusa, ideally placed to interfere with communications between Tunisia and Malta, the assault-base for Husky. Pantelleria had a large airfield within easy range of western Sicily, while aircraft based in Lampedusa, some ninety miles farther south and about the same distance west of Malta, would be able to assist with convoy protection. Seizure of these islands would also permit the installation of radar and navigation aids and air–sea rescue bases and deprive the enemy of these advantages. Coningham, however, found it hard to take the massive air–sea bombardment planned by Spaatz seriously and Spaatz, stung by some light-hearted remarks, sent Robb to tell him that 'he should correct his attitude'. The bombardment of Pantelleria began on 7 June. British troops landed on the 11th and garrisons there and in Lampedusa promptly surrendered. More than 11,000 prisoners were taken and the sole British casualty was a soldier bitten by a mule!

Nevertheless, the operation was grossly over-rated by Spaatz who wrote at length about it to Arnold in Washington. Useful as Pantelleria and Lampedusa were, Coningham was much more concerned with the fact that the beaches chosen for the assault on Sicily lay in the south-east corner of the island (between Licata in the west and Cassibile in the east, a distance of about 100 miles), at extreme range from his fighter bases in Tunisia. Early in June, he sent the Spitfire wings of 242 Group and the Desert Air Force to

6. The Sicilian and Italian Campaigns, 1943–4

Malta, a total of twenty squadrons. These filled Park's existing airfields to capacity, but a new airfield was constructed on Gozo (near Malta) for American Spitfires and by the end of June Coningham had brought into use a dozen airfields (either newly-built or improved) on the Cap Bon Peninsula, the nearest point to Sicily.[8]

The Husky air plan exhibited in even more perfect form than in the Tunisian Campaign the four merging phases of air action: to neutralise the enemy air force, to destroy his communications, to isolate the expected battlefield and to give direct support to ground forces. The plan also included support of naval operations, convoy cover, airborne landings, protection of base and rear areas against air attack and ample air–sea rescue. During May and June, however, complaints arose from Army and Navy commanders about the plan's alleged vagueness, but Tedder's attitude, warmly seconded by Coningham, was: 'Tell us what you want done and we'll deliver – in our own way.' This attitude, however justifiable in military terms, was mistaken in human terms. Neither Tedder nor Coningham appeared to realise that ground commanders needed more than lofty assurances that 'it would be alright on the night'. 'Even when pressed,' wrote Bradley, 'they would tell us nothing about how they would support our landings . . . It would have been immensely comforting to know positively that our massive air power would be overhead to help us if we needed it.'[9]

On the other hand, recorded Butcher on 13 July, 'Ike spoke vigorously to Patton about the inadequacy of his reports of progress reaching headquarters at Malta . . . we were unable to determine just what assistance, particularly in the air, he needed.' Despite their Tunisian experience, both British and American ground commanders remained unwilling to accept that aircraft might usefully be employed out of sight of frontline troops. For Patton, in particular, arguments over the air plan's merits or defects were quite beside the point. He flatly refused to accept that Coningham – or even an American airman – could exercise a legitimate, independent authority on the battlefield; aircraft, in his view, were flying tanks, subject to the orders of the senior soldier. The work of the air planners was complicated by numerous changes made to the overall plan by soldiers and sailors and by the markedly different methods of the British and American services. Even so, their major objective – the destruction of the Axis air forces in the air and on the ground – was achieved and, in consequence, soldiers and sailors suffered little interference from aircraft, despite Bradley's assertion that the 'air support provided us on Sicily was scandalously casual, careless and ineffective'. What *was* scandalous, from start to finish of the Sicilian Campaign, was the readiness with which Allied gunners, Army and Navy, fired on sight at all aircraft, thus causing numerous avoidable casualties to Allied airmen.[10]

Elmhirst wrote on 7 July:

We hope to keep the ships and beaches free from interference by enemy airmen, but our bases are all sixty miles or more from the beaches and we have hardly enough bases within range to keep an air umbrella over the beaches every minute of the day. However, the heavy bombers have done great work lately, smashing every airfield in Sicily, so what is left of the Hun air force should not be large nor in the best of spirits.

But the 'big effort,' he recognised, must be made by sailors 'who have to put the soldiers ashore at the right place and then it is the soldiers who have to fight it out. I don't think anyone here underestimates the difficulties. Getting into Europe is no light task.' Operation Husky, beginning on 10 July, was the first major landing in the Second World War of seaborne troops against a fully-defended shore and air superiority was clearly essential. More than 4,000 aircraft ensured that superiority for the massive surface force employed: 160,000 men were landed in the first wave, with 600 tanks, 14,000 vehicles and nearly 2,000 guns. They were transported to Sicily by an Allied armada of 2,600 vessels under the command of Admiral Cunningham, who described Husky as 'the most momentous enterprise of the war' to that date because the Allies were 'striking for the first time at the enemy in his own land'.[11]

Because of 'the negative attitude' of the Italian authorities in Sicily, wrote Luftwaffe Colonel Christ in 1947–8, it proved impossible to prepare camouflaged landing strips away from established airfields to permit effective dispersal; every attempt met with 'energetic resistance from property owners who were afraid their land would be spoiled or damaged'. By 10 July, continued Christ, all the island's airfields 'were so destroyed in continuous attacks by massed forces that it was only possible to get this or that airfield in running order again for a short time'; promised reinforcements never arrived, the ground organisation broke down and 'dilatory behaviour' by the Italians on the mainland was a constant handicap. Kesselring often thought it would be easier to manage *without* Italian help, but he had problems even with his Germans: the leadership of the *Hermann Göring* Division under General Konrad 'was not fortunate' and although General Hube conducted the retreat skilfully, 'the Axis High Command had plenty of luck in every mishap. The extraordinarily regular behaviour of the Allied forces especially helped them; I used to count on that.'[12]

Coningham wrote to Park in Malta on 4 July, asking if he might arrive three days before D-Day, as he had to tag along with Alex. 'Am bringing a special bottle of mine,' he added, 'for us to drink to a spot of good luck.' He spent ten days in Malta, directing operations through Park before returning to La Marsa. 'Our feeling of strain here has lifted,' wrote Elmhirst on 15 July.

The invasion has, of course, gone far better than anyone of us here had dared to hope. The German air force might have ruined the whole show. There were literally thousands of ships as a target on their front door step such as they might have been waiting the whole war for and they could not take advantage. It shows to what straits their air force has come and to what extent they must be committed in Europe against our bombing offensive and the Russians.

On the 17th he added: 'We are now all congratulating ourselves' and rightly, with one exception: 'If we had had some control of the airborne effort, it might have gone far better with far less casualties. No-one is in closer touch with the frontline soldiers and knows the local situation – ground, sea and air – better than ourselves. We think that there were too many amateur enthusiasts controlling the airborne operation.'[13]

On 27 July, Coningham visited Montgomery to discuss plans for coming operations. They agreed to aim at isolating the enemy in the north-east corner of Sicily, stop supplies coming in and then, as land fighting intensified and better targets appeared, concentrate on the enemy army. Next day, they flew to Palermo to see Patton, who welcomed them exuberantly. 'The Americans,' wrote Montgomery, 'do not realise the need for a combined Army–Air plan and the airman is left out and hardly knows what is going on. What they really need is an Air Force; at present, their Air is part of their Army.' Coningham moved his headquarters to Cassibile, ten miles south of Syracuse, on 31 July. 'Mary has every intention of going home for a week once we are firmly established,' noted Elmhirst, 'and I will go with him. Fusing of RAF and US has been a *very* tricky job. Tedder has said *again* that he, Mary and I are likely to be at home before next Spring at the latest.'[14]

That 'fusing' was crumbling during July, as Butcher observed on the 17th. Tedder, he wrote, had taken 'active charge' and Spaatz had been 'virtually squeezed out of his job, yet the vast majority of all aircraft in the operation is American'. Spaatz, however, was attempting to ensure his personal control of US air units by creating a highly-secret communications network, known as *Redline*, manned exclusively by Americans and used to bypass Coningham. Officers were to be trained to take over at a moment's notice as soon as Spaatz got permission to separate his forces from those of the RAF. Eisenhower, deeply concerned to encourage American and British forces to work together, required Spaatz to act in fact, though not in name, as Tedder's Deputy. He had his say in overall strategic direction and continued to champion zealously the separation of those forces, but day-to-day operational control of Allied air power in the Mediterranean remained in Tedder's hands – and Coningham remained his principal instrument. 'Nationalism has reared its ugly head,' wrote Tedder to Portal on 7 August. The feeling was 'all underground' at present and sprang, he thought, 'from Spaatz himself and the little coterie of pleasant incompetents he keeps round him'. Tedder had done his best to build him up and let him run his own show, but 'he is a Dutchman and is full of the suspicions which one has found typical of Dutchmen and, moreover, suffers from a violent inferiority complex. One spends much of one's time and energy jollying him along – very wearing!'[15]

William Mitchell, an ai. man driver, recalled taking Coningham right across Sicily early in August – from Palermo, on the north-west coast, to Augusta, on the south-east – a distance of about 120 miles. Mitchell thought him 'a pleasant individual, who did not stand on ceremony'. In answer to his questions, Mitchell described enemy air raids, but drew attention 'to the complete freedom we had to drive on the roads in daylight', unlike Tunisia.

> Then I dropped a bombshell into Coningham's lap, but it was done in all innocence, as I just naturally assumed, like everyone else, that we would trap the enemy forces at Messina. I said: 'I suppose after what we were able to do at Pantelleria, the air forces will be able to stop the enemy forces from escaping across the Straits?' Coningham did not reply and I kept my face towards the road . . . After what must have been minutes he said: 'That's always been my intention.'

The car then suffered a puncture in the middle of nowhere and Mitchell had to repair it, having no spare wheel, while his passenger stood by, grimly silent. As it happened, Coningham already suspected that he would be unable to prevent an orderly evacuation.[16]

The battle area in Sicily remained Coningham's first priority, but flak in the Messina area was now practically prohibitive for all aircraft except heavy bombers at high levels. Broadhurst raised with Coningham on 3 August the problem of preventing an evacuation and Coningham replied next day. The night, he said, 'is our problem and though the increasing moon will help the air, only a positive physical barrier, such as the Navy can provide, would be effective. The difficulties of operating naval surface forces in the narrow part of the strait is obvious and I do not see how we can hope for the same proportion of success as at Cap Bon.' Nevertheless, he issued instructions. The enemy, he advised, might be expected to evacuate Sicily at any moment, using initially beaches between Milazzo to Taormina and later those close to Messina because of the short crossing and intense flak which he could provide in such a restricted area.[17]

The Allied land forces did not press the enemy closely enough to prevent them withdrawing most of their men; the naval forces would not risk the loss of large vessels by bringing them into the confined waters of the strait; and the air forces did not employ their full tactical power, let alone their full strategic bombing force. The Allied High Command had not foreseen an opportunity to prevent a massive evacuation and took too long to accept that it had begun. As late as 4 August, the Allied Joint Intelligence Committee found 'no sign that the enemy intends an evacuation of Sicily and there is evidence that reinforcements still continue to reach the island'. It was not until 10.10 pm on 14 August that Alexander, having discounted 8th Army warnings for nearly a week, at last advised Tedder that an evacuation really seemed to have started.[18]

In fact, the Germans considered Sicily lost by the 7th and orders were issued next day to prepare a planned withdrawal across the strait. Operation *Lehrgang* began on 11 August and continued until the early hours of the 17th. During that time, ferries and landing craft (using four routes across the strait) carried at least 40,000 men, 10,000 vehicles and tanks and 15,000 tons of equipment to the mainland. It was a well-planned operation, carried out with great skill and courage, under the protection of formidable flak defences on both sides of the strait as well as aboard the ferries themselves. Thousands of Italian troops were also successfully evacuated with their heavy equipment in a separate operation under Italian control. Although *Luftflotte 2* was unable to protect the hard-pressed troops from the air, wrote Colonel Christ, it was able to set up 'an extremely effective anti-aircraft defence at least over the Strait of Messina. By concentrating all anti-aircraft forces that were in any way suitable from the whole of Italy, thereby recklessly depriving airfields and industrial installations, a cover of some 400 guns was set up over the Strait of Messina which beat off every raid by the Allied air force,' thus permitting a successful evacuation.[19]

Coningham chose not to use Doolittle's heavy bombers to impede the evacuation. Heavy bombers, in his opinion, were not an efficient 'battlefield weapon' and he preferred to see them reserved for their 'proper' role: attacks upon industrial plants, military bases or transport systems in Italy. Constant, heavy bombing of access roads and landing places might have stopped the movement of material and delayed that of troops, but it was next to impossible, as Admiral Ruge pointed out, 'even with exceptionally heavy attacks, to knock out enough ferries and landing places to block the traffic effectively'. The absence of persistent daytime bombing persuaded the Germans and Italians to shift most operations to daytime, but even at night they suffered few losses. Although British destroyers were frequently seen at the southern entrance to the strait, they rarely ventured further. Torpedo boats and gun boats, operating from Augusta, made brave efforts to interfere with the evacuation, but were usually thwarted by searchlights and shore batteries. The Navy's main armament was not used. From dusk on 29 July to dusk on 17 August, only one-quarter of nearly 10,000 sorties flown by bombers or fighter-bombers of the entire Mediterranean Air Command were directed at targets in the strait; few attacks were pressed home over the most sensitive areas, for total losses amounted to no more than thirty-one aircraft in those nineteen days.[20]

As early as 3 August, Alexander had signalled Tedder and Admiral Cunningham to inform them that the Germans were preparing a withdrawal to the mainland. 'We must be in a position to take immediate advantage of such a situation by using a full weight of Naval and Air power. You have no doubt coordinated plans to meet this contingency.' Tedder and Cunningham, in fact, had done nothing of the sort, as Alexander probably knew perfectly well. Neither he nor they, nor any other commander in any of the services, had hitherto given this problem a moment's serious thought. It would be unjust to say that they took 'no thought for the morrow', but they were guided by the rest of St Matthew's advice: 'Sufficient unto the day is the evil thereof.' The sight of Germans moving backwards was rare enough in 1943 to give widespread satisfaction and they were tenacious fighters even in apparently hopeless circumstances, as Tunisia had already shown and the rest of the war would abundantly confirm. The Allies gladly accepted any victory in those days and the official historians of British Intelligence, reflecting at their leisure many years later, pronounced it still an 'open question' whether the evacuation could have been prevented.[21]

As soon as Coningham and Admiral Cunningham realised the strength of Axis defences in the strait, they decided against an all-out, hastily improvised effort in sky and waters where fearful casualties were certain. On 11 August, however, Coningham told Tedder that there were as yet no signs of substantial evacuation movements by day. If it begins, he added, 'we can handle it with our own resources and naval assistance'. He was lucky not to be haunted by these careless words, for the evacuation – beginning that very day – quickly confirmed his earlier fears that neither he nor Cunningham could 'handle' it.

Reflecting on this campaign in February 1946, Coningham naturally emphasised its positive aspects: 'Fighting proceeded so successfully,' he wrote, 'that within forty days the campaign was over.' Among the 'new experiences' he identified and found repeated in later campaigns was the fact that the Germans, fighting without air support, eagerly sought protection in numerous villages which therefore suffered severe damage by aircraft during the rest of the war. 'We found also,' he concluded, 'that our own forces could be seriously delayed and impeded by the results of our own bombing and finally, the escape of a large number of the enemy at Messina proved that a density of flak can be provided so lethal that air attack can be held off sufficiently to maintain communications.'[22]

CHAPTER THIRTEEN

'A Grand Time in the Air'

Coningham in Italy, August 1943 to January 1944

Although so closely linked in time and space, the conquest of Sicily and the invasion of Italy were widely separated in terms of strategy. The former ended a struggle to clear the enemy from Africa and open the Mediterranean to Allied shipping, the latter opened a struggle which saw the invasion of North-west Europe and the destruction of Nazi Germany. The Mediterranean, hitherto the primary theatre, now became secondary and once the Allies were securely established in southern Italy, the thoughts of Coningham and his fellow commanders dwelt increasingly on their hopes for exciting new appointments in England. Meanwhile, they all had plenty of fresh challenges to meet.

Not until campaigns began in Sicily and Italy did Coningham face an enemy with a well-developed communications network, though by then the Luftwaffe was weakening rapidly. Consequently, these campaigns were the most serious test so far posed in the war of what medium bombers and fighter-bombers (as opposed to heavy bombers) could do to enemy lines of supply. Upon which targets should Coningham concentrate? Which types of aircraft would hit them most effectively? How best should these aircraft approach them? Lessons learned here would be applied in North-west Europe in 1944–5. Did Coningham believe that road and rail bridges were better targets than, for example, marshalling yards and rolling stock? The former, if destroyed, took much longer to repair and (because there were so many of them) were less well defended by anti-aircraft fire. Medium bombers and fighter-bombers seemed capable of taking on these targets. However, marshalling yards (being so extensive and amply provided with anti-aircraft defence) were perhaps best left to heavy bombers. Coningham pondered these questions continually during his last months in the Mediterranean and was also able to profit from reports of further experience in Italy during the first five months of 1944.[1]

Just as planning for Operation Husky had been hampered by the fact that key officers actively engaged against the enemy in Tunisia, so planning for operations Avalanche (an Anglo-American assault upon Salerno) and Baytown (a British assault upon the Italian 'toe') was hampered by the need to complete the conquest of Sicily. Responsibility for detailed air plans was delegated to Coningham's headquarters for Avalanche and to Broadhurst's for Baytown; Sinclair's Tactical Bomber Force, based in Sicily, would assist both. But Montgomery's demands for Baytown, as Tedder told Portal on 7 August, 'were such as to put Avalanche right out of court' if accepted. Moreover, the Italian 'toe' was an 'absolutely ideal' target from a German viewpoint: encouraging Montgomery to make a typically pedestrian advance, throwing away all the advantages offered by command at sea and in the air and ending any prospect of striking at Germany by air from Italian bases before winter set in. Eisenhower agreed with Tedder, but was reluctant to press either Montgomery or Alexander. 'I have signalled privately to Coningham,' Tedder ended, 'asking him if he can manage for Monty to be "inspired" to make alternative proposals which will make Avalanche possible. We've managed to work the oracle before, but I'm not very hopeful this time.'[2]

Even though Coningham had much else on his mind – in particular, the effort that he could or should ask of his air crews to disrupt the evacuation of Sicily – he summoned up yet again the energy needed to massage Montgomery's ever-inflating ego. Three days later, helped by Coningham's efforts, the decision was taken to make a maximum effort at Salerno and not across the strait. Coningham was now anxious to see his wife Nan in August if he could, and he was, in any case, very much in need of a break from responsibility. Cassibile, moreover, was proving to be the most uncomfortable of all his wartime headquarters. It was too far from the sea, too hot and several members of his hard-pressed staff, notably the hitherto indestructible Elmhirst, succumbed to illness there. Coningham packed him off to rest at the villa in Hammamet on 19 August and two days later he himself escaped to England (for nine days), having just received a most welcome letter of congratulations from Lord Trenchard for his achievements in Sicily: you must have had 'a tremendously hot time,' he wrote, but no details were yet known in London. As for Elmhirst, his Mediterranean service was over and he flew to England on 19 September: 'The parting was made much easier by Chief Tedder telling me just before I left that as soon as I was fit I was earmarked for the same job, again under Mary, in the 2nd Tactical Air Force now getting together in England, preparatory to the invasion of the Continent from Britain next spring.'[3]

On 22 August, Montgomery found time to select his team to win the war. Alexander, he decided, should command it and 'I believe that I am necessary to Alex'. Tedder must have a place, as 'a very brilliant airman on the big strategic side' who was also 'a delightful person' and Broadhurst should be his tactical assistant. 'Some would advocate Mary Coningham,' wrote Montgomery, 'but he is a dangerous man, being of a highly jealous nature and not to be trusted to "pull" in the team; he is out for himself.' On the naval side, Montgomery chose Ramsay (not Cunningham, who had disagreed sharply with Montgomery over his Baytown proposals) and wanted a place found for Mountbatten, who had influence in high places. With such fancies did Montgomery beguile his leisure hours. Not content with leading his own army, this champion of teamwork had tried hard to take control of the entire campaign in Sicily and, thanks to Alexander's ineffectuality, succeeded well enough (in Michael Howard's words) 'to cause confusion, unnecessary delay and much bad blood'. Disapproving of the plans for invasion of the mainland, added Howard, 'he then sulked, Achilles-like, in Calabria and allowed the Salerno landings to risk disaster'.[4]

Resenting the fact that Eisenhower had assigned him a supporting role in the first invasion of mainland Europe, Montgomery took even longer than usual to get ready. Operation Baytown therefore did not begin until dawn on 3 September, days later than his fellow commanders had hoped. The crossing of the strait was easy, air cover ample, opposition negligible, progress stately. Operation Avalanche (commanded by Lieutenant General Mark Clark) was an altogether larger, more complex undertaking and began six days later, in the early hours of the 9th. Coningham controlled all tactical air units and Broadhurst handled air support for the 8th Army, assisted by some of Sinclair's medium bombers. Coningham could also call (through Tedder's Command Post at La Marsa) for heavy bombers if necessary. Edwin House (Commander, 12th ASC) was responsible for fighter and fighter-bomber cover of the Salerno landings, helped by the rest of Sinclair's bombers and Fleet Air Arm fighters, operating from aircraft carriers accompanying the invasion fleet. That fleet was protected by Hugh Lloyd (Coastal Air Force) and Keith Park (Malta). These air forces far outnumbered their German opponents, the Italians having surrendered on the 8th – news which aroused less enthusiasm among Allied forces in Sicily than it did in the United States and Britain. Both countries, wrote Harry Butcher, were in for a 'serious letdown' when they realised that Italy's surrender would not stop the Germans from fighting hard there all winter.[5]

For the attack upon Salerno, recalled Coningham in February 1946, a complete break with past practice was accepted. Before Operation Husky, a distance of fifty to eighty miles ahead of Allied lines had been thought as much as fighters could cover, but a great increase in air power – together with a great decline in enemy air power – now enabled him to accept the hazard of covering a landing by a large force 180 miles from base. Coningham followed his well-tested three-pronged tactics: intended to defeat the Luftwaffe in the air and on the ground; to impede the movement of enemy reinforcements and supplies to the battle area; and to provide Allied soldiers with close support. The main danger to those soldiers came some days *after* their landing when the enemy, despite aerial attack, had gathered greater strength than the invaders yet had ashore and attempted to push them back into the sea. Although airstrip construction had begun at once and an excellent aerodrome was captured at Montecorvino, little use could be made of them during the most critical days – 13–15 September – because of German artillery fire. The bravery and resolution of the Allied soldiers, aided by the timely arrival of paratroops, naval gunfire and intensive bombing, day and night, repelled what an official RAF historian called 'a highly dangerous, mathematically timed, elaborate and impressive attack, which shook the Allied system to its foundations'.[6]

'It is of the utmost importance,' Alexander told Montgomery, 'that you maintain pressure upon the Germans so that they cannot remove forces from your front and concentrate them against Avalanche,' but Montgomery refused to hurry and actually stopped moving altogether for no better reason, admitted Nigel Hamilton (his authorised biographer) than 'to make Alexander pay for his mistakes,' as Montgomery saw them. Not only did he wait to see the outcome of the fighting at Salerno, he then falsely claimed credit for saving a situation already under control by the time his forces arrived, late as usual. After the crisis on the fourth day of the invasion, wrote Coningham, when heavy bombing stopped a dangerous counter-attack, all went well and steady progress was made until winter weather arrived. He had frequently warned his Army colleagues that this would seriously reduce air support: 'German armies,' he said, 'had learned to fight without air support and our ground forces should be ready to do the same when flying was impracticable.'[7]

Without the advantage of tactical surprise, the beachhead at Salerno had been stormed, won, almost lost, established and extended. By 1 October, the prime tasks of Baytown and Avalanche had been achieved. Three excellent ports (Naples, Bari, Taranto) and well-equipped airfields at Foggia and Naples were in Allied hands. The Germans had suffered heavy losses in men and material. The air forces' contribution had been vital in ending the last remnants of Italian will to fight on, in nullifying German air reconnaissance, in protecting the assembly, convoying and landing of invasion troops and in halting a fierce counter-offensive.[8]

Having sweated through the critical days at Salerno, Coningham was able to inform Tedder on the evening of the 16th that Clark's Anglo-American forces had switched to the offensive, linking up with the 8th Army under the cover of aircraft able at last to use Montecorvino safely as well as several temporary airstrips. Coningham now had time for less urgent problems. Grahame Dawson, for example, had written to say that he was still seeking him a twin-engined aeroplane and 'a car as big as those used by the American commanders'. These were perks that Coningham relished, although imposing offices did not interest him. On 26 September, he ruled that the best rooms in his new headquarters at San Spirito in Bari (a major port on the Adriatic coast) were to go to his senior staff and administration officers; Joe Cannon (his Deputy) was to be considered next and he himself would make do with a smaller room. 'The organisation of the building,' he said, 'is to be based on the importance of 'the machine working' and not on any question of seniority insofar as General Cannon and I are concerned.'[9]

Next day, 27 September, Coningham sent a stiff letter to Spaatz concerning a dispute which began when Cannon reported to Coningham 'his great concern' that 12th ASC was dealing direct with Spaatz's headquarters 'on certain operational requests'. Even after Cannon reminded House (Commander, 12th ASC) and Spaatz's, headquarters of the correct procedure to follow, Spaatz had personally given House direct instructions and then told Coningham that he intended to continue doing so. 'Both Cannon and I,' wrote Coningham, 'explained how wrong this arrangement would be and the confusion that would result. Spaatz having agreed, Coningham was therefore surprised to learn of his latest improper intervention and formally warned Spaatz that he would not accept another such incident:

> Either my exercise of command is satisfactory, or it is not. In the latter case, the remedy is to change. But as commander, I cannot be responsible for the force and at the same time have my superior headquarters cut across and undermine my authority. This leaves me no alternative but to request to be relieved and that would not only be deplorable in this happy and closely integrated force, but to me personally would be a disastrous act. I feel so strongly on the matter, however, that it would be my duty.[10]

Coningham sent copies of this letter and several signals to Tedder, knowing that he would support his brusque rebuke of Spaatz. Neither British commander had any regard for Spaatz's professional abilities – an opinion Portal shared and conveyed to Trenchard when advising him what lines to follow during a proposed visit to the United States: 'Soft-pedal as hard as you can on Spaatz,' wrote Portal on 8 November. 'Of course, you cannot tell them he is no good, but perhaps you can suggest that others are better.' Trenchard's words evidently fell on stony ground because Spaatz would be given command of the US Strategic Air Forces for Operation Overlord, the invasion of Normandy. On 10 December, however, Tedder's Mediterranean Air Command became Mediterranean Allied Air Forces by absorbing Spaatz's command (North-west African Air Forces) and RAF Middle East in Egypt. The Tactical, Strategic and Coastal commands of Coningham, Doolittle and Lloyd at last lost their 'North-west African' prefixes and formally became what they had long been: 'Mediterranean Allied'.[11]

Early in October, Portal intended that Keith Park should move from Malta to replace Coningham when the latter went to England, but Tedder demurred: 'We must now give the Americans their turn,' he told Portal on the 15th, and Cannon was 'good, sound, and now, experienced'. Cannon had done very well as Coningham's Deputy, added Tedder two days later, and now had more practical experience of air support to the Army than

173

anyone else available. Coningham, Alexander and Broadhurst all thought highly of him.

Tedder wrote:

> Up to the present this business has been kept too much in the hands of two or three people and we have not been spreading the experience wide enough. This, of course, is largely my fault, but I feel it was inevitable, since when we came over from Middle East at the beginning of the year, it was only the fact that Coningham, Beamish, etc., had had experience and been successful which made it possible for them to lead the Americans the right way.

As for current operations, he continued, Montgomery and Clark 'have been quite firm in stamping on anyone who showed a tendency to bellyache' about enemy air activity, of which there was little. On the other hand, the Air was providing ample direct support to the ground forces by interrupting communications, preventing or breaking up concentrations and disrupting counter-attacks before they could be launched. 'When one compares our own crowded and unimpeded lines of communication,' he ended, 'with the enemy L of C which we attack day and night from the Brenner to the front line, one cannot but sympathise with Eisenhower's reliance on the Air as one of the major factors in the land battle.' On 18 October, however, Tedder learned from Coningham that the growth of German strength in country easy to defend was worrying Alexander: without the means for a flank attack, 'he saw no reason why we should ever get to Rome'. The German ability to resist successfully without air support impressed Coningham, although he pointed out that rain and cloud frequently handicapped his airmen and he doubted whether the Germans could mount an offensive of their own.[12]

On 22 October, Churchill forbade Sir Archibald Sinclair (Secretary of State for Air) to make any changes in the Mediterranean air commands until the senior appointments to Operation Overlord had been decided. 'The movement of Air Marshal Coningham to Overlord cannot even be considered,' ruled Churchill, 'before Rome is taken. I am, however, not at all inclined to move him from the Mediterranean theatre since he is so closely linked with Alexander, who will need him, and all the more if Spaatz became Chief of the Air' in that theatre, for Churchill agreed with Portal, Tedder and Coningham that Spaatz had little capacity for high command. Happily, rumours of Churchill's ruling had reached neither Dawson nor Coningham when they corresponded early in November. 'A little bird told me,' wrote Dawson on the 1st, 'that you would soon be making a big jump to new fields of action where I know you will continue your success until you end up in the vanguard at the final showdown, where we hope all our troubles may end and real peace for the world dawn again.' 'I hear that I am expected to leave here some time in December,' replied Coningham on the 7th, 'to go to

England to take over the Tactical Air Force at home. There is no confirmation of this report and therefore it is extremely confidential and not to be talked about at the moment.'[13]

Coningham wrote to 'My dear Tommy' Elmhirst (then in England) from Bari on 2 November. Harry Broadhurst had just returned from England, he said, 'and reports you on the job in TAF with George [Beamish] doing some important Army/Air work.' Broadhurst had also reported a tendency for 'people at home' to resent replacement by Mediterranean experts, but where else was operational experience available? 'I understand I am to go home in December (Chief says New Year) to take over TAF' Coningham continued, and he and Nan proposed to have 'a one room flat in Town', although they would welcome Elmhirst's advice about that and about accommodation in Bracknell or wherever TAF Headquarters was located. Joe Cannon was to take over in Italy and have an RAF Deputy. 'We are having a grand time in the air,' Coningham told Elmhirst, but 'the Army will be slow and I fear Rome will not be reached until next year. It's a shame, but the tap was turned off the ship supply too soon and the momentum went.' He liked the new Lady Tedder, a Scottish widow whom Tedder had married a week earlier and taken off to Coningham's villa at Hammamet for a brief honeymoon. During the coming year, she and Nan would become good friends – a friendship that encouraged Tedder, as Eisenhower's Deputy, to stand as resolutely by Coningham in North-west Europe as he always had in the Mediterranean.[14]

On the afternoon of 2 December, Coningham held a press conference in Bari, assuring everyone that the Germans had been defeated in the air. 'I would regard it as a personal affront and insult,' he declared, 'if the Luftwaffe should attempt any significant action in this area.' He used these foolish words in spite of the fact that German bombers operating from northern Italy had attacked the Naples port area four times in November and carried out successful raids on other Mediterranean targets. Bari, moreover, as he knew better than anyone, lacked any real defence. The American heavy bombers based there were of no defensive use and no RAF fighter squadrons were based at Bari. Those fighters within range had escort or offensive duties; none were assigned to port defence. Ground defences were neither adequate nor efficiently organised. Within a few hours of ending his press conference, Coningham was visiting improvised hospitals all over Bari, offering what words of comfort he could to victims of the worst shipping disaster suffered by the Allies since Pearl Harbor.

At 7.25 pm, two or three German aircraft had circled the harbour at 10,000 feet, dropping numerous small tinfoil strips to confuse the signals received by ground radars. They also dropped flares, though these were hardly needed for the harbour was working at full pressure and there were lights everywhere. Consequently, during the next hour a hundred Ju 88 aircrews enjoyed the time of their lives. Fourteen merchant ships laden with over 34,000 tons of cargo were destroyed, three more carrying 7,500 tons were sunk (but later salvaged) and six others were damaged. A bulk petrol pipe was pierced, several serious fires started and the port closed for three weeks, with serious effects on land–air operations; it would not be fully restored until February. A subsequent inquiry exonerated Coningham, but found that the absence for some time of aerial attacks had given rise to a feeling of complacency in the whole area and generous tribute was paid to the skill and bravery of the German airmen responsible for the 'best and most cleverly executed raid yet experienced', in the judgment of one senior RAF officer.[15]

One of the Allied ships destroyed had been carrying 540 tons of mustard gas in the form of 100-pound bombs. That ship, the *John Harvey*, was hit and exploded. Many of the bombs broke open, releasing a deadly poison that spread across the harbour, mingling with clouds of smoke from burning ships and cargoes. The *John Harvey*, wrote Stephen Roskill, an official Royal Navy historian, had been brought to Bari because the Germans had threatened to use gas against Italy, and the Allies, in turn, had threatened to retaliate against Germany herself, 'using the full weight of their air power'. In fact, Eisenhower ensured that this poison was available in all his combat theatres, though for reprisal use only, though he never made it his business to know which ship carried it nor the location of the storage depot.[16]

Churchill insisted that no public mention be made of mustard gas aboard an Allied ship in Bari. This decision delayed proper treatment, adding to the toll of casualties, and served no short-term purpose because German radio broadcasts taunted Allied personnel in Bari for days afterwards with remarks about them enjoying their own poison. Long-term, the cover-up was maintained for many years after the war to avoid adverse comment. Churchill's decision was widely supported by Anglo-American authorities, civilian and military. It proved to be the only major poison gas incident, outside the Nazi concentration camps, of the Second World War. There were 617 known gas casualties among soldiers and seamen in Bari of which about ninety proved immediately fatal. Others were certainly affected as well as an unknown number of Italians. According to *The Times*, 6 March 1986, up to 600 British seamen contaminated by mustard gas at Bari were to receive backdated war pensions as a result of an official admission in December 1985 that the substance affecting them was indeed mustard gas.[17]

As a relief from this horror and believing that he would soon leave the Mediterranean, Coningham wrote to Sir Louis Greig (a close friend of the Secretary of State for Air) on 6 December about his long connection with the 8th Army, a matter in which he took great pride.

As you know, my one essay in military midwifery was the preparation for and accouchment of 8th Army in September–October 1941. I then saw it through a most troublous adolescence – what black eyes and a dirty face it had!!! Since then I have, aerially speaking, guarded it through the present phase of lusty manhood. I am, I think, the only battle commander of land, sea and air forces, British, German and Italian, who has remained with it continuously since its birth.

He therefore asked Greig to seek a dispensation from current regulations and permission for him to wear an '8' on his 1939–43 service ribbon as a 'tangible link' with that Army. His request, though evidently well justified, was not granted.[18]

Churchill arrived in Tunis on 11 December and remained there, in poor health, until the 27th. Together with every other Mediterranean commander, Coningham made his way there during those days in part to commiserate with the unhappy Prime Minister, but mostly to learn whether they had in fact landed a top job in England or whether they must soldier on in Italy. Despite Churchill's illness, momentous decisions were taken: Eisenhower would be the Supreme Commander of Operation Overlord with Tedder as his Deputy, but Eisenhower's wish to have Alexander as his land commander was blocked by General Brooke (head of the British Army) who managed to persuade Churchill to appoint Montgomery instead. As soon as he knew his own fate, Montgomery wrote to Brooke, urging him to press for the appointment of Broadhurst as tactical air commander, not knowing that Coningham was already home and dry.[19]

While in Tunis, paying court to Tedder, Coningham took the opportunity to gossip with Robb and Larry Kuter, who had escaped briefly from a Washington desk. On learning that he could uncross his fingers, Coningham visited Algiers briefly and while there, on 17 December, replied to a 'helpful and cheery' letter from Elmhirst, telling him that his appointment as commander of 2nd TAF had been confirmed and that he would leave Italy about 10 January; 'Ike in the party and already under orders.' As for the land war in Italy, it was 'very sticky and a bet that we shall be in Berlin before Rome is not so wild!!!' He was grateful for Elmhirst's advice about accommodation in London and had told Nan that a flat would suit perfectly. 'I hope to go straight to the New Forest to see the children,' he ended, 'and then to town and a spot of leave' before taking over. Coningham returned to Tunis, lunched with Robb and Spaatz and celebrated his escape from a bogged-down campaign in Italy by risking a long overdue visit to a dentist.[20]

Robb, as always, could not but admire Coningham's nerve – whether in asking to get permission for him to wear an '8', the Army symbol, or in asking Dawson for a four-engined aircraft (a B-24 Liberator, as used by the Prime Minister) to take him home in January. In this, as in other matters, Coningham and Montgomery had more in common than either would have cared to admit, for the General, like the Air Marshal, believed that the importance of his new appointment also required a ride home in the largest aircraft available – in his case, a Douglas DC-4. But Robb regretted the 'complete upheaval' among senior air commanders in the Mediterranean at this time: it 'has done the RAF anything but good' and originated, he thought, 'with Mary pulling strings to prevent Keith Park following him in

TAF' and continued with Park pulling more strings to prevent his own posting to India. 'Whatever the cause, my faith in the higher direction of the RAF has suffered a rude blow.' However, having refused a position in Italy as Cannon's Deputy, Robb himself would follow the great ones to England to take part in the liberation of North-west Europe.[21]

Returning to Bari, Coningham received a choice example of Montgomery's childish malice: a Christmas greeting carefully addressed to Air Marshal 'Cunningham'. Less happily, he also received word that the newly-formed Mediterranean Allied Air Forces Headquarters intended to break up his fighter-bomber force, employing four of the Groups as escorts for long-range bombers. The fighter-bomber, he told that headquarters on 29 December, 'is the most important single factor which consistently contributes to success on land' in North Africa, Tunisia, Sicily, Italy or any subsequent campaign. Without this weapon, it would often be impossible for troops to advance because their artillery could not reach enemy positions and they would in fact be in danger of defeat from counter-attacks. A fighter-bomber force, like any other effective weapon, could only achieve and maintain a high standard of performance if it was kept together, to gain experience and train hard; to switch its units to other duties was, in Coningham's view, 'unthinkable'. Neither bombers nor fighters could replace fighter-bombers. All three types had their particular – and different – duties and both their air and ground crews needed to specialise in them if they were to carry them out well. Such, in sum, was one of the chief lessons he had learned during numerous hard-fought campaigns; a lesson, moreover, that he intended to teach in England.[22]

On 8 January 1944, recorded the official British historians of the Mediterranean and Middle East campaigns, the air forces lost to Operation Overlord 'a great commander', Coningham, who had taken over 204 Group on 30 July 1941 and transformed it into the Desert Air Force. In their judgment, Coningham was an airman of the highest quality – as leader, commander or organiser – with a sure grasp of the complicated relation between air and land operations. He worked constantly to foster a strong sense of unity, of single purpose, among every member of his air forces and yet *esprit de corps* was but one part of his achievement. 'With profound originality,' wrote the historians, Coningham 'thought out from first principles what should be the shape of a tactical air force in the conditions of fast-moving desert warfare. He then brought his conceptions to life, step by step', creating a weapon in which every component part, in the air and on the ground, worked in harmony to produce maximum mobility and maximum striking power. 'He never for a moment forgot the land forces and devised for them methods of providing a tremendous direct support which applied familiar principles in a new and most effective way.' His doctrine and methods were the foundations, 'never to be bettered, of the successes of Tactical Air Forces until the end of the war'. Coningham and

John Lancaster (his pilot and personal aide) arrived in Tunis on 8 January and Robb took them to the villa at Hammamet, where Coningham presided over his last African party on the 9th with all the style for which he was famous. Next morning, at 10 am, he left for England.[23]

CHAPTER FOURTEEN

'Approaching a Very Great Day' in a 'World of Paper and Talk'

Coningham in England, January to June 1944

In 1946, Air Marshal Sir Thomas Elmhirst had a private talk with Eisenhower in Washington about the respective merits of Alexander and Montgomery as candidates for command of the invasion troops in Operation Overlord, the Allied assault upon Normandy. Eisenhower, admitting that Roosevelt and Churchill had rejected his preference for Alexander, asked Elmhirst for his opinion. Although 'Monty was a showman,' replied Elmhirst, he did send his troops to the beaches believing in themselves and in him: 'that confidence was something Monty could radiate and something that I did not think was in Alex, for all his great qualities; he was to some extent a shy man.' Eisenhower smiled and sighed, wondering as he often did in post-war years whether Montgomery's undoubted talents had not been too dearly bought. 'There's a lot in what you say,' he said.[1]

On 30 December 1943, shortly after the decision was made to give this vital command to Montgomery rather than Alexander, Coningham flew with Alexander to Vasto (on the Adriatic coast, ten miles south of the Sangro river) to farewell Montgomery, who was leaving for England next day. At lunch, reported Coningham to Tedder that evening, 'I was seated on Montgomery's right – for the especial purpose, so far as I could see, of being 'grilled' about my new appointment in England,' but Coningham had spent too many hours in conversation with Montgomery on Tedder's instructions to be so easily caught. He merely kept his mouth shut and his ears open while 'Napoleon' expounded his own ambition to command all the armies taking part in Overlord.

'I have since discussed this further with Alex,' wrote Coningham, 'and he says undoubtedly the trouble is that General Ike is disinclined or even unable to command separate groups of armies and that he wishes Monty to do it while he stays back as Supreme Commander. It is this factor that Monty has seized upon for his own idea of the organisation,' proposing that 'he should in effect be a deputy commander to Ike for the land forces, and at the same

9a. Coningham and Major General Neil Ritchie, commander of the 8th Army, early in January 1942. As they approached their aircraft, after posing for this photograph, a Junkers JU 88 suddenly appeared and dropped several bombs, one of which exploded about a hundred yards from where the top brass were busily burrowing into the sand.

9b. Coningham and Montgomery in November 1942. They first met in August, when Coningham said: 'We now have a man, a great soldier if I am any judge, and we will go all the way with him.' And they did, but their personal relations grew steadily worse as the triumphs in which they shared grew steadily greater.

10a. The Americans begin to make their presence felt. Tedder (at left) senior airman in North Africa, and Coningham, his field commander, share a jeep in November 1942 with Brigadier General Auby C. Strickland, USAAF. During the following year, 'Mary' and 'Strick' would become close friends.

10b. Auchinleck and Smuts attend a series of momentous meetings in Egypt with Churchill, Brooke, Tedder and Coningham which resulted in what Churchill called 'drastic and immediate' changes: Alexander became Commander-in-Chief the Near East, Montgomery became commander of the 8th Army and three other generals were dismissed.

11a. 'Bing' Cross and Fred Rosier somewhere in the desert early in 1942. Like Cross, Rosier was an exceptional pilot and commander who would later be knighted and reach Air Chief Marshal rank.

11b. 'Morning Prayers' at Ain Beida, Tunisia, in early April 1943. George Beamish (left) and Tommy Elmhirst (right), Coningham's two senior British Officers, discuss the day's plans with Coningham and his American Deputy, Major General Laurence S. Kuter, USAAF.

12a. Throughout the war, Coningham regularly made time to talk informally to all men under his command, not merely the air crews. Here he addressed members of the RAF regiment, who played such a vital role in protecting airfields, at the end of the Tunisian Campaign in May 1943.

12b. Eminent New Zealanders at Castel Benito, near Tripoli, in February 1943. Sir Keith Park, Malta's air commander, and Coningham were then concerned with the Tunisian Campaign and preparing, at the same time, for its successor – the invasion of Sicily.

13a. In January 1943, James Robb, Coningham's oldest service friend (at left) was appointed British Chief of Staff to Major General Carl A. Spaatz, soon to become head of the North African Air Forces – and Coningham's first American boss.

13b. Teddy Hudleston (left) whose abilities had greatly impressed Coningham in Italy, took command of 84 Group on 10 November 1944. They are seen here in earnest consultation with Portal, Chief of the Air Staff, probably about helping British and Canadian troops to clear access to the vital port of Antwerp.

14a. Five very senior Allied commanders surround a mere Group Captain (C. R. Dunlop) while inspecting an RAF Bomber Wing 'somewhere in England' in April 1944. Clockwise from the top, they are Brereton, Coningham, Eisenhower, Leigh-Mallory and Vandenberg.

14b. Coningham and Elmhirst, whose complementary talents and mutual respect made them a formidable partnership. This photograph, recorded Elmhirst, was taken in Brussels on 28 February 1945: 'the day we had completed three years together in the field'.

15a. Churchill flew to Brussels on 2 March 1945 and lunched at Coningham's 'sumptuous villa' (as his secretary described it). Among those present were Freddie de Guingand, third from left, and (on Churchill's left) Brooke, Victor Groom (Coningham's Chief of Staff), Mary Churchill, Clementine Churchill and Hastings Ismay.

15b. Relaxing at Villa Rosalia, Cannes, in the first post-war summer. Coningham arm-in-arm with Lucienne Rolando (the Villa's housekeeper) on his left, with John Lancaster (his ADC and personal pilot) on her left. It is thought that Rita Hayworth is the person on Coningham's right.

16a. Coningham and Lieutenant General Lewis H. Brereton, head of the 9th US Air Force, found it easier than some Allied commanders to smile cheerfully in each other's company while touring airfields during the anxious weeks before D-Day. 'Mary is always good company,' wrote Brereton in February 1945.

16b. On 22 January 1948, Coningham and Nan attended the Wedding at St Columba's Church in Pont Street, Chelsea, of Nigel Tapp (his old Sudan Defence Force colleague) and Dorothy, a particular friend of Nan's. The other members of the party were Sir Denholm Fraser (left), Nigel's brother Donald (right) and, at the rear, Dorothy Hutchinson, her husband and Ted Fernyhough. This is the last known photograph of Coningham.

time command from a small advanced headquarters. I mentioned your appointment, but he brushed it aside and said you were merely the Air Adviser to the Supreme Commander. The cheek of the blighter!' Alexander thought Montgomery's proposals would be rejected. Coningham continued:

'But as you know, Monty oozes confidence (except when Rommel is about): he is most persuasive and he will arrive home with an aura of invincibility, with clear-cut ideas, and the force to put them through . . . I hope all the foregoing turns out to be merely a Monty flurry, but I thought it desirable to let you know the position, as Montgomery let loose in London by himself at the present stage could get into serious mischief which may later affect us all.[2]

Montgomery would remain a cross for Coningham to bear for the rest of the war and Leigh-Mallory, who had emerged – with Portal's backing – as head of the Allied Expeditionary Air Force (AEAF), became for most of 1944 another. Neither Coningham nor Elmhirst had any regard for him because he 'failed to pull well' with Keith Park, in their view, during the Battle of Britain. 'I had not thought LM in the same class' then, wrote Elmhirst, and his opinion did not improve on renewing acquaintance in October 1943; few other senior officers, British or American, liked Leigh-Mallory and his position in the Anglo-American hierarchy was never settled.

The AEAF, formed on 25 November, comprised the 2nd Tactical Air Force (which would be, said Leigh-Mallory, 'the spearhead of the assault'), Lewis Brereton's 9th US Air Force and Roderic Hill's Fighter Command (renamed Air Defence of Great Britain). Coningham, already experienced in the command of large forces of many aircraft types, crewed and serviced by men from all parts of the world, found every aspect of his work in 1944 vastly increased in scale: his new air force, divided into three (later four) principal Groups, would grow to more than a hundred squadrons based on some fifty airfields, many of them temporary and ill-equipped, scattered throughout southern England. By D-Day, there were about 11,000 operational aircraft on hand: nearly 7,000 American, over 4,000 British. Of these, in round numbers, 4,200 were heavy bombers; 1,100 medium or light bombers; 4,500 fighter types, used by day or night as fighter-bombers or for reconnaissance; and 730 troop-carriers. The balance was made up of Observation and Air-Sea Rescue machines.[3]

Coningham's first task, delegated to Elmhirst, was to bring home to his squadrons that they were about to go on *campaign*. That meant separating thousands of men from snug permanent bases in the middle of a bitterly cold winter, giving them tents and transport and making them set up temporary camps on the edge of airfields. There they would learn to live as so many of their predecessors had once lived in France and later in North Africa, Sicily and Italy: as comfortably as their native wit would allow off whatever they could cook or scrounge for themselves. Brereton, echoing Coningham, emphasised 'Keep Mobile' as his motto. 'Since our job is to support the invasion and cooperate with the Ground Forces,' he said, 'once D-Day comes we'll be a travelling circus. I don't want any of our forces to get too comfortable or to think in terms of static warfare. All training must be with mobility in mind.'[4]

In addition to this massive upheaval, which began as soon as Coningham arrived from Italy, pilot training was reorganised to allow much more time for low-level attacks with guns, rockets and bombs on ground targets and much less for high-level aerial dogfighting. The fight for air superiority, although Coningham's first priority, was in fact the least of his worries, for many pilots under his command were adept in that task, though few were skilled in ground attack. As Coningham wrote after the war, 'years of intensive air-to-air fighting without any accompanying land operations' meant that pilots 'had to have their minds reorientated on to ground attack and be made to think first, foremost and almost all the time of land operations': a concentration only possible because there was adequate air strength available to ensure air superiority over the battle area.[5]

As soon as he returned to England, Coningham formed an Advanced Headquarters at Uxbridge, handy for visits to his Main Headquarters at Bracknell, AEAF Headquarters at Bentley Priory, the Air Ministry and Montgomery's headquarters in St Paul's School, Hammersmith. John Lancaster set up a mess and sleeping quarters in a cottage which proved 'a very comfortable billet', in Elmhirst's words, 'until we all flew over to our next headquarters, in a Normandy orchard, in July'. A notable absentee from this billet was George Beamish, replaced in Italy as Senior Air Staff Officer by Edmund Hudleston and now in England by Victor Groom, who had long been head of the RAF's Overlord planners. Groom's special knowledge could not be matched by Beamish, but Coningham helped his old friend into an important job as head of 44 Group in Transport Command, and on 10 February Coningham wrote to the Air Ministry on his behalf, expressing displeasure that Beamish – whom he had recommended for the CB – got nothing in the New Year List and refusing to accept 'the excuse' that this was because Beamish was not at the time of Air Commodore rank. On 4 March, Brereton wrote to Coningham to tell him that Beamish had been awarded the Legion of Merit. Coningham was delighted and replied at once, thanking him for this American recognition of Beamish's devoted efforts in North Africa and the Mediterranean.[6]

Squadron Leader Frank Instone, deputy commander of 2nd TAF's police and security force, thought Coningham and Elmhirst infused a lively spirit throughout their headquarters: 'the one a handsome extrovert, the other calmly efficient in ensuring that the organisation would fail in no respect'. Instone and other members of headquarters staff had been sorry to hear of the departure of John D'Albiac, their original commander, but Coningham at once summoned all officers to a meeting 'and struck just the right note, saying that he didn't doubt for one moment that most of us thought his predecessor had had a raw deal'; D'Albiac, he said, 'was a fine fellow and a personal friend,' but he had been sent to replace D'Albiac because of his experience in the Middle East both in operations and in managing a vast, allied headquarters. 'Before he got halfway through his opening address,' wrote Instone, 'his electric personality made itself felt on those who had not served with him before and we all realised that here was a man who not only knew his stuff, but was one of immense personality and quite clearly an inspiring leader.' Coningham later sent for Instone, telling him that his officers and men were used to 'a free life' overseas and he did not want them chased from pillar to post. Instone assured him that *security*, which was essential to the success of the invasion, was his 'particular pigeon' and his staff would not be 'bloody-minded' in other matters. Coningham smiled and thereafter Instone had his full support.[7]

The Chief Signals Officer at 2nd TAF Headquarters, Group Captain Kenneth Porter, shared Instone's high opinion of Coningham. 'The headquarters ran like a well-oiled clock,' he remembered, 'everyone knew what they were responsible for, there were no passengers and relations between all members of the staff were exceptionally harmonious.' Porter had liked D'Albiac and offered his condolences on learning that he was to go: 'His response was to say that he knew Mary, thought very highly of him and considered that his experience of providing air support in the Desert and in Italy made him much better qualified for the job.' During the rest of the war, Porter would learn that D'Albiac had been right.

Coningham, said Porter, was an outstanding operational commander: 'He understood how best to support ground forces, he made up his mind very quickly, he was decisive and having made a decision or stated his policy, he delegated the responsibility for carrying it out to his subordinates and did not interfere with them.' Moreover, 'Mary admired the Americans as much as they admired him' and thought the drive and ability to exploit success of the US Army compared more than favourably with that of the British Army. Porter planned and had manufactured mobile VHF equipment to provide speech and teleprinter communications which could only be guaranteed if the terminals were sited to give a line-of-sight path between them. The advantage of being able to talk and send teleprinter messages between 2nd TAF Headquarters and the Group Headquarters and between these and their units, even when landlines were unavailable, was obvious. Coningham therefore ruled that Porter was responsible for the siting of all headquarters throughout the campaign in North-west Europe and supported him even against the fiery Basil Embry, head of 2 Group: 'Mary not only decentralised, but supported the decisions of the subordinates to whom he had decentralised.'

Porter concluded:

In my experience, Mary never dithered or panicked. He always seemed to me to be fully in control of events, to be completely self-confident and to have Army–Air support buttoned up in the same way as Park had fighter defence buttoned up . . . I was fortunate to have served under two commanders who were masters of their respective fields and who inspired complete confidence that their operations would be successful. Of the two, whereas Park was highly-strung, always seemed to be on a short fuse and when I had to go to see him in his office, usually went to some lengths to impress me with the importance of what he was doing, Mary seemed to me to take things much more easily, not to be concerned with the impression he was creating and to be a more balanced character.

When Porter knew Park, however, the outcome of the war was very much in doubt; when he served with Coningham, that was no longer the case.[8]

Meanwhile, late in January 1944, details of Overlord's leadership were released to the press. 'Of all the appointments for the high staff positions for the Western Front,' wrote Wing Commander Charles Bray in the *Daily Herald* on the 26th, Coningham's 'will be one of the most popular. It means that the old highly-successful Montgomery-Coningham partnership is to be maintained in our greatest operation of the war.' Bray rejoiced to know that this 'pair of friends', as he supposed them, were together again. Next to Tedder's appointment as Eisenhower's deputy, wrote Frederick Tomlinson in the *Observer* on the 30th, 'nothing could give greater pleasure to students of military aviation' than Coningham's appointment. During his recent tour of the Mediterranean, Tomlinson had found 'general agreement among soldiers and airmen that Sir Arthur Coningham is an ideal commander for any air formation cooperating with land and sea forces'. He appreciated military situations, through his close contact with Alexander, and by his knowledge of what aircraft could and could not do, unquestionably contributed much to recent Allied successes. Tomlinson had evidently listened to Coningham more closely than some soldiers, observing that he was 'inclined to be impatient with those who expect aircraft to achieve miracles, for he holds that some military successes can only be gained on the ground, however good the air support and preparation may be'. He did not, for example, 'expect the Army to ask him to winkle out isolated machine-gun positions and thereby to neglect the bombing of a large concentration of German transports a few miles away'.[9]

From February onwards, Coningham attended numerous conferences at AEAF Headquarters, Bentley Priory, where matters great and small were exhaustively discussed. He stressed the urgent need for realistic training in both TAFs 'on their legitimate Overlord tasks' and a great reduction in the time spent escorting bomber raids. Brereton, however, was 'less concerned' than Coningham about his pilots' state of training: some were getting the best possible training over Italy, while three fighter Groups at a time could be withdrawn from Spaatz's operational control. Coningham remained anxious about training and signalled Hudleston (now Senior Air Staff Officer to Joe Cannon in Italy) on 25 February, asking for a report on the latest methods of ground attack on road transport. Concerned as ever about gallantry awards, he found time on the 29th to point out to Leslie Brown (head of 84 Group) that of fifty names put forward for such awards, only two had been for airmen aircrew. In future, ruled Coningham, they must account for at least one-fifth of Brown's recommendations.[10]

After a very long Chiefs of Staff meeting on 3 March, Portal asked for the room to be cleared of secretaries and then explained his problems regarding the air forces. Tedder, recorded Brooke, the Army Chief, 'is now to assume more direct command: as far as I can see, this can only be done by chucking out Leigh-Mallory.' Butcher (Eisenhower's naval aide) also thought Leigh-Mallory's days were numbered because neither Harris nor Spaatz, the top 'bomber barons', was prepared to work under him. Butcher had gone with Eisenhower to Tedder's house the previous evening to discuss the matter.

> It seemed inevitable that LM would ask to be relieved and Tedder thought there was a vacancy in the Far East to which he might be assigned . . . Ike has nothing against LM, but is seeking harmony in the Air Service and there is considerable rivalry among the marshals of the RAF who seem to be divided roughly into Tedder's School and the Leigh-Mallory Camp.

Eisenhower preferred Tedder, partly because of his record, but mostly because Tedder helped him to prevent Churchill and the British Chiefs of Staff issuing orders direct to British Units under his command.[11]

Hudleston responded promptly to Coningham's request for an account of Operation Shingle, the Allied landings at Anzio, south of Rome. Coningham, anxious to benefit from experience gained in Italy while planning for Overlord, replied to Hudleston on 4 April, thanking him most warmly for his notes. 'As you, know,' he continued, 'the Army cannot be blamed, so in all reports over here the Air Force bombing of Cassino was quoted as the reason for the Army's failure – in other words, the attack was used as a weapon to beat us,' but 'if ever the Army try to press us to take wrong air action near the frontline, I shall use the word "Cassino" and say no.' Coningham carefully annotated Hudleston's notes, dated 6 March, and made full use of them in his own planning.

In general, wrote Hudleston, Shingle had followed the pattern of Husky and Avalanche. Tactical bombers were employed until six days before D-Day (D-6) on the disruption of rail communications and attacks intended to conceal the actual target area; from D-5 to D-Day, they were to isolate the target area by attacks on roads and railways leading into it; and from D-Day onwards, while continuing with this task, they would give the maximum possible close support. Hudleston then summarised the lessons learned. Bombing of marshalling yards proved effective, he wrote, but only for about twenty-four hours: by then, at least a single line would be working again. Successful attacks on railway bridges, though more difficult, closed lines for longer. Such breaks were particularly valuable in bad weather, when continuous attacks on communications became impossible. At least ten per cent of all bombs dropped should be delayed-action. Fighter-bombers did much better with cannon fire than with bombs against moving targets on roads or railways, but only if they were prepared to fly low and press home attacks at close range. Their successes obliged the enemy to carry out essential movement at night and this could not be prevented, nor could much be done about heavy guns operating out of range of Allied artillery or naval gunfire. The soldiers made strident demands for attacks on these guns, but they were carefully concealed and, if found, put up fierce flak. Requests for artillery spotting, both from the Army and the Navy, were intense and observation squadrons operating in the bridgehead proved invaluable, as did mobile radars in all activities.[12]

Coningham's exasperation with the direction by Spaatz and Doolittle of the American heavy bomber force was mounting daily and on 25 March he drafted (but did not send) a letter to Leigh-Mallory about its operations the previous day. Although the 8th AF had not used all its own escort fighters, it took about 250 of Coningham's. Worse still, he wrote, 'If 600 fighters are required for 220 heavies over 10/10th cloud in Western Germany, what is going to be demanded when 1,000-plus go deeper during fine weather? I feel that 8th AF judgment in this matter is unreliable and that is why they go on the simple rule of using every available fighter for every show.' Moreover, he added, 'an enormous attack' was made on two French airfields which were practically devoid of enemy aircraft: 'How much more valuable to have attacked our railway targets!'[13]

Three days later, on 28 March, he had the opportunity to discuss these matters further with Leigh-Mallory and Spaatz when they went with Eisenhower to a subordinate headquarters of Pete Quesada's 9th Fighter Command at Middle Wallop in Hampshire, although the main concern of Coningham and Quesada on that visit was to demonstrate to the Supreme Commander the much-vaunted mobility of air formations. Eisenhower, having been suitably impressed, then asked what happened when the Army requested air support and none was forthcoming because of prior commitments. Quesada explained, to Coningham's gratification, that cooperation between American and British tactical air forces was so close that somebody would be found to help.[14]

Next day, 29 March, Coningham attended a conference at Bentley Priory and voiced his complaint about 8th AF calling on 9th AF for fighter support without using all its own fighters first. This practice, he said, was preventing essential training. Eisenhower agreed, ruling on 1 April that tactical air force operations should be 'directed more closely towards the preparation for Overlord' and that their first priority henceforth should be attacks on railway targets in France rather than escort for heavy bombers over Germany. In an attempt to protect French civilians as much as possible, he further ruled that 'attacks on these targets be made under conditions that will allow definite visual identification'. Missile launching sites were ranked second in priority, 'industrial targets' third and airfields fourth, all to be selected from given lists. However, Coningham and Brereton soon learned that Eisenhower's ruling was unreliable, for Spaatz and Doolittle simply *required* the fighters of 9th AF to join their own fighters in providing massive escort for strategic bombing missions.[15]

While Leigh-Mallory supervised the activities of his air force from Bentley Priory (and chaffered with Spaatz and Harris for heavy bomber support), Coningham and Brereton were discussing how best to coordinate and control actual operations from a Combined Control Centre at Uxbridge. Bentley Priory and Uxbridge had been chosen because Fighter Command had long-established communication networks there which were not available in Portsmouth, where Eisenhower had based himself near to Ramsay and Montgomery, his naval and land force commanders. Keith Park, a New Zealander, had directed the fighter defence of Britain from Uxbridge in 1940; now, four years later, another New Zealander would share with an American the direction of the Allied fighter offence from there.[16]

Brereton had lunch with Leigh-Mallory and Coningham in London on 20 April 'at which,' wrote Brereton, 'the command setup of the AEAF was batted around again'. Leigh-Mallory wanted Coningham to command both TAFs, but Brereton was '100 per cent opposed because it subordinates one air force to the control of the commander of another'. That afternoon, at a meeting between Portal, Tedder and Leigh-Mallory, it was decided to appoint Coningham 'AOC *Advanced* Headquarters AEAF instead of AOC Allied TAF as at first proposed. This decision', according to Wing Commander Leslie Scarman, Tedder's diarist, 'was due to representations by LM: (1) that his position as AC-in-C AEAF likely to be embarrassing with an Allied TAF and (2) that there is serious danger of too many headquarters formations being established.' Coningham would direct the operations of both tactical air forces during the assault phase of Overlord and thereafter the two commanders would be directly responsible to Leigh-Mallory for the operation of their respective forces. AEAF's authority was, in fact, more nominal than real, for Coningham and Brereton worked in constant association to achieve an effective collaboration in the execution of directives which *reached* them via Leigh-Mallory, but had their *origins* in conferences between Coningham, Brereton, Tedder, Spaatz and Harris. Advanced AEAF dealt directly with Ramsay and Montgomery, whose representatives in Uxbridge relayed requests and provided information necessary to sea–ground–air cooperation.[17]

On Anzac Day, 25 April, Colin Bednall wrote fulsomely (though none too accurately) about '"Mary" Coningham: Number One Anzac' in the *Daily Mail*. He began with a reference to his father, 'the first man ever to represent Queensland in Test cricket' who travelled home to Brisbane from his first – and only – Test match in Melbourne, arriving just in time for the birth of a boy 'who now has the greatest and most responsible job ever given to an air commander in the field'. Bednall thought it fitting to tell Coningham's story on Anzac Day, for he 'has become the most important Anzac of all'. Though born in Australia, he preferred to be considered a New Zealander and saw nothing odd in that: Lloyd George, he observed, was no less a Welshman for being born in Manchester.[18]

Coningham attended a particularly important conference at Bentley Priory next day, 26 April. Leigh-Mallory announced that he was anxious 'to determine the precise functions of the different Air HQs'; as for his own role, he saw himself coordinating the strategic and tactical effort throughout the battle. This, he thought, could best be done by means of a daily conference at Bentley Priory, which either Coningham or Brereton would attend. Coningham immediately replied that he would be quite unable to visit Bentley Priory every day because he intended to keep in very close touch with Montgomery's headquarters in Portsmouth. He suggested that the strategic effort be allocated at least twenty-four hours ahead, since heavy bombers and their large crews took longer to prepare and brief than the mediums, fighter-bombers and fighters of the tactical air forces. The strategic effort having been decided, Coningham proposed that the tactical effort be agreed at an evening conference not at Bentley Priory but in Uxbridge. As Commander Advanced AEAF, Coningham would naturaly keep Leigh-Mallory fully informed of the battle's progress, but did not propose to give orders to his Group Commanders while he himself remained in Uxbridge. Leigh-Mallory queried the control of all tactical air forces from Uxbridge, suggesting decentralisation in view of the huge numbers of aircraft involved, but Coningham and Hugh Saunders (head of 11 Group) confirmed that the Combined Control Centre was perfectly capable of adequate control.

It was then agreed that Leigh-Mallory would lay down general policies for the employment of strategic and tactical bombers, which latter policy Coningham would implement; that Tedder would allot the strategic effort, when such forces would be used in a tactical role; that most tactical tasks for strategic bombers would be arranged twenty-four hours in advance; and that a tactical conference would be held nightly at Uxbridge to determine allotment and employment for the following day. Until such time as Leigh-Mallory could establish himself in France, Coningham would act in a duel role similar to that of Montgomery: i.e., he would command 2nd TAF and also Advanced AEAF. Thereafter, he would command only 2nd TAF. Leigh-Mallory wrote to Portal after this conference ended. In the early stages of Overlord, he had learned, Montgomery was to fulfil a dual role as head of 21st Army Group and overall commander until Eisenhower took charge. It therefore seemed 'a reasonable organisation to make Coningham also fulfil a dual role. My Advanced Headquarters would go out and would parallel the Supreme Commander's Advanced Headquarters and 2nd TAF Headquarters would go out and parallel 21st Army Group. Coningham would act as Commander Advanced Headquarters and as Commander of the 2nd TAF.'

Everybody seemed 'most satisfied' with this arrangement, thought Leigh-Mallory, which could not be made earlier because of 'certain allied factors'.[19]

Coningham wrote to Philip Wigglesworth, Leigh-Mallory's SASO, on 29 April, asking for a directive implementing the conclusions reached at the conference on the 26th. This would enable Coningham to call a meeting with Brereton, Saunders and Quesada to decide the organisation needed for laying on operations and supporting Montgomery. He enclosed a draft of what he wanted which was published on 1 May. Under Leigh-Mallory's direction, Coningham was to 'coordinate the planning and operations' of both TAFs from his headquarters in Uxbridge where a Combined Control Centre (managed by Saunders and Quesada) would issue his instructions. Advanced AEAF would be an operational headquarters with no administrative responsibilities and during 'the assault phase' Coningham would coordinate all requests for direct support and reconnaissance and pass to Leigh-Mallory requests for heavy bombing beyond the capacity of his own forces. This organisation, the directive announced, would provide for 'one Air authority' with whom Montgomery would deal.[20]

Some American commanders were unhappy with this directive. Hoyt S. Vandenberg – Leigh-Mallory's American Deputy, but Spaatz's agent – read the 'Control of Air Units' section of the air plan, noting Coningham's dual role. He was told that Brereton did not agree and promptly raised the matter with Leigh-Mallory who produced the conference minutes to show that Brereton had in fact agreed to the decisions reached. This unwelcome news, noted Vandenberg, 'temporarily blocked further action by me'. Next day, he discussed the matter further with Spaatz and Brereton, who now found the directive 'unsatisfactory' and intended to complain to Tedder; Spaatz would complain to Eisenhower. Spaatz told Vandenberg on 16 May that Eisenhower had agreed to Coningham's dual role, 'if he was detached from 2nd TAF while on the AEAF job'. Vandenberg thereupon gave this news to Coningham and Brereton and later proposed certain changes in the air plan. 'All amicable and changed as US desired,' he recorded.[21]

Throughout 1944, Coningham kept in close touch with his former colleagues of the Italian Campaign, Cannon and Hudleston, partly to draw upon their daily experience of operations similar to those facing him; partly because he liked them. On 29 April, he wrote warmly and at length (in his own hand) to 'Joe', having just enjoyed a visit from 'Teddy'. As well as cheerful gossip about his family ('Our Jane is home from school and we have had a lot of laughter') and mutual friends (including the enigmatic comment, 'Tooey remains Tooey'), Coningham felt able to discuss with Cannon his major worries, chief of which was 'to get people's minds down to attacking ground targets'. His force was unbalanced, with too much 'fighter v fighter strength' and too many untried rockets for pilots trained in conventional weapons. Also, he confided, 'I'm getting into a private flurry at our delay in producing jet-propelled aircraft': the Germans would soon get rid of the

189

bugs in an aircraft as far ahead of the latest Spitfire as it was of the pre-war biplane; jets, he feared, 'could wash out our great air superiority tomorrow'.

As for daily life, Coningham told Cannon, he had no sympathy for his hassles with other headquarters, as related by Hudleston: 'You are in a haven of peace,' he wrote with feeling, 'compared to my world of paper and talk. It will be such a relief to get the show started.' However, 'General Ike' was still 'the grandest value' and another consolation was the great number of 'old Med. sweats' at all the conferences. 'I have just been given my third new title in two and a half weeks' he added, 'and am now organised to work with Monty, both of us filling two positions.' He outlined the system in words and diagrams, ending: 'See? Damned awful thing to explain, but there you are.'[22]

Tedder's famous 'Transportation Plan', based upon Mediterranean experience and strongly supported by Coningham, was intended to disrupt a vast railway network and oblige the enemy to use roads which were much less suitable for the rapid movement of large forces and heavy equipment. The plan stretched – and therefore weakened – defences and extended over such a large area that flyable weather could usually be found somewhere. Another advantage that weighed heavily with Coningham was the fact that it spared French towns and villages as much as possible. A German study, completed on 18 November 1944, concluded that the paralysis of the railway network and the destruction of bridges before D-Day had had a 'most damaging effect' on German plans. Although arguments in favour of creating 'choke points' by bombing road junctions in towns and villages were strongly advanced, it was agreed on 3 May to begin attacks on bridges about D-14 and that the American heavy bombers should undertake a full-scale attack on three Seine bridges and (as a deception) three Meuse bridges. Spaatz was reluctant to see his heavy bombers thus employed and was therefore no less delighted than Coningham on 7 May when eight fighter-bombers of the 9th AF destroyed a railway bridge over the Seine at Vernon: this feat encouraged both men in their aversion to the sight of heavy bombers over the battlefield.[23]

At this time, Coningham was concerned about the very heavy losses to be expected from attacks on radar stations and Leigh-Mallory agreed that they might be left until nearer D-Day. Coningham was even more concerned about evidence that the Luftwaffe would 'shortly' be operating squadrons of jet aircraft. Such machines, he said, would give the Germans an immense advantage and all possible pressure must be brought to get the early introduction of British jets: if necessary, at the expense of Typhoon production. Leigh-Mallory agreed to raise the matter with Portal. Other matters that Coningham raised included, as usual, the employment of fighter-bombers as escorts for heavy bombers; the need to conserve stocks of 1,000-pound bombs during 'the preparation period' for extensive use against bridges after D-Day; the lag in production of fragmentation bombs and especially his efforts to train a dozen squadrons in the use of rocket projectiles. He was convinced that the rocket was a more accurate weapon than the bomb, although admitting that its proper use required much practice. Not least, Coningham asked Leigh-Mallory to take up with Ramsay his 'grave concern' about the misuse by the Navy of vessels specially equipped to assist fighter direction. These Fighter Direction Tenders, said Coningham, were nothing like ready for their critical role in the initial stages of the assault.[24]

At a conference on 17 May, Coningham asked whether sufficient weight of attack was being carried out in the 'Neptune' (assault) area. He thought it unwise to leave the Seine bridges untouched much longer, given the risk of bad weather. The Germans, argued Coningham, clearly regarded the 'Fortitude' (Pas de Calais) area as the principle Allied objective and Neptune as its cover. Heavier attacks in Neptune, so far from compromising security, would therefore *strengthen* it. Moreover, the Army wanted him to attack those bridges, but Leigh-Mallory decided that an even balance must be maintained between Neptune and Fortitude and attacks on the Seine bridges did not resume for another week.

Convinced that the major task of the air forces from D-Day onwards would be to delay enemy movement into the battle area, Leigh-Mallory then made a bid for personal control of the medium bomber force to impede such movement. Coningham was adamantly opposed. Montgomery, he said, might call for direct support which could not be met by fighter-bombers alone because of intense flak; in such cases, simultaneous raids by medium bombers would be called for. Although Leigh-Mallory 'guaranteed' that if this should happen, the Army's needs would be met instantly, Coningham thought divided control would not work in practice and informed Montgomery that he might not always be able to offer direct air support promptly. As Coningham intended, Montgomery complained at once to Eisenhower, saying that he would only deal with one Air Commander. Eisenhower agreed and announced on 19 May that Coningham was to have 'the necessary executive authority to implement all requests for air action required by the Army' and Leigh-Mallory was merely 'to exercise general direction of air operations', about which Coningham would keep him informed.[25]

On the afternoon of the 17th, recorded Scarman, Tedder had had a long meeting with Leigh-Mallory, 'who is worried at his position vis-à-vis Coningham. Monty has demanded ONE Air Force authority to deal with. He is to be Coningham, as Commander Advanced AEAF (Allied TAF has died). Chief [Tedder] impressed on LM that scheme would work, given tact and goodwill. As Chief says, "LM requires educating to School Certificate standard."' Quite apart from the fact that so many of his colleagues disliked him, few officers would have found Leigh-Mallory's position tenable. Although nominally responsible for the success or failure of the air plan, he had in fact no control whatever over the air forces: Coningham managed the tactical air forces; Tedder 'directed' on Eisenhower's behalf the strategic air forces; and Leigh-Mallory was reduced to endorsing the decisions they made.[26]

Nevertheless, Coningham was invited to attend the wedding of Leigh-Mallory's daughter on 20 May. Among the guests was Vandenberg who found an opportunity to advise Coningham that he should set at rest fears in the mind of Admiral Alan G. Kirk, US Naval Force Commander, about his likely air support. Coningham agreed to attend yet another meeting, arranged by Vandenberg for 9.30 am on 22 May in his own office, where Kirk was asked by Vandenberg to 'present his fears and questions, that we might get everything on the table'. The entire plan was then explained in detail and Kirk departed, 'apparently much relieved', expressing his appreciation. Coningham had received that morning a most welcome letter from his friend Larry Kuter in Washington: 'your activities', wrote Kuter, 'are a source of the greatest interest at this time, both publicly and in official circles. That fact makes duty in the Pentagon Building less fascinating day by day.' Kuter assumed that Vandenberg 'has undoubtedly given you an inside look into the way things are happening in Washington', so Coningham showed him the letter. Vandenberg, an ambitious young man and widely regarded as a rising star, was impressed – as Kuter and Coningham desired that he should be – by this evidence of top-level American approval of at least one British Air Marshal.[27]

Next day, 23 May, the principal Allied air commanders began a new series of meetings at Bentley Priory – first of their 'Overlord Conferences', with Leigh-Mallory as chairman – to decide target priorities and allocation of effort between strategic and tactical forces. Four more meetings were held before D-Day, after which they continued every morning at 11 am throughout the summer and early autumn. Leigh-Mallory surpassed even himself at the first meeting by asking for the immediate relief of all US officers employed in the War Room, declaring in effect, wrote Vandenberg, 'that British methods of operation, which he understood', must be introduced. Vandenberg at once contacted Spaatz, told him Leigh-Mallory's attitude was 'an outrage' and said he was ready 'to bring a very fine fight out in the open', if Spaatz thought the time appropriate. After a pause for thought, Spaatz advised him to say nothing to upset relations for the present.[28]

'It is quite impossible for any one service to win a modern war,' said Coningham in a talk to Spitfire pilots on 24 May. His next sentence – 'There is no short cut to beating the Germans and you cannot do it by bombing alone' – revealed how far he was from the camp of the bomber barons, but it was the following sentence which many newspapers quoted next day: 'We are approaching a very great day on which a tremendous amount depends.' Coningham then went on to say that although the Germans had given up hope of winning the war, they would fight hard to achieve a stalemate and so avoid defeat.[29]

His preparations for that 'very great day' had made astonishing progress since January. Most of his aircrews knew how to refuel and re-arm their aircraft, to remedy minor mechanical defects and even to use some ground weapons. Although immensely expanded in numbers, they were, in spirit, his old Desert Air Force in that they did not live in large, well-appointed messes, but slept four to a tent and ate in big marquees; nor did they have batmen. Ground crews had also been taught 'Desert methods', for a TAF unit had to be fully and quickly *mobile*, with workshops and offices that could be driven or towed to practically any flat space where a temporary airfield could be set up at short notice. This method of running an air force, common enough in the Great War and revived in France in 1940, had been brought to a fine art under Coningham during the North African and Mediterranean campaigns. He was well aware that many otherwise excellent staff officers simply could not give of their best in the rough-and-tumble of mobile warfare; others could not handle rapidly enough the daily, sometimes hourly – and often heated – arguments with Army, Navy or USAAF representatives over where and when to employ aircraft. Such officers would neither be useful nor happy in 2nd TAF and few were to be found in senior positions by D-Day.

Having assembled a staff suitable for the task in prospect, Coningham left it to get on with detailed planning while he concentrated on high-level negotiations and low-level visits. 'Just as he did in Africa,' wrote Flight Lieutenant Anthony Vandyk in the *Daily Telegraph* on 30 May, Coningham 'turns up unexpectedly at all hours and talks informally with all ranks about their work – as often as not during a meal, for he always expresses great determination not to interfere with their duties.' Most pilots, added Vandyk, have had little experience of working with an army, for their targets had hitherto been in the air and not on the ground, but under Coningham's direction they were learning how an army worked and how best to help it. Hard, dangerous fighting during the coming year would teach them much more.[30]

CHAPTER FIFTEEN

Cooperating with Brereton, Cajoling Montgomery, Scuppering Leigh-Mallory

Coningham and the Battle for Normandy, June to August 1944

Throughout the Second World War, Lord Trenchard found it hard to keep away from the scenes of high drama, and officers who had justified his early patronage by rising to senior rank learned to expect his appearance – full of apologies for any inconvenience caused, but equally full of determination to see everything. Coningham was therefore not at all surprised to receive a letter from the great man on 3 June, inviting himself for a guided tour once Operation Overlord had been safely launched: 'because really,' he wrote, 'outside the official set-up, you are the person chiefly concerned.'[1]

Much as he relished flattery from a man of Trenchard's eminence, Coningham was at that moment too busy to respond. He had just emerged from a long, tense meeting at Bentley Priory where Leigh-Mallory, having outlined his unsolicited views on the employment of aircraft to a hostile audience of British and American airmen, lost his temper and was publicly rebuked by Tedder. It was then decided, as Tedder, Coningham and the Americans wanted, to use heavy bombers as soon as the invasion began to isolate the battlefield, by destroying bridges, railways and blocking roads deep in enemy territory; medium bombers would be used to inhibit movement towards the landing area as well as against beach defences; fighter-bombers would cover the infantry's advance and break up enemy concentrations of troops or armour; and fighters would cover everything, with a strong reserve held ready to counter any unexpected emergency.[2]

Coningham then left for Admiral Ramsay's headquarters at Southwick House, near Portsmouth, to attend the dramatic meetings at which Eisenhower would decide when to launch Overlord, the largest and most complex combined operation in history. The first meeting, at 9.30 pm on 3 June, was told to expect very poor weather during the next few days and a second meeting began at 4.30 the following morning. At this meeting, Montgomery announced that he was prepared to go on the 5th even if bad weather prevented air support; Ramsay said he was reluctant to go, but would if

Eisenhower asked. After a shocked silence, Eisenhower exploded: for months he had been told that air support was essential and now his chief soldier and chief seaman blithely said they could manage without. 'No,' he said, 'we'll postpone Overlord twenty-four hours.' Already a confirmed Eisenhower man, Coningham agreed: as in past crises, so in those to come, he preferred the Supreme Commander's judgment to Montgomery's. Later that day came news of a break in the weather and at 9.45 pm Eisenhower decided to go. As Chester Wilmot later explained, the issue was clear-cut: 'take a chance on the Tuesday [6 June], or wait for two weeks' until tide conditions were right again – and even then there would no longer be moonlight and, of course, no guarantee of calm water and clear skies. The risk of a major security breach was growing, the morale of men packed tightly together in ships was causing concern and promises had been made to the Russians that an invasion would be launched in the first week of June. These were compelling reasons and Coningham smiled when Eisenhower said: 'After all, we have a great force of fighter-bombers.'[3]

All the Allied commanders, Coningham among them, expected the Luftwaffe to respond immediately and with great vigour to the assault, none realising how gravely it had been weakened in France in order to strengthen defence of the homeland against day and night attack by American and British heavy bombers. Moreover, the prior destruction of radar stations on the coasts of France and the Low Countries combined with a brilliantly executed cover plan – Operation Fortitude – blinded the enemy to the size, direction and purpose of the Allied landings. Long after the armies were safely ashore, the Germans continued to assume that the real blow would be made against the Pas de Calais and that the assault on Normandy was no more than a feint.[4]

From Coningham's viewpoint, the outstanding fact about the assault was the complete lack of aerial opposition, but before noon on D-Day he knew that cloudy weather was making it impossible to carry out carefully-laid plans to prevent enemy movement towards the Allied invaders while they were at their most vulnerable. He therefore ordered Typhoons armed with rockets or bombs to patrol all roads in the assault area. Other aircraft carried out similar missions farther afield and found road convoys escorted by fighters. Although movement was not stopped, the Germans were obliged to disperse or take to side roads or wait for darkness. A maximum effort was made for two days, regardless of wear and tear upon men or machines, but on the third morning – 8 June – Coningham told Montgomery's representative at Uxbridge that he and Brereton had agreed that this degree of intensity could no longer be sustained. Until reliable information about enemy intentions became available, he must allow time for rest and repair because even though the Luftwaffe had not yet proved a danger, many aircraft had been destroyed or damaged by accurate German ground fire – supplemented, as in the Mediterranean landings, by reckless fire from Allied ships and soldiers ashore. Coningham repeatedly implored the Naval and Army commanders to insist that gunners identify aircraft before opening fire, but such 'incidents' continued at a distressing rate for weeks.[5]

'The situation is changing as the German reinforcements come up,' said Leigh-Mallory to his diarist, Hilary St George Saunders, on 8 June. 'The weather is still bad, but our fighter-bombers have certainly delayed their movements.' By that day, however, Coningham was more concerned about the armies placing the bombline too far forward. This imaginary line was intended to protect forward troops from accidental attack by friendly aircraft, but if placed too far forward would also spare enemy forces in the protected zone. Montgomery took up Coningham's point in a letter to his Chief of Staff (Freddie de Guingand, still in England) on 9 June. 'I think the bombline has got to be a bit out just at present,' wrote the Army Commander, because 'the troops are mostly new to fighting and we do not want to create a loss of confidence in the air.' He therefore accepted – on their behalf – less close support than Coningham was willing to provide.[6]

Nevertheless, at a meeting of Air Commanders on the 10th, Coningham again asked for the line to be brought nearer to Allied troops. A few squadrons were then operating from landing strips within the beachhead and Coningham immediately delegated their control to Broadhurst because, as he wrote later, 'there should be only one point of contact between the Army and Air Force commanders fighting the battle'. Broadhurst (83 Group) and Dempsey (2nd British Army) worked together. As soon as direct radio-telephone and wireless communications were established across the Channel between Uxbridge and Broadhurst's headquarters, wrote Coningham, 'I was able to keep him fully informed of my intentions and learn his requirements for carrying them out.' At the Air Commanders' meeting on 12 June, Coningham summarised operations the previous day, outlined those proposed for that day and announced that three landing strips had been made and were being used by Typhoons and Spitfires.[7]

Once they were securely established ashore, the Allies needed both a good deepwater port (to permit a rapid build-up of supplies) and the capture of flat, open terrain for airfield construction and the effective deployment of tanks. Consequently, the Americans aimed to seize Cherbourg and the British to seize Caen. Whatever doubts the Germans had about the purpose of the Allied landings, they had none at all about the significance of Caen as a route centre or the suitability of the country east and south of that town for aircraft and tank operations. Both were defended fiercely for weeks. But the breakout from the bridgehead, recalled Coningham, 'had been planned with the particular intention of providing sufficient air bases to the east and southeast of Caen' to enable him to get his short-range aircraft based in Normandy as quickly as possible. He needed these in order to maintain air superiority and so permit the growth and free movement of Allied land forces while denying – or at least impeding – the growth and free movement of German forces encircling the bridgehead. Unfortunately, continued Coningham, choosing his words with care, Montgomery's plan could not be

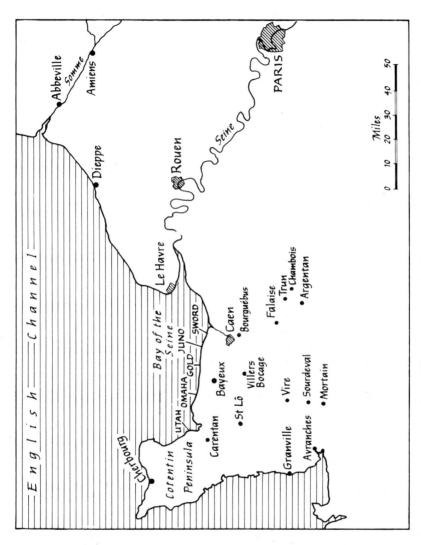

7. The Normandy Campaign, 1944

carried out. Before D-Day, Montgomery had made it clear to commanders in all services that he intended to make a major effort in the Caen area to capture terrain suitable for airfield construction; after D-Day, however, the strength of German resistance obliged him first to abandon that intention and then to deny that it had ever existed. Coningham, having seen Montgomery play this particular game before, did not allow his anger and exasperation to blind him to the hard work and bravery of the Army's five Airfield Construction Groups: these, he wrote, 'enabled me to take a justifiable risk in concentrating more aircraft on each airfield than was originally planned'.[8]

On the morning of 14 June, Wing Commander Leslie Scarman (Tedder's diarist) recorded that the 'complacency' of a meeting at Bentley Priory was 'disturbed' when Coningham bluntly announced that his information on the Army situation – received from Broadhurst – did not agree with that given by Brigadier Charles Richardson, Montgomery's representative. Units of the 7th Armoured Division, reported Coningham, had suffered a severe setback the previous day; the situation was 'near crisis' and there could be no disguising it. Finding a weakly-defended point between two Panzer divisions, British tanks had rolled into Villers Bocage, but a fierce counter-attack destroyed many and drove out the rest. The position was made worse, Coningham said, by the fact that no fresh Allied formations were due to land on the 14th or the next day and those currently engaged had been fighting almost continuously for a week and were becoming exhausted.

As for air action, he continued, the fact that German forces were reaching the front in very small detachments from various directions made it difficult to strike severe blows and the weather had been bad on the 13th, limiting the number of sorties that could be flown. But 'a terrific air punch', said Tedder, would be put in that day on targets close to the frontline, 'largely for morale purposes'. According to Scarman, Tedder was already considering the abolition of AEAF Headquarters and the dismissal of Leigh-Mallory, as Coningham and the Americans wanted, for 'LM, though earnest, does not inspire confidence. Even Harris [head of Bomber Command], who cooperates magnificently, is irritated at AEAF delay in giving him his targets for the night. This is due to LM's request "for a think", as he puts it, at the daily conference.' Tedder visited Eisenhower after the meeting and they decided to go to Normandy next day and see for themselves what substance there was in Coningham's claim.[9]

Leigh-Mallory chose to visit Montgomery on the 14th, proposing a heavy bomber attack to break the stalemate at Caen and sending representatives to Dempsey's headquarters to discuss aiming points, all this without consulting either Spaatz or Coningham. Tedder, however, had already advised Coningham to go to Normandy himself, await his arrival with Eisenhower, and then – with American support – they would scupper Leigh-Mallory's proposal. This they did, arguing that high-level bombers would find it difficult to identify targets and would be obliged to leave such a wide safety margin that the subsequent advance would be over untouched ground. Tedder also told Montgomery that Coningham, not Leigh-Mallory, was his opposite number and Broadhurst's was Dempsey – as had been made perfectly clear before D-Day. 'Monty,' noted Scarman, merely said he 'was relieved to get this laid down with authority' and continued to play Leigh-Mallory and Coningham against each other on the grounds that one provided strategic and the other tactical air support. Tedder and Coningham, wrote Leigh-Mallory on 10 July, 'agreed between themselves that the Army should be supported only by the Tactical Air Force' and 'there was nothing that I could do except acquiesce or clear out'. In fact, Leigh-Mallory found a third alternative: he aligned himself with Montgomery.[10]

Coningham, meanwhile, returned to England and made another blunt statement to his fellow commanders at their meeting on 16 June. The Army, he said, must 'keep in mind what they had planned and where they had planned to be by D+10 and admit that the plan had failed'. Nothing was to be gained by claiming that all was well and 'a greater sense of urgency was needed'. Major General Kenneth Strong, Eisenhower's Chief Intelligence Officer, agreed with Coningham and Scarman recorded that Strong told Tedder he was 'anxious lest we delay through excess of caution. We have won the build-up race: exploit it.' During the night of 15–16 June, however, an alarming attack on London by flying-bombs had begun, distracting attention from the Normandy campaign. Leigh-Mallory 'regretfully observed' on the 16th that 'help against the flying bomb would be required from 2nd TAF as well as from the Strategic Air Forces if launching sites were to be effectively neutralised'. Coningham announced next morning that seven of his squadrons had been assigned to assist attacks on those sites, codenamed 'Crossbow' operations, but the targets were difficult to hit and neither strategic commanders (eager to destroy German capacity and will to fight on) nor tactical commanders (equally eager to help ground forces break out of Normandy and advance across France into Germany) welcomed such operations.[11]

On 19 June, Coningham reported that the 9th Air Force was giving excellent close support to an American advance in the Cotentin Peninsula towards Cherbourg and that as many as seven wings – four British, three American – of fighters and fighter-bombers were now based in France. Spaatz having told Bradley (Commander, US 1st Army) that 1,200 heavy bombers could be assigned to help him capture Cherbourg, the air commanders met on 21 June to consider the offer. Coningham saw no more use for heavies at Cherbourg than at Caen and the American airmen agreed: the tactical air forces could cope and in any case bad weather ruled out the heavies. Brereton then asked Coningham, wrote Vandenberg, 'if he wanted to take this over, but was informed that it was purely an American show and that Brereton had the ball. Coningham added, however, that his force was available for use by Brereton.' Next morning, at the usual meeting in Bentley Priory, Air Vice-Marshal Stephen Strafford (Coningham's Chief of Plans and

Operations) outlined Brereton's plan. Inexcusably, he referred to the support from the air 'as being provided by 2nd TAF and elements of the 9th': words which upset the Americans and earned him a sharp rebuke from Coningham.[12]

Operation Epsom, Montgomery's latest plan to capture Caen and open country to the south and south-east which was suitable for airfields and tank movements alike, began on 25 June. The plan, explained by Coningham to Leigh-Mallory on the previous day, required the air forces to bombard strongpoints around Caen airfield in order to protect the Army's left flank during its advance. Leigh-Mallory thought the plan tame and unambitious and wanted to use heavy bombers to get Montgomery moving: the Russians, he said, were advancing in the east and might reach Berlin while the Allies were still west of the Rhine. Coningham replied that he would ask for heavies if he thought they could help, but for the moment Montgomery was content with the support of mediums and fighter-bombers.

Tedder visited Portsmouth on 28 June, recorded Scarman, to see de Guingand and 'examine the allegation of hitches in air–ground cooperation'. Next morning, he flew to France with de Guingand to discuss the matter further with Coningham and Broadhurst over lunch at 83 Group Head-quarters. Tedder then met Montgomery in an attempt 'to allay Army fears of Coningham'. Epsom had become bogged down amid recriminations all round and Eisenhower told Tedder on the 30th that he was worried about Army–Air cooperation. Montgomery, Scarman noted, had suggested to Eisenhower that Coningham was 'being too critical and a little uncooperative. Chief's view is matter will not be settled till, as in Africa, the Army and Air commanders live side by side.' Tedder then saw Portal to brief him 're Mary and Monty' and urge, yet again, the abolition of AEAF.[13]

Nevertheless, despite hard words exchanged on paper or round tables, the superiority of German soldiers in sheer fighting skill ensured that actual cooperation between all Allied forces in the field was becoming closer. Coningham and Brereton spent a couple of days together in France at the end of June discussing first with Broadhurst and Quesada how best to improve the mutual support of their air forces and then with Bradley how best to support his next attack. They also inspected flying-bomb sites in the Cotentin Peninsula which had been expertly camouflaged. 'These sites,' said Brereton, 'can be built more quickly than they can be destroyed' and Coningham agreed that this fact made still more urgent the need for the Allied armies to break out of their bridgehead and overrun the missile sites for 'they are not profitable targets for air attack'.[14]

Whatever rivalries existed between airmen – British or American, strategic or tactical – they all agreed that newspapers and radio bulletins gave inadequate attention to air operations and that this neglect had an adverse effect on morale. Harris, head of Bomber Command, observed on 30 June that he had lost 4,000 men during the past two months – about twice the number of British soldiers so far killed in Normandy – and Coastal Command had played a vital part in eliminating the U-boat menace in the Channel, yet the press continued to regard ground action as the 'real' war. Coningham supported Harris. Dempsey, he said, could not move without Broadhurst's support and yet the press never mentioned Broadhurst, but Leigh-Mallory thought much of the blame for this lack of attention lay with the Air Ministry and advised Harris and Coningham to direct complaints there.[15]

At the end of June, however, Coningham had more cause for satisfaction – or at least relief – than complaint. As in earlier campaigns, Ultra provided Allied commanders with so much information about enemy intentions that operational planning contained little guesswork; and Elmhirst provided 2nd TAF with the detailed, efficient management of men and material which enabled Coningham to make the best use of Ultra. It was Elmhirst who weedled out of the Air Ministry the loan of one Dakota per fighter squadron for the day of its move across the Channel. A week before that move, ground crews and heavy equipment were despatched by road to embarkation ports and thence to Normandy while pilots and aircraft continued to operate from permanent Fighter Command airfields (with the help of a few key people) until their ground crews reported that they were ready to receive them. The squadron then combined a routine operation with escort for the Dakota carrying its key people and all the personal kit and bedding of the pilots. 'The scheme was a great success,' wrote Elmhirst, 'and enabled me to report to Mary every morning during the invasion period that he had the full strength of his force available.' Elmhirst also persuaded the Air Ministry to let him form a 'support unit' for each Group going to Normandy. 'They were big units,' he recalled, 'some thousand men in each, and they held three reserve pilots per squadron and some 150 aircraft, three in reserve for each squadron.' Like Coningham, Elmhirst was acutely aware that 'fighter pilots are a very highly-tempered weapon which bad handling can blunt very easily . . . Other than bad leadership, probably the worst thing for a squadron's morale is gaps. Pilots expect losses among themselves and their aircraft through battle and airfield crashes, but they become depressed if those gaps are not quickly made good.' His support units solved that problem.[16]

Coningham and Larry Kuter had been delighted to renew their friendship at intervals between meetings in mid-June and as soon as he returned to Washington Kuter wrote to thank Coningham for 'the dinner and delightful evening with you and your Lady. That evening was also not only a high point in fine company, in quality of fine food, fine wine and liquor but, as far as I was concerned, it was also a high point in consumption of the latter. That seven passenger Packard the ETO provided was just barely big enough for me to get into.' Kuter had visited 'our old friends' Joe Cannon and General Alex in Italy and passed on their best wishes as well as news about their excellent progress. Coningham's recommendation that he be awarded the CBE had been approved and Kuter deeply appreciated the honour 'and particularly the fact that the citation came from you'. 'Can't you do something about getting this fighting business over', Kuter ended, 'so that the orderly course of holidaying may be resumed', for he and his wife looked forward very much to entertaining the Coninghams in the United States.[17]

Eisenhower, who visited Tedder on 1 July was 'worried at dilatoriness of Monty outside Caen', noted Scarman, 'and at frankness of Coningham's criticism of Army. Monty and de Guingand would not mind the removal of Mary. Chief has told Ike his removal would be a disaster and his frankness is justified.' Eisenhower then flew to Normandy with Coningham in Brereton's C-47, *Debonair Duke*. Brereton wrote:

> On the way over, I had a very frank conversation with General
> Eisenhower about my differences with AEAF. This in no way involved
> Coningham, with whom my relations could not have been better. The
> outcome was that Coningham would run the 2nd TAF and I would run
> the 9th AF. Any matters between us that needed a decision would go
> through AEAF Headquarters to a higher authority.

Eisenhower spent the night at Montgomery's headquarters and Brereton entertained Coningham at Grandcamp. It was just the kind of evening Coningham most enjoyed: 'a nice dinner, prepared by French chefs' (recalled Brereton), followed by 'some excellent Courvoisier, which had been "liberated" by my aides' and convivial company, including Quesada. Thus fortified, they easily survived the following morning – a Sunday – as Montgomery's guests at Bayeux. The General read the lesson at a church service and then explained his latest interpretation of the Master Plan: that the early capture of Caen had never, in fact, been part of it and that his intention had always been to use the British and Canadian armies to hold tight in the east, attracting maximum German opposition in order to permit an easier American breakout in the west. Coningham did not hide his contempt for this shuffling and Eisenhower returned from France on 5 July, still 'very worried over Monty's relations with the Air', wrote Scarman. 'Situation is that Monty thinks Air is not sufficiently vigorous in support of immediate battle, Coningham is highly critical of the slow progress of the Army.'[18]

Coningham completed a memorandum, *Reorganisation for Future Operations*, on 6 July. Reorganisation, he wrote, was needed for three reasons: 'The dual appointment (and personality) of General Montgomery; the division of Air Force needs between England and the Continent; the comparative redundancy and unwieldy nature of AEAF, as at present constituted.' Efficient operations depended upon 'a proper and simple chain of command' and that required Eisenhower to assume executive command of both Army groups, but at present, wrote Coningham, 'Montgomery is under the impression that SHAEF and the Supreme Commander will remain based in England, dealing largely with political matters and the broadest direction of land operations, whilst he, Montgomery, conducts field operations' and retains control of both British and American forces: 'I cannot see how this can continue.' Coningham wanted SHAEF *in England* to control the Allied TAFs (as well as Air Defence of Great Britain and the two heavy bomber commands) through a small, purely operational, air staff *on the Continent*. With regard to command, an 'interim suggestion' (pending approval of a reorganisation) 'is that I and Brereton should be commander and deputy respectively of Allied TAF and at the same time command our respective forces', an arrangement that 'has the advantage of keeping both of us in command of our forces at a time when the armies need educating'. Coningham gave copies of his memorandum to Leigh-Mallory and Tedder on 6 July. 'His views are like ours,' remarked Scarman, 'an air staff in SHAEF and elimination of AEAF.'[19]

Eisenhower despatched a most carefully-composed letter to Montgomery on 7 July. 'When we began this operation,' he said, 'we demanded from the air that they obtain air superiority and that they delay the arrival of enemy reinforcements in the Neptune [beachhead] area. Both of these things have been done.' That beachhead must now be expanded. Advance on the right, the American flank, had been 'slow and laborious, due not only to the nature of the country and the impossibility of employing air and artillery with maximum effectiveness, but to the arrival on that front of reinforcements'. On the left, the Anglo-Canadian flank, 'a major full-dress attack . . . supported by everything we could bring to bear', had not yet been attempted. 'Through Coningham and Broadhurst,' emphasised Eisenhower, 'there is available all the air that could be used,' ending with a promise to 'back you up to the limit' in any effort made to break the deadlock. Montgomery replied next day, assuring the Supreme Commander that he was still 'quite happy about the situation' and 'working throughout on a very definite plan'. Part of that plan called for the dismissal of Coningham. Like Tedder and the principal American commanders (ground and air), Coningham had the rank, experience and independent authority necessary to criticise Montgomery's conduct of operations and draw influential attention to the gulf between his words and deeds; unlike them, thought Montgomery, Coningham could be silenced.[20]

To that end, Montgomery had complained to both Tedder and Brooke (head of the British Army) about him on 7 July. 'The Army,' according to Montgomery, was unhappy: it lacked confidence in Coningham; it knew that he said 'unpleasant things about it – behind its back'; it was having difficulty in getting full value from the available air support because of his rivalry with Leigh-Mallory; and was, in short, 'beginning to wonder if Coningham is a loyal member of the team'. Tedder passed these opinions on to Coningham, who visited Montgomery to hear them for himself and left, said Montgomery, 'almost in tears', aware at last, presumably, that loyalty should exclude criticism. 'Since then,' Montgomery assured Brooke, 'his attitude has been very different and his advances almost an embarrassment!!'

Montgomery, that apostle of loyalty, then explained to Brooke his use of Dempsey (Commander, 2nd Army) to undermine Coningham: 'Dempsey and his staff do not know a very great deal *yet* about how to wield air power,' wrote Montgomery, but Dempsey is 'very teachable and will soon get "the form"; just at present, he is inclined to rush his fences somewhat and to be impatient; whereas the only real answer is to proceed very carefully and to lead "the air" down the garden path – but we must always be right and must remember that the path is a bit slippery.' Brooke, apparently, did not consider such conduct reprehensible, nor was he able to have Coningham dismissed. In fact, so far from contemplating his removal, Portal was at that time planning to bring Leigh-Mallory back to England (as Air Member for Personnel) and divide his duties between Tedder and Coningham.[21]

The next attempt to capture Caen, Operation Charnwood, began in the late evening of 7 July with a massive raid by heavy bombers on the city's northern suburbs. Coningham opposed the raid, knowing that it would merely create huge holes and mounds of rubble, as at Cassino in Italy, to impede an advance by ground forces and provide defenders with excellent concealed firing-points. Heavy bombers, in his view, were not a battlefield weapon, but Montgomery – acutely aware that Churchill was listening to growing criticism of his handling of the campaign – urgently demanded their support and Eisenhower backed him in the hope of seeing some forward movement on the British front. A creeping artillery barrage began at 4.20 next morning and behind it Dempsey's troops moved forward, supported all day by Broadhurst's aircraft. But the going was so difficult and German opposition so fierce that only four tanks and a few troops had entered Caen by nightfall. Next day, bulldozers and tanks cleared lanes through the rubble and by evening the ruins north of the Orne river were in British hands: an achievement of no immediate advantage as long as the Germans continued to hold a line along the river, the eastern suburb of Colombelles (where they observed British movements from the towers of steelworks) and the heights of Bourgébus Ridge, four miles to the south-east.[22]

Montgomery's claim that the bombing 'played a vital part in the success of the operation' is contradicted by the report of an investigation on 12 July by a group of senior officers, Army and Air Force. The report concluded that the raid, though cheering up British troops and depressing enemy morale, killed few Germans. 'Many divisional officers expressed puzzlement as to the object of the bombing as they had seen no signs of road blocks or any other defences in that area. The French inhabitants also said that there had been no Germans or German-prepared positions in the area destroyed.' The conclusion was therefore unavoidable that 'a great deal of French property was devastated without sufficient justification and some scepticism was felt about the existence of the batteries and other targets listed by the 2nd British Army'.[23]

Refusing to allow such details to clutter his mind, Montgomery turned instead to Operation Goodwood (an offensive east of the Orne) due to begin on 18 July. Eisenhower – knowing his man – heaped praise upon it, adding that Coningham 'has already given you the assurance you desire concerning air. All senior airmen are in full accord because this operation will be a brilliant stroke which will knock loose our present shackles.' Goodwood, alas, proved yet another example of the gulf between Montgomery's words and deeds, yet another example (as Major-General Sir Percy Hobart told Liddell Hart after the war) of a 'lack of sufficiently bold leadership on the part of the armoured divisional commanders' coupled with a readiness to make excuses.[24]

Coningham told his fellow commanders on 19 July that his airmen had had a heavy day on the 18th, working in close support of Dempsey's Army. The Americans, however, had 'held the ring', permitting the British freedom of action over the battle area; cooperation and performance alike, he thought, had been excellent. Scarman noted on 19 July that relations between the Army and Air commanders remained very bad: 'Montgomery will NOT deal with Coningham, but only with LM. This entails Broadhurst, Coningham's subordinate, dealing *direct* with LM' who had nevertheless moved his personal caravan from Broadhurst's headquarters to Montgomery's and 'seems to be cashing in on the discomfiture of his own subordinate'.[25]

The facts of the military situation, however, argued powerfully for Coningham and against Montgomery. Tedder telephoned Eisenhower about 9 pm on 19 July to say that the British Chiefs of Staff would support 'any recommendation' he cared to make: 'meaning' (according to Butcher) 'that if Ike wanted to sack Monty for not succeeding in going places with his big three armored division push, he would have no trouble, officially.' 'The Air people', added Butcher, 'are completely disgusted with Monty' and though Eisenhower shared their opinion, he had agreed to Montgomery's request for a private meeting: 'i.e., no airmen or top rankers along to stifle Monty's anticipated belly ache'. Butcher thought 'Chief Big Wind' had a 60–40 chance of avoiding the sack, largely because of 'the British system of limiting the number of names of British generals who may be written about in the public prints or publicised on the BBC'. Tedder spent the following afternoon (20 July) with Portal, who was 'most concerned' (recorded Scarman) 'about the Army failure and, as Chief, regards Monty as cause'. They also discussed 'LM's flirtation with Monty at Coningham's expense', a misjudgment that would not only cost Leigh-Mallory his place in the campaign, but also his appointment as Air Member for Personnel.[26]

Montgomery, meanwhile, had 'put Ike fully in the picture', as he told Major General Frank Simpson (Brooke's Secretary) on 21 July, 'about the friction in "air" circles between LM and Coningham; and told him the Army views on Coningham – all most confidentially.' But Eisenhower, writing to Montgomery that day, showed himself more concerned with the General's performance than with the Air Marshal's. When the armoured divisions, wrote Eisenhower, 'assisted by tremendous air attacks', broke through the enemy's forward lines, he had been 'extremely hopeful and optimistic . . .

205

that at last we had him and were going to roll him up. That did not come about.' 'Right now,' he pointed out, 'we have the ground and air strength and the stores to support major assaults by both armies simultaneously' and 'do not need to fear, at this moment, a great counter-offensive.'[27]

Eisenhower's rebuke, characteristically courteous, disappointed Tedder: 'Not strong enough,' he told Scarman that afternoon. 'Montgomery can evade it. It contains no *order*.' Tedder therefore drafted a long, blunt letter (approved by Portal) which he sent to the Supreme Commander on 23 July.

> I cannot forget that for weeks after the initial landing, while our build-up proceeded to programme, the enemy was struggling from hand to mouth with quite inadequate forces split up in bits and pieces along a line, disorganised in command, short of weapons and material of all sorts. On the western flank, despite difficulties of terrain, we were able to widen the beachhead and clear the Cotentin Peninsula. On the eastern flank, despite our overwhelming superiority, we were apparently unable to exploit our advantage and now, more than six weeks after the landing, one of our beaches, and the only port of any size, is still under enemy shell fire.

Tedder had 'no faith', he concluded, in the General's latest plan and urged Eisenhower to take personal command of all the Allied armies in France. Until then, Tedder advised, Eisenhower should ensure that Montgomery gave 'clear and unequivocal' orders for 'energetic and decisive action'. Unfortunately, as the historian Max Hastings observed, 'He whom propaganda has made mighty, no man may readily cast aside': on this principle, Portal found (a few months later) that he could not get rid of Harris; Tedder could not get rid of Montgomery for the same reason.[28]

Coningham reverted to command of 2nd TAF on 5 August ('Advanced AEAF' ceasing to exist) and moved his headquarters from Uxbridge to a site near Montgomery's Main Headquarters, newly established at Le Tronquay, just south of Bayeux. 'Our camp here is delightfully set up in an orchard,' wrote Elmhirst on the 9th, with caravans for himself, Groom and Coningham. 'Cows feeding around my caravan and butter, milk, cream and cheese such as we have not seen since before the war. Wonderful weather and the surroundings ideal for a quiet life: no bombs, doodlebugs or sirens, much quieter than London' though Frank Sayer, Coningham's driver, remembered naval shells roaring overhead like express trains. As in Tunisia, Coningham ensured that his headquarters was lavishly supplied with American rations, far superior to British, and arranged for supplies of fresh bread from England to be dropped by Spitfire each morning. The ground and air battles, though going well, would go better (Elmhirst thought) now that the Army and Air headquarters were at last together.

> It has been a nightmare for Mary and Victor these last two months and little less for me, trying to run our show under Leigh-Mallory's HQ at

Stanmore who were 'supposed' to be in direct touch with Monty's 21st Army Group HQ at St Paul's. I have been able more or less successfully to sidetrack LM's HQ and work with those I should, Air Ministry and 21st Army Group, but not so Mary and Victor. I only hope now that LM's HQ will quietly fade out, it's a big 'empire' which should never have been allowed to arise.[29]

Morning meetings with the soldiers had resumed, to Elmhirst's delight, but Montgomery, 'living as a recluse two miles away', did not attend. While in seclusion, he received a letter from Sir James Grigg, Secretary of State for War, written on 1 August.

> I am convinced, that Conyngham [sic] is continuing to badnam [sic] you and the Army and that what he says in this kind is easily circulated in SHAEF via Tedder and again that Bedell [Smith] – who seems to have become very conceited and very sour – listens too readily to the poison. If I am right, then you will have no comfort until you have demanded and obtained the removal of Conyngham from any connection with Overlord whatever. He is a bad and treacherous man and will never be other than a plague to you.

Montgomery replied next day. Your letter, he said, 'is quite first class and I had a real good hearty laugh when reading it; a good "lash out" all round is an excellent thing. What we really need is an extensive use of weed killer; we would then progress rapidly towards the end of the war.'[30]

Unaware of this key to victory, Bradley tried another one. On 25 July, he had begun a major American offensive – Operation Cobra – from St Lô in the west of the bridgehead. Intended primarily to escape at long last from the dreaded bocage (a region of numerous tiny fields enclosed by earth banks and dense hedges, a gift to cunning defenders), the offensive actually burst through the hitherto impenetrable German ring. With his forces in Avranches by the 30th, Bradley realised that his original intention (to concentrate on the conquest of Brittany) should now be replaced by a massive thrust eastward; and that it should be led by Patton, a man ideally suited to exploit an unexpected opportunity by driving his newly-formed 3rd Army both harder and faster than any other Allied commander of his day would have thought possible. The early days of August proved the most decisive of the Normandy campaign because not only were the Allies at last on the move, but Hitler himself was helping them. He ordered a counter-offensive (aimed between Sourdeval and Mortain) and refused to permit a controlled withdrawal to the Seine. Left to themselves, the Germans would have resisted the Allied advance, stubbornly and fiercely, for weeks to come; as it was, thanks to Hitler, the last of their strength was wasted in days. They then fled eastward, were trapped and slaughtered in thousands.[31]

The Germans launched their attack on 7 August, capturing Mortain and other villages. Coningham and Vandenberg (who had replaced Brereton as head of the 9th Air Force on 1 August) agreed that 2nd TAF's rocket-armed aircraft should tackle the armoured columns while the 9th Air Force put up a fighter screen and used its fighter-bombers to attack transport moving into the battle zone. Once this decision was made, wrote Coningham, Broadhurst and Quesada worked out the details between them 'and proved the wisdom of our insistence on good lateral communications'. For the first time in Normandy, air forces had a chance to strike at a German armoured concentration and 'as the day developed, it was obvious', in Coningham's opinion, 'that air history was being made'. There were no fixed positions at which heavy bombers could have aimed, for this was a battle of armoured columns 'striking with speed in what might be a decisive concentration against our ground forces'. When the fighter-bomber pilots saw the spearheads of the enemy columns being engaged by American armour and anti-tank weapons, they turned their attention to the centre and rear of the enemy columns. Overall, he concluded, the day had seen one of the war's best demonstrations of the tactical use of air power. 'It proved that a Tactical Air Force may be a decisive battle-winning factor and it showed the smooth coordination of air effort which could be achieved at short notice by the teamwork which had been perfected between the 9th Air Force and 2nd TAF.' And now, added Elmhirst, 'with the American Army running round his flank and our Army hammering hard here and taking a heavy toll, the Hun is in a tight corner and will have to run shortly. He will be in for a very sticky retreat if the weather holds, as we have a very fine force of fighter-bombers here now. I guess we will be in Paris before the end of the month.'[32]

On that same day, 7 August, Montgomery mounted Operation Totalize. The newly activated 1st Canadian Army was to drive south (with the 2nd British Army covering its right flank) and take Falaise. Next morning, Bradley ordered Patton to swing north towards Argentan, some twenty miles south of Falaise. He had forces there by the 13th, but Bradley ordered them to stay in Argentan. The Canadians, being inexperienced, were moving slowly and though Montgomery urged the British to join up with them as quickly as possible, he did not send units to reinforce them. It was late on the 16th before they reached Falaise and a gap – now notorious in military history – lay between them and the Americans which was actually sealed ten miles farther east, between Trun and Chambois, on the 19th. The gap, in fact, was converted into a *funnel* and a great part of the German armies which had so effectively bottled up the Allies for ten weeks was destroyed in it.[33]

A week later, Coningham flew over the battlefield, but the sheer immensity of the wreckage and still more the stench rising from thousands of bodies, human and animal, so appalled him that he soon left. It had been 'an astounding day', wrote Elmhirst to his wife at midnight on the 18th: 'I think Dunkirk is nearly avenged and I see no reason why we should not shortly go forward with some ease and capture the flying-bomb coast and take that menace off you and all in and around London.' The destruction was perhaps more complete and Allied casualties were certainly fewer than would have been the case if the Falaise-Argentan gap had been closed earlier. Those Germans who escaped were determined to do so; but they were unable to transport their heavy equipment across the Seine, even if they managed to get it so far; they therefore could not make a stand at that river and had no choice but to continue their flight towards Germany.[34]

During these exhilarating days, Coningham flew his own Fieseler Storch from airfield to airfield, as in North Africa, and often had Elmhirst for company. On 12 August, they were flying back to their orchard when the engine cut out: 'Dare I say it,' wrote Elmhirst, 'we had run out of petrol!', but Coningham found an airfield, made a good forced landing and was refuelled without comment by some very straight-faced airmen. Elmhirst noted:

> He is in good form, and directing his side of the battle to perfection, but much bothered by LM above him. We now realise how lucky we were having 'Ted' behind us in Cairo, Algiers and Tunis. He told me last night that LM had not accepted his recommendation that I should get a CB in the Normandy honours list. No matter, it will come yet and this smooth-running show here is my recompense.[35]

As in North Africa, the slowness of Allied troops in pursuit disappointed Coningham. The Canadians, he told Robb on 29 August, had reported that they would be opposite Rouen on the 27th and therefore pressed him to stop bombing the railway bridges from 1 pm on that day, but two days later they were still three miles away and during all that time the German withdrawal continued undisturbed. 'I have made a big row about this incident here,' wrote Coningham, 'and find that de Guingand and his staff fully agree with my view. This is not the first time that optimism and ridiculous bomblines have let the Germans escape.' He had ordered his Group Commanders ('and am advising the 9th Air Force for like action') to continue their attacks until pilots *see* Allied ground forces within artillery range of targets. Montgomery's headquarters had promised to ensure that spearhead formations were lavishly provided with smoke and special markings so that they could be easily identified. Coningham was certain, as he wrote in his official report after the war, that 'we could have captured a much greater proportion of the enemy west of the Seine, or turned pursuit into a rout'.[36]

Even so, he particularly commended the efforts of Embry's medium bombers, supported by the 9th Air Force, for devastating attacks on the left bank of the Seine at Rouen in the last week of August when vehicles of all kinds were waiting to cross the river. The achievement of the air forces at Rouen were not challenged, but the Operational Research Section of 21st Army Group, reporting on the 'Falaise Gap' battle and the advance to the Seine, found that many pilots had over-claimed and considered the rocket an over-rated weapon. By the time of the investigation, replied Coningham, 'salvage parties, looters and the tide of battle had covered the ground so that it was difficult to ascertain exactly what were the causes of destruction'. More important, his task had been to cause confusion and prevent a planned withdrawal: consequently, he did not aim to destroy tanks or vehicles one by one, but to attack the heads of convoys and so disorganise enemy troops that they were incapable of disciplined action. 'This was undoubtedly achieved,' Coningham believed, 'by the 2nd TAF in the Shambles area and by British and US fighter and medium bombers west of Rouen. They carried out interdiction in the true meaning of the term – the prevention of enemy movement.' The Army claimed all the credit for the withdrawal, but Coningham argued, with justice, that it was 'the result of a combined effort by both air and ground forces'.[37]

Pondering the 'Lessons of Normandy' in 1952, Liddell Hart observed that Allied attacks had rarely succeeded unless they had a superiority in strength of *more than five to one*, accompanied by command of the air 'which at least doubles the value of attacking ground forces and in some staff calculations has been reckoned as trebling it'. On the other hand, the land and rivers of Normandy proved easy to defend and immense material resources encouraged the Allied armies to let the machine win the battle. British troops in particular, as the Germans often remarked, showed much greater determination in defence than in attack. Not least, there was a feeling that the end of the war was near and no-one wanted to be the last man killed. Had it not been for the airmen, Liddell Hart concluded, who hampered the enemy at every turn, results would have been much worse. Nevertheless, massive superiority in manpower, equipment and supplies eventually prevailed and by the end of August, the last German troops had crossed the Seine and their domination of France was clearly at an end.[38]

CHAPTER SIXTEEN

Commander-in-Chief and 'Renaissance Prince'

Coningham in Brussels, September to December 1944

Early in September 1944, at the height of rejoicing over the triumphant end to the Normandy Campaign, Coningham came close to losing his great command. Portal and Sinclair (Secretary of State for Air) had been anxious for some time to find a new Air Member for Personnel to deal with overall manning policy and, in particular, senior appointments and promotions. The present incumbent, Bertine Sutton, was becoming worn out by the burdens of a demanding task and Leigh-Mallory had been a serious contender to replace him before the Normandy Campaign, but Sinclair now much preferred Coningham. He had no doubt, he told Portal on 2 September, about Coningham's 'high reputation in the Service. He is versatile and a man of the world . . . has breadth of understanding, good judgment and a strong character.' He had no experience of the Air Ministry, however, and this lack, together with the fact that the war soon took an alarming turn for the worse, kept Coningham in the field and Sutton in his office until the following April. It was then decided that this influential position should go to Jack Slessor, an officer whose administrative experience far surpassed Coningham's.[1]

Meanwhile, as Elmhirst wrote home from Normandy on 1 September, 'Things out here are going like wildfire.' He expected the Allies to be in the Low Countries in two or three weeks 'and then it is a case of whether the Hun will fight it out in his own country or give in. He *ought* to give in, but Hitler is a madman!' Coningham, wrote Elmhirst, had already taken a 'residence' in Paris: 'he had fixed the one he wanted before we left England and his French ADC was in Paris the day the troops went in [25 August] with a signed letter from our old friend General Koenig, now Governor there, allotting him the house of a supposed collaborator.' Elmhirst added that Coningham had also chosen the location of a future headquarters in northern Germany: 'He says it's the best possible place in view of the fact that the RAF ought to be there for twenty years!'[2]

Eisenhower had moved his headquarters to France on 1 September and taken personal command of the Allied ground forces there, divided between the Anglo-Canadians of 21st Army Group (under Montgomery) and the Americans of 12th Army Group (under Bradley). After breaking out of Normandy, the original plan had been to pause and regroup at the Seine, but events now dictated immediate pursuit of disorganised foes. Eisenhower favoured pursuit on a broad front, with Montgomery advancing north of the Ardennes, through Belgium towards the Rhine and Bradley driving south of the Ardennes, towards the Saar and the Frankfurt Gap. Montgomery's demand for a *combined* thrust to the Ruhr was rejected, but his own thrust was approved on the understanding that he make Antwerp his first major target: the largest and best-equipped port in Europe, Antwerp's capture was vital, for the Norman ports were proving quite unable to handle Allied supply needs. To protect Montgomery's right flank, Eisenhower gave him the 1st US Army (Commander, Courtney Hodges) and priority in petrol supplies. Bradley, resenting both decisions, permitted Patton to move rapidly east to Metz, where a shortage of petrol (despite 'diversions' from Hodges' army) combined with Eisenhower's support for Montgomery's complaints and stiffening enemy opposition halted him at the end of August.[3]

Coningham gave to 83 Group (operating with the 2nd British Army) the mobile role of maintaining air supremacy ahead of pursuing columns and close support during their advance. To 84 Group (working with the 1st Canadian Army) he gave the task of protecting the western flank of that advance and support for the several combined operations needed to capture ports between Le Havre and Antwerp. As in the Desert campaigns, he emphasised mobility at the expense of numbers, conscious of the need to use every possible flying day to press the enemy hard. Captured airfields, he ruled, were to be cleared of mines and booby traps and no time wasted making new airfields; many squadrons were to be left behind in order to release their ground transport to supply petrol and ammunition for the rest, while air transport was to be used whenever possible to carry forward both men and equipment. The actions of 83 Group, recorded Coningham, were 'singularly successful since the country through which the pursuit passed was of an open rolling nature with few places for concealment and eminently suitable for successful attacks by low-flying fighters and fighter-bombers, which by this time were highly experienced after the closing of the Falaise pocket'. The Group drove as far as Eindhoven, north-east of Antwerp, before it was halted by bad weather and enemy resistance along the Meuse.[4]

The Canadians, meanwhile, demanded the help of heavy bombers as well as 84 Group's tactical aircraft in operations against Le Havre, Dieppe and Boulogne, much to Coningham's anger. 'The Army,' he wrote later, in words carefully vetted by Air Ministry officials, 'had been impressed with the reduction in casualties and the economy in artillery support which resulted from the use of strategic air forces for tactical support', but 'it was inevitable that, owing to the size and location of the targets in and near built-up areas, large numbers of friendly civilians were killed'. Given the air superiority achieved by the tactical air forces, Coningham thought more use should have been made of light, unarmed Auster aircraft, which were under Army control, to direct artillery fire accurately and dispense altogether with the 'wastage of effort' and 'unnecessary damage' caused by heavy bombers. Sir John Colville, Churchill's Private Secretary, observed that Coningham had 'an obsessive hatred for the Germans, combined with over-strong sympathies for the French'. Shortly before D-Day, a couple of padres had complained to Colville about a speech Coningham made to pilots at Odiham in which he stressed the need to take as much care as possible not to kill French men and women or destroy their property, but they could do what they liked to the Germans. Although Colville admired Coningham's 'forcefulness', he was 'mildly shocked by his flamboyance and somewhat excessive outspokenness'.[5]

Coningham's headquarters moved north from the orchard at Le Tronquay in Normandy to a school in Amiens on 5 September and thence to the Residence Palace, Rue de la Loi, in Brussels on the 14th. The palace's most recent occupants had been the Luftwaffe, a fact which gave Coningham immense satisfaction. Coningham, his Personal Assistant (John Lancaster), Groom, and Elmhirst lived in a large house in the Avenue des Nations, now Avenue Franklin Roosevelt, off which lies an avenue named after Coningham. 'All very comfortable,' admitted Elmhirst, 'but I hope we shall be on our way forward and back into tents and caravans shortly.'[6]

Elmhirst, Groom and Broadhurst had been to Paris with Coningham on 3 September for a house-warming dinner in his new 'retreat', taking food with them from Normandy because there was so little in the city. They had all claimed to be too busy, but Coningham insisted: 'The Hun is on the run, and if your jobs are not well enough organised to run without you for 24 hours, they ought to be.' When the dinner guests departed, wrote Elmhirst, 'Victor, Harry and I ran riot and inspected the house from top to bottom, even to trying on the latest Paris hats of the owners. They had departed at an hour's notice and left everything.' The sight – and silence – of Paris shocked them: no fuel for cooking or heating, no trains, buses, trams, taxis or cars, not even the Metro was running, but bicycles – 'including bicycle taxis, a sort of bathchair pulled by two men on a tandem bicycle' – were everywhere. It was 3 am before the Air Marshals fell into bed, but within eight hours they were back on duty, 'all the better for the outing' as a relief from intense pressure.[7]

Coningham and Elmhirst had often flown low over northern France in recent days to see what could be done to repair communications wrecked on their orders which they now needed. At the moment, Elmhirst noted, 'all bridges are down, road and rail junctions and marshalling yards shattered, engines shot up and not one with smoke or steam showing'. As for the towns, Caen, Rouen and parts of Amiens were 'dreadful to see. One feels of

Caen, was it necessary? Mary says no and was very much against it, but was overruled.' However, Elmhirst enjoyed his first visit to Brussels on 9 September: 'not so coldly fastidious as Paris,' he thought. 'People seemed more genuine, more cheerful and more welcoming.' The Germans had departed their offices in evident haste, leaving behind a mass of papers and photographs of Hitler. 'Victor and I,' he added, 'are bidden to join Mary for another party in Paris tomorrow, Sunday night. It's no distance from Amiens and I think we deserve it, but our consciences prick and I don't know whether or not we shall make it.'[8]

Coningham certainly felt he deserved a break, having endured yet another exasperating meeting on 10 September with Leigh-Mallory, who was energetically wringing whatever authority he could out of an office regarded by other commanders as a fifth wheel on the waggon. Leigh-Mallory had crossed to France with Eisenhower, setting up his headquarters alongside, but Coningham and Vandenberg continued to arrange the day-to-day conduct of the fighting in direct consultation with their associated Army Group Commanders, by-passing Leigh-Mallory whenever possible. The meeting on the 10th therefore opened with his complaint that news from 2nd TAF was not reaching him and Coningham's reply that recent rapid movements had upset his communication systems. These ritual exchanges over, Leigh-Mallory announced that Roderic Hill's Air Defence of Great Britain (formerly Fighter Command) must have bases in Belgium and Holland from which to escort Bomber Command raids and carry out offensive operations. Coningham objected that as yet there was no room in newly-liberated territory for Hill's aircraft and even when there was, he could only countenance their presence under his own command. He urged Leigh-Mallory to agree to allot two wings of Tempest aircraft to 2nd TAF, to return a wing of Mustangs presently on loan to Hill and to place the squadron of Meteor jet aircraft under his command as a counter to the growing threat of German jets. He also urged Leigh-Mallory to support his strong belief that 2nd TAF should control its own transport aircraft – and that it needed many more of them.[9]

On the following day, 11 September, came the sickening news that Sir Howard Frank, Nan's elder son by her first marriage, had been killed. A Lieutenant and tank commander in the Guards Armoured Division, he had come safely through the Normandy campaign, but was killed while attempting to capture a bridge over the Escaut Canal, south of Eindhoven. Coningham had had only fleeting chances to meet Howard since his 21st birthday celebration in April and could not then fly home to comfort Nan, though Robert (her younger son, an RAF officer) was in England. Next morning, he broke the news to Elmhirst and Groom. 'Nan and I thought very well of him,' he said, quietly and calmly: 'he seemed a nice young chap.'[10]

By that time, Coningham wrote, 'we could not maintain the momentum of any further advance without the use of Antwerp' – captured on 3 September – 'but with its approaches denied to us by the enemy who had taken up firm positions on either side of the Scheldt Estuary'. Montgomery neglected to clear those approaches and chose instead, against the advice of his own staff, to launch a drive to the Rhine at Arnhem. Operation Market, carried out by the 1st Allied Airborne Army (Commander, Lewis Brereton) between 17–25 September, was intended to seize vital bridges across the Maas (Meuse), Waal and Lower Rhine and establish a corridor through Holland and into Germany for the British 2nd Army. Operation Garden was the code name for that Army's advance from the general line of the Albert and Escaut canals in Belgium to the Zuider Zee in Holland, a distance of about 100 miles – on a very narrow front, with only one road for most of the way. 'We have reached a vital moment in the war,' Montgomery told Simpson (Director of Military Operations in the War Office) on 7 September, 'and if we now take the right decision we could be in Berlin in three weeks and the German war would be over.' Some part of the blame for the subsequent disaster lies with Eisenhower, who did not actually *order* Montgomery to secure Antwerp's approaches first and Montgomery himself admitted after the war that he made 'a bad mistake' in not giving that task priority. Even Brooke agreed on 5 October that Montgomery's strategy had 'for once' been at fault: 'Instead of carrying out the advance on Arnhem, he ought to have made certain of Antwerp in the first place.' Ramsay, the Allied Naval Commander, 'brought this out well in the discussion,' added Brooke, 'and criticised Monty freely. Ike nobly took all the blame on himself as he had approved Monty's suggestion to operate on Arnhem.'[11]

Even so, as John Terraine has written, 'there is no aspect of the preparation of that tragic fiasco' – Operation Market Garden – 'that does not fill one with dismay': not least 'the failure to coordinate Tactical Air action'. Coningham had been unable to give maximum support to the airborne troops because the air plan forbade 2nd TAF to operate over the landing/dropping zones while troop carrier aircraft and gliders were about. Thus opportunities to strike at the enemy were missed, especially when poor weather delayed the arrival of the troop carriers. According to Brereton's Chief of Staff, the commander of the British airborne division (Sir Frederick Browning) thought the disaster was caused in part by 'the prohibition of the area to 2nd TAF during the time when airborne forces and re-supply were flying in'. 'Everybody thought it would be a romp,' recalled Roy Urquhart, who led the descent on Arnhem, though later he realised that 'Air support should have been given high priority. Wireless communications should have been far better and the relieving force should have been able to fight its way through,' but 30 Corps (Commander, Brian Horrocks) which was to cross the bridges taken by the American airborne divisions and relieve the British at Arnhem, 'had lost some of their edge for war,' in Urquhart's opinion.[12]

The operation had been mainly planned by the 1st Allied Airborne Army in England and Coningham's staff composed a report on it, sent to SHAEF Air Staff on 5 January 1945. The numerous mistakes made, they concluded,

> clearly showed that the Tactical Air Force through whose area and on whose front the airborne operations were conducted must have a very considerable say with regard to the provision and coordination of air escort, air support subsequent to the landing, air cover day and night and emergency re-supply when weather conditions prevent flying from bases outside the tactical area.

As a result of the Arnhem disaster, the next airborne operation intended to cross the Rhine – Operation Varsity – was planned at Coningham's headquarters in Brussels with the cooperation of all the air and ground commanders concerned.[13]

Some twenty years later, in June 1964, Robb learned that Groom had recently visited Major L. F. Ellis (at work on an official history, *Victory in the West*) to discuss his draft. With regard to Arnhem, Groom assured Ellis that the planning took place in England, not Brussels, and 2nd TAF was ignored; Robb agreed. In November 1978, David Belchem, Chief of Operations at 21st Army Group Headquarters, supported these claims in a letter to Elmhirst. In his book, *All in the Day's March*, Belchem had been obliged, he said,

> to play the Arnhem story in a low key: so much emotion remains that one cannot be frank. But at Woolwich I was able to make it clear that failure in the Arnhem sector was not the fault of the air forces and bad weather . . . It is correct that the whole planning procedure was too rushed. It was done in London, so that we had no influence upon it, but worse still, the TAF people *did not know* there was to be a battle for Arnhem (apart from the part they were to play) until D-2 (15 September).

Major General J. M. McNeill, then a member of the Air Staff at 21st Army Group Headquarters, clearly remembered in 1986 'our frustration caused by the grounding of 2nd TAF during the re-supply of Arnhem, allegedly because of the danger of misidentification'. The problem, he believed, 'was *not* lack of accord between Monty and Mary (it worked well enough in the Western Desert) but between TAF on the Continent and Bomber Command and Airborne Forces based on English airfields'.[14]

At the end of September, the great advance which began with the breakout from Normandy came to an end. The Allied armies, stretching from the North Sea to the Mediterranean, were halted before the natural obstacles of the Rhine, Meuse, Moselle and the fortifications of the West Wall. Eisenhower's strategy had been to advance on a broad front towards the Ruhr and the Saar, Germany's two great industrial areas, and at the same time open up ports to maintain that advance. Montgomery's flanking movement across the

Lower Rhine had failed and the need to open Antwerp for the receipt of essential supplies of fuel and ammunition was now desperate. The 21st Army Group, crammed into a narrow salient between the North Sea and the Meuse, lacked the strength to conduct operations to the east and at the same time clear the enemy from the Scheldt Estuary. But German armies, strengthening as the Allied advance slackened, were determined to protect the Ruhr and the Saar. Both areas were served by many roads and railway lines and along these reinforcements poured west of the Rhine to confront the surprised and disappointed Allied armies.[15]

On a more cheerful note, as far as Coningham was concerned, the long-heralded dissolution of Leigh-Mallory's headquarters took effect at midnight on 14 October and Tedder became at last formally responsible, unobstructed by 'a fifth wheel', for the coordination of all air operations. To Coningham's delight, he had Robb appointed Chief of Staff (Air) at SHAEF Headquarters and delegated that task to him. The Americans resisted Tedder's attempt to exercise through Robb the authority to which Leigh-Mallory had aspired, arguing that cooperation between Coningham and Vandenberg needed no formal organisation: their own experience, common sense and mutual respect ensured that operations would be wisely conducted. Robb's headquarters, like Leigh-Mallory's, thus became a source of irritation, but the official historians of the USAAF found that Eisenhower, Tedder, Spaatz, Coningham and Vandenberg all had a gift for 'effective cooperation without reference to the legalities inherent in a defective command structure' and left the squabbling to 'lesser men'. Tedder, of course, was aware that Coningham and Robb were firm friends as well as outstanding officers and therefore that he could rely on them to run the British side of the air war and leave him free, as Deputy Supreme Commander, to keep up his keen interest in ground operations.[16]

Coningham, wrote Portal to Sinclair on 5 October, was to be 'solely responsible direct to the Air Ministry for the administration of a very considerable Air Force on the Continent' – four groups, 88 squadrons, 97,000 officers and men by 18 October – and must be raised to Commander-in-Chief status, but for reasons doubtless obvious to Air Ministry bureaucrats he could not at the same time be promoted to Air Chief Marshal rank, equivalent to full General. Nevertheless, after Tedder, he was now the senior RAF officer on the Continent and Robb was not far behind. Both men, on the rare occasions when they could be alone together, wondered at their present eminence when it seemed such a little time ago that they themselves were frontline pilots, fighting the same enemy in the same skies.[17]

Harold Balfour (Under-Secretary of State for Air) wrote to Coningham on 8 October, thanking him for arranging a visit to Falaise. Coningham replied at once, hoping that Balfour now realised why he was so averse to bombing Allied villages just because the Army thought that as road centres their destruction would hinder the enemy: a view that was making him unpopular 'in high places'. Chief of those highly-placed critics was Montgomery who complained to Eisenhower on 8 October about Leigh-Mallory's departure. Eisenhower's assurance that Tedder – Coningham's unwavering patron – would henceforth command all air forces in the west encouraged the Field Marshal's already notorious inclination to prefer the company of 'young and adoring acolytes' (as Michael Howard called them) who became old and adoring apologists and to avoid regular contact with his fellow commanders: men who had the rank, character and experience to argue with him.[18]

Leigh-Mallory sent a farewell message to 'My dear Coningham' on 11 October. 'Our role in the battle,' he wrote, 'was threefold: we had to ensure air supremacy, to paralyse the enemy's communications and generally disorganise the German battle force to facilitate the defeat of the enemy in the field. These tasks you have carried out with speed, efficiency and great gallantry.' Coningham, touched by these generous words, replied in similar terms. Within a few weeks, Leigh-Mallory would be dead, killed when the Avro York taking him to India struck a ridge in the Belledonne Mountains, some fifteen miles east of Grenoble. A little more than three years later, Coningham himself was killed in another aircraft accident. Whatever quarrels went before, it is good to know that their last exchange was friendly.[19]

The dissolution of AEAF, wrote Coningham, simplified the command structure. He and Montgomery were responsible for planning and executing all ground and air operations in the British area, but Montgomery spent most of his time at a forward Tactical Headquarters whereas Coningham remained at his Main Headquarters in Brussels. Close to his senior operational staff and in the centre of the communication network, he was able to make the rapid decisions necessary to exploit the flexibility of air power and, he added, 'study the personalities' of his staff and 'watch for any signs of overstrain during the critical periods of the campaign'. However, what Coningham called the 'deliberate disassociation' of Montgomery from his Main Headquarters caused problems. 'He and I used to meet at his Tac HQ at intervals to discuss and to decide upon our joint plan for the conduct of the battle by the Army and Air Forces in the British sector', but the absence of Montgomery from daily meetings meant that the 'responsible Soldier' was not in touch with the 'responsible Airman'. This method of doing business, thought Coningham, was wrong.

> My year with General Alexander, covering all the complications of Allied command in Tunisia and the series of difficult amphibious operations up to the advance on Rome, proved the point. As is usual in such cases, more junior commanders copy their chief and both General Leese in Africa and General Dempsey in Europe lived at a similar Tac HQ away from the Main Army/Air HQ.

This disassociation, not found among the Americans, was 'a luxury which only a winning force with overwhelming strength can afford'.[20]

Sir Wilfrid Freeman, currently Chief Executive in the Ministry of Aircraft Production, formerly Vice-Chief of the Air Staff and throughout the war Portal's closest friend, gave himself the pleasure of frequent and unrestrained comment to Portal on the RAF's men and affairs. Coningham was the object of his displeasure on 14 October for spreading 'alarm and despondency' over the danger from German jet aircraft and 'instigating politicians and others to demand the immediate production of jets no matter what the cost'. The answer to low-flying jets, wrote Freeman, was AA fire and 'if Coningham has allowed this aspect of defence to be neglected (as he has) he should, I think, be asked why and if his reply is inadequate he can be replaced by someone who has a better understanding of air warfare.' In Freeman's opinion, jets were not an immediate danger. However, if Coningham had 'cold feet with the first touch of frost in the air, he should try mustard in his bath or return to a warmer climate and at all costs he should be prevented from passing on this distressing and by no means universal complaint to his subordinates'. No-one else would have dreamt of writing in such terms to Portal, though this letter, by Freeman's standard of invective, is extremely mild. For example, he described Douglas Evill as 'a pathological case'; Bertine Sutton as 'hopelessly senile'; Arthur Barratt as 'incredibly stupid' and Sholto Douglas as 'beneath contempt', socially and morally, though he at least was 'well equipped mentally'. Portal no doubt found this abuse a refreshing change from the rest of the correspondence flowing across his desk and distilled from it, in Coningham's case, the admission that jet aircraft were a *potential* threat to be guarded against – precisely the point Coningham had been urging.[21]

Eisenhower held a conference in his headquarters at Versailles on 18 October at which he instructed Montgomery to devote all his resources to the clearance of the Antwerp Estuary. He also decided that the 1st US Army should undertake an offensive to gain a footing across the Rhine south of Cologne in the first week of November and approved Montgomery's plan to capture Walcheren Island at the same time. This 'unfortunate island', wrote Coningham, 'was rapidly becoming inundated due to the breaching of the dykes by Bomber Command, thereby isolating and disorganising the perimeter defences and coastal batteries on the island'. During attacks on the Breskens Peninsula, repeated demands were made by the Canadians to Brown (head of 84 Group) for heavy bombing, quite regardless of the fact, pointed out by Coningham on many occasions, that if ground forces would follow closely behind fighter-bombers using bombs, rockets and cannons, the peninsula would be efficiently cleared without indiscriminate destruction of Dutch lives and property.[22]

On 29 October, Coningham attended a meeting with Eisenhower, Portal and Tedder to discuss the Army's demand for heavy bomber attacks on Flushing. As ever, Coningham insisted that fighter-bombers fully met the Army's real needs, that heavy bombers killed too many Dutch civilians and, not least, that the bombers were better employed over Germany. Tedder agreed, forbidding heavy bomber attack on the town and accepting Coningham's proposal to employ Mosquitoes just before the assault, which was timed to take place at dawn. Portal took up Coningham's point about using the heavies over Germany, saying that their escorts needed bases on the Continent where they could refuel and re-arm, but suitable airfields were few and far between. Coningham's men were doing their utmost to improve the situation, Tedder told Portal, by repairing existing fields, making new ones and ripping steel planking out of the Normandy mud and hauling it north. 'Even so, the congestion is appalling: for example, two fighter wings on one field which is within artillery fire and three fighter wings on the only other available field in the forward area.'[23]

After the capture of the Breskens Peninsula, two combined operations were carried out on 1 November: Infatuate I (an assault in the Flushing dock area) and Infatuate II (an assault through a breach in the dyke at West Kapelle). The principal feature of the planning for these operations, wrote Coningham, was the readiness of Ramsay (Naval Commander) and Simmonds (Canadian Army Commander) to press on even if bad weather prevented adequate air support. During the planning, Coningham insisted that the air forces could not undertake to knock out well-sited gun emplacements by heavy bombing. His arguments, he said, 'were clearly proved to be correct' by later reports and the 'main lesson' learned from Infatuate I and II 'was the ineffectiveness of heavy bombardment in neutralising coast defence or mobile batteries'. Both Ramsay and Simmonds expressed surprise that these batteries remained active despite aerial attack, even though officers of 2nd TAF and Bomber Command had warned them that this would be so. They were also warned that an assault which failed to follow hard upon aerial attack would find gun crews recovered from their initial shock.[24]

Attacks by Typhoon fighter-bombers, reported Groom to Kenneth Cross (Director of Tactical Operations in the Air Ministry) on 20 November, 'saved a very critical situation. Without their help, operating when clouds were at a very low altitude, it is probable that the craft would not have reached the shore.' Coningham instructed Groom to add that 'in his opinion, 2 Group during the night before the landing at Flushing, and 84 Group on the day of the landings, gave one of the most effective and efficient examples of air support' since Overlord began. On 10 November, as Coningham had long wanted, Teddy Hudleston took over 84 Group from Leslie Brown, who had never convinced the Canadians that aircraft were a support, not a substitute, for ground action. Antwerp received its first convoy on 27 November. Thereafter, in spite of missile attack, the port's rate of effort increased steadily until the daily tonnage passing through reached a peak, on 29 March 1945, of 66,500 tons of stores and 733 vehicles.[25]

Coningham became directly concerned in the campaign against missiles when the Germans switched from attacks on London to attacks on Antwerp and Brussels. Between 21 October and 11 November, 733 flying-bombs were aimed at Antwerp and 132 at Brussels. Hill, head of Fighter Command (the much-disliked title 'Air Defence of Great Britain' had disappeared at the same time as Leigh-Mallory's headquarters), was responsible for dealing with the missile offensive and looked to Coningham for help. Missiles were no longer launched from static sites, but from 'well-camouflaged ramps,' wrote Coningham, 'which could be quickly erected on widely-dispersed sites. By air observation and ground reports, these ramps were detected in disused factories, woods and sometimes along minor roads'. Moreover, the Germans appreciated his unwillingness to attack sites in built-up areas and so Coningham chose to try and reduce their rate of fire by disrupting communications to the sites, while heavy bombers were used to destroy storage depots and factories where rockets were made. Even so, in Coningham's opinion, 'the only way to neutralise such weapons is by over-running the launching sites with ground forces'.[26]

At that time, with the 2nd British Army penned between the Albert Canal and the Lower Rhine, 83 Group trying to operate from three soggy airfields and everyone aware that a long cold winter of hard fighting lay ahead, grumbles were voiced – especially in army circles – about the splendid state maintained by Coningham in Brussels. These he heard without any qualm whatever. As a pilot on the Western Front during the no less bitter winter of 1916–17, when every flight not only put his life at risk but ended with him frozen stiff, Coningham had decided that life off duty, as long as it lasted, must be made as pleasant as possible. Throughout the years that followed, he mastered the art of combining duty with pleasure – hard work, good company, the best available surroundings – in many a bleak hole between Iraq and Belgium. Inevitably, as he rose higher, there were observers quick to believe that his cat-like shrewdness in pursuit of comfort was becoming a desire, inappropriate in wartime, to live in splendour.

However, the joint Army–Air Headquarters in Brussels, recalled Sir Kenneth Porter, had been furnished by the *Germans* with Belgian loot, 'each office having magnificent furniture, pictures and wall-to-wall carpets. Whilst we took the place as we found it and appreciated the unaccustomed comfort, the Army had all the carpets and furniture removed and replaced with field office furniture. Perhaps this is the origin of the story that Mary lived like a Renaissance Prince in Brussels.' Sir John Colville admired Coningham's dynamic energy but was less impressed 'by the somewhat ostentatious grandeur of his headquarters in Brussels, where a great deal of money was obviously spent on expensive flowers and still more expensive wines. It all seemed a little bit excessive while the fighting was still going on and while austerity ruled almost everywhere else.'[27]

Coningham believed that breaks from austerity, fairly earned, might actually *help* the war effort. For example, the *Daily Mail* reported on 17 November that Diana Barnato, 'beautiful daughter of the millionaire racing motorist, and her husband, Wing Commander Derek Walker, DFC, have flown on a honeymoon trip to Brussels and back, each piloting their own Spitfire'. Married just before D-Day, they then had no time for a honeymoon – Walker was serving with 2nd TAF, Barnato with the Air Transport Auxiliary, a civilian organisation of ferry pilots – but now they had and Coningham invited them to enjoy it in Brussels. Freeman, of course, thought Coningham's action 'quite monstrous' and told Portal so on the 27th. The fact that Coningham had brought his wife to Brussels also annoyed Freeman, even though he knew that her son Howard had been killed on active service only a few weeks earlier. 'It is well known,' he added, 'that Lady Tedder is in Paris, Lady Coningham in Brussels and that Lady Leigh-Mallory was accompanying her husband to Ceylon. There may be no harm in all this, but nonetheless it is being widely commented on and I strongly advise you, in the interests of the RAF, to recall both Lady Tedder and Lady Coningham to this country.'[28]

These redoubtable ladies regarded themselves as working wives, taking their welfare work so seriously that Elmhirst and Groom had already been driven to protest. 'Much too much "welfare" in the villa this past week,' complained Elmhirst in mid-October. The ladies are doing good work, 'but even so Victor and I eventually lodged our protest to Mary at the end of it. Since we started the mess for the three of us at Uxbridge, we have always got a good deal of work done over meals; now we have to talk "welfare" at lunch and worse still, after a long day's work, at and after supper.' The complaint, added Elmhirst, was met, even though Coningham knew that since the death of her son Nan needed to throw her energies more than ever into demanding work among a great many people.[29]

Field Marshal Walter Model (Commander, German Army Group B) issued on 1 November a summary of recent failed attacks. 'Enemy No. 1,' he wrote, was 'the hostile air force, which, because of its absolute superiority, tries to destroy our spearheads of attacks and our artillery through fighter-bomber attacks and bomb carpets and to render movements in the rear areas impossible.' Two weeks later, on 15 November, Air Ministry Intelligence circulated a German appraisal of Tedder (among others) under whom 'Cooperation between Army and Air Forces has become excellent'. Nevertheless, Coningham recorded after the war that at that time he faced five 'serious problems'.[30]

First among them, he wrote, was the provision of all-weather airfields to enable aircraft on forward bases to continue offensive action and escort for heavy bombers flying from England. The construction, repair and mainten-ance of airfields was the responsibility of 21st Army Group's Chief Engineer, but his labour force was often reduced without warning by Army Command-ers who considered they had more urgent tasks for it. A second problem was winter accommodation for men in an area which had suffered heavy war damage. On 1 October, more than half Coningham's men had been living under canvas, but within three months that figure was reduced almost to zero and he readily acknowledged his debt to the Army for that achievement.

Thirdly, Coningham singled out the need for welfare facilities by which health and morale could be maintained at a high level in preparation for spring offensives. Welfare centres such as Malcolm Clubs were set up, also leave hostels in Brussels and other large towns. 'I attach great importance,' wrote Coningham, to such facilities: 'We have shown a great improvement in this war in raising living conditions and amenities to a standard which ensures the most efficient functioning of the human element.' Fourthly, he turned to the building up of a reserve of aircraft and trained pilots to support those offensives. Planners, he said, had supposed that the German war would end much sooner than it did and apportioned men and materials according to rates of wastage which also proved optimistic. Coningham was therefore obliged to instruct his Group Commanders 'to restrict the intensity of their operations' in order to maximise their resources by 1 March 1945 because he appreciated that a 'maximum effort would then be required from the 2nd TAF to provide cover for and to support the crossing of the Rhine'. His final 'serious problem' was a shortage of experienced pilots, having lost more than 650 since D-Day.[31]

Tedder had just had 'a long private talk with Ike,' he told Portal on 4 December, 'about his visit to 21st Army Group, the command set-up and the broad strategy of the campaign'. Montgomery, wrote Tedder, reiterated his opinion that the campaign had been mismanaged ever since Eisenhower took personal command, demanded yet again that he himself be placed in overall command and that Tedder, the Deputy Supreme Commander, be regarded as 'just the airman' and told not to accompany Eisenhower on visits to Army Commanders. Three days later, Eisenhower, Tedder, Bradley and Montgomery met at Maastricht. Montgomery urged Eisenhower to transfer the whole of Bradley's Army Group north of the Ardennes and place it under his (Montgomery's) command to assist the Anglo-Canadian forces in a massive attack on the Ruhr. Eisenhower offered the Field Marshal command of William Simpson's 9th US Army and two American airborne divisions to help his attack, but also accepted Bradley's proposal that the Americans launch their own offensive, aimed at Frankfurt, from north and south of the Ardennes.[32]

Montgomery rejected Eisenhower's offer, refusing to admit, as Bradley wrote, 'that there was any merit in anybody else's views except his own' and immediately fired off 'bellyaching' letters to sympathisers in England, among them Sir James Grigg, Secretary of State for War: 'I played a lone hand against the whole three,' he lamented. 'That Tedder should take their side is too dreadful.' (Grigg underlined these words.) Montgomery's misery engulfed de Guingand, his Chief of Staff, as Coningham learned next day when he took him out for a couple of hours' snipe shooting. 'On the war situation,' Coningham told Robb on 9 December, de Guingand 'was in one of his most depressing moods . . . It took the form of great concern at our disagreement with the Americans on matters of high policy. I think this was due to a talk with Montgomery after the latter had come from his conference with the Supreme Commander and the Chief.'[33]

Montgomery's argument that the Allies lacked the infantry, armour and supplies to support two major drives into Germany was strong, but undermined by his grossly offensive manner, his naked personal ambition, his disregard for the fact of overwhelming American preponderance in the alliance and, above all, his own disastrous failure to clear access to the great port of Antwerp. That failure obliged Eisenhower to pursue a broad front strategy which he favoured anyway; and that strategy left the Allies extended over a front of at least 500 miles from the North Sea to Switzerland with only two major concentrations: one north of the Ardennes aimed at the Ruhr, the other south of the Ardennes aimed at the Saar. The Ardennes themselves were therefore vulnerable to a counter-offensive and it was precisely there that the greatest German attack in the west since 1940 began at 5.30 am on 16 December. It involved more than a million men and its impact was all the greater because it achieved complete surprise.[34]

CHAPTER SEVENTEEN

'Plenty of Knives Will Be Out Now'

From the Ardennes to Bad Eilsen via Haagsche-Bosch, December 1944 to May 1945

The enemy's situation, announced Montgomery on 16 December 1944, 'is such that he cannot stage major offensive operations'. On that point at least, all Allied commanders – ground and air – were agreed and all were proved wrong that very day, having ignored or discounted numerous indications to the contrary that conflicted with the assessments of their Intelligence experts. Even when the German attack began (on the front of Courtney Hodges' 1st US Army), Bradley refused for several days to recognise that it was more than an attempt to disrupt a planned American offensive and, consequently, did little to help Hodges. Coningham and Vandenberg, however, got together at once and agreed on 17 December that all available 2nd TAF aircraft would assist the 9th Air Force next day. American aircraft would give close support to their respective armies, covered by British aircraft, which would also attack enemy ground forces east of a line chosen by Vandenberg, but 'Hitler Weather' – fog, drizzle and low cloud – kept most of them grounded.[1]

James Robb (senior airman at Eisenhower's headquarters in Versailles) attended a meeting on 20 December at which the Supreme Commander decided to put Montgomery in temporary charge of *all* forces north of Bastogne: two American armies, the 1st and 9th (Commander, William Simpson), as well as his own British and Canadian armies. This was because Bradley's headquarters in Luxembourg City, which he would not leave, was too far south of the battle area to permit effective control of operations; also, the threat endangered Montgomery's communication and supply lines and he had a reserve in hand (30 Corps) whereas Bradley had not. Tedder, recorded Robb, added that there was also a problem of air coordination and Coningham should control part of the 9th Air Force, 'not necessarily on geographical grounds'. It was therefore agreed that the 9th and 29th Tactical Air Commands, (Pete Quesada and Richard Nugent) should come under Coningham's operational control and some of his 'extremely strong force of fighter-bombers' was placed at the disposal of 19th TAC (Otto Weyland) to support Patton. By this 'rearrangement of command,' wrote Coningham, he controlled all air forces north of the 'bulge' in Allied lines; Vandenberg those to the south, and no difficulties arose, thanks to the excellent working relations developed between British and American airmen since the invasion began. Group Captain Kenneth Porter, Coningham's Chief Signals Officer, visited the two American headquarters to arrange communications to 2nd TAF Headquarters and received total cooperation, which 'would not have happened,' he emphasised, 'if the Americans had not had a high opinion of 2nd TAF and of Mary and his conduct of operations'.[2]

The Hun attack, wrote Elmhirst on 20 December, was 'a hell of a gamble on his part and if the clouds would lift only a few feet, he would find himself in an awful mess which might well put a finish to the war much earlier than expected'. Complacency nevertheless vanished overnight and with it all talk about how best to move forward into Germany. Instead, eyes measured the distance to Brussels and Antwerp from the foremost point of what Elmhirst called 'the ominous bulge' thrusting through the American line. Telephones rang constantly and, it seemed, more insistently; doors slammed more loudly; people moved faster, talking importantly, between offices and found good reasons to race here and there in cars and jeeps. All this scurry reminded Coningham of similar crises in the Desert and he noticed, as there, that some otherwise competent men quickly wilted under such pressure. He himself, wrote Elmhirst, 'as always when things get exciting, is at his best, radiating confidence and good cheer. As he says: "Give us 300 feet lift of clouds and a mile of visibility and we and Vandenberg's tactical air force alongside will put 4,000 aircraft over them and they haven't a chance."'[3]

Writing after the war, Coningham thought the Ardennes offensive 'particularly interesting' in three respects. Firstly, because the plan of attack followed closely the plan employed in 1940 'by the same German commander, von Rundstedt, using approximately the same ground forces and the same faulty tactics in using his air forces primarily in direct support of his Army instead of ensuring first that he established air superiority in the tactical area of the battle'. Secondly, because the Allied air forces prevented the Luftwaffe from concentrating in the battle area by attacking its bases whenever weather permitted. And thirdly, because 'the extreme flexibility and smooth cooperation of the 9th Air Force and the 2nd TAF' demonstrated their adoption of 'the same basic organisation, procedure and tactics in air operations'. The German rate of advance was more than twelve miles a day between 16–23 December, a week in which bad weather grounded the air forces, but with nearly 600 sorties a day possible from the 24th, the enemy advance practically ceased on Christmas Day.[4]

At 9 am each morning during the crisis, recorded Robb, a Chiefs of Staff conference was held in the Trianon Palace Hotel at Versailles to review the ground, air, naval and supply situation. It lasted about half an hour and was followed immediately by an Air Staff meeting. Robb then telephoned

8. From Brussels to Bad Eilsen, 1944–5

Coningham, who had by that time finished his own morning conference and attended 21st Army Group's conference. He was therefore able to give Robb the latest air and army news from the northern part of the front. Thus armed, Robb joined his fellow Chiefs – Bedell Smith (Staff), Harold Bull and John Whiteley (Operations, American and British respectively), Kenneth Strong (Intelligence) – and Tedder in Eisenhower's office, where the current situation was presented to the Supreme Commander, who usually consulted Bradley over the telephone. 'It is noticeable, however,' added Robb, 'that no calls are ever made either to or from Field Marshal Montgomery, though General Whiteley usually rings up General de Guingand during the day.'[5]

Between 23–27 December, there was neither time nor need for elaborate planning, for the airmen's task was simple: to impede and disrupt the thrust into Belgium until sufficient ground forces had been assembled to halt it and drive it back. 'Christmas Day was the worst,' wrote Elmhirst on 27 December, 'and few in the know here could hide a look of gloom, Mary of course excepted.' Coningham insisted that Elmhirst and Groom accompany him – with smiling faces – on the traditional Christmas duties for senior officers: visiting hospitals and airmen's messes, serving dinner to their own batmen and drivers. 'We had tasted so much turkey and plum pudding by 3 o'clock,' wrote Elmhirst, 'that we did without lunch and worked in our offices till 8 pm.' He and Coningham were then entertained by some prominent Belgians, and did their best to appear relaxed and confident, for everyone was very much on edge, fearing that the Germans might re-occupy Brussels in the next couple of days.[6]

Ground and air staffs at SHAEF Headquarters believed that Montgomery had responded expertly to the immediate crisis, but when the time came for rapid offensive action, his 'inherent over-carefulness' (in Bedell Smith's words) would cause him to miss opportunities to inflict serious damage. Moreover, he had invited Bradley to his headquarters on Christmas Day, lectured him on the failure of American strategy in general, his own performance in particular and sent him away enraged (and, incidentally, without anything to eat or drink). On the 29th, Montgomery again demanded overall command of Allied ground forces when the drive into Germany was resumed. Eisenhower's patience broke at last and Montgomery would have been dismissed had not de Guingand persuaded him to sign a grovelling apology next day. Eisenhower, having accepted the apology, urged Montgomery to begin an attack on the northern flank of the 'bulge' in the American lines no later than 1 January, but de Guingand said (according to Robb): 'If you want something out of him [Montgomery], you must give *a direct order*, otherwise, he'll go his own way.' The attack did not begin until the 3rd and Montgomery proceeded with great caution, even though intelligence and reconnaissance reports alike indicated that the Germans had suffered heavy losses and were seriously short of fuel and ammunition.[7]

Elmhirst was admitted to hospital exhausted on New Year's Eve and awoke next morning to learn that he had been awarded the CB and that the Luftwaffe 'had had the cheek to shoot up all our airfields' in an attempt to prevent Allied fighter-bombers intervening in German attempts to capture Bastogne. When the Luftwaffe appeared over Brussels, Frank Sayer (Coningham's personal driver) remembered him running up a grassy bank to get a better view, as excited as a schoolboy. The Air Marshal, said Sayer, always showed plenty of concern for his daily comfort, but none whatever for his personal safety. Coningham had been pressed for airfield space throughout the winter and the enemy, aware of this fact (as he later wrote), 'carried out a well-timed simultaneous attack' by more than 800 Fw 190s and Me 109s on 27 congested airfields in good weather which caught the defences unprepared. Nevertheless, the attack ended disastrously for the Luftwaffe, which lost over 400 aircraft and as many of its dwindling band of experienced pilots. These were the heaviest losses suffered in a single day in what proved to be the Luftwaffe's last major attack. Although some 465 Allied aircraft were destroyed or damaged (mostly on the ground, so that very few pilots were killed), even losses on such a scale were quickly made good and Allied air superiority thereafter was more complete than ever.[8]

'Aircraft are available without delay to replace those destroyed,' Portal told Churchill on 1 January, 'and AM Coningham has assured us that the losses will not involve any reduction in our air effort for the battle.' Anticipating the Prime Minister's frosty response, Portal went on to explain that 'in order to employ our superior numbers, we have had to accept very great congestion at our forward airfields and I am sure we were right to do so because of the complete lack of enterprise shown until today by the GAF since D-Day. We take the same risks on the roads and again I am sure we are right to do so.' Churchill was not convinced, but by the time he next visited Brussels – on 5 January – the scale of the Luftwaffe's defeat was clear and Coningham repeated Portal's arguments to good effect, adding that his ideal was one wing of three squadrons per airfield, but this proved impracticable 'on the watery fields of the Low Countries where hard standings and concrete runways were so scarce'.[9]

Squadron Leader Frank Instone, Deputy Provost Marshal, left 2nd TAF in January. He was not sorry to go, for the war was clearly in its last stages and the 'exuberant crusading spirit' which had so inspired him at Bracknell, Uxbridge and in Normandy was gone. To his surprise, Coningham sent for him on his last day.

> That a man directing the day-to-day action should find time to send for a comparatively junior member of his staff and one with whom he had had relatively little personal contact was, I felt, a pretty decent gesture, the more so as he had just had his airfields heavily bombed and lost many aircraft, including his own, newly-delivered from the UK the previous day.

229

Like all great commanders, Coningham gave Instone his whole attention for the time he was with him, making him feel not only that his work had been particularly important, but also that Instone had given him a new insight into its value: 'I didn't think much of your security sections when I first took over,' said Coningham, 'but I must tell you now that they have added a new dimension to our type of warfare.'[10]

Early on 5 January 1945, de Guingand telephoned SHAEF Headquarters to ask if the press could be told that Montgomery had had command of two American armies for the past fortnight. A little later, Groom made a similar request on Coningham's behalf. The answer in both cases was a firm 'no', but on that very day a New York newspaper got hold of the story and SHAEF was obliged to admit that it was true. The fact that Coningham had exercised 'operational control' of American air forces was widely emphasised in the British press on 9 January: *The Times*, wisely and correctly, spoke of a 'temporary transfer', but the *Daily Herald* headed its account with the words '"MARY" BOSSES US PILOTS' while other newspapers caused equal offence by carelessly referring to Generals Vandenberg, Nugent and Weyland.[11]

Of 600,000 Americans eventually involved in the fighting, 19,000 were killed; only 55,000 British troops were involved, of whom about 200 lost their lives. In the air as on the ground, Americans predominated, as was emphasised in a report on the battle by the Operational Research Section of Coningham's headquarters in April 1945. The Germans, suffering at least 100,000 casualties – killed, wounded or captured – among the 500,000 men employed, failed even to reach the Meuse river, let alone Brussels and Antwerp. Although hard fighting continued until the end of January, the attempt to split the Anglo-American armies had clearly failed. Worse still, the Russians opened their long-awaited offensive along the upper Vistula in Poland on 12 January and swept westward at such a furious pace that the last resources of the Third Reich were consumed in a vain effort even to delay them. Resistance to the Anglo-Americans became a matter of holding actions, though nonetheless savagely fought for that.[12]

By 18 January, Eisenhower was aware that the Germans were retreating in good order from the Ardennes. Consequently, he proposed to hold on that front and attack in the north. The object was to be the Rhine, north of Düsseldorf, in two main operations – 'Veritable' and 'Grenade' – under Montgomery's command. A fortnight later, when it was clear that the Russian offensive had forced the Germans to withdraw troops from the western front, Eisenhower instructed Montgomery to begin Veritable not later than 8 February and Grenade two days later. Coningham delegated the planning and execution of air support for Veritable to Hudleston, head of 84 Group, working with the 1st Canadian Army. Richard Nugent (head of 29th TAC, working with the US 9th Army) had once again been placed under Coningham's operational control and Coningham delegated responsibility for Grenade to him. Broadhurst's 83 Group was charged to hold the outer ring and prevent the movement of enemy land or air forces into the area concerned: between the Rhine and the Meuse, opposite the Ruhr. Before these operations began, Coningham ordered constant sweeps over enemy territory and standing patrols over known airfields to deny the Germans information about the regrouping of Allied forces and thus ensure tactical surprise, but low cloud and poor visibility often thwarted his pilots.[13]

Operation Veritable, launched on 8 February, was a strong offensive aimed south-eastward from Nijmegen between the Rhine and the Meuse as far as the general line Xanten-Geldern to clear the enemy and form a firm flank on the Rhine to prepare crossing places for the next offensive, Operation 'Plunder'. In Coningham's opinion, 'a bold decision to attack earlier when the ground was hard, even though we had fewer ground forces available,' would have achieved success sooner and saved casualties. By the time Montgomery was ready, a thaw had turned roads to mud and armoured vehicles bogged down. An endless demand for road repair work greatly reduced the labour and resources Coningham needed for new airfields to cover the advance beyond the Rhine. In addition, the heavy going so slowed the Canadians that the Germans had time to rush reinforcements into the area of the Reichswald Forest and hard fighting there required Coningham to devote a far greater effort to close support than would have been the case if Veritable had begun sooner; that effort detracted from the attention he wanted to give to isolating the battle area in preparation for Operation Plunder. On 14 February, for the first time in a week, the weather was good and Coningham's aircraft flew more sorties that day than on any other since the end of the campaign in Normandy.[14]

As for Operation Grenade, it did not begin until 23 February and consisted of an attack by the US 9th Army eastward from the line of the Roer river between Roermond and Julich, aiming at the Rhine between Mors and Düsseldorf. The enemy, his back to the Rhine, was acutely conscious of the need to protect its bridges and ferry points; Coningham was equally aware of the need to destroy them to prevent him moving back heavy guns and tanks to consolidate a defensive line east of the Rhine. Coningham found, however, that the AA defences of vulnerable points became more intense as the campaign advanced and flak units which had hitherto been scattered over wide areas of France and the Low Countries were concentrated to protect the Fatherland. The difficulties of ensuring accurate bombing of such pinpoint targets as bridges by tactical bombers flying at low levels therefore increased. A dangerous downward spiral of a kind with which Coningham was only too familiar had been created: only the bravest and most experienced crews could carry out the most hazardous tasks efficiently, but inevitably these were the crews who suffered the heaviest losses and thus the overall performance of the force steadily declined even though its numbers were growing all the time. Nevertheless, Coningham resisted Montgomery's demand for heavy bombers to attack nine bridges over the Rhine between Wesel and Cologne and an Air Staff meeting at SHAEF

Headquarters on 27 February supported him. Throughout the campaign, Coningham consistently argued that heavies were best employed over Germany; they were an inefficient battlefield weapon and even if they did destroy the bridges in question, the Germans had numerous ferries, barges and pontoons which were vulnerable only to attack by mediums and fighter-bombers.[15]

Hard as he worked in the office, Coningham worked equally hard out of it to maintain his reputation as a generous and entertaining host. On 22 February, for example, Lewis Brereton visited him in Brussels to discuss air plans for Operation 'Varsity' and noted in his diary next day that 'Mary is always good company': words which he would cheerfully have accepted as an epitaph. A few days later, Coningham sent Elmhirst to a conference in Cannes, lending him his own Dakota and designating the trip 'Operation Mimosa' because he wanted Elmhirst 'to fill up the aircraft at Cannes with mimosa or any other flowers to brighten us up in the winter weather in Belgium'. These flowers were still in bloom on 2 March when Churchill, Colville (his secretary) and Brooke flew to Brussels and were met at the airfield by Coningham. They all lunched at Coningham's 'sumptuous villa', as Colville described it, and afterwards he unctuously recorded his opinion that 'massed flowers, expensive furniture and rare foods combine to create an effect too luxurious for the HQ of an operational commander'. Next day, however, Colville accompanied a tour of service clubs for men and women in Brussels and observed that good living was rampant even there: 'Never can the welfare of the troops,' he exclaimed, 'have been so lavishly and painstakingly cared for': another epitaph that would have pleased Coningham – and his wife. Coningham's own suffering in the Great War was never far from his thoughts, convincing him of the need, as he put it, to 'feed, clothe, house and entertain' those under his command better than they expected.[16]

On 3 March, however, a raid by medium bombers of 2 Group went tragically wrong and Coningham's sluggish response severely shook his standing with Portal and Churchill. About forty medium bombers appeared over The Hague at 9 am that morning, intending to attack Haagsche-Bosch (Hague Wood), an area on the eastern outskirts of the city, where the Germans stored V-2 rockets. Their aiming-point was incorrect and the bombs killed at least 520 Dutch civilians as well as causing massive destruction of public buildings, churches and houses. Coningham failed to recognise that a major disaster had occurred, requiring prompt and thorough action. He did nothing, in fact, until asked for a report on this 'deplorable accident' by Norman Bottomley, Deputy Chief of the Air Staff. Even then his report, written a full week later, was almost perfunctory. 'It would appear,' he wrote, 'that a bad assessment of the wind may have been made,' though the crews were properly briefed. He had received messages from Prince Bernhard and consequently arranged for leaflets to be dropped, regretting and explaining the accident.[17]

Bottomley, meanwhile, was writing to Sinclair, Secretary of State for Air (sending copies to Portal, among others) on 10 March to answer an allegation by the Dutch Ambassador that the attack 'constituted a breach of faith'. When the general plan of bombing rocket sites in Holland was drawn up in November 1944, wrote Bottomley, a conference was held in the Air Ministry to ascertain the reactions of the Dutch government to the likelihood of casualties and damage. Commander Moolenburgh, representing that government, had declared that there would be no objections to attacks 'if they were likely to be effective and were considered necessary'. The Haagsche-Bosch area was one of those selected for attack and therefore the Dutch could not claim that the raid was launched without prior consultation.

Portal was 'far from reassured' by Coningham's report and Churchill himself was furious. The Dutch protest, said the Prime Minister, 'reflects upon the Air Ministry and the RAF in two ways. First, it shows how feeble have been our efforts to interfere with the rockets and secondly, the extraordinarily bad aiming which has led to this slaughter of Dutchmen'; the matter required 'a thorough explanation' and would be brought before the Cabinet. Coningham was informed that the incident had been the subject of conversations between Sinclair and the Dutch Ambassador, that Moolenburgh was to be consulted before any further attacks were made on rocket targets in or near built-up areas and that Kenneth Cross (Director of Tactical Operations in the Air Ministry) would be visiting him and the units concerned to seek further information.

Basil Embry, (head of 2 Group) told Coningham on 18 March that he had had 'no idea' until that morning that 'the consequences of our inaccurate bombing were so serious'. When 2 Group received instructions from 2nd TAF that the target was to be bombed visually or by radar, Embry had personally queried the advisability of radar bombing and told Coningham's Duty Ops Officer that he was not prepared to take on the target by radar unless it was confirmed that the built-up area within 500 yards of the edge of the target area, which was 1,000 yards from the aiming points, was uninhabited. That officer, having spoken to the Air Ministry, assured Embry that the area specified was clear of inhabitants when in fact it was not. Embry later learned that the Duty Intelligence Officer in 137 Wing gave an aiming-point 'in the middle of a built-up area approximately 1,250 yards from the correct aiming-point' and that squadrons accurately bombed this incorrect point. The Intelligence Officer was clearly at fault, Embry concluded, and would be court martialled. Next day, Coningham sent Portal a copy of Embry's account, 'which,' he said, 'for the first time shows that there was a mistake that affected the briefing. My report that all the briefing was correct must in the light of this new information be amended.'

Portal informed Churchill (on 21 March) that the cause of the incident was 'a most unfortunate lapse by one or more officers concerned in the briefing' and Court Martial proceedings were likely to follow. Knowing Churchill of old, he then went on to the attack. 'In spite of heavy pressure from yourself and the Minister of Home Security "to do more", we have resisted the employment of heavy bombers against these sites, but it was in answer to this pressure that the use of 2nd TAF's medium bombers to back up the Spitfires was authorised.' Arrangements were made to drop leaflets carrying the text of a radio explanation and apology on the night of 24–25 March. Churchill accepted on 15 April a report of what he called 'this unfortunate episode' and the Dutch did not raise the matter again. Portal, however, did not forget that Coningham's immediate response to this crisis had been neither quick nor straight and afterwards was readier to listen to critics of his princely manner. Coningham himself knew how vulnerable he had become: 'Plenty of knives will be out now,' he told his friends.[18]

Meanwhile, back at the war, Eisenhower had directed Montgomery on 8 March to begin new operations on the 24th. They were intended to cross the Rhine on a front of two armies between Rheinberg and Rees, the US 9th Army under Simpson on the right (Operation 'Flashpoint') and the 2nd British Army under Dempsey on the left (Operation 'Plunder'). The communication centre of Wesel and a crossing point near there would be secured by an airborne assault (Operation 'Varsity'). The initial lodgement on the east bank of the Rhine would be expanded until three armies (those of Simpson, Dempsey and Henry Crerar's 1st Canadian Army, all under Montgomery's overall command) were positioned east of the Rhine and north of the Ruhr so that further thrusts deeper into Germany could be developed quickly in any direction required by Eisenhower.[19]

In order to make 'the most economical use' of the Anglo-American air forces, Eisenhower instructed Coningham to produce 'a single overall air plan' and coordinate its execution through his own headquarters. Brereton (Commander, 1st Allied Airborne Army) set up a small advanced headquarters in Brussels to assist him. Their plan had two bases. One, that the airborne strike should *follow* the ground force assault instead of *preceeding* it. And two, that only air forces familiar with the terrain and the position of ground forces and which could be closely controlled to meet rapidly changing situations should operate over the battle area and for some distance beyond. Fighter Command and the US 8th Air Force, for example, would escort troop carriers *to* that area but not *over* it. 'Only in this way,' thought Coningham, 'was it possible to avoid mistakes in air-to-ground action, ensure close support without interfering with the airborne drop and prevent mutual interference in the air from air forces of different commands.' Detailed planning was delegated to Broadhurst, who could ask Hudleston and Nugent direct for help if necessary.[20]

'By the end of the week,' wrote Elmhirst on 18 March, 'we should see most of the Germans back across the Rhine and a good number of our American friends after them.' Several important persons had called on Coningham in recent days: Mrs Churchill and her daughter Mary, Mr Attlee, the British Ambassador to Belgium, the Archbishop of York, two members of the Air Council (Jack Slessor and Peter Drummond) and, of course, Lord Trenchard. 'I think it is time we were out in the blue and under canvas again,' grumbled Elmhirst, who was not yet ready to admit that those exhilarating days – as they now seemed – had gone and duller days were at hand. Coningham would normally have been in his element with such a galaxy of famous, influential people to entertain, but since the Haagsche-Bosch tragedy, Elmhirst noticed, he avoided most visitors and spent more time touring his vast command as well as attending meetings at SHAEF Headquarters in Paris. A few days later, Drummond would lose his life when a Liberator carrying him to Canada disappeared in the Atlantic. Coningham, deeply moved, wrote to Portal as soon as he heard the news on 30 March.

> Peter was a close personal friend of mine, and his place as a fellow
> antipodean cannot be filled. But your loss is greater, especially as it
> follows the tragedies of L-M [Leigh-Mallory] and John Linnell. Poor
> Lala [Drummond's wife], whose world will have dropped out –
> presumably she will receive all possible aid. I cannot do anything from
> here. If only these disasters will stop.[21]

D-Day for Operation Varsity was 24 March. It went perfectly and ample close support for ground forces was constantly available in the absence of aerial opposition. 'For the first time in 140 years, since Napoleon's time,' exulted Brereton, 'hostile armies are operating east of the Rhine' and the way to Berlin lay open. Even so, Coningham had no great faith in such methods of waging war. 'Paratroop losses can be kept down,' he reflected later, 'if the dropping zones are widely dispersed, close to their objectives and within range of artillery support.' This last point was vital in his view because of the low altitude at which airborne forces and their supplies must be transported across enemy territory and their vulnerability even to machine-gun fire. Once paratroops had been landed, however, the enemy could concentrate mobile AA guns and take a heavy toll of supply aircraft, as happened at Arnhem, so re-supply by air must therefore be kept to a minimum. Although Coningham had recognised and planned against this danger, enemy flak still inflicted serious losses and after D-Day he pressed hard for re-supply by land. His conclusion, consequently, was unenthusiastic: the operation went according to plan, but the Rhine crossing would have succeeded without it. Nevertheless, he valued Brereton's generous words written on 4 April – 'You and your command were largely responsible for the success of this operation' – and also Elmhirst's appraisal: at last, he wrote, 'an airborne operation in front of a field army was allowed to be controlled from the one place that could properly exercise control: RAF HQ alongside the Army Group HQ, and with the help of perfect weather there was no hitch. All so different from those airborne army efforts in Sicily and at Arnhem.'[22]

A rapid advance of over 200 miles from the Rhine to the Elbe, closely supported by numerous aircraft attacking fleeing Germans, put Coningham very much in mind of exciting days at the end of the Great War. The advance in this war was carried out by Simpson's army (heading for Magdeburg with Nugent's support) and Dempsey's (heading for Hamburg with Broadhurst's support). On reaching the Elbe, both were to halt. The Americans would then help Bradley to mop up opposition in the Ruhr; the British would help the Canadians under Crerar (supported by Hudleston) to open a supply route through Arnhem and then clear north-east Holland, the coastal belt eastward to the Elbe and western Holland in that order of priority. The large area of Germany thus occupied by Montgomery's Army Group would be placed under military government. On 31 March, Coningham gladly forwarded to Broadhurst and Hudleston rare praise from Montgomery: 'Over a long period of very high-class performance,' wrote the Field Marshal, 'the standard reached before, during and since the crossing of this great river obstacle [the Rhine] has been remarkable; the splendid support given by the whole of 2nd TAF has been the admiration of the soldiers.' By now, Coningham's chief anxiety was for the safety of Allied prisoners and both Group Commanders had been ordered to maintain reconnaissance over all known POW camps in the British zone. 'A simple code of ground strips,' he recalled, 'had been devised whereby the prisoners could indicate if they were short of water, food or medical supplies, or if they were being attacked.'[23]

'The war is running out very fast now,' wrote Elmhirst at the end of March, but he wanted it to continue until 'the ordinary German in the countryside' realised that Germany was well beaten – 'which is the lesson we are here to teach and didn't in 1918'. On 7 April, Coningham's Advanced Headquarters moved (together with Montgomery's) to Suchteln, near Krefeld in Germany. It was not, thought Elmhirst, an ideal site: 'a lunatic asylum in the Ruhr with a barbed-wire fence around it. But it will give the troops a good laugh and we don't expect to be there long.' Nor were they, for Coningham sent forward a reconnaissance party, protected by a detachment of the RAF Regiment, to occupy and prepare the permanent location of his headquarters in one of Germany's most beautiful places: Bad Eilsen, near Bückeburg, in the province of Schaumberg-Lippe. It lay in an area allotted to Bradley's Army Group, but the Americans permitted Coningham's men to capture it, together with the design staff, drawing office and a large quantity of valuable documents belonging to the Focke-Wulf aircraft firm which had been evacuated to Bad Eilsen from Bremen in 1942. Coningham knew that Bad Eilsen had been a pleasant spa before the war, recalled Sir Kenneth Porter, and that the leading Nazis had subsequently enjoyed themselves there. 'All the furniture, crockery, linen, etc., had been safely stored,' wrote Porter, 'and my Wing Commander was able to have the two hotels and gardens restored to their former glory before we moved in' at the end of May, for Coningham still saw no moral worth in discomfort.[24]

'Mary is in good form,' wrote Elmhirst on 19 April, 'but now that the war is as good as over and won he cannot settle or take further interest in it. He is here one day, Brussels another; Holland, Paris, London or Cannes.' He had earned his relaxation, thought Elmhirst, having commanded air forces fighting against the Germans from the first day of the war and would do so until the last. Moreover, 'Victor and I can run this show while Harry Broadhurst, Basil Embry and Teddy Hudleston certainly don't want teaching their jobs.' Trenchard, who shared Elmhirst's admiration for Coningham's conduct throughout those strenuous years, attempted a summary of his achievement on 30 April. The Air, he wrote, had found four principles. Firstly, to maintain air superiority and with that went the others: to destroy the enemy's means of production and communication; to enable the Army to build up; and to prevent the enemy build-up. 'This is what you and your Air Force have done,' he concluded.[25]

At the end of April, Coningham summoned to his headquarters Wing Commander 'Laddie' Lucas, who had earned a high reputation as a fighter pilot. Before the war, however, he had already made his mark as an international-class golfer and a journalist in Beaverbrook's employment. Coningham struck him at once as 'a senior officer with time to think and talk . . . there were no files on his desk, no bumph' and he came straight to the point: would Lucas write a history of the tactical air forces from the Desert to Germany? Given his exceptional background, Coningham thought him ideal for the job. He would have an office in Wales, a small staff and his own aeroplane; the job might last two years, was obviously worth doing and, not least, would set Lucas up nicely for a peacetime career in the service. But for Lucas, civilian life – including the lure of politics – seemed then to offer more attractive openings and he refused the offer. It had been a shrewd move on Coningham's part, for Lucas would have produced an account both well-informed and well-written; one that would, moreover, have been well-publicised in the powerful Beaverbrook press. Although the staff of 2nd TAF prepared an official report on their part in the Overlord campaign, which Coningham himself rewrote extensively, he made no attempt to compose his own overall account of the years 1941–5 and foresaw that the RAF would prove slow to publish detailed narratives matching those written by soldiers who, naturally, paid little attention to the deeds of airmen.[26]

'It's hard to realise how far and fast the war has gone this past week,' mused Elmhirst on 3 May. 'Hitler, Mussolini and Göbbels dead. Berlin and Hamburg captured' but 2nd TAF was still fighting, causing havoc behind what was left of the front and on the German Baltic coast, where numerous boats were trying to escape north to Sweden or Norway. 'The slaughter was so great yesterday,' he wrote, 'that Mary called them off in places, as it was obvious that the Hun would be caught between the British and Russian armies a few hours later.' Flying operations ceased on 5 May 'and the night before, Mary and I sat alone here [in Krefeld] gossiping over the whole length of the war until two in the morning'. They decided that the devastated Ruhr was no place to celebrate victory and returned next day to Brussels, where the end of the war was signalled by a flood of congratulatory messages

237

headed by the King, President Truman, Churchill and Eisenhower. Coningham flew to Copenhagen on the 9th for the official entry of British forces to that city, a ceremony that dissolved into joyful chaos as exuberant Danes burst through the guard of honour to voice their feelings at close range to the Allied commanders. By 11 May, however, Sholto Douglas knew – though Coningham perhaps did not – that the RAF in Germany would soon have a new Commander-in-Chief. 'It was generally known,' wrote Douglas, 'that I had always worked well with Montgomery' and that Coningham had not: Montgomery having been appointed Military Governor of the British Zone of Germany, it was therefore decided to provide him with a senior airman more to his liking.[27]

CHAPTER EIGHTEEN

'A Ballerina Leaving Borneo'

The End of Coningham's Career,
May 1945 to January 1948

Sholto Douglas, Coningham's designated successor, wrote to him on 1 June 1945, saying that he intended to take over about 15 July: 'I gather that you are then going on a triumphal tour of America before taking up a new appointment.' Douglas had gathered correctly, but meanwhile Coningham was setting up a most elegant residence for himself, Groom and Elmhirst, furnished by the Germans with Gobelin tapestries and pictures by Rubens and Rembrandt. His partners, however, men of less elevated taste, complained that there were no comfortable chairs, 'so we have each imported one from the local hotel and are happier, even if they don't quite tone in with the furnishing scheme'. According to Elmhirst's reckoning, Bad Eilsen was the thirtieth home he had shared with Coningham since joining him at Tobruk early in 1942.[1]

Elmhirst's letters from Germany end on 8 July, a few days before he, Coningham and Groom left on posting to other jobs in England. On the day they left, 2nd TAF changed its name to British Air Forces of Occupation and Elmhirst thought everyone was glad 'that the good old name goes with Mary'. They spent their last fortnight working normally each morning, but flying somewhere every afternoon for a farewell party, a practice they all agreed was unavoidable, exhausting and depressing. 'All our goodbye hosts have said the same,' wrote Elmhirst, 'that the TAF has been a very efficient and happy party and we shall not see its like again.' Nothing appeared in the Victory Honours List to sweeten their departure: 'Mary very shattered,' noted Elmhirst, not only by his own omission, but also by Elmhirst's. 'I gave you as good a recommendation for a KBE', he said, 'as I thought it was possible to give.' On his last day at 2nd TAF, 14 July 1945, he circulated throughout the command a final signal ending: 'Once more we bow our heads in humility for all our comrades who died and in depth of feeling we assure their families that their sacrifice was more than vindicated. You all share the victory we have helped to win.' A few days later, on the 26th, he went with his oldest service friend – James Robb, newly-appointed head of

Fighter Command – to Eisenhower's headquarters in I. G. Farben's palatial offices in Frankfurt to receive from President Truman the American Distinguished Service Medal. Five months later, on 1 January 1946, both Coningham and Elmhirst were made Knights Commander of the British Empire (KBE) and Coningham became a substantive Air Marshal.[2]

Coningham's new appointment, as head of Flying Training Command, was announced by the Air Ministry on 30 July 1945. 'Although the appointment was not unexpected,' wrote the *News Chronicle* next day, 'it was none the less surprising. One of the greatest air generals Britain has produced is being relegated to a comparatively minor command' and 'will not have a voice on the Air Council' which that newspaper thought he should have because, with the exception of Tedder, Coningham had greater operational experience of coordinating air power with that of other services than any other airman and, the *News Chronicle* reminded its readers, 'during von Rundstedt's thrust into the Ardennes, he took over command of the US 9th Air Force's fighter units'. Other newspapers, though welcoming Coningham's appointment, did not think he had been slighted. The *Evening Standard*, for example, considered him 'one of the most popular and highly-respected commanders this war has produced. A splendid leader, entirely free from starch and red tape. In command of the Desert Air Force, he proved himself a master of air–ground cooperation. He invented new tactics and kept his mind always receptive to new ideas.' Coningham 'may have an unorthodox way of dealing with future problems', thought the *Observer*. 'Shrewd, candid and confident – and an often successful prophet.'[3]

Best of all was *Flight*'s tribute. Coningham's appointment, in that magazine's well-informed opinion, was 'a guarantee that flying training of the RAF in postwar days will be on the right lines'. His experience of operational flying was unrivalled for duration and variety and he would tolerate no shortcomings in the system. Moreover, he was a man who had proved capable of taking long views and would not make the mistake of re-fighting the last war. *Flight* continued to think well of Coningham and published a profile on 6 December 1945 (illustrated by an excellent caricature) in which he was described as '*par excellence* the air friend of the Army. It may be said, with regrets, that in 1940–1 the Army and the Air Force had no very real idea of how to work together', but Coningham changed all that. 'Up to the time of the surrender of Germany, he continued his masterly work of giving the Army everything which could possibly be expected from the air' and careful study of his methods would ensure that Army-Air cooperation did not wither as it had done after the Great War.[4]

For the moment, however, Coningham had had enough of high command responsibility and spent most of August with his family in Cannes, enjoying an untroubled holiday – except for a visit from yet another official artist – for the first time in seven years. The Tedders stayed with them and they all went swimming, sailing or fishing together. Sometimes the Air Marshals simply lay in the sun, content to know that nothing they decided cost men their lives. Other guests that summer included Maurice Chevalier and the Duke and Duchess of Windsor. On returning to England, Coningham began at last to believe that the blissful days of the late Thirties might really come again when he was elected Commodore of the RAF Yacht Club, a mark of distinction deeply gratifying to a man for whom off-duty life in peacetime England had revolved around yachts and those who owned or sailed them. He would be re-elected in 1946 and 1947.

Coningham then enjoyed a more public mark of distinction, spending three weeks in September on what Douglas called his 'triumphal tour' of the United States. A booklet entitled *British Commanders* had recently been published in New York by British Information Services (an agency of the British government) which helped to introduce him to Americans. It contained sketches of ten soldiers, five sailors and six airmen: Portal, Harris, Tedder, Douglas, Park and Coningham, who was described as 'this war's greatest expert on ground support and the inventor of many of the most devastating and ingenious tactics used by the Allied air forces'. In Tedder and Coningham, Churchill was quoted as saying, 'we have two air leaders of the very highest quality: not technicians, but warriors who have worked in perfect harmony with the generals.'[5]

During his tour, Coningham was a guest of the USAAF and rejoiced in the opportunity to meet on their home ground American officers with whom he had served, in particular Larry Kuter, whose career was thriving. Coningham arrived in New York on the 7th to attend a gala premiere of *The True Glory*, an Anglo-American film about the liberation of Occupied Europe. It was his first visit to New York and he greatly amused some pressmen by flourishing an Italian five lire note signed by General Patton, who had lost it to him during the invasion of Sicily by betting – wrongly – that sooner or later the soldiers would find themselves short of air support. Coningham raised another laugh by proposing that the cities of New York and London should erect statues in memory of Rommel 'for his great contribution in directing the training of the US and British Armies'. Wherever he went, he made speeches that were well received, urging a continuance in peacetime of the better understanding forged between Britons and Americans in wartime. There could be joint development work in aviation, he thought, to a much greater degree than had been the case pre-war and it need not be at the expense of healthy competition. As for military aviation, there should certainly be cooperation in the production of new jet aircraft. The atomic bomb, however, had probably ended the need for vast fleets of strategic bombers because he supposed that even fighters would soon be able to carry these fearful weapons. By 25 September 1945, he was back in New York and at the end of what he hoped would be the first of many exhilarating visits to the United States.[6]

On 6 October, nearly three months after leaving Bad Eilsen, Coningham took up his duties at Shinfield Park, Reading, as head of Flying Training

Command. Having learned to value the ability and diligence of Tommy Elmhirst as his senior administration officer, he was careful to secure the services of another exceptional man, Victor Groom, for that key appointment. As well as getting to know a new staff and the numerous units of a vast command, Coningham revelled in a succession of grand occasions at this time: a dinner at Claridge's Hotel, London, to commemorate the battle of El Alamein on the 23rd, luncheon next day with the Duchess of Kent at her home in Buckinghamshire, an audience with the King at Buckingham Palace on the 31st to mark his new appointment, a visit to Brussels on 8 November to be invested in the Royal Palace by the Prince Regent with the Order of Leopold (Grand Officer) and the Croix de Guerre (with Palm) and, a week later, a return to that city as the Prince's guest at a dinner in honour of Churchill.[7]

Throughout 1946, Coningham continued to find good reasons for leaving his Shinfield Park office. He lectured at the Royal United Services Institute in London on the development of tactical air forces and was invited to give other lectures on that subject at staff colleges (Army and Air Force) in England, Belgium and Palestine. Brussels remained his favourite place to visit, most notably in April when he flew there to receive the Freedom of the City and also to open an avenue re-named in his honour. He was an indefatigable traveller on more or less official business: opening an RAF exhibition in Zurich, presenting certificates to former members of the Resistance in Brussels and Paris, attending rugby matches in Hamburg and boxing championships at South Cerney in Gloucestershire. After one visit to Germany, he brought home a whole stag which he had shot himself. As president of the RAF Yacht Club, he negotiated successfully to take over the Luftwaffe's surviving fleet and twenty vessels reached Calshot safely in June, manned by airmen flown to Germany to sail them home (other vessels were left in Germany for the use of airmen serving there). He attended a session of the Allied Military Tribunal in Nuremberg, then conducting the trial of Nazi war criminals and (more cheerfully) ceremonies in March and May at which Alexander and Tedder respectively were given the Freedom of London. Coningham was invested by the King with the KBE at Buckingham Palace in March and in June took part in the Victory March in London, attending the subsequent reception at Hampton Court Palace for the victorious commanders. Not least, he spent almost the whole of August in Cannes with his family and some close friends. At Claridge's in September he was presented by the King of Greece with the Grand Cross of the Order of the Phoenix.[8]

The *Yorkshire Evening Post* wrote about Coningham at length on 17 January 1947, recalling him as a pioneer of early night bomber raids on Germany. 'The tall, willowy figure of this smiling New Zealander' had once been well known in and around York, according to the reporter, who went on to recall his subsequent career and present appointment as 'the man responsible for the training of all air crews in the RAF (except flight

242

engineers) and the Air Forces of all the Dominions, as well as France and Belgium,' which look to his command for a lead. Comment followed on his father's record as a Test cricketer, the nickname 'Mary', his alleged deeds as a fighter pilot in the Great War ('in one memorable fortnight, he destroyed 19 enemy aircraft'), his athletic prowess, representing the RAF at polo, and his flight from Cairo to Kaduna ('still celebrated by the natives of Northern Nigeria . . . his only map was a sheet torn from an atlas'). Coningham's log book currently showed some 5,000 hours as a pilot and a further 10,000 as a passenger. York men who served with him, concluded the reporter, 'will well remember how he laughed off their first mistake; how, perhaps, they tried to laugh off their second and how, if they were unfortunate enough to make a third, nobody laughed!'[9]

Ever since the end of the European war, the question of composing and possibly publishing an official record of 2nd TAF's part in Operation Overlord had loomed over Coningham. Portal had decided on 27 November 1945 that except for Dowding's despatch on the Battle of Britain, those written by other Commanders-in-Chief should only be published if required to 'balance' despatches produced by soldiers and sailors, but Coningham did not know this when he wrote to Air Commodore Theodore McEvoy (Director of Staff Duties in the Air Ministry) on 4 December. He sent McEvoy four copies of 'our third effort' and sought guidance on its present form and content before spending any more time on it. Coningham was aware, he added on the 10th, that the Air Ministry wanted him to 'match or answer' any point made by Montgomery, but he could hardly do this unless he knew what the Field Marshal intended to say.[10]

McEvoy circulated Coningham's draft to various officials before replying on 5 February 1946. In general, he told Coningham, they found it 'valuable and interesting', although it placed 'more emphasis on the higher direction of the campaign, the organisation of the command and the broad trend of events' than on the detailed operations of 2nd TAF. All were distressed, however, by Coningham's specific criticism of Montgomery in regard to his insistence on a rigid inter-Army Group boundary, his demand for the use of heavy bombers over battlefields where (Coningham claimed) 'unnecessary casualties to Allied civilians and property' were caused and his conduct of ground operations, all of which, in the opinion of Air Ministry officials, 'might conceivably be resented by the Army as coming from an Air Commander'. With regard to matching Montgomery's points, the Air Ministry had as yet no idea what he might say, but McEvoy would forward a copy of his draft as soon as it came to hand to enable Coningham, if necessary, to 'adjust' his own draft.[11]

There matters rested until July, when Montgomery's draft reached the Air Ministry. Air Marshal Sir William Dickson (Vice Chief of the Air Staff) told Tedder on the 8th that it was 'brief and uncontroversial', paying full tribute throughout to the value of air power, whereas Coningham's report, though dealing with operations 'in far greater detail', included 'a large amount of controversial and contentious matter which, while useful to the Air Staff, is unsuitable for publication'. Dickson therefore recommended that Coningham's report be retained in the Air Ministry and that Montgomery's despatch be balanced by the publication of the 'uncontroversial' despatch written on Leigh-Mallory's behalf by his staff and a SHAEF (Air) report. In February 1947, McEvoy loaned 'our only copy' of Coningham's report to Air Commodore Dermot Boyle (head of the RAF Staff College, Bracknell). It was not being published, he said, 'though it may later be circulated confidentially to Staff Colleges and Air Ministry departments' and Coningham was currently at work on 'an abridged and non-controversial' version.[12]

At that time, February 1947, Robb was visited by Forrest Pogue, who had been given the task by Eisenhower of writing SHAEF's official history. 'He has had full access to all records and documents and Ike's personal files,' wrote Robb to Coningham on the 5th, and was in England 'chiefly to obtain background material and information on the personalities involved.' During a three-hour session, Robb answered some very pertinent questions about AEAF. 'I was absolutely frank with him about Monty, the difficulties he made, the fact that LM was an additional link in the RAF chain of command, how Monty seized upon this weakness and also such points as Monty's discourtesy in never once visiting Ike.' Robb thought it most important that Pogue get the facts straight and had therefore told him to get in touch with Coningham. 'He is a studious but pleasant type,' Robb thought, 'who before he undertook this task had not met any of the individuals concerned. I had him out to lunch and let him rummage through my papers for two or three hours.' On the same day, Robb wrote to Leslie Scarman, formerly Tedder's diarist, advising him also to talk to Pogue. 'Incidentally,' he added, 'I found that Mary Coningham was not on his list for interview and I have corrected that.'[13]

Pogue spoke to Coningham at Shinfield Park on 14 February, finding him 'the bitterest critic of Monty' whom he had yet encountered. Coningham showed Pogue part of his report on the Overlord Campaign 'which was so strong,' wrote Pogue, 'that the Air Ministry told him to rewrite it since, as the Air Marshal puts it, "they thought I out-Ingersolled Ingersoll and they don't want to start a war with the War Office."' (Ralph Ingersoll, formerly a member of Bradley's staff, had recently published a critical account of the campaign, entitled *Top Secret*, which profoundly agitated generals on both sides of the Atlantic.) 'To be blunt,' said Coningham, 'Monty and I had constant trouble', especially before the Arnhem disaster cut him down to size. Whenever they disagreed, Montgomery went over his head to anyone who might listen – in the RAF as well as the Army – and on at least three occasions tried to have him dismissed, but Tedder saved him. Although Montgomery frequently urged Coningham to bomb French towns, in order to block roads and so prevent the Germans using them, Coningham always refused, saying they would merely drive round such obstacles, through fields if necessary, and the lives and property of friendly civilians would have been destroyed for no purpose.[14]

In Coningham's opinion, according to Pogue, Montgomery's slowness and jealousy of the Americans (Patton in particular) prevented more complete Allied victories at Falaise and the Seine. He failed to overrun missile-launching sites quickly enough and could have secured seaborne access to Antwerp by September 1944 had he not been obsessed by leading a drive to Berlin. The Allies could also have reached the Rhine on Patton's front in September if fleets of transport aircraft standing by in England to carry paratroops on operations that were never mounted had instead been used to carry petrol to the man who could use it most effectively. Unhappily, pressure in the American as well as British armies to find employment for their large, highly-trained airborne forces was very strong, but the best chance to end the war early had already gone when the disastrous Arnhem operation began, hastily and badly planned, with the tactical air forces excluded. 'After that,' said Coningham, 'Monty had to sit quietly. When it came to planning for the Rhine crossing, they left the whole business to me.'

In the last stages of the war, said Coningham, it became possible for nearly every soldier in a foxhole to call down a fighter to strafe a machine-gun nest in front of him. This was the happy payoff for years of effort devoted to beating the Luftwaffe and building countless aircraft. Until then, Coningham had laboured hard to persuade both American and British generals to accept his conviction that only airmen could handle air power and use its flexibility to the best overall advantage. Now, however, he was very anxious lest Allied armies were basing plans for any future war against a major power on having the total air cover enjoyed in 1944–5. If so, they were going to be disappointed, for the British and Americans could expect to be at their usual disadvantage on the outbreak of a new war and air superiority took years to achieve. In conclusion, Coningham reminded Pogue of the lighter side of decision-making. 'Perhaps you wonder,' he said, 'why we extended the northern boundary of 21st Army Group to Bergen-op-Zoom? It wasn't so done at first and when I saw it, I said: "But the best oysters in the world are there!", so they changed the boundary to bring that town in.' Coningham was never convinced that in wartime a commander should rest content with bully beef and biscuits.[15]

By the time Pogue came to publish *The Supreme Command* in 1954, he needed no reminding of a more vital point, that readers should not be unduly impressed by accounts of differences between commanders: they argued frequently and sometimes quarrelled bitterly, but day-to-day cooperation between services and nations on the Allied side was close at all levels throughout the war. On 23 May 1945, for example, Coningham had warmly thanked Brigadier Panet (head of the Airfield Construction Group at 2nd TAF Headquarters) for devoted services. 'You know fully, and I have but an inkling,' he said, 'of the difficulties and heartbreak periods that have occurred, but always the job has been done.' In 2nd TAF, replied Panet, 'we have had the exhilarating experience of feeling that our work had a direct part in helping to win the war' under 'your inspiring leadership'. Coningham also wrote to Major General Inglis (Chief Engineer, 21st Army Group) on the 23rd. During the past year, airfield conditions had varied through the whole range of possible hazards and Coningham freely admitted that 2nd TAF could have done nothing without the devoted efforts of Inglis and his men. At first, he recalled, there had been the 'heat, dust and restricted space of Normandy' to trouble Inglis, followed by 'a grand rush ahead' which brought him German airfields to repair; then came 'the mud and rain and ice of winter to be again followed by a bound ahead over German airfields that were mined or bombed or otherwise unsuitable.' It was out there, on the cheerless airfields where it mattered, that the Army–Air cooperation advocated in comfortable offices was really to be found.[16]

Anthony Powell, the novelist, once reflected on 'the whole question of senior officers, their relations with each other and with those of subordinate rank'. The longer one dealt with them, he concluded, the more one developed the habit of treating them like members of the opposite sex:

> specifically, like ladies no longer young, who therefore deserve extra
> courtesy and attention; indeed, whose every whim must be given thought
> . . . Perhaps the cumulative effect of such treatment helped to account
> for the highly strung temperament so many generals developed. They
> needed constant looking after . . . 'They're like a lot of ballerinas,' agreed
> Pennistone. 'Ballerinas in Borneo, because their behaviour, even as
> ballerinas, is quite remote from everyday life.'

As Eisenhower put it on 20 December 1942 and on many occasions thereafter, 'Ch-ee-r-i-s-t, anyone who wants the job of Allied Commander-in-Chief can have it.'[17]

At some time during 1946, Coningham had learned that his ballerina days would end on 1 August 1947, as soon as he completed thirty years of commissioned service. He kept this news very much to himself, however, telling Elmhirst (then in India) as late as 23 June 1947 that 'I have just asked Air Ministry if I can retire at my own request on 1 August.' In fact, an Air Ministry official minuted on 30 June that Air Marshal Sir John Slessor (Air Member for Personnel) had 'accepted Sir Arthur's plea that his retirement, when Gazetted, may be shown as taking place at his own request . . . notwithstanding that he will actually retire as a compulsory case and receive retired pay and benefits appropriate to that form of exit.' At the invitation of the Belgian Air Force, Coningham paid his last official visit to Brussels early in July and received from Sir James Barnes (Permanent Under-Secretary of State for Air) his last 'marching orders' on the 10th. In his letter, Barnes added to the usual 'with regret' and recognition of 'distinguished service', the most unusual concession that the *London Gazette* would show Coningham as having retired at his own request even though both men knew this to be untrue.[18]

The author of this biography found no documentary explanation for this concession. There are rumours that Coningham ended his career under a cloud, rumours that are based in part on certain facts: he was not promoted to the rank of Air Chief Marshal, as were several contemporaries whose records as operational commanders bear no serious comparison with his; and he was not awarded the GCB (Grand Cross of the Bath, the grade of chivalry above that to which he had been tardily admitted after El Alamein and distinctly superior to the KBE, awarded on New Year's Day, 1946). But the award of the GCB was linked to four-star rank and in promoting officers at the highest level, the question of personal reward for exceptional merit did not outweigh the authorised value of the position occupied: at Shinfield Park, Coningham occupied an Air Marshal's position and that was that. There are also rumours about him that seem to be based less on facts than on the notoriety he earned – and undoubtedly relished – as a 'Renaissance Prince' in Belgium and Germany, where he exploited his authority for all it was worth. For example, as Frank Sayer (his personal driver) wrote, he had a Dakota fitted out 'like something from the King's flight' and certainly used it on unofficial jaunts. Coningham's pursuit of his own comfort led to rumours that he did more than *enjoy* the beautiful furnishings and treasures in the residences he occupied, but regarded them as *spoils of war* which might be taken to England; legitimate prizes in compensation for years of anxiety and misery. Together with many others who joyfully laboured to smash Hitler's evil empire, it seems likely that Coningham held this view and possible that he went too far, but no evidence on this point has been discovered.

The fact that Coningham was *required* to retire is not in itself mysterious: indeed, given the lack of demand for senior operational commanders from mid-1945 onwards and his own lack of Staff College, Imperial Defence College or Air Ministry experience, he was lucky to receive any post-war employment. As soon as the war ended, the RAF was drastically reduced in size and many senior officers with excellent records had to go in order to make room, in a smaller service, for the next generation. Tedder must have recommended Coningham to Portal for further employment in mid-1945; after he himself became Chief of the Air Staff on 1 January 1946, Tedder must also have told Coningham that Flying Training Command would be his last job; and Tedder must finally have agreed to the singular formula used to ease Coningham's return to civilian life and indicate to prospective employers that the RAF had not wanted to lose him. It seems unlikely that Portal and Tedder would have shown such consideration to Coningham if they had regarded him as a thief.

Coningham, his wife and daughter spent August and September in Cannes and southern France, casting off the burdens of an old life and considering what best to do about a new. At fifty-two, in good health, with well-proven management powers and a wide circle of influential friends, he could reasonably hope to fashion a second career, one which would not separate him so long and so often from his dearly-loved family: especially his daughter – now 13 – of whom he had seen far too little in recent years. While the Coninghams were thus occupied, Philip Noel-Baker (Secretary of State for Air) sent him two letters. One conveyed the King's formal thanks for 'long and valuable services', the other expressed, informally, the Air Council's gratitude 'for all you have done for the RAF' in the Western Desert and the 2nd TAF. Since then, Noel-Baker wrote, 'you have turned to the equally important work of training members of aircrew' whose future performance will afford you great satisfaction. Among less exalted mail, Coningham received details of 'emergency clothing coupons' for the 'issue of a civilian outfit on prepayment'.[19]

During his sojourn in France, Coningham learned that an air accident had cost him another famous acquaintance: Roy Chadwick, Avro's Chief Designer, who was killed in August when the Mark II version of his new airliner, named the Tudor, crashed on takeoff. An enquiry found that the accident was not caused by a design fault; so Donald Bennett, Chief Executive of British South American Airways and formerly head of Bomber Command's élite Pathfinder Force did not cancel his order. Bennett was anxious to establish a transatlantic service; he preferred British to American aircraft and trusted Chadwick, the man responsible for the excellent Lancaster bomber. By January 1948, therefore, three enlarged and improved versions of the Tudor – designated Mark IVs – were flying. One of these, named *Star Tiger*, had by then made eleven return journeys across the Atlantic, amounting to a total of 575 hours in the air, since its initial test flight on 4 November 1947. Coningham booked a passage aboard this aircraft for its twelfth journey, scheduled to begin on 27 January 1948.[20]

Flight of the *Star Tiger* II

Lisbon to a Place Unknown, 28–30 January 1948

Coningham received two invitations to dine on his night in Lisbon, one from an air force general who claimed to have met him in Gibraltar, the other from a business executive who claimed to have met him at Cowes. Though declining both, promptly if politely, he now regretted his decision, for he had finished his letter to Nan and time passed slowly when one was alone in a cold hotel bedroom. Before the war, with his career to make, Coningham had rarely missed an opportunity (as he confided to Nan) 'to meet and match'. By making him famous, he reflected wryly, the war had unexpectedly cooled his ardour in that direction: but now, with a new career to make, it was essential to start meeting and matching again. The successful entrepreneur, like the successful Air Marshal, could afford neither to be tired nor to spurn boring company. He had been slack for two years now – not idle, as some thought – but definitely in need of a long, slow unwind after six years of wartime command and so, as 'Poley' Rowley told Nan, he had merely done *one* day's work each day. However, a new year had begun and with it new resolutions: 1948 would see the Coningham Career pick up a fresh breeze.

By 8.45 next morning, 28 January, the six crew members and twenty-five passengers (two more had joined the flight) were back on board *Star Tiger*. Half an hour later, Captain McMillan having told the passengers that the port inner engine needed a little attention and that there was still a slight problem with the heating system, the two air hostesses – 'Stargirls', as BSAA liked to call them – were shepherding them back into a bleak and draughty waiting room. There, Sheila Nicholls and Lynn Clayton distributed blankets, served coffee and thought of something cheerful to say to everyone. At 11.45, two and a half hours late, *Star Tiger* at last took off again. The heating system, in fact, worked no better than on the first leg of the flight and everyone was chilled to the bone by the time the aircraft reached the island of Santa Maria in the Azores later that day, landing into a sixty-knot wind which brought it to an abrupt halt.

A refuelling stop of seventy-five minutes had been scheduled there, but the weather report was so poor that McMillan decided to stay overnight. Both crew and passengers were accommodated in a so-called 'hotel' near the airfield: a single-story, prefabricated building with only basic facilities, including a room designated as a lounge where they huddled to drink something hot. At Santa Maria, another BSAA aircraft – a civilian version of the Lancaster bomber, known as the Lancastrian – was awaiting a favourable opportunity for continuing its flight to Bermuda with freight which was to be trans-shipped there to *Star Tiger*. That night, a Mexican passenger (one of the two who boarded in Lisbon) wrote to his wife. 'The weather is still bad,' he said. 'We do not know if we will leave tomorrow or next day by way of New York.' Coningham, having written again to Nan, encouraged Tony Mulligan and Ernest Brooks, a Treasury official, to help him relieve the overworked hostesses by circulating among those passengers who had not gone early to bed, too full of cold or too miserable for company.

Next morning, the 29th, Captain McMillan, his First Officer (David Colby) and the Lancastrian captain (Frank Griffin) went together to the Meteorological Office to get the latest forecast. 'There's a strong wind,' Griffin later recalled telling McMillan. 'I expect I can make it in the Lancastrian, but I've got long-range tanks and an endurance of nineteen hours. I don't know about you.' Nevertheless, McMillan decided to go and they agreed to fly at no more than 2,000 feet throughout the journey in the hope of avoiding the worst winds and to permit drifts to be observed on the surface of the sea during daylight hours.

No weather ships were stationed along the route, unlike the routes between Europe and North America, and there was little commercial shipping, so weather conditions had to be 'inferred' mainly from observations made on either side of the Atlantic or on its islands. Griffin and McMillan therefore also agreed to fly with one hour between them: the Lancastrian, flying ahead, would pass valuable weather information back to *Star Tiger*. In order to get accurate position-fixes, methods of astronomical navigation were used, based on sextant observation of stars. Consequently, flights were planned so that the greater part of the journey – especially the latter part – was made in darkness. In good conditions, a star-fix should not be in error by more than fifteen miles and could be corrected by radio bearings transmitted to the aircraft from ground stations. For its final approach, the aircraft would home on to a Eureka radar beacon at Kindley Field, Bermuda.

The Tudor IV's fuel tanks would hold 3,300 gallons, but McMillan learned that the maximum amount he could take without overloading the aircraft was 3,150 gallons. However, he risked a slightly overloaded takeoff, knowing that he faced one of the world's longest civil aviation journeys – 1,960 nautical miles across the open Atlantic – and knowing also that his employers would not wish him to leave a passenger behind (there being no freight on board that he could leave instead). The aircraft had a maximum range of 2,900 miles: more than sufficient, in theory, to reach Bermuda safely, but the prevailing winds in winter were strong westerlies. Twice before, on westward flights, *Star Tiger* had had to divert to Gander in Newfoundland and just two months before this flight, another Tudor IV captain found himself still airborne with petrol gauges showing 'nil'. He alerted the air-sea rescue organisation and prepared to ditch, but managed a safe landing with no more than a hundred gallons to spare: less than the amount by which *Star Tiger* was overloaded on leaving Santa Maria. Frank Griffin took off at 2.22 pm on 29 January and Brian McMillan followed at 3.34 pm.[1]

Soon after takeoff, heavy rain and strong winds lashed *Star Tiger*, causing her to plunge and rear alarmingly, but at least the passengers and crew were no longer freezing. Flying at first some 200 miles behind Frank Griffin's Lancastrian, Brian McMillan slowly closed the gap and both aircraft maintained radio contact with each other and with Bermuda, their next destination. During this leg of their long journey, scheduled to last more than twelve hours, the Air Marshal resumed his close interest in *Star Tiger*'s navigation. He could navigate like a homing pigeon, recalled Frank Sayer, and in a car, a boat or an aircraft always knew exactly where he was. In his own aircraft, he would follow the progress of the flight, minute by minute, mile by mile, assessing the weather better than any professional forecaster. *Star Tiger*, however, was not his own aircraft and 'never interfere' was for him a strict rule of command – 'except, of course, to sack a chap altogether,' he added with a smile. Throughout the journey so far, however, Coningham felt only sympathy for the airliner's crew: looking back on his own exhausting long-distance flying days in Iraq, Egypt, the Sudan and across Africa, he knew only too well how weary they would be when the journey ended.

By 1.26 am on 30 January, after ten hours in the air, *Star Tiger* was only 150 miles behind the Lancastrian. At that time, Griffin's navigator got an astral fix and found that unforecast south-westerlies had blown the aircraft more than sixty miles north of its intended track during the previous hour. While Griffin was hearing this unwelcome news, McMillan was passing his Point of No Alternative, the point at which he might have diverted to Newfoundland; thereafter, he was committed to maintaining course for Bermuda. Griffin promptly radioed news of the wind change to *Star Tiger* and asked the operator on duty in Bermuda (a Mr Richards) for wind information. He had to wait forty minutes – and repeat the request twice – before he got it. *Star Tiger*, following the Lancastrian's course and in regular contact with it, did not make its own requests for such information.

At about 2 am, Cyril Ellison (*Star Tiger*'s navigator) got his own astral fix and learned that he, too, had been blown off course and was in fact crabbing away from Bermuda. Ellison at once gave McMillan a new course which turned the aircraft into the teeth of a gale. Even so, McMillan would not as yet have had cause for alarm, for he expected to reach Bermuda with at least an hour's fuel in hand. At 3 am, with cloud once more obscuring the stars, McMillan reported his position by dead reckoning. He believed that he was now making good his course for the island and amended his estimated time of arrival from 3.56 to 5 am, although it would in fact have been closer to 5.30 before he landed. Griffin called McMillan just after 3 to say that he was changing to voice telephony to contact Bermuda Approach Control, used for the last stage of the flight. 'See you at breakfast,' he added. Griffin later testified that he heard nothing from *Star Tiger* to indicate that it was in trouble and from that time until touchdown at 4.11 his own aircraft encountered nothing worse than head winds: no turbulence, icing, fog or electrical storms.

Meanwhile, at 3.04 am, *Star Tiger* had requested a radio bearing from Richards. To obtain this, the aircraft's radio operator simply depressed his key, transmitting a continuous signal to enable the receiving station to fix his bearing. On that occasion, a satisfactory bearing could not be given and the request was repeated ten minutes later. This time, Richards was able to give a first-class bearing of 72 degrees. He advised the aircraft accordingly and received an immediate acknowledgement at 3.15. Any doubts McMillan had about his position would seem to have been dispelled, for a series of such bearings would have guided him safely to the airfield, but if such requests were made, they were not heard. Richards called the aircraft at 3.50. Receiving no reply, he thought it might have gone over to direct radio contact with Bermuda Approach Control and asked that control if it had made contact. It had not. Nevertheless, Richards allowed another fifteen minutes to pass before trying again to contact *Star Tiger*. Still no response; still no action from Richards. At 4.40 he called again and only then, eighty-five minutes after losing contact, did he at last declare a state of emergency.

He heard no distress message, neither did anyone else, and yet many radio receiving stations were listening on the aircraft's frequency. If anyone aboard *Star Tiger* had so much as touched the transmitting key, it is likely that he or she would have been heard. The USAAF personnel operating the airfield immediately organised a maximum effort to find survivors that went on for five days, despite rapidly worsening weather: twenty-six aircraft flew 882 hours between them and surface craft also searched, but found nothing.

If *Star Tiger*'s radio failed shortly after 3.15 am, her captain and navigator would have been set the task of finding a small group of islands, extending twenty-two miles from north-east to south-west, covering a total area of twenty square miles and provided with powerful marine lights visible from about thirty miles in all directions at the aircraft's presumed altitude. It was at that time only 340 miles – about two hours and fifteen minutes' flying time – from those islands with sufficient fuel to fly for at least three and a half hours. Having received an accurate bearing, McMillan's task of making a landfall was not in itself difficult, except that he was acutely aware of the fact that there was no alternative landing ground: the nearest point of the

American mainland – Cape Hatteras – lay 580 miles to the west, far beyond *Star Tiger*'s range. No evidence survives to suggest that radio failure or navigational error were responsible for the disaster.

As for engine failure, the aircraft could have reached Bermuda comfortably on two of its four engines. Its low altitude, however, would mean that any handling problem was very dangerous. The altitude chosen by both aircraft was much lower than usual and no previous BSAA flight is known to have flown so low for so long. Wind forecasts throughout the journey were unreliable, especially at lower altitudes. Consequently, a sudden strong gust may have plunged the aircraft abruptly into the sea or inattention on the part of tired pilots combined with a faulty altimeter may have allowed it to slide in quietly, giving the radio operator no time in either case to send a distress signal. In the absence of such a signal, it seems probable that no-one aboard realised until the last moment of their lives that anything was amiss.[2]

'Mary is Always Good Company'

As soon as he learned that *Star Tiger* had crashed, the Minister of Civil Aviation in Britain (Lord Nathan of Churt) grounded BSAA's remaining Tudors as 'a measure of prudence'. A few weeks later, however, they were permitted to carry cargo – not passengers – between Santa Maria and Bermuda, but only via Newfoundland: a diversion that reduced the longest oversea passage by 250 miles. Although Sir Roy Dobson (Avro's Managing Director) and Bennett both publicly regretted any implication that the aircraft itself might be faulty, the Minister decided that a judicial investigation into the cause of an aircraft accident was necessary for the first time since the loss of the R.101 airship in October 1930. Bennett objected so strongly that BSAA sacked him. Lord Macmillan was appointed to carry out the investigation with two assessors, a Professor of Aviation in the University of London and the Chief Pilot of British European Airways. The investigation, held in public at Church House, Westminster, opened on 12 April 1948 and lasted for eleven days, with two short adjournments. Macmillan and the assessors visited Heathrow to inspect a Tudor IV (the assessors later taking a short flight in it) and on 21 August they presented their report to Lord Pakenham (Nathan's successor).[1]

The inquiry emphasised that McMillan, Colby and Ellison were vastly experienced airmen, all former members of Bennett's highly-regarded Pathfinder Force, before joining BSAA. As for the Radio Officer, Robert Tuck, he had followed his profession for twenty years at sea and in the air. All four had experience of the London to Havana route, although they had not previously flown together. Of the two cabin attendants, one – Lynn Clayton – had already survived an aircraft accident, when an Avro York crashed at Dakar in April 1947 and four passengers were killed. Though praising the crew, the enquiry found 'want of care and attention to detail' in the flight plan, but nothing serious enough to explain the accident. According to his biographer (Alan Bramson), Bennett did not always support his Operations

254

Manager against his ex-Pathfinder pilots, some of whom resisted simulator and instrument training and even the use of pre-takeoff and pre-landing checklists. The enquiry also found that BSAA 'did not sufficiently ensure that significant changes in the weather ahead of an aircraft would be known to it', but was unable to say whether that failing caused the accident. 'In closing this Report,' wrote Lord Macmillan, 'it may truly be said that no more baffling problem has ever been presented for investigation. In the complete absence of any reliable evidence as to either the nature or the cause of the disaster to *Star Tiger*, the Court has not been able to do more than suggest possibilities, none of which reaches the level even of probability.' The aircraft's fate must therefore remain 'an unsolved mystery'.[2]

On 17 January 1949, almost exactly a year after the loss of *Star Tiger*, another Tudor IV – named *Star Ariel* – crashed between Bermuda and Jamaica, again in unexplained circumstances. Bennett claimed that both aircraft were sabotaged (in Bramson's words) 'on the orders of those who felt threatened by the possibility of a successful challenge to their interests'. Although he learned that 'a known war-registered saboteur' had been seen standing near *Star Tiger* shortly before its last takeoff, Prime Minister Attlee (said Bennett) ordered enquiries abandoned. Bramson admits, however, that he could find no 'real support' for Bennett's assertions. The Tudor IV was converted to freighter use, but Bennett – while head of his own company – had a couple restored to carry passengers. One of these crashed near Cardiff in March 1950 and eighty lives were lost: at that time, the gravest aircraft disaster suffered in Britain. Despite Bennett's protests, an enquiry found that incorrect loading was the cause and the Tudor's tragic career ended.[3]

Jane-Mari, Coningham's daughter, well remembered a succession of cables, telephone calls and visitors to her mother on the day that *Star Tiger* went missing. Even though the airliner was overdue and perhaps down in the sea, every message and messenger reminded her that extensive searches for survivors were continuing. Then came another knock at the door which Jane-Mari answered. A small man, wearing a shabby raincoat, stood there. 'My name is Tedder,' he said, quietly and shyly. 'May I come in?' He had come to tell Nan that there was no longer any hope of finding her husband alive.[4]

Coningham's death had shared the front page of the *New York Times* on 31 January 1948 with news of the assassination of Gandhi in India and the death of Orville Wright in the United States. A long obituary described Coningham as 'one of the early advocates of the employment of tactical air power in close cooperation with ground forces and certainly one of its most successful practitioners'. The *New Zealand Herald* recorded on 2 February the death of 'one of the Empire's most distinguished air leaders in the war' as well as the fact (flattering to the people of such a small and isolated country) that both the *New York Times* and the *New York-Herald Tribune* had printed news of the search for the airliner on their front pages and devoted double column headlines to Coningham's career.

In both newspapers, the biographical sketches made the point that he preferred to be known as a New Zealander even though he was born in Australia. This point was emphasised by the *New Zealand Herald* in its own tribute, although admitting that he 'advanced in his chosen profession of arms far from either land in which he spent his youth'. History, the paper continued,

> may reveal him as one of the great Allied commanders in the Second World War. When he first assumed command of air formations in the Western Desert, the Air Force was extremely jealous of its separate entity and in danger of developing an unwarranted exclusiveness. Coningham changed all that and, at the same time, through the force of his own personality, sent into the air squadrons which outclassed the Luftwaffe in its own highly-specialised art of army cooperation.

The newspaper also emphasised Coningham's belief in *tactical* air operations 'as distinct from the massed bombing offensive'.[5]

An obituary in *The Times* on 10 February described Coningham as one of the war's 'outstanding air commanders'; he and Tedder 'were the main architects of the air side of the plan by which the action of the three Services was integrated. Though such a system had long existed in theory, it was first applied in North Africa' and then transferred to Europe. 'Coningham was much more than an efficient air commander,' the obituarist wrote, he was 'a brilliant strategist' as well.

> Not only could he form a sound judgment himself, but he had the ability to explain a situation lucidly and succinctly to others. With the aid of maps and by moving rulers, inkwells and similar objects on a table, he would convey a clear picture of what the enemy was planning and what steps would be taken to thwart him. Tall, handsome and invariably immaculate, even in the field, he was an impressive figure. One could not fail to appreciate his clear thinking, his power of grasping essentials and rejecting trivialities, his courtesy and his charm. He was an admirable speaker, animated and fluent.[6]

Coningham was one of the war's great men, announced C. G. Grey in the *Aeroplane* on 13 February with characteristic trenchancy. A famous aviation pundit, Grey had edited that magazine from 1911 to 1939 and had strong views on all aspects and personalities. Even though Coningham had inspired, as well as commanded and organised, men who were the spearhead of victory from El Alamein to Luneberg Heath, Grey was still more impressed by his conduct as head of 4 Group, Bomber Command, long before those dramatic days. 'The way he kept up the spirit of his aircrews and those on the ground during the grim winter of 1939–40 was extraordinary,' wrote Grey, because 'everything seemed so futile', whereas once the German conquest of Western

Europe began, everyone in Britain became perversely cheerful and military
command that much easier. 'I doubt whether any officer in the RAF has
been better beloved than Mary Coningham,' thought Grey. 'He had the
gentle and kindly way with him which one so often finds with big and
warlike men,' yet Grey also thought 'he would have made such a magnificent
Captain of Condottiere' in the Renaissance and had as well 'a quickness of
wit and a genius for phrase which would be worth a fortune if they could be
set on paper'. Had he been spared, he would certainly have made his mark
outside the RAF.[7]

Tedder's appreciation of Coningham appeared in *The Times* on 14 February. 'It was a grand Air Force team we had in Middle East in the difficult
days,' he wrote: 'a team led by a handful of individuals, outstanding alike in
their vision, courage and initiative, but each with his own strong individual
personality.' Sadly, three members of that little band had already been killed
in air accidents: Drummond, who 'bore so much of the burden and took so
little of the credit'; Dawson, who 'built up an aircraft industry in the slums
of Cairo and in the quarries of the Pharoahs, made bricks without straw and
aircraft from scrap'; and now Coningham, 'the airman personified'.

Coningham, wrote Tedder, had 'the alert, active, inquiring mind, the
imaginative, highly-strung temperament, the perennial youth' of 'a brilliant
commander of air forces. War, to him, was an art rather than a science;
insistent though he was on administrative and technical efficiency, he always
put morale first and material second, quality before quantity. His weapon
was the rapier not the bludgeon.' In Tedder's opinion, Coningham's greatest
contribution to victory was in the lead he gave to Army–Air cooperation.

> It was to him personally more than to anyone else that we owe the
> initiation and development of the joint land-air technique which became
> the doctrine and practice of the 8th Army and the Desert Air Force and
> subsequently of the Allied Armies and TAFs in North Africa and Europe
> . . . At times a candid critic, but at all times a loyal colleague of his Army
> team-mates he, more than any other man, fulfilled the wish expressed by
> Mr Churchill in a message to the RAF, Middle East, in July 1942: 'We
> are sure you will be to our glorious Army the friend that endureth to the
> end.' Coningham was that friend.[8]

The last, but not least, of the informed tributes came, appropriately, from
Elmhirst. 'To have heard him speaking every morning through those exciting
years at his 8 am staff meetings and again every evening to have discussed
with him, over a gin in his caravan, the events of the day was an education
in itself,' wrote Elmhirst in the *Aeroplane* on 2 April, and all his appointments, forecasts and plans were sound. Like Montgomery, 'his great
contemporary', Coningham refused to be immersed in detail and Elmhirst
well remembered days 'when a battle was raging in the desert and Mary
could not be found, but later admitted to having taken his sandwiches to lie

on the beach and have "a quiet think"'. Crises brought the best out of him and Elmhirst was sure that the

> tonic of his gay and confident presence in the 8th Army Commander's Mess in the dark days of defeat and retreat from Gazala is something the members of that Mess will not forget. Ever remembered will be his inspiration to the pilots under German fire at Gambut and about to withdraw to El Alamein when they saw their commander piloting himself around the airfields in an unarmed and unarmoured aircraft. He always radiated quiet confidence in difficult days, such as those in Tunisia in February 1943 and on those other critical evenings before the landings in Sicily and Normandy and again in Brussels during those four dark days of the Ardennes offensive before Christmas Day, 1944.

Coningham's greatness, Elmhirst concluded, lay in

> his detailed study of enemy intelligence from hour to hour, his ability to choose correctly his junior commanders; his youthful spirit, which infused confidence into and made a team of his junior commanders and staff; his absolute loyalty to his superiors; his ruthlessness where inefficiency was concerned; his quick and wholehearted commendation for those whose gallantry or services deserved it; his technical knowledge as a very competent airman and, lastly, his undoubted flair for the conduct of air operations.

His name would be remembered whenever tactical air forces were under consideration, for he was 'the original architect of them and unsurpassable in their leadership'.[9]

A memorial service attended by numerous RAF officers, past and present, had been held in St Margaret's, Westminster, on 17 February. Among Coningham's family and friends, were Nan, Jane-Mari and his stepson, Sir Robert Frank; Nan's mother and sister were also there, but Coningham's mother, brother and sister were all at that time in New Zealand. The RAF's Chaplain-in-Chief, John Jagoe, said that the service brought back memories of Sunday, 8 July 1945, the last Sunday of 2nd TAF's existence. Coningham, he said, had been anxious that he and at least some of the men and women in 2nd TAF should make an act of worship before the force dispersed. 'Never in all my experience,' said Jagoe, 'have I been privileged to take part in such a service as that held at Malmaison.' Coningham had asked Jagoe to include his own favourite hymn – 'Immortal, invisible, God only wise' – and many who sang it with him in Malmaison now sang it for him.[10]

Later that year, Wellington College in New Zealand decided to honour 'one of its most distinguished sons' with a Memorial Chair. There is nothing grand about it: apart from a small inscribed plate, it is just an ordinary wooden chair (though it has survived the hurly-burly of daily use for more than forty years now), but Coningham would have valued this uncommon mark of distinction in a school and in a city which had for him mixed memories. Still more would he have appreciated the special service in the Assembly Hall on 14 October 1948 at which Sir Bernard Freyberg, VC – then Governor General of New Zealand and also an old boy of the college – dedicated the memorial in the presence of many senior members of the New Zealand government, armed forces and citizens, some of whom clearly remembered a time when Coningham's name was derided. Freyberg himself was one of them and this knowledge added piquancy to his remarks about New Zealand's 'national loss' mingled with her 'national pride' in the knowledge that few people in the British Commonwealth had earned as high a place in history as this son of the notorious Arthur and Alice. Freyberg and Coningham had travelled many of the same roads in two world wars and in the Western Desert the General had noticed that the Air Marshal always took the keenest interest in the New Zealand forces and proudly counted himself among them. After emphasising the 'selflessness and humility which drew everyone to him', Freyberg ended by saying: 'I have lost a great companion and war comrade, the RAF has lost one of its most distinguished airmen and the Commonwealth one of its greatest sons.'[11]

In 1949, Nan gave a cup in memory of her husband to the RAF Sailing Association for competition between vessels of all three services at an annual regatta off Seaview, Isle of Wight. For some years, she herself presented it to the winner; her daughter then took over and now it is done by Sarah, her granddaughter. Nan died in June 1985 and early in July an RAF launch scattered her ashes, as she had requested, in the Solent. It would have struck Coningham as a fitting end to their earthly existence that Nan's remains should join his in the sea that they loved and that it should happen in July, always his favourite month. It would also have pleased him that a granddaughter whom he never knew played a part in the ceremony because, she said, she was proud of her connection with the Royal Air Force.[12]

NOTES

Prologue (pp. 1–3)

1. Letters, Jan–Apr 87, from source wishing to remain anonymous, re Mulligan; Report of the Court Investigation; Barker, *Great Mysteries of the Air*, 87–96; *NZ Herald*, 2 Feb 48 (McMillan); Runyon, *The Snatching of Bookie Bob*; C's last letters now lost, but tenor recalled by family members.

Chapter One (pp. 5–11)

1. *Australian Dictionary of Biography* (Nairn on C.); Martin-Jenkins, *The Complete Who's Who of Test Cricketers*; *Wisden*, 1894.
2. 'Zero' [Daniel Green]; *The Secret History of the Coningham Case*; Anon, *Coningham v Coningham*; O'Farrell, *The Catholic Church in Australia*, 182–3; *Catholic Press*, Sydney, 22 Dec 1900; *Courier*, Brisbane, 5–16 Dec 1900.
3. 'Zero', Anon, Pearl & O'Farrell; *Australian Dictionary of Biography* (Crick & Green); *Courier*, Brisbane, 11 Mar to 3 Apr 1901.
4. *Bulletin*, Sydney, 12 Nov 1903.
5. Wellington College records & corresp. with Ray Michael, Archivist; *Wellingtonian* (1910), 8–9.
6. Conningham [sic] v Conningham (1912), *NZ Law Reports*, xxxi, 956–7; National Archives, Wellington, D1106/12 & D1114/12; *New Zealand Truth*, 18 May 1912; *Wellington Evening Post*, 13, 14 May 1912 (divorce) & 28 Jul 59 (death of Alice); *Australian Dictionary of Biography* (C.); *Sydney Morning Herald*, 15 Jun 39.

Chapter Two (pp. 12–23)

1. Tomlinson, *Remembered Trails*, 50–1; conv./corresp. with Tomlinson, Peter Coote, John Blechynden, 1987–8.
2. Ministry of Defence, Wellington (C's Army service); Davidson, *Samoa Mo Samoa*, 90–1; Leary, *New Zealanders in Samoa*; Puttick Diary, 1–6; Waite, *New Zealanders at Gallipoli*, 326–7.
3. Raleigh & Jones, *War in the Air*, iii, 296–8; *Wellingtonian* (1917), 39.
4. For 32 Sqn see: AIR 1/691/21/20/32 (History composed by Air Historical Branch, London, 1927); Chamberlain, 'A Short History of No. 32 Squadron', *Cross & Cockade, USA*, xxii (1981) 39–70; AIR 1/1492 & 1493/204/38/3 (Record Book); AIR 1/1494/204/38/4 (Combat Records); AIR 1/

2218–2220/209/40/2–9 (V Brigade War Diary); AIR 1/1812/204/162/11 (22 Wing Reports). Lewis on Cairnes in *Over The Front*, iii (1988) 23 & on Lealvillers in *Wings over the Somme*, 95; Falconer Diary.
5. Lewis, *Wings over the Somme*, 100–1.
6. Bruce, *Aeroplanes of the RFC*, 41–6; Bridgman, *Clouds Remember*, 97–100; Robb Papers, AC71/9/68 & 105; *Wellingtonian* (1917), 31.
7. Rochford, *I Chose the Sky*, 68–9.
8. Bruce, 61–6; Bridgman, 101–3; Lewis, 103, 114 & in *Over The Front*, 23.
9. AIR 1/1592/204/83/13 (Gough's commendations).
10. AIR 1/1032/204/5/1434 (C's decorations).
11. C's Record of Service; *Southland Times*, 3 Nov 17; *Wellingtonian* (1918) 39–40.

Chapter Three (pp. 24–32)

1. For 92 Sqn see: Russell, 'History of 92 Squadron', *Journal of the Society of World War I Aero Historians*, vii (1966) 1–15; AIR 1/1836/204/206/3 & 4 (Record Book & Field Returns); AIR I/1835/204/206/1 & 2 (Record Book & Air Combats); AIR 1/1227/204/5/2634 (Combat Reports); AIR 1/976/204/5/1132 & AIR 1/977/204/5/1135 (V Brigade Summary of Work); AIR 1/176/15/194/1 (History of 92 Squadron); AIR 1/2386/228/11/13 (Douglas on SE 5a); Bruce, 471–81 & Bridgman, 90–3 (on SE 5a).
2. Robb Papers, AC71/9/30, 80, 104, 140 & letter to Russell, 13 Jun 63.
3. AIR 1/1030/204/5/1433 (Strange commendation).
4. Jones, *King of Air Fighters*, 251.
5. Gascoyne Interview, 15–24; Revell, 'Memories of J. V. Gascoyne, DFC', *Cross & Cockade, GB*, iv (1973) 128–33.
6. Strange, *Recollections of an Airman*, 187–93 (description of C. refers to 11 not 17 August).
7. AIR 1/1056/204/5/1550 (Haubourdin & Lomme); Kilduff, *Germany's Last Knight of the Air*, 144–50; Cutlack, *Australian Flying Corps*, 345–51.
8. AIR 1/677/21/13/1887 (Charlton & Cairnes's Instructions); Simkins, *Air Fighting*, 77.
9. AIR 1/1030/204/5/1433 (Gascoyne's DFC).
10. Reid to Bateman, 30 Apr 88; AIR 1/1064/204/5/1596 ((Inspection).
11. Coningham, 'The Development of Tactical Air Forces', *RUSI Journal*, xci (1946) 211–2.

Chapter Four (pp. 33–48)

1. Peyton-Ward, *RAF in Maritime War*, i, 47–53; Longmore, *From Sea to Sky*, 84–5.
2. C's Record of Service; conv./corresp. with Groom & Groom to Bateman, 19 Jul 88.
3. Douglas, *Years of Combat*, 15–16; *Flight*, 8 Jul 20, 705 & 709; conv./corresp. with Gibbs, 1986–8.
4. Taylor, *CFS*, 94–5; Macmillan, *RAF in the World War*, iii, 141.
5. Draper, *Mad Major*, 103–5.

6. C's Record of Service; conv./corresp. with McEvoy; *Spearpoint* (55 Sqn newsletter) lii (1987). On Iraq, see: AIR 5/1287 (Record Book); AIR 8/34 & AIR 19/109 (RAF Control).
7. Glubb, *War in the Desert*, 69; Embry, *Mission Completed*, 28–57.
8. Robb Papers, AC71/9/34; Long Interview.
9. Andrews & Morgan, *Supermarine Aircraft*, 184–6 (Kinkead).
10. AIR 5/1287; Longmore, 109–110.
11. Air 1/2389/Box (Groom & Williams).
12. McEvoy's foreword to Carr, *You are not Sparrows*, 5.
13. AIR 23/542 (Salmond Report); AIR 10/1115 (Army-Air Cooperation); AIR 1/2387/Box (Pirie).
14. AIR 19/109; Glubb, preface.
15. On C's trans-African flight see: AIR 5/820 (his Report); *Flight*, 1 Oct 25, 644; 15 Oct 25, 665–6; 5 Nov 25, 713–14; 26 Nov 25, 775–6; 3 Dec 25, 801; 7 Jan 26, 13; 14 Jan 26, 23; Jones, *Time Shrinkers*, 54–60 & 226–9; Robb Papers, AC71/9/35; *Aeroplane*, 25 Nov 25, 616; *Nigerian Pioneer*, 6 Nov 25, recorded aircraft numbers as J.7093, J.7339 & J.7337; *The Times*, 20 Nov 25. C's Record of Service; AIR 30/62/1–9 (awards to Coningham & Grant).
16. Brooke-Popham Papers (Trenchard's Speech & Air Staff Memo).
17. *Aeroplane*, 27 Feb 48. Rowley retired as Air Cdre & died 9 Apr 66; Baggs killed in Snipe accident at CFS, Wittering, 16 Jun 27.

Chapter Five (pp. 49–59)

1. C's Record of Service; Haslam, *History of RAF Cranwell*, 19–31, 38; AIR 29/699 (Cranwell ORB); *Journal of the RAF College*.
2. Conv./corresp. with Hudleston, Rosier, Sinclair, Kyle, 1986–8.
3. Conv./corresp. with Wall, 1987–8.
4. C's Record of Service; Taylor, 110, 122–3; Air Estimates, 1932; *The Times*, 8 Aug 31.
5. C's Record of Service; AIR 20/673 & 675 (Khartoum ORB); press notices, *Who's Who* (Frank family); letters from C to Nan & information from family members.
6. Principal Registry of Family Division, Somerset House, London.
7. Tapp to Bateman, 6 Apr 88.
8. C's Record of Service; *The Times*, 7 Jan 37 (17 Group & C's appointment); AIR 25/376 (17 Group ORB); AIR 28/120 (Calshot ORB).

Chapter Six (pp. 60–76)

1. AIR 25/93 (4 Group ORB); AIR 14/318 (4 Group organisation); Elworthy Interview.
2. Webster & Frankland, *Strategic Air Offensive against Germany*, i; Werham, *RAF in the Bombing Offensive*, ii, 5–8.
3. Air Ministry Propaganda Leaflets (2 vols.); Ludlow-Hewitt Papers, Box 2 (Nickel operations).
4. Ludlow-Hewitt Papers, Box 3.
5. AIR 14/111 (Reports by Group Commanders).

6. AIR 35/159 (Targets for Night Bombing); AIR 14/111.
7. AIR 14/205 & AIR 14/546 (C's Reports); Ludlow-Hewitt Papers, Box 3; Werham, ii, 72–3; Middlebrook & Everitt, *Bomber Command War Diaries*, 30.
8. Webster & Frankland, i, 140–1, 163, 201–12.
9. Ludlow-Hewitt Papers, Box 3; AIR 14/448 (Portal's Reply).
10. Werham, ii, 77–9, 81–5, 105–10.
11. Werham, ii, 113–19, 129–42.
12. Robb Papers, AC71/9/124 & AIR 14/1932 (C's promotion) AIR 14/1940 (Peirse-C corresp.).
13. Werham, ii, 149, 153–7, Appx. C3; Middlebrook & Everitt, 111.
14. Yarburgh-Bateson Papers; conv./corresp. with Stephen's brother Arthur, 6th Baron Deramore.
15. AIR 14/1940; AIR 14/811; Peirse Papers, AC71/13.
16. Werham, ii, 146–8; AIR 14/1927 (Portal-Peirse); AIR 14/1940.
17. AIR 14/1956.
18. AIR 14/654 (C-Saundby); AIR 14/102 (tactical problems); AIR 14–1940; Werham, ii, Appx C5 & 149–50.
19. AIR 14/102.
20. AIR 14/1940.
21. Yarburgh-Bateson Papers; Webster & Frankland, i, 241; Middlebrook & Everitt, 185.

Chapter Seven (pp. 77–94)

1. Tedder, *With Prejudice*, 37.
2. Liddell Hart to Cassells, 1/339/20, 26 Apr 66; Tedder, 55–6.
3. Drummond, 'The Air Campaign in Libya and Tripolitania', *RUSI Journal*, lxxxviii (1943) 251–7.
4. Lee, *Special Duties*, 113, 129; Joubert, *Third Service*, 209; Harding, *Mediterranean Strategy*, 13; Liddell Hart to Cassells, 26 Apr 66.
5. Coningham, 213; Bidwell & Graham, *Fire Power*, 275.
6. AIR 41/25 (RAF Narrative, June 41–Jan 42), ii, 20; Portal Papers, File 12.
7. AIR 41/25, ii, 25, 30, 34; West African Reinforcement Route (AHB, London).
8. AIR 41/25, ii, 38–9, 52–3.
9. AIR 41/25, ii, 56–8.
10. AIR 41/25, ii, 59–62; Bidwell & Graham, 263–9.
11. Portal Papers, File 12; Embry, 209–28; member of C's staff who wishes to remain anonymous.
12. AIR 41/25, ii, 22–3.
13. AIR 39/20.
14. AHB Trans. VII/104; Hinsley, *British Intelligence in the Second World War*, ii, 287–91, 313–19.
15. AIR 41/25, ii, 85–6.
16. AIR 41/25, ii, 99–103.
17. AIR 41/25, ii, 130–1; *The Times*, 25 Mar 81 (Auchinleck obituary).
18. *Star*, 20 Nov 41; *Daily Mail*, 21 Nov 41; *Life*, 1 Dec 41; *Time*, 1 Dec 41; Houghton, *They Flew Through Sand*, 173–4.

19. AIR 41/25, ii, 157–8.
20. AIR 41/25, ii, 151–3; Brown, *Eagles Strike*, 96–8; Alan Cunningham to CIGS, Dec 41, in Admiral Andrew Cunningham Papers, BM Add. 52570.
21. Portal Papers, Box C, File VIII.
22. AIR 41/25, ii, 196–7, 203.
23. AIR 41/25, ii, 222–30, 237–41, 262–3, 267.
24. Behrendt, *Rommel's Intelligence in the Desert Campaign*, 145–6; AHB Trans. VII/104.
25. AIR 23/1773; AIR 41/26 (RAF Narrative, Jan–Jun 42), iii, 16, 20–3, 28.
26. Portal Papers, Box C, File VIII.
27. AIR 41/26, iii, 37–43; AIR 23/1773.
28. Cross Papers; Elmhirst Papers, 6/1 (p. 66) & Rec. 16 (Jun 78).
29. Elmhirst Papers, Rec. 20 (Nov 78) & 6/6; *The Times*, 14 Nov 67 & anon member of C's staff on Beamish.
30. Elmhirst Papers, Rec. 20 (Nov 78), 6/2 (vii, 2) & 6/6.
31. Elmhirst Papers, Rec. 20 (Nov 78).
32. Elmhirst Papers, Rec. 20 (Nov 78); AIR 41/26, iii, 92, 94.
33. Portal Papers, File 12.
34. Portal Papers, Box C, File VIII; AIR 41/26, iii, 95.
35. AIR 40/2323.
36. AHB Trans. VII/104; *The Times*, 25 Mar 81 (Auchinleck's obituary); Behrendt, 155, 166.

Chapter Eight (pp. 95–110)

1. AIR 41/26, iii, 135, 214–15; Elmhirst Papers, 6/2 (vii, 6–8).
2. AIR 23/904.
3. Elmhirst Papers, 6/6; AIR 41/26, iii, 216–17.
4. AIR 23/904; Brown, 166, 174–5.
5. Brown, 164; AIR 41/26, iii, 159–60; AHB Trans. VII/II; Owen, *Tedder*, 160.
6. Tedder Papers; Elmhirst Papers, 6/2 (vii, 8).
7. AIR 41/26, iii, 175–6; Hinsley, ii, 373–80.
8. AIR 41/26, iii, 177–8; Elmhirst Papers, 6/2 (vii, 8); Brown, 180.
9. AIR 41/26, iii, 186–7; BBC *Listener*, 4 Jul 74 (interview with Auchinleck).
10. AHB Trans. VII/104.
11. Portal Papers, Box C, File VIII.
12. Portal Papers, Box C, File VIII; Elmhirst Papers, 6/6; Brown, 189; AIR 41/26, iii, 195.
13. Portal Papers, Box C, File VIII; Elmhirst Papers, 6/2 (vii, 7–8); Wilmot to Liddell Hart, no date, 1/753.
14. Portal Papers, Box C, File VIII.
15. Portal Papers, Box C, File VIII.
16. Portal Papers, Folder 8; Brereton Diaries, 130–1, 136.
17. Elmhirst Papers, 6/2 (vii, 8); AIR 41/26, iii, 195; AIR 41/50, xxix.
18. AIR 41/50, 1; Lee, 158, 163–5.
19. Brereton Diaries, 137–8.
20. AIR 41/50, 3–4, 6; AIR 19/557.

21. Lee, 162.
22. Elmhirst Papers, 6/2 (vii, 9) & 6/6; Coningham, 214.
23. Portal Papers, File 12.
24. Portal Papers, File 12; Brereton Diaries, 141–3.
25. Portal Papers, File 12.
26. Elmhirst Papers, Rec. 14 (May 78) & 6/6; Portal Papers, File 12.
27. Elmhirst Papers, 6/2 (vii, 10) & 6/6; Portal Papers, File 12.
28. Elmhirst Papers, Rec. 14 (May 78), 6/2 (vii, 12) & 6/6.
29. Elmhirst Papers, 6/2 (vii, 13); AIR 41/50, 160–4.
30. Elmhirst Papers, 6/2 (vii, 14); AHB Trans. VII/104; AIR 41/50, 172, 186; Lewin Papers, 8/8 (letter, 17 Dec 79).
31. AIR 23/8294; Guingand, *Operation Victory*, 150; Brereton Diaries, 151–2; Elmhirst Papers, 6/2 (vii, 16); AIR 41/50, 205–7; AHB Trans. VII/104.
32. AIR 37/760.
33. AIR 37/760.
34. AIR 41/50, 220–1.
35. Elmhirst Papers, 6/2 (vii, 17–18); AIR 41/50, 223.
36. AIR 41/50, Appx II.

Chapter Nine (pp. 111–126)

1. Elmhirst Papers, 6/2 (vii, 19); Brown, 264–5; AIR 41/50, 236–7; Kuter Papers, Reel 2.
2. Elmhirst Papers, 6/2 (vii, 19) & 6/6; Montgomery Papers, BLM 27, Reel 4; AIR 41/50, 107; corresp. with McNeill, Apr 86.
3. Elmhirst Papers, 6/6.
4. Elmhirst Papers, 6/6; AIR 41/50, Appx 9.
5. AIR 41/50, 227–8, 264–5, 240–3; AHB Trans. VII/104.
6. Elmhirst Papers, 6/2 (vii, 19–20) & 6/6; AIR 41/50, 263–4.
7. *TLS*, 12 Jun 81 (Carver, review of Hamilton, *Monty: The Making of a General*); AIR 41/50, 357; Hinsley, ii, 430–8.
8. AIR 41/50, 357–9; Hinsley, ii, 438–48.
9. AIR 41/50, 361.
10. AIR 41/50, 361–2.
11. Trenchard Papers, MFC 76/1/469.
12. *Sunday Times*, 27 Oct 57; Elmhirst Papers, 6/2 (vii, 23–5); AIR 41/50, 325–6.
13. Elmhirst Papers, 6/2 (vii, 25); AIR 41/50, 327, 333–9.
14. Elmhirst Papers, 6/2 (vii, 26); AIR 41/50, 367–8; Brown, 292.
15. AIR 41/50, 367–8; Hinsley, ii, 452–3.
16. AIR 41/50, 387–9, 406–8.
17. AIR 41/50, 372–4.
18. AIR 41/50, 391–7.
19. Elmhirst Papers, 6/2 (vii, 28–9); AHB Trans. VII/III.
20. Elmhirst Papers, 6/2 (vii, 29).
21. Portal Papers, File 12; AIR 23/904.
22. Portal Papers, File 12.
23. AIR 41/50, 417–21.
24. Pogue Interviews.

25. Elmhirst Papers, 6/2 (vii, 30–1) & 6/6.
26. Portal Papers, File 12.
27. Portal Papers, File 12.
28. Portal Papers, File 12.
29. Portal Papers, File 12.
30. Portal Papers, File 12; Alanbrooke Papers, 3/A/VII.
31. AIR 41/50, 431–2.
32. AIR 41/50, 432–6.
33. Elmhirst Papers, 6/6; Portal Papers, Box A, Folder 8; *Daily Telegraph*, 26 Nov 42; *Daily Mail*, 27 Nov 42.
34. Freiherr von Heydte (commander of Rommel's rearguard) in Purnell's *History of the Second World War*, 1230–2.
35. Heydte, 1327–9.
36. Power Papers, BM Add. 56097; AHB Trans. VII/106; Guingand, 231; AIR 41/50, 463; Drummond, 265.
37. Brereton Diaries, 167–8, 172; *Daily Telegraph*, 11 Dec 42; Spaatz Papers, Box 9 (Craig to Spaatz, 23 Dec 42).

Chapter Ten (pp. 127–142)

1. AIR 41/33, 23–4; Mortensen, *A Pattern for Joint Operations*, 47–65.
2. AIR 41/33, 113; Hinsley, ii, 463–505.
3. Bradley & Blair, *A General's Life*, 135, 137, 140.
4. Bradley & Blair, 132.
5. Davis, *Bomber Baron*, 206–8; AIR 41/50, 478–9.
6. Davis, 177–8; Kohn & Hanrahan, *Air Superiority*, 30–1; Power Papers, BM Add. 56097.
7. AIR 41/33, 121; *Decatur Herald*, 6 Feb 42; Kuter, unpublished autobiography [hereafter, u.a.] 267 & Diary; Mortensen, 74–84.
8. Portal Papers, Box C, Folder 5; Quesada Papers, Interview, May 75: Section 3, 3–5.
9. Robb Papers, AC 71/9/68; Belinda Montagu (née Crossley) to Bateman, 1 Apr 88.
10. Davis, 205, 237 & 'Eisenhower's Airman', 38; Spaatz Papers, Box 10, Private Diary.
11. Davis, 'Eisenhower's Airman', 42; Montgomery Papers, BLM 31, Reel 4; Robb Papers, AC71/9/68.
12. Kuter, u.a., 274–8.
13. Robb Papers, AC 71/9/68; Coningham, 215.
14. AIR 23/1709.
15. AIR 41/50, 479; Robb Papers, AC 71/9/109 (copy of pamphlet); Tedder to Liddell Hart, 1/339/20, 26 Apr 66.
16. Craven & Cate, *Army Air Forces in World War II*, iii, 806–7.
17. Parton Papers, Series 6, Box 3, Reel 2.
18. Kuter Diary & u.a., 271.
19. Kuter, u.a., 279; Elmhirst Papers, 6/2 (viii, 2–3) & Rec. 15 (May 78).
20. AIR 41/33, 153; corresp. with Wiseman, Oct 87; Kuter, u.a., 279.
21. Kohn & Hanrahan, 32–4; Mortensen, 70–4 & corresp., Dec 87.

22. Lewin, *Life & Death of the Afrika Korps*, 234; Irving, *Trail of the Fox*, 279–80.
23. Lewin, 234–7; Irving, 280–90.
24. AIR 41–33, 124; Hinsley, 586–92.
25. Kuter, u.a., 279–82.
26. Butcher, *Three Years with Eisenhower*, 231; Kuter, u.a., 282.
27. Elmhirst Papers, 6/7; AIR 41/33, 156–7.
28. Portal Papers, PM Minutes, File 4; Montgomery Papers, BLM 49, Reel 4.
29. Elmhirst Papers, 6/2 (viii, 4); Spaatz Papers, Box 11 & Robb Papers, AC71/9/65 (C's directive).
30. Allfrey Papers, 3/9.
31. AHB Trans. VII/106.

Chapter Eleven (pp. 143–156)

1. Bradley & Blair, 140–2; AHB Trans. VII/V; Hinsley ii, 574–82.
2. AIR 41/33, 170; AIR 41/50, 503, 509; Hinsley, ii, 597–605.
3. Kuter Diary & Papers, Reel 2; Montgomery Papers, BLM 32, Reel 4; conv./corresp. with Cross, 1986–8.
4. Kuter, u.a., 282–3; Bradley & Blair, 143.
5. Parton Papers, Series 1, Box 1, Folder 3.
6. AIR 41/33, 157–8; conv./corresp. with Sinclair, 1986–7.
7. Elmhirst Papers, 6/7; Coningham, 215.
8. Bradley & Blair, 146–7; Blumenson, *Patton Papers*, ii, 205, 216; Kuter, u.a., 287.
9. Kuter, u.a., 284–5.
10. Spaatz Papers, Box 11 (Diary); Kuter, u.a., 286; Bradley & Blair, 148; Blumenson, ii, 207 (8 April should be 3 April).
11. Blumenson, ii, 208–11; Kuter, u.a., 286.
12. Spaatz Papers, Box 11 (Diary); Butcher Diary, 6 Apr 43.
13. Blumenson, ii, 209, 217; AIR 23/7439.
14. Portal Papers, Box C, File VIII; *The Times*, 14 Apr 43 (C's signal).
15. Leigh-Mallory Papers; AIR 41/66, 3–10.
16. Elmhirst Papers, 6/2 (viii, 6–7) & 6/7; AHB Trans. VII/106.
17. AIR 41/33, 180; Lewin, 247.
18. Bradley & Blair, 151.
19. Kuter, u.a., 291–2; Robb Papers, AC71/9/68.
20. AIR 41/33, 184–6; Quesada Papers, Interview May 75: Section 2, 30; Davis, 265–9; *The Times*, 20 Apr 43 (C-Broadhurst); AIR 41/50, 256.
21. Davis, 292–3; Hinsley, ii, 605–14; Montgomery Papers, BLM 34, Reel 4.
22. *Daily Telegraph*, 10 May 43 (Balfour); Coningham, 215.
23. Elmhirst Papers, 6/2 (viii, 9) & Rec. 15 (May 78).
24. Kuter Diary & Papers, Reel 4.
25. Robb Papers, AC71/9/153; Kuter Papers, Reel 4.
26. AHB Trans. VII/106.

Chapter Twelve (pp. 157–168)

1. Elmhirst Papers, 6/2 (viii, 11–13) & 6/7; Robb Papers, AC71/9/65 & 68; conv./corresp. with Mills, 1986.
2. Kuter Papers, Reels 2 & 4; AIR 23/7439; Kohn & Hanrahan, 22, 35–6 (manual printed here as appendix).
3. Butcher Diary, 30 Apr 43; Blumenson, ii, 236–7.
4. Butcher Diary, 4 Jun 43; Hamilton, *Monty: Master of the Battlefield*, 333–4.
5. Portal Papers, Box C, Folder 8.
6. Brereton Diaries, 188–9; Butcher Diary, 11 Jun 43.
7. AIR 41/59, 17–18.
8. AIR 41/59, 25–8.
9. Robb Papers, AC71/9/65; D'Este, *Bitter Victory*, 165–8; Bradley & Blair, 177.
10. Butcher Diary, 13 Jul 43; Bradley & Blair, 178.
11. Elmhirst Papers, 6/2 (viii, 13); Craven & Cate, ii, 446–87.
12. AHB Trans. VII/94 (Christ), VII/93 (Kesselring).
13. AIR 23/7439; AIR 41/59, 40; Elmhirst Papers, 6/2 (viii, 13–14).
14. Montgomery Papers, BLM 39, Reel 4; Elmhirst Papers, 6/7.
15. Butcher Diary, 17 Jul 43; Davis, 365–7, 370–2; Parton Papers, Series 1, Box 1, Folder 3; Portal Papers, Box C, File 8.
16. Mitchell, *No Medals for the Airmen*, 139–42.
17. AIR 41/59, 80–1.
18. Hinsley, iii, part 1, 95–9; Davis, 372–7; AIR 41/59, 88–9.
19. AHB Trans. VII/161 (Lehrgang), VII/94 (Christ).
20. D'Este, 523–49.
21. AIR 41/59, 80; Hinsley, iii, part 1, 99.
22. AIR 41/59, 81; Coningham, 215–16.

Chapter Thirteen (pp. 169–179)

1. Parton, '*Air Force Spoken Here*', 379–82; Craven & Cate, ii, 488.
2. AIR 41/34, 12–13, 32–3; Portal Papers, Box C, File 8.
3. Elmhirst Papers, 6/7 & 6/2 (viii, 14); Trenchard Papers, MFC 76/1/469; Robb Papers, AC71/9/68.
4. Montgomery Papers, BLM 41, Reel 4; Cunningham Papers, BM Add. 52571; *Sunday Times*, 30 Oct; 83 (Howard review of Lamb & Hamilton on Montgomery).
5. Martin & Orpen, *Eagles Victorious*, vi, 41–2; Craven & Cate, ii, 510–2; Butcher, 356; Hamilton, 375–87.
6. Coningham, 216; Craven & Cate, ii, 491–4, 529–36; AIR 41/34, 103.
7. Hamilton, 401, 406; AIR 41/34, 168.
8. AIR 41/34, 177.
9. Tedder, 466; AIR 23/7439 (Dawson) & 7441 (San Spirito).
10. AIR 23/7439.
11. Portal Papers, Box D, Folder 5; AIR 41/34, 194–5.
12. Portal Papers, Box D, Folder 5; Tedder, 487–8.
13. Portal Papers, Box D, Folder 5; AIR 23/7439.

14. Elmhirst Papers, 2/12; Robb Papers, AC71/9/68.
15. Infield, *Disaster at Bari*; AIR 41/34, 227–9; AIR 23/1481; AHB Documents, 5/110 & 5/244.
16. Roskill, *War at Sea*, iii, 210.
17. *The Times*, 6 Mar 86.
18. AIR 23/7440.
19. Gilbert, *Road to Victory*, 603–51; Hamilton, 464–6.
20. Elmhirst Papers, 2/12; Robb Papers, AC71/9/68; Kuter Papers, Reels 2 & 4.
21. Robb Papers, AC71/9/68; Hamilton, 471.
22. AIR 23/7441; Robb Papers, AC71/9/153.
23. Moloney, *Mediterranean & Middle East*, v, 641–2; Robb Papers, AC71/9/68.

Chapter Fourteen (pp. 180–193)

1. Elmhirst Papers, Rec. 15 (May 78).
2. Tedder Papers.
3. Elmhirst Papers, Rec. 27 (Apr 79); Wynn & Young, *Prelude to Overlord*, 30–3.
4. Elmhirst Papers, 6/2 (ix, 2–3); Brereton Diaries, 222–3, 261.
5. Coningham, 216–17.
6. Elmhirst Papers, Rec. 27 (Apr 79); AIR 37/1237.
7. Instone, *Deputy Provost Marshal*, 93–4, 105.
8. Corresp. with Porter, 1987.
9. *Daily Herald*, 26 Jan 44; *Observer*, 30 Jan 44.
10. AHB Narrative, North-west Europe [hereafter NW Europe], i, Appx 1/26; AIR 37/1237; AIR 37/609; Brereton Diaries, 240.
11. Alanbrooke Papers, 3/B/XI; Butcher Diary, 3 Mar 44; Portal Papers, Box A, Folder 6.
12. AIR 37/1237.
13. AIR 37/1237.
14. Brereton Diaries, 254–5.
15. AIR 37/609; NW Europe, i, Appx 1/26; AIR 41/66, 19–20.
16. Craven & Cate, iii, 139–40 & 110.
17. AIR 41/24, 50–2; Brereton Diaries, 259; Tedder Papers (Desk Diary, 19 & 20 Apr 44); AIR 37/1213.
18. *Daily Mail*, 25 Apr 44.
19. NW Europe, i, Appx 1/60/1; Portal Papers, File 12.
20. AIR 37/537; AIR 37/1213, para. 245.
21. Vandenberg Papers, Box 1; Brereton Diaries, 264.
22. Cannon Papers, Reel A.1724.
23. Kingston-McCloughry Papers, Box 417; AHB Trans. VII/19; Hinsley, iii, part 2, 106, 111–12.
24. AIR 37/1213, paras. 429–33; AIR 37/609.
25. AIR 37/1213, paras. 433, 246–50.
26. Tedder Papers (Desk Diary, 17 May 44); 41/66, 53.
27. Vandenberg Papers, Box 1; Kuter Papers, Reel 4.
28. AIR 41/24, 50; Vandenberg Papers, Box 1.

29. *News Chronicle*, 25 May 44.
30. *Daily Telegraph*, 30 May 44.

Chapter Fifteen (pp. 194–210)

1. Trenchard Papers, MFC 76/1/469.
2. Brereton Diaries, 270–2; AIR 37/564.
3. Robb Papers, AC71/9/26; Wilmot, *Struggle for Europe*, 236–43; Kingston-McCloughry, *Direction of War*, 137–8.
4. Hinsley, iii, part 2, 126–32; AIR 41–24, 71, 157–9.
5. AIR 41/193–4; AIR 37/564; AIR 37/876 (C's Report), paras. 22–5.
6. AIR 37/784; Montgomery Papers, BLM 126/M.500.
7. AIR 37/564; AIR 37/876, para. 26.
8. AIR 41/67, 1–3; AIR 41/24, 81; AIR 37/876, paras. 16–9; Hinsley, iii, part 2, 133–5.
9. Tedder Papers (Desk Diary, 14 Jun 44); AIR 37/564.
10. AIR 37/1213, paras. 477–8.
11. AIR 37/563; Tedder Papers (Desk Diary, 16 Jun 44); AIR 41/67, 5–7.
12. AIR 37/563; Vandenberg Papers, Box 1.
13. Tedder Papers (Desk Diary, 28–30 Jun 44).
14. Brereton Diaries, 296–7.
15. AIR 37/563.
16. Hinsley, iii, part 2, 171–224; AIR 41/66, 189; Elmhirst Papers, 6/2 (ix, 4–5).
17. Kuter Papers, Reel 1.
18. Tedder Papers (Desk Diary, 1 & 5 Jul 44); Brereton Diaries, 300–1; Montgomery Papers, BLM 75–1; AIR 41/67, 21–2.
19. AIR 37/1012; Tedder Papers (Desk Diary, 6 Jul 44).
20. Montgomery Papers, BLM 126/M.509.
21. Montgomery Papers, BLM 126/M.508; Portal Papers, Box D, Folder 4, Item 8.
22. AIR 41/67, 22–4; D'Este, *Decision in Normandy*, 308–20.
23. Kingston-McCloughry Papers, Box P.414.
24. AIR 41/67, 38–9; Hobart-Liddell Hart, 11/1947/15.
25. AIR 37/564; Trenchard Papers, MFC 76/1/469; Alanbrooke Papers, 3/B/XIII; Tedder Papers (Desk Diary, 19 Jul 44).
26. Butcher Diary, 20 Jul 44; Tedder Papers (Desk Diary, 20 & 21 Jul 44).
27. Montgomery Papers, BLM 94–6.
28. AIR 41/67, 56; Tedder Papers (Desk Diary, 21 Jul 44); Hastings, *Overlord*, 243.
29. Elmhirst Papers, 6/2 (ix, 7); corresp. with Sayer, 1986–8.
30. Elmhirst Papers, 6/2 (ix, 8); Grigg Papers, 9/8/19a.
31. AIR 41/67, 85–8; Hinsley, iii, part 2, 235–8.
32. AIR 37/876, paras. 42–8; Elmhirst Papers, 6/2 (ix, 8).
33. AIR 37/876, paras. 49/53; Hinsley, iii, part 2, 249–54.
34. Elmhirst Papers, 6/2 (ix, 9–11).
35. Elmhirst Papers, 6/2 (ix, 8–9).
36. AIR 37/674; AIR 37/1; AIR 37/876, paras. 97–8.

37. AIR 37/876, para. 99; Air Ministry, *Operational Research*, 137–8; AIR 41/67, 122.
38. Liddell Hart Papers, 11/1944/45a.

Chapter Sixteen (pp. 211–224)

1. Portal Papers, Box D, Folder 4.
2. Elmhirst Papers, 6/2 (ix, 12).
3. D'Este, *Decision in Normandy*, 433, 463–8; Hinsley, iii, part 2, 377–82.
4. AIR 37/876, paras. 103–5.
5. AIR 37/876, paras. 108–15; corresp. with Colville, Jan 87.
6. AIR 37/876, para. 120; corresp. with Mrs Waterhouse; Elmhirst Papers, 6/2 (ix, 13).
7. Elmhirst Papers, 6/2 (ix, 13–15).
8. Elmhirst Papers, 6/2 (ix, 15–16).
9. AIR 37/876, paras. 57–62; AIR 37/880.
10. Forbes & Nicolson, *Grenadier Guards*, ii, 96, 119; conv. with Groom, 1986.
11. AIR 37/876, paras. 122–9; Brereton Diaries, 340–2; AIR 41/67, 168–74; Hamilton, *Monty: The Field Marshal*, 30, 103; Alanbrooke Papers, 3/B/XIII; Hinsley, iii, part 2, 382–95.
12. Terraine, *Right of the Line*, 668; AIR 41/67, 150; Brereton Diaries, 363–4; *Press*, Christchurch, 29 Oct 88 (Urquhart interview, reprinted from *Daily Telegraph*).
13. AIR 37/876, paras. 130–2.
14. Robb Papers, AC71/9/78; Elmhirst Papers (private letters); corresp. with McNeill, 1986.
15. AIR 41/67, 174–5.
16. AIR 8/1181; Craven & Cate, iii, 620–2.
17. AIR 41/68, 12–3.
18. AIR 37/1237; *Sunday Times*, 30 Oct. 1983 (Howard review of Lamb & Hamilton on Montgomery); Grigg Papers, 9/8/28g.
19. AIR 37/674.
20. AIR 37/876, paras. 73–9; AIR 37/1060.
21. Portal Papers, Box D, Folder 3.
22. Portal Papers, Box D, Folder 3 & Folder D, Item 22; AIR 37/1237; *Sunday Chronicle*, 5 Nov 44; AIR 37/876, paras. 137–9.
23. AIR 41/68, 22–3; Portal Papers, File 12.
24. AIR 37/876, paras. 140–4, 161 & Appx H.
25. AIR 41/68, 26–8.
26. AIR 41/68, 40; AIR 37/876, para. 154.
27. Corresp. with Porter & Colville, 1987.
28. Portal Papers, Box D, Folder 3; *Daily Mail*, 17 Nov 44.
29. Elmhirst Papers, 6/2 (ix, 18).
30. Portal Papers, Box C, Folder 1; AIR 40/1497.
31. AIR 37/876, paras. 173–88; AIR 41/68, 48–9.
32. Portal Papers, Box C, Folder 1; Hamilton, 163.
33. Grigg Papers, 9/8/37a; AIR 37/1.
34. MacDonald, *Battle of the Bulge*, 11, 49–51; Hinsley, iii, part 2, 417–30.

Chapter Seventeen (pp. 225–238)

1. AIR 37/876, paras. 189–93; AIR 41/68, 69.
2. Robb Papers, AC71/9/26; AIR 37/876, para. 194; corresp. with Porter, 1987.
3. Elmhirst Papers, 6/2 (ix, 20–1).
4. AIR 37/876, paras. 194–6.
5. Robb Papers, AC71/9/26.
6. AIR 41/68, 78; Elmhirst Papers, 6/2 (ix, 21–2).
7. Robb Papers, AC71/9/26; AIR 41/68, 91.
8. Elmhirst Papers, 6/2 (ix, 22); AIR 37/876, para. 197; Cooper, *German Air Force*, 364–5; corresp. with Sayer, 1986–8.
9. Portal Papers, PM Minutes, Jan–Dec 45; AIR 41/68, 102–3.
10. Instone, 183–4.
11. Robb Papers, AC71/9/26.
12. MacDonald, 415–29, 587–603, 611; AIR 41/68, 108.
13. AIR 37/876, paras. 199–206; Hinsley, iii, part 2, 663–690.
14. AIR 37/876, paras. 211–14; AIR 41/68, 152–3.
15. AIR 37/876, paras. 215–17; AIR 41/68, 161.
16. Brereton Diaries, 397; Elmhirst Papers, 6/2 (ix, 24); Colville, *Fringes of Power*, 567–8; AIR 37/876, part IV, paras. 74–5.
17. AIR 20/794 & 5; Gilbert, 1256–7; Bowyer, *2 Group*, 390–1, 512.
18. AIR 20/794; conv./corresp. with Cross, Groom, McEvoy, 1986–8.
19. AIR 37/876, paras. 220–3.
20. AIR 37/876, paras. 224–38; Brereton Diaries, 403–5.
21. Elmhirst Papers, 6/2 (ix, 24–5); Portal Papers, Box A, File 11, No. 17.
22. AIR 37/876, paras. 234–48; Brereton Diaries, 406–15; AIR 41/68, 177; AIR 37/674; Elmhirst Papers, 6/2 (ix, 25).
23. AIR 41/68, 237–8; AIR 37/876, paras. 254–5, 258–64; AIR 37/674.
24. Elmhirst Papers, 6/2 (ix, 25–6); AIR 37/876, paras. 268–76; AIR 41/68, 221; corresp. with Porter, 1987.
25. Elmhirst Papers, 6/2 (ix, 26–7).
26. Corresp. with Lucas, Feb 87.
27. Elmhirst Papers, 6/2 (ix, 28–9); AIR 41/68, 262–3; AIR 55/161; Sholto Douglas, *Years of Command*, 280–1.

Chapter Eighteen (pp. 239–248)

1. AIR 55/161; Elmhirst Papers, 6/2 (ix, 30–1).
2. Elmhirst Papers, 6/2 (ix, 31) & 6/8; AIR 24/1792; AIR 37/674; Robb Papers, AC71/9/41.
3. *News Chronicle*, 31 Jul 45; *Evening Standard*, 31 Jul 45; *Observer*, 5 Aug 45.
4. *Flight*, 9 Aug & 6 Dec 45.
5. *British Commanders*, 10–11.
6. *Daily Telegraph*, 12 & 28 Aug, 8 & 10 Sep 45, 5 May 47; *Star*, 18, 22 & 26 Sep 45.
7. AIR 24/660.
8. AIR 24/1792; *Evening Standard*, 17 Jun 46.

9. *Yorkshire Evening Post*, 17 Jan 47.
10. AIR 20/6344.
11. AIR 2/7910.
12. AIR 20/6345; AIR 20/1593.
13. Robb Papers, AC71/9/26.
14. Pogue Interviews; D'Este, 488–9.
15. Pogue Interviews.
16. Pogue, *Supreme Command*, xii; AIR 37/674.
17. Powell, *Military Philosophers*, 148–9; Butcher Diary, 20 Dec 42.
18. C's personal file, AHB, London.
19. AIR 24/1792.
20. Brown, *Wings of the Weird & Wonderful*, 19–23; Bramson, *Master Airman*, 122–4; Report of the Court Investigation [hereafter Report].

Finale (pp. 249–253)

1. Report; Barker, 87–96.
2. Report; Barker, 87–96; corresp. with Sayer, 1986–8.

Aftermath (pp. 254–259)

1. Report.
2. Report; *Aeroplane*, 13 Feb 48, 201; Bramson, 120.
3. Brown, 24; Bramson, 125, 131–5.
4. Conv. with Mrs Jane-Mari Shearing, 1986.
5. *New York Times*, 31 Jan 48; *NZ Herald*, 2 Feb 48.
6. *The Times*, 10 Feb 48.
7. *Aeroplane*, 13 Feb 48.
8. *The Times*, 14 Feb 48.
9. *Aeroplane*, 2 Apr 48.
10. *The Times*, 18 Feb 48; AIR 8/1555; *Aeroplane*, 5 Mar 48; *Daily Telegraph*, 18 Feb 48.
11. *Wellingtonian* (1948), 10.
12. Family information via Bateman.

BIBLIOGRAPHY

Unpublished Sources

(Note: AHB = Air Historical Branch; IWM = Imperial War Museum; LHC = Liddell Hart Centre for Military Archives, King's College; MOD = Ministry of Defence; NA = National Archives)

Allfrey Papers: LHC, London
AIR: numbered Air Ministry records, Public Record Office, London
Air Ministry Propaganda Leaflets, 2 vols.: AHB, MOD, London
Alanbrooke Papers: LHC, London
Brooke-Popham Papers: LHC, London
Butcher Diary: Dwight D. Eisenhower Library, Abilene, Kansas
Cannon Papers: Albert F. Simpson Historical Research Center, Maxwell AFB, Alabama
Coningham's NZ Army service: MOD, Wellington
Coningham's RFC/RAF service: AHB, MOD, London
Coningham Divorce: NA, Wellington
Cross Papers: private
Cunningham Papers: Admiral Andrew, British Museum, London
Davis, Richard G., *Eisenhower's Airman: General Carl A. Spaatz and the USAAF in Europe, 1942–5* (Ph.D thesis, George Washington University, 1985)
—, *The Bomber Baron: Carl Andrew Spaatz and the Army Air Forces in Europe, 1942–5* (ms. submitted to Publication Committee, Office of the Chief of Air Force History, Bolling AFB, Washington, DC, 1987)
Elmhirst Papers: some in Churchill College, Cambridge; others private
Elworthy Interview: IWM, London
Falconer Diary: IWM, London, under reference W. H. D. Hawkins
Gascoyne Interview: IWM, London
Grigg Papers: Churchill College, Cambridge
Kingston-McCloughry Papers: IWM, London
Kuter Papers: some in USAF Academy Library, Colorado; others private
Leigh-Mallory Papers: RAF Museum, Hendon
Lewin Papers: Churchill College, Cambridge
Liddell Hart Correspondence: LHC, London
Long Interview: IWM, London
Ludlow-Hewitt Papers: AHB, MOD, London
McDonald Papers: USAF Academy Library, Colorado

Bibliography

Montgomery Papers: IWM, London
Parton Papers; USAF Academy Library, Colorado
Peirse Papers: RAF Museum, Hendon
Peyton-Ward, D. V., *The RAF in Maritime War*, vol. i, *The Atlantic and Home Waters: The Prelude, April 1918 to September 1939* (AHB, London, n.d.)
Pogue Interviews: US Army Military History Institute, Carlisle Barracks, Pennsylvania
Portal Papers: Christ Church, Oxford
Power Papers: British Museum, London
Puttick Diary: Account of Samoan Expeditionary Force, 1914–15, NA, Wellington
Quesada Papers: US Army Military History Institute, Carlisle Barracks, Pennsylvania
Robb Papers: RAF Museum, Hendon
Somerset House, London: Principal Registry of Family Division
Spaatz Papers: Manuscript Division, Library of Congress, Washington, DC
Tedder Papers: private
Trenchard Papers: RAF Museum, Hendon
Vandenberg Papers: Manuscript Division, Library of Congress, Washington, DC
Werham, R. B., *The RAF in the Bombing Offensive Against Germany*, vol. ii, *Restricted Bombing, September 1939 to May 1941* (AHB, London, n.d.)
West African Reinforcement Route: AHB, MOD, London
Yarburgh-Bateson Papers: IWM, London

Published Sources

Air Ministry, *The Origins and Development of Operational Research in the Royal Air Force* (HMSO, London, 1963)
Andrews, C. F. & E. B. Morgan, *Supermarine Aircraft Since 1914* (Putnam, London, 1981)
Anon, *The Celebrated Divorce Case, Coningham v Coningham, O'Haran Co-respondent: a full account of the first hearing of the most startling Divorce case of the 19th Century* (Sir Robert Bear, Sydney, 1901); a second edition covered the 2nd hearing
Australian Dictionary of Biography, vols. 7& 8, ed. Bede Nairn & Geoffrey Serle (University of Melbourne Press, 1979–81)
Barker, Ralph, *Great Mysteries of the Air* (Chatto & Windus, London, 1966)
Barnett, Correlli, *The Desert Generals* (2nd ed., Allen & Unwin, London, 1983)
Behrendt, Hans-Otto, *Rommel's Intelligence in the Desert Campaign* (Kimber, London, 1985)
Bidwell, Shelford & Dominick Graham, *Fire-Power: British Army Weapons & Theories of War, 1904–1945* (Allen & Unwin, London, 1982)
Blumenson, Martin (ed.), *The Patton Papers, vol. 2: 1940–1945* (Houghton Mifflin, Boston, 1974)
Bowyer, Michael J. F., *2 Group, RAF: A Complete History, 1936–1945* (Faber & Faber, London, 1974)

Bradley, General Omar N. & Clay Blair, *A General's Life: An Autobiography of General of the Army Omar N. Bradley* (Simon & Schuster, New York, 1983)

Bramson, Alan, *Master Airman: A Biography of AVM Donald Bennett* (Airlife, Shrewsbury, 1985)

Brereton, Lieutenant General Lewis H., *The Brereton Diaries: The War in the Air in the Pacific, Middle East & Europe, 3 October 1941–8 May 1945* (Morrow, New York, 1946)

Bridgman, Leonard, *The Clouds Remember: The Aeroplanes of World War I, with a commentary by Oliver Stewart* (Arms & Armour Press, London, 1972)

British Commanders (British Information Services, New York, 1945)

Brown, Captain Eric, *Wings of the Weird and Wonderful* (Airlife Publishing, Shrewsbury, 1983)

Brown, James Ambrose, *Eagles Strike: South African Forces in World War II*, vol. iv (Purnell, Cape Town, 1974)

Bruce, J. M., *The Aeroplanes of the Royal Flying Corps (Military Wing)* (Putnam, London, 1982)

Butcher, Captain Harry C., *Three Years with Eisenhower: the Personal Diary of Captain Harry C. Butcher, USNR, Naval Aide to General Eisenhower, 1942 to 1945* (Heinemann, London, 1946)

Carr, S. J., *You are not Sparrows* (Ian Allan, London, 1975)

Chamberlain, Paul, 'A Short History of No. 32 Squadron, RFC/RAF, 1916–1918' in *Cross & Cockade, USA*, vol. 22, no. 1 (Spring 1981) pp. 39–70

Colville, Sir John, *The Fringes of Power: Downing Street Diaries, 1939–1955* (Hodder & Stoughton, London, 1985)

Coningham, AM Sir Arthur, 'The Development of Tactical Air Forces' in *RUSI Journal*, vol. 91 (1946) pp. 211–26

Cooper, Matthew, *The German Air Force, 1933–1945: An Anatomy of Failure* (Jane's Publishing, London, 1981)

Cranwell, *Journal of the RAF College*

Craven, Wesley F. & James L. Cate (eds.), *The Army Air Forces in World War II* (7 vols., University of Chicago, 1948–58; new imprint by Office of Air Force History, Washington, DC, 1983)

Cutlack, F. M., *The Australian Flying Corps in the Western & Eastern Theatres of War, 1914–1918* (Angus & Robertson, Sydney, 1923)

Davidson, J. W., *Samoa Mo Samoa: The Emergence of the Independent State of Western Samoa* (Oxford, 1967)

D'Este, Carlo, *Decision in Normandy: The Unwritten Story of Montgomery and the Allied Campaign* (Collins, London, 1983)

—, *Bitter Victory* (Collins, London, 1988)

Douglas, Sholto (MRAF Lord Douglas of Kirtleside) with Robert Wright, *Years of Combat* (Collins, London, 1963); *Years of Command* (Collins, London, 1966)

Draper, Christopher, *The Mad Major* (Air Review, London, 1962)

Drummond, AM Sir Peter, 'The Air Campaign in Libya & Tripolitania' in *RUSI Journal*, vol. 88 (1943) pp. 249–66

Embry, ACM Sir Basil, *Mission Completed* (Methuen, London, 1957)

Forbes, Patrick & Nigel Nicolson, *The Grenadier Guards in the War of 1939–1945* (2 vols., Gale & Polden, London, 1949)

Gilbert, Martin, *Road to Victory: Winston S. Churchill, 1941–1945* (Heinemann, London, 1986)

Glubb, Lieutenant General Sir John Bagot, *War in the Desert: An RAF Frontier Campaign* (Hodder & Stoughton, London, 1960)

Guingand, Major General Sir Francis de, *Operation Victory* (Hodder & Stoughton, London, 1947)

Hamilton, Nigel, *Monty: The Making of a General, 1887–1942* (Hamish Hamilton, London, 1981)

—, *Monty: Master of the Battlefield, 1942–1944* (Hamish Hamilton, London, 1983)

—, *Monty: The Field Marshal, 1944–1976* (Hamish Hamilton, London, 1986)

Harding, FM Lord, *Mediterranean Strategy, 1939–1945* (Cambridge, 1960)

Haslam, E. B., *The History of Royal Air Force Cranwell* (HMSO, London, 1982)

Hastings, Max, *Overlord: D-Day and the Battle for Normandy, 1944* (Michael Joseph, London, 1984)

Heydte, Freiherr von der, 'Afrika Korps Escapes' in Purnell's *History of the Second World War*, pp. 1230–2

—, 'Chase to Mareth: The German View', *ibid.*, pp. 1327–9

Hinsley, F. H. (& others), *British Intelligence in the Second World War* (3 vols, 3rd in two parts, HMSO, London, 1979–87)

Houghton, George W., *They Flew Through Sand* (Schindler, Cairo, 1942)

Infield, Glenn B., *Disaster at Bari* (Robert Hale, London, 1974)

Instone, Frank, *Deputy Provost Marshal* (Pallaton Press, Tunbridge Wells, 1977)

Irving, David, *The Trail of the Fox: The Life of Field-Marshal Erwin Rommel* (Weidenfeld & Nicolson, London, 1977)

Jacobs, W. A., 'Tactical Air Doctrine and AAF Close Air Support in the European Theater, 1944–1945' in *Aerospace Historian*, vol. 27, no. 1 (March 1980) pp. 35–49

—, 'Air Support for the British Army, 1939–43' in *Military Affairs*, vol. xlvi, no. 4 (December 1982) pp. 174–82

Jones, David, *The Time Shrinkers* (David Rendel, London, 1971)

Jones, Ira, *King of Air Fighters* (Ivor Nicholson & Watson, London, 1935)

Joubert, ACM Sir Philip, *The Third Service: The Story Behind the Royal Air Force* (Thames & Hudson, London, 1955)

Kilduff, Peter (ed.), *Germany's Last Knight of the Air: The Memoirs of Major Carl Degelow* (Kimber, London, 1979)

Kingston-McCloughry, AVM E. J., *The Direction of War* (Cape, London, 1955)

Kohn, Richard & Joseph P. Harahan (eds.), *Air Superiority in World War II & Korea* (USAF Warrior Studies, Office of Air Force History, USAF, Washington, DC, 1983)

Leary, L. P., *New Zealanders in Samoa* (Heinemann, London, 1918)

Lee, AVM A. S. G., *Special Duties* (Sampson, Low & Marston, London, 1947)

Lewin, Ronald, *The Life and Death of the Afrika Korps* (Batsford, London, 1977)

Lewis, Gwilym H., *Wings over the Somme, 1916–1918* (Kimber, London, 1976)

— & Keith Caldwell, letters in *Over The Front*, vol. 3, no. 1 (Spring 1988) pp. 20–6.

Longmore, ACM Sir Arthur, *From Sea to Sky: 1910–1945* (Geoffrey Bles, London, 1946)

MacDonald, Charles B., *The Battle of the Bulge* (Weidenfeld & Nicolson, London, 1984)

Macmillan, Captain Norman, *The RAF in the World War* (3 vols., Harrap, London, 1942–9)

Martin, Lt. Gen. H. J. & Colonel Neil D. Orpen, *Eagles Victorious: South African Forces in World War II, vol. vi (May 1943 to May 1945)* (Purnell, Cape Town, 1977)

Martin-Jenkins, Christopher, *The Complete Who's Who of Test Cricketers* (Orbis, London, 1980)

Middlebrook, Martin & Chris Everitt, *The Bomber Command War Diaries: an Operational Reference Book, 1939–45* (Penguin, London, 1985)

Mitchell, William, *No Medals for the Airmen* (Northwood Publishing, Aylmer, Ontario, 1982)

Moloney, Brigadier C. J. C. (& others), *The Mediterranean and Middle East, vol. v* (HMSO, London, 1973)

Mortensen, Daniel R., *A Pattern for Joint Operations: World War II Close Air Support, North Africa* (Office of Air Force History & US Army Center of Military History, Washington, DC, 1987)

NZ Law Reports, vol. xxxi, pp. 956–7

O'Farrell, Patrick, *The Catholic Church in Australia: A Short History, 1788–1967* (Thomas Nelson (Australia), Sydney, 1968)

O'Neal, Mary Lee Strickland, *Why did you start without me?* [biography of Brigadier General Auby C. Strickland]

Owen, Roderic, *The Desert Air Force* (Hutchinson, London, 1948)

—, *Tedder* (Collins, London, 1952)

Parton, James C., *'Air Force Spoken Here': General Ira Eaker and the Command of the Air* (Adler & Adler, Bethesda, Maryland, 1986)

Pearl, Cyril, *Wild Men of Sydney* (W. H. Allen & Co., London, 1958)

Pogue, Forrest C., *The Supreme Command* (Office of the Chief of Military History, Department of the Army, Washington, DC, 1954)

Powell, Anthony, *The Military Philosophers* (Heinemann, London, 1968)

Raleigh, W. & H. A. Jones, *The War in the Air* (6 vols., Oxford, 1922–37)

Report of the Court Investigation regarding the loss of Tudor IV aircraft 'Star Tiger' G-AHNP on 30 January 1948: Presented by the Minister of Civil Aviation to Parliament, September 1948 (HMSO, London, 1948)

Revell, Alex, 'Memories of J. V. Gascoyne, DFC' in *Cross & Cockade, GB*, vol. iv, no. 3 (1973) pp. 128–33

Rochford, Leonard H., *I Chose the Sky* (Kimber, London, 1977)

Roskill, S. W., *The War at Sea, 1939–45* (3 vols, 3rd in two parts, HMSO, London, 1954–61)

Runyon, Damon, 'The Snatching of Bookie Bob' in *Guys and Dolls*
  (Penguin, London, 1956) pp. 98–110
Russell, H. H., 'History of 92 Squadron' in *Journal of the Society of World
  War I Aero Historians*, vol. 7, no. 1 (Spring 1966) pp. 1–15
Simkins, Peter, *Air Fighting, 1914–18: The Struggle for Air Superiority over
  the Western Front* (Imperial War Museum, London, 1978)
Skelton, Marvin L., Letter of Prinz Friedrich Karl in *Cross & Cockade*,
  GB, vol. 13, no. 3 (1982) p. 144
Spearpoint (The 55 Squadron Association newsletter) no. 52, August 1987
Strange, L. A., *Recollections of an Airman* (Hamilton, London, 1933)
Taylor, John W. R., *CFS: Birthplace of Air Power* (Jane's Publishing Co.,
  London, 1987)
Tedder, Lord, *With Prejudice: The War Memoirs of MRAF Lord Tedder,
  GCB* (Cassell, London, 1966)
Terraine, John, *The Right of the Line: The Royal Air Force in the European
  War, 1939–1945* (Hodder & Stoughton, London, 1985)
Tomlinson, Jack, *Remembered Trails* (*Timaru Herald*, 1976)
Waite, F., *The New Zealanders at Gallipoli* (Whitcombe & Tombs,
  Christchurch, 1921)
Webster, Sir Charles & Noble Frankland, *The Strategic Air Offensive
  Against Germany, 1939–1945* (4 vols., HMSO, London, 1961)
Wellingtonian (Wellington College magazine)
Wilmot, Chester, *The Struggle for Europe* (Collins, London, 1952)
Wisden: *John Wisden's Cricketers' Almanack for 1894*, ed. Sydney H. Pardon
  (Wisden, London, 1895)
Woodman, Harry, 'Captured Enemy Aircraft Exhibition of 1918' in *Cross &
  Cockade, GB*, vol. 2, no. 3 (1971) p. 81
Wynn, Humphrey & Susan Young, *Prelude to Overlord* (Airlife Publishing,
  Shrewsbury, 1983)
'Zero' [Daniel Green], *The Secret History of the Coningham Case (Illustrated
  with Photographic Facsimiles of the Documents in the Case and many others
  that were not produced in Court)* (Finn Brothers, Sydney, 1901)

INDEX

in Western Desert, 106, 121, 123–4; in
Tunisia, 132, 136, 138–9, 143, 146, 150–2,
154–5, 157; in Operation Husky, 160–1,
164, 166–7; in Italy, 170–2, 174, 201; and
Operation Overlord, 177, 180–1; and
Coningham, 184, 218, 242
Alexandria, 51, 54, 55, 102, 114–15
Algeria, 118, 127
Algiers, 127–8, 130, 132–3, 138, 149, 151,
153, 159–60, 177, 209
Amiens, 213–14
Amiriya, 114
Anderson, Lieutenant General Sir Kenneth,
128, 130–1, 136, 141–3, 145, 152–4
Andover, Staff College, 34–5, 50, 54, 61–2
Antelat, 88–9, 120
Antwerp, 212, 215, 217, 219–21, 224, 226,
230, 245
Anzac Cove, 14
Anzio, 185
Arab Legion, 36
Ardennes, 212, 223–4, 226, 230, 240, 258
Argentan, 208–9
Armies, Allied: 1st Allied Airborne, 215, 234
—American: 1st US, 212, 219, 225; 3rd US,
207; 7th US, 161; 9th US, 223, 225,
230–1, 234; 12th Army Group, 212; II
Corps, 132, 135–8, 143–4, 146, 148,
151–2, 155
—British: 1st, 128, 132, 135, 136, 139, 143,
146, 152; 2nd, 196, 204, 208, 212, 215,
221, 234; 8th, 79, 85, 95, 102–3, 112, 118,
125, 130, 132, 134, 136, 138, 143, 146,
152, 161, 166, 171–2, 176, 257–8; 15th
Group, 161; 18th Group, 132; 21st Group,
188, 207, 209, 212, 216–17, 223, 228,
245–6; 5 Corps, 135, 152; 9 Corps, 152; 13
Corps, 84, 87, 92, 115; 30 Corps, 84, 86,
159, 215, 225; 4th Indian Division, 151;
New Zealand Division, 103; 6th Armoured
Division, 148; 7th Armoured Division,
108, 132, 198; Guards Armoured Division,
214; 128th Brigade, 148
—Canadian: 1st Canadian, 208, 212, 230, 234
—French: XIX Corps, 132
—New Zealand: 5th Wellington Regiment,
13, 14; Expeditionary Force (4th
Reinforcements), 14; Canterbury Mounted
Rifles, 14
Arnhem, 215–16, 235–6, 244–5
Arnim, General Jurgen von, 137–8, 142–4
Arnold, General Henry H., 134, 155, 161
Arras, 29
Arras, Battle of, 19, 20
Atlantic, Battle of, 72
Attlee, Clement, 234, 255

Auban, District Commissioner in Gambeila,
57
Auchinleck, Field-Marshal Sir Claude, 78,
86–8, 92–4, 97, 99–106
Augusta, 167
'Avalanche', 170–2
Avranches, 207
Azores, 2, 250

Bad Eilsen, 236, 239, 241
Baggs, Flight Lieutenant Humphrey, 45
Baghdad, 36, 40, 41
Bagush, 119
Baheira, 93
Bahr-el-Ghazal, 54
Bailleul, 25
Balfour, Harold, 154, 217
Baltic, 64
Bapaume, 18
Bardia Pass, 99
Bari, 172, 175–6, 178
Barnato, Diana, 221–2
Barnes, Sir James, 246
Barratt, Air Marshal Sir Arthur, 108–9, 219
Basrah, 36
Bastico, Marshal Ettore, 99
Bastogne, 225, 229
Batas, 39
'Baytown', 170–2
Bazeul, 31
Beamish, Air Marshal Sir George, 90–1, 93,
107–8, 111, 119, 136–7, 151, 158, 174–5,
182
Beaumont, 32
Beaverbrook, newspapers, 237
Becelaere, 21
Bedell Smith: *see* Smith, General Walter
Bedell
Bednall, Colin, 187–8
Behrendt, Hans-Otto, 88
Belchem, Major General David, *All in the
Day's March*, 216
Belledonne Mountains, 218
Belgium, 212, 214–15, 221, 228, 242
Benghazi, 85, 87, 89, 96, 115, 120–1, 155
Bennett, Air Vice Marshal Don, 1, 248,
254–5
Bentley Priory, 89, 182, 184, 186–8, 192,
194, 198–9
Bergen-op-Zoom, 245
Berlin, 67, 200, 215, 235, 237, 245
Bermuda, 1, 2, 250–4
Bernhard of The Netherlands, Prince, 232,
242
Bertangles, 18
Bicknoller, 11
Bir Hacheim, 97–8